From Indus to Independence

A Trek Through Indian History

From Indus to Independence
A Trek Through Indian History

Volume VI

Medieval Deccan Kingdoms

Sanu Kainikara

Vij Books India Pvt Ltd

New Delhi (India)

Copyright © 2019, *Sanu Kainikara*

Dr Sanu Kainikara
416, The Ambassador Apartments
2 Grose Street
Deakin, ACT 2600, Australia
sanu.kainikara@gmail.com

First Published in 2019

ISBN : 978-93-88161-59-6 (Hardback)

ISBN : 978-93-88161-61-9 (ebook)

Designed and Setting by

Vij Books India Pvt Ltd

2/19, Ansari Road, Darya Ganj, New Delhi - 110002, India

(www.vijbooks.com)

All rights reserved.

No part of this book may be reproduced, stored in a retrieval system, transmitted or utilized in any form or by any means, electronic, mechanical, photocopying, recording or otherwise, without the prior permission of the copyright owner. Application for such permission should be addressed to the author.

For

'Puju'

Priyanka Kainikara-Sen

I believe, my dearest daughter,
That when you came into this world, the angels gathered
And sprinkled moondust on your hair and starlight in your eyes.
When you smile and hold my hand,
Time stands still and my world is at peace;
For you are my breath and life itself.

OTHER BOOKS BY SANU KAINIKARA

National Security, Strategy and Air Power

Papers on Air Power
Pathways to Victory
Red Air: Politics in Russian Air Power
Australian Security in the Asian Century
A Fresh Look at Air Power Doctrine
Friends in High Places (Editor)
Seven Perennial Challenges to Air Forces
The Art of Air Power: Sun Tzu Revisited
At the Critical Juncture
Essays on Air Power
The Bolt from the Blue
In the Bear's Shadow
The Sword Arm

Political Analysis

The Asian Crucible
Political Musings: Turmoil in the Middle-East
Political Musings: Asia in the Spotlight

The Indian History Series: From Indus to Independence

Volume I: Prehistory to the Fall of the Mauryas
Volume II: The Classical Age
Volume III: The Disintegration of Empires
Volume IV: The Onslaught of Islam
Volume V: The Delhi Sultanate

CONTENTS

Author's Preface		xi
Introduction to Volume VI		xix
Section I	**The Deccan and South India**	**1**
Chapter 1	The Deccan – A Broad Overview	3
Chapter 2	The Bridge Between Two Eras	11
Chapter 3	A Tale of Three Kingdoms	27
Chapter 4	Prologue to Hindu Revival	39
Section II	**The Bahmani Dynasty**	**49**
Chapter 5	Origins	53
Chapter 6	The Gulbarga Sultans	61
Chapter 7	The Bidar Sultans	77
Chapter 8	Last Days and Break-Up	91
Chapter 9	The Bahmanis – Concluding Deductions	107
Section III	**The Successor Kingdoms of The Deccan** **The Adil Shahis of Bijapur**	**115**
Chapter 10	Yusuf Adil Shah Establishes A Kingdom	119
Chapter 11	Entrenching the Dynasty	129
Chapter 12	Growing Strength	143

Chapter 13	The Zenith	153
Chapter 14	The Final Collapse	165
Chapter 15	A Concluding Evaluation	181
Section IV	**The Successor Kingdoms of The Deccan — The Nizam Shahis of Ahmadnagar**	**189**
Chapter 16	The Founding of A Kingdom	193
Chapter 17	Consolidation: Burhan Nizam Shah I	205
Chapter 18	Turmoil: Hussein Nizam Shah	221
Chapter 19	The Zenith of Power: Murtaza Nizam Shah	233
Chapter 20	Stagnation and Confusion: Murtaza's Last Days	247
Chapter 21	The Beginning of The End	263
Chapter 22	The End: Chand Bibi's Finest Hour	277
Chapter 23	Malik Ambar – The Rise and Rise of A Slave - The Habshi Ascendancy	287
Section V	**The Successor Kingdoms of The Deccan — The Qutb Shahis of Golconda – Hyderabad**	**305**
Chapter 24	A Kingdom is Established	309
Chapter 25	Containing Instability	319
Chapter 26	Ibrahim Quli Qutb Shah: Increasing Power and Stature	327
Chapter 27	Muhammad Quli Qutb Shah Focus on Cultural Development	339
Chapter 28	Plateauing and Decline	351
Chapter 29	The Obliteration of a Dynasty	365
Section VI	**Deccan Shahis – Other Aspects**	**377**
Chapter 30	Administration, Military and Foreign Affairs	379

Chapter 31	The Cultural Front	391
Section VII	**Medieval Deccan – A Concluding Analysis**	**399**
Chapter 32	Chaotic Administration	401
Chapter 33	The Social Environment	409
Chapter 34	Economy, Trade and Commerce	423
Chapter 35	The Cauldron Bubbles…	431
Bibliography		443
Index		449

AUTHOR'S PREFACE

A Sense of History

There is continuing debate regarding the Indian 'sense of history' with most academics tending to state that unfortunately the people of India do not have an entrenched sense of history. Even after a great deal of research, I have not been able to find any logical explanation for such an assertion. My search however continues, since the assertion has been made for a number of years and seems to have taken root. In this context it has to be accepted that historic monuments have not been maintained in pristine conditions or even in good repair in modern India. The reasons are many and also include the fact that there is bound to be a certain apathy towards old buildings in a civilisation as old as mankind itself. However, this reason is not being put forward as an excuse for the noticeable lack of care in India for historic monuments.

A dichotomy in this aspect needs to be pointed out. At the same time that the neglect of historic structures are bemoaned as indicative of Indians being devoid of a sense of history, any mention of the really glorious past of the Hindu civilisation is dismissed as being against the 'secular' aspects of modern India. It is obvious the two opinions cannot co-exist and thrive, one or the other has to be committed to oblivion. Unfortunately, for the better part of India's 'independent' existence, the advocates of a secular society—secular according to how they have defined it—have prevailed and so the modern India continues to be labelled one without a sense of history, rightly or wrongly.

It would seem that the concept of history itself is not very well understood in India. Therefore, it is difficult to fathom as to how the claim that an entire people do not have a 'sense of history' has been made so often and so vociferously. What is history? Very broadly, history is the study of the past. It is research aimed at studying emerging patterns in human development based on the examination of past events, their sequence, cause and effect. Such a study must also provide a perspective, based on historical tradition, on current challenges facing a people as a whole, in order to ensure that the study has relevance.

In order to ensure its relevance, history must include two aspects in its narrative—the what, and the how. It must provide a description of what happened, as accurately as possible; and then the narrative must investigate how it happened. Only such a two-pronged analysis will provide details that in turn would lead to an understanding of the impact of the event being discussed. Taken together, it will indicate the immediate and long-term value of an event and its contribution towards the evolution and development of a particular group of people.

Contrary to the arguments of some modern historian, I believe that the Indian-Hindu ethos has an eternal root in history. For example, the epics—*Mahabharata and Ramayana*—are still recited in the oral tradition despite them having been written down as texts centuries ago. Normally during these recitals, each couplet is explained for its meaning and commentaries are made to relate them to the current circumstances. These commentaries connect the basic narrative to the prevailing times; essentially the elaboration of the meaning of the couplets, the significance of the events, and their value to the group is clearly explained. Thus the age-old oral tradition has become an agent of transformation of history from stating mere facts to describing its value to society, which is the inherent strength of the Indian historical narrative.

Another unique influence on the Indian perception of history is the Hindu concept of Time as being cyclic that permeates into the core of understanding history in a holistic manner. The cyclical nature of Time creates an inimitable blend of the past, present and future in the general view of the historic narrative. This is one of the main reasons for the preservation of Indian history over the centuries, starting even before written or recorded narratives became common place.

*   *   *

Author's Preface

Scholarly dissertations on history, over a period of time, have become increasingly removed from examining the compulsions that a king, chief or leader faced while initiating a particular action in the distant past. The tendency is to be completely dispassionate about the individual while the analysis also carries some amount of bias. Empathy for the individual being discussed is now considered 'unprofessional' while judging his actions through the lens of current day sensibilities has become de rigour. I feel that this attitude is incompatible with the necessity to produce work that provides a readily understandable analysis of history. Yes, it is necessary to maintain a formal distance between the historian and the individual or event being analysed. However, it is equally important for the historian to have a clear understanding of the personality of the leadership in order to ensure that the analytical conclusions that are arrived at stand the test of fairly intense scrutiny. Identifying the compulsions under which a king or warlord functioned in a particular case will enhance the veracity of the analysis. The historian's job is complex, to say the least.

History and its analysis cannot be about remembering dates, events and some other mundane facts. Past events, even ones that have been studied and discussed innumerable times, merit new historical analysis as time goes by. As contemporary sensibilities alter, the people whose ancestors are being evaluated in history also tend to change their attitudes and appreciation of their forefathers. It is the responsibility of the historian to ensure that these tendencies do not unduly influence the common understanding of events past and their significance for the present. If checks and balances are not carefully maintained the risk of a people re-writing history to suit their beliefs becomes real and palpable. The historian has an onerous responsibility to ensure that the narrative adopted by a people remain true to the past, irrespective of the interpretations that are made. History, after all will indicate the path that a people trode to reach the place where they are now, in a broad socio-politico-economic sense.

In terms of knowing the past, both history and mythology fulfil the same need—to provide an understanding of the distant past of a people. The difference between the two is that historical analysis is based on fact, whereas mythology is based on fantasy. It is once again the historian's responsibility to ensure that fantasy is not confused with evidence. A clear and visible line must define one from the other. Most ancient civilisations suffer from the malaise of having to cater for an increasing popular demand to authenticate and date their epics. This phenomena has become very clearly visible in the Indian context in the past decade or so. Such moves are detrimental to creating a visibly authenticated narrative that leads to a clear understanding of the history of the people. The need of the hour, particularly in India, is to acquire and make available evidence-based knowledge of events past so that mythology can be separated from history in the minds of the common people. I accept that history and mythology are both explanations of the past, but the difference is the basis for their individual explanations—one is based on irrefutable evidence, the other on imagination.

* * *

This volume of the series on Indian history, *From Indus to Independence: A Trek Through Indian History*, deals with the Islamic entrenchment in the Deccan Plateau—the flow of events, the reasons and the consequences of this development. It is inevitable that the volume will have, especially in its concluding analysis, a detailed analysis of the meeting and the subsequent clash of two dissimilar religions. The fundamental differences between Islam and Hinduism—that finally led to the partition of the sub-continent in 1947—can be clearly appreciated in an analysis of the developments that took place in the Deccan. I have tied to ensure that the narrative of events is as close to the truth as possible and also to remain completely unbiased and objective in my analysis. While studying this period in the history of the southern peninsula, I have been overwhelmed at times by the magnanimity and great sensibilities displayed by some rulers while being disgusted and sickened by the actions of depravity by some others. In the middle of such extremes, I have made a conscious attempt to tread the centreline without stepping out on either side.

The interaction of Islam and Hinduism in the peninsula, after the initial marauding expeditions, was on a much more even keel than had happened in North India. As a result, the Islam that was practised in medieval Deccan was a much more flexible variety, as compared to the more rigid version of the religion followed elsewhere. In a fundamental manner this can be attributed to the influence of Hinduism. Hinduism,

Author's Preface

then as now, was and is the embodiment of diversity, which in turn makes it a living religion. It has never been threatened to being ossified because it is chained to some archaic dogma. Hinduism has never been defined by one set of beliefs, effectively there is no 'one' Hinduism—diversity is inherent in the religion.

I have a particular grouse against modern historians who dabble in Indian history—uniformly they attempt to play down the atrocities that invading armies committed against the local population. The fact remains that in the Indian context the invaders were neither extraordinarily brutal nor were they kindly towards the local opposition. This was the norm across the medieval world and the Indian sub-continent was no exception. The fact that the two sides were divided by religion seems to have inhibited modern historians in recounting events as they took place. I believe that this is a disservice to the broader recounting and comprehension of history.

The fact remains that both the Hindus and the Muslims in India were parochial and tribal in their outlook and subscribed, at the basic level, to an entrenched mistrust of the 'other'. It has also to be pointed out that a majority of the common men—both Hindus and Muslims—were impoverished and far too busy eking out a living to worry about the so-called clash of religions that was supposed to have been taking place. This particular narrative of the 'clash' was created at a later stage by historians studying the flow of events and the actions of kings, sultans and the nobility. There is no doubt that the Muslim rulers were as tyrannical or as benign as any other despotic ruler of medieval times, anywhere in the world.

*   *   *

This volume, detailing the events of medieval Deccan contains some very minor discrepancies in the account of invasions, wars and battles, especially the ones of the Shahi kingdoms laid out in different sections. This is so because each section was researched from all available information of a particular Shahi kingdom and the chronicles of one kingdom may not match with those of the others. There will always be a bias on the part of a chronicler towards his own king and master that is bound to cloud the narrative. In such a situation it becomes difficult to determine the exact flow of events and also the factuality of what transpired. This is the unique nature of Indian history. I have not made any attempt at reconciling the apparent differences of opinion between the different chronicles that were available for my research.

I have attempted to provide a feasible outline of the events as they transpired. However, the focus in this volume has been to analyse the consequences and impact of these events on the broader flow of the historical narrative of the peninsula and indirectly, the entire the sub-continent. I believe that in recounting historic events, the minor details of how exactly an event unfolded is less important than the understanding of the impact of that event on the subsequent progress and future of the kingdom, dynasty and the people at large. This has been the emphasis in this volume, as in the other volumes in this series.

I believe that the past is not a singular entity but a learned interpretation of a sequence of events that in turn must gather a history of its own over time.

Sanu Kainikara
Canberra
March 2019

The Despot

The garden mould was damp and chill,
Winter had had his brutal will
Since over all the year's content
His devastating legions went.

Then Spring's bright banners came: there woke
Millions of little growing folk
Who thrilled to know the winter done,
Gave thanks, and strove towards the sun.

Not so the elect; reserved, and slow
To trust a stranger-sun and grow,
They hesitated, cowered and hid
Waiting to see what others did.

Yet even they, a little, grew,
Put out prim leaves to day and dew,
And lifted level formal heads
In their appointed garden beds.

The gardener came: he coldly loved
The flowers that lived as he approved,
That duly, decorously grew
As he, the despot, meant them to.

He saw the wildlings flower more brave
And bright than any cultured slave;
Yet, since he had not set them there,
He hated them for being fair.

So he uprooted, one by one
The free things that had loved the sun,
The happy, eager, fruitful seeds
That had not known that they were weeds.

— Edith Nesbit

INTRODUCTION TO VOLUME VI

Tumult and Upheaval in the Deccan

Deccan, a modified version of the word 'Dakhin' meaning south, literally alludes to the southern part of the great Indian sub-continent. The region was referred to as Dakshinapatha in both the epics, *Mahabharata* and *Ramayana* while Periplus mentions it as Dachinabades. The *Markandeya*, *Vayu* and *Matsya Puranas* also mention the term Dakshinapatha to denote the lands south of the River Narmada, encompassing the entire peninsula. However, in keeping with the uncertainties that crop up every now and then in the Indian historical narrative, there is continuing debate regarding the origin of the term 'Deccan'.

In the relatively more modern age Deccan has been taken, at times, to include in its widest sense, 'the whole of the peninsular South India lying to the south of the Vindhya mountain ranges and the Narmada River, which separate it from the north of the sub-continent'. This is perhaps a slightly confusing description, since the term Deccan refers to only the plateau within the peninsula and does not incorporate the region deeper to the south of the plateau. Therefore, in more recent historical writings, the Deccan Plateau is considered to be the region that formed the core territory of the kingdoms of the Rashtrakutas and the Chalukyas in ancient times and was ruled in medieval times by the Bahmani dynasty initially and thereafter by the successor Shahi states. Geographically, this norm has been followed in this narrative.

Most histories of India concentrate on the core regions of the sub-continent; the regions where political and cultural stability periodically prevailed, areas that attracted not only foreign invasions but also were the recipients of a plethora of scholars and travellers, sufficient to create enough information to attract the attention of modern historians. On another plane, the core regions also provide the most coherent narrative of the broad history of India since the major events that have shaped the landscape over the eons also took place there. Consequently there are some understudied regions in the Indian sub-continent, which continues to remain in the shadows, although the events that transpired in those regions did have a limited direct and a more elaborate indirect influence on the broader flow of Indian history. These regions have also have gone through turmoil similar to the ones faced by the core regions, although they arrived at significantly different end-states. This difference, between the core regions and the peripheral ones, is itself worth studying to understand the influence of local factors on the flow of history. The Deccan is such a region.

For centuries, the Deccan Plateau never possessed a core political centre, which is essential to carry out a worthwhile detailed study of the region from a modern historian's point of view. However, the Deccan holds a uniquely important position in the broader narrative of Indian history with some of the events that took place there reverberating across the sub-continent.

Till the second half of the 13th century, the Deccan remained isolated and devoid of any Muslim influence, referred to derisively as 'pagan' country. Only limited and incoherent information regarding the plateau and the peninsula made its way to North India. The arrival of the Muslims into the Deccan can be traced back to the migration of the Central Asian Turks into the sub-continent after being displaced from their homelands by the Mongol invasions of the 13th and 14th centuries. They were mainly refugees, but brought with them a vibrant literary and cultural tradition as well as a cosmopolitan attitude since the timing of their move coincided with the later part of the Persian Renaissance that took place between the 10th and 13th centuries. Persian-influenced Muslim culture took root in North India and gradually diffused southwards with the armies of the Delhi Sultanate that started to probe the region. (The Delhi Sultanate's invasion of the Deccan and the peninsula has been covered in *Volume V* of this series.)

The northern most kingdom in the Deccan was that of the Yadavas who ruled form their capital at Devagiri. The Yadavas, already

Introduction

in decline, were taken by surprise by the invasion of Ala ud-Din Khilji in 1294. The very first contact between Islam and the Hindu Deccan was a traumatising display of the uncompromising, vicious and rapacious attitude of the Islamic rulers who did not display even the slightest sympathy for, or understanding of, the culture and religion of the people of the invaded lands.

Devagiri in the north-west of the plateau and Warangal in the east coast, were the two centres of the kingdoms to the north of the Deccan Plateau. Devagiri was a great city and also considered an impregnable fort. The Yadava kingdom was aesthetically highly evolved, although the dynasty was in decline. The kingdom boasted of the caves at Ajanta and Ellora that displayed great advances in art and architecture; and the people were prosperous, happy and brave. It was the wealth of the kingdom that attracted the covetous eyes of the Muslim invaders, who were initially merely raiders and looters. However, the invading warlords realised that the region was easy to conquer and hold. Within a short span of three decades, both the Devagiri and the Warangal kingdoms had been destroyed and the regions were under Muslim rule. Devagiri was renamed Daulatabad. Simultaneously, migrants who had arrived in North India were gradually transplanted to the south, settling around Daulatabad, establishing the first permanent civilian Muslim presence in the Deccan. Accompanying this migration were the Sufis—Muslim holy men and mystics. In medieval times, the Sufis had great spiritual authority, which is believed to have transcended the temporal authority of political rulers and military commanders—they were more exalted than kings and generals.

The invading forces of the Delhi Sultanate marched all the way south and reached Rameswaram in the eastern tip of the peninsula, attracted no doubt by the scope for plunder of the enormous wealth concentrated in the Hindu temples. The wealth in these temples were the collective submission of the local people for centuries and the prevailing conditions in the region did not necessitate any protection for these temples. The invading Islamic armies aimed at looting this readily available wealth that proved an easy task. This parallel thread of the greed for the lucre of gold and wealth as a driving force in the invasions has been carefully camouflaged—both by contemporary chroniclers of the time and by modern Indian historians—under the hypocritical cover of the invading army and its commanders being strict followers of Islam, which required them to lay waste the places of worship of all non-believers, the dreaded kafirs. It never gets a mention that the invading army broke all the fundamental tenets of their own religion during their raids.

The arrival of the Islamic armies altered the Deccan and the Peninsula, they were never again the same tranquil, stable region. The inherent urge within the Islamic religion to be belligerent and its in-built intolerance of other religions and cultures made it oppressive by nature. There is a strong streak of selfishness and a lessening of humanity that was very visible in the medieval Islamic armies that invaded the sub-continent.

Even though in a broad-sweep-narrative it would seem that the Islamic armies were always victorious in battles and wars in the sub-continent, it was really not the case. The established Hindu kingdoms invariably put up vehement and brave opposition to each invasion. Every single Islamic victory was contested and many of the results hung in the balance, both in battles as well as in long-drawn campaigns. It took all out efforts by the Delhi Sultans to establish a foothold in the Deccan and thereafter to put down a continuous series of rebellions that carried on for years at a stretch. The people of the Deccan did not take kindly to Muslim rule, however nominal the Islamic administration may have been. As a result of the rebellious attitude of the local people, the conquests were almost inevitably followed by ruthless suppression of the people and destruction of religious institutions that provided a central focus point for the uprisings. The more astute Hindu chieftains and kings realised the extreme threat posed by the Islamic invasion of the Deccan. They did attempt to present a united front to resist the invaders, however they were not always very successful. On the other hand, these efforts led to the establishment of a strong Hindu kingdom in South India, that of Vijayanagar. (The illustrious history of the Vijayanagar Empire will be covered in detail in the next volume in this series).

The Bahmanis – Forging a Regional Deccan Identity

By late 13th century, the Muslim settlers in the Deccan were unhappy with the arbitrary nature of Delhi's imperial rule. In Delhi the ruling

Introduction

Tughluq dynasty was in the process of self-destructing because of the ill-conceived policies of the sultan, Muhammad-bin-Tughluq. Rebellion was in the air in the Deccan. By the early years of the 14th century the rebellion was in full swing, led by a local warlord who detached himself from Delhi and declared independence, establishing the Bahmani dynasty. This act of defiance laid the seed for the creation of an independent Muslim identity in the Deccan, far removed from the Islamic culture that had spread in North India. At the end of the nearly two centuries of the Bahmani rule that followed the initial rebellion, the Deccanisation of the Islamic religious process was complete.

The Bahmani kingdom was the first Indo-Persian state to be established in the Deccan and lasted for slightly over 180 years—in different stages of growth, consolidation, grandeur, splendour, decline and decay. The founder established strong roots and was a devoted king, which was one of the main reasons for the longevity of the dynasty. However, the basic fact remains that the dynasty was founded only because the warlord found himself at the 'right place at the right time' and not because of any concerted individual effort at carving out a kingdom. Without doubt, he did carve out a kingdom when the opportunity presented itself, but it is highly doubtful that he would have created the opportunity himself. This lucky favour continued to haunt the future generations of the dynasty throughout its rule—the question of their 'fitness' to rule always being placed on the balance and questioned.

The kingdom was resource-rich and the people generally docile. The conquered population was predominantly resident in rural areas and suffered from an inexplicable sense of lethargy, being comfortable with the fact that they were not particularly oppressed by the change in rule. In fact they did not care who ruled them, since the Panchayat system of governance that was of immediate concern to them was left untouched by the Muslim kings. In effect, the influx of Islam into the Deccan was not an earth-shattering event, not even particularly noticeable at this stage in the rural areas. It did not take a great effort for the new rulers to control and rule the rural areas through the establishment of military garrisons.

Persian Influence

At the infancy of the Bahmani kingdom, Timur invaded India and sacked Delhi. However, the Deccan was a step too far and so was spared the depredations of Timur's battalions. The Bahmani kings adopted the Central Asian style of governance, with all power concentrated in the person of the king/sultan, patronage for the development of art and learning and emulating the architecture of the region. It was the Bahmani king, Firuz Shah Bahmani, who first introduced the animal motif as a royal insignia in Indo-Muslim architecture. The Bahmani rulers provided patronage for persons with knowledge of Persian culture, seeking out soldiers, educators and administrators who were well-versed in Persian for advancement in royal service. As a result, settlers from Persia and Arabia flocked to the Deccan. They were provided favoured status and were locally referred to as 'phirangis' and/or 'gharbiaris', both terms meaning foreigners.

This favouritism was the beginning of a deep and intractable division in the ranks of the nobility—into the phirangis and the Deccanis—which led to poisonous intrigues and self-defeating civil strife in the Deccan throughout the rule of the Bahmanis and the successor states. This division played an important role in starting a large number of rebellions and internecine conflicts. It was also a major contributory factor in the fall of the Bahmani dynasty. In an indirect manner the Muslim obsession with the more sophisticated Persian culture, as opposed to the more mundane Turko-Afghan societal norms, contributed to the fall of a dynasty in faraway Deccan in the Indian sub-continent.

Other Aspects

The Islamic code of succession of the fittest to the throne being selected by the elders as the leader of a tribe or clan on the demise of the ruling chief had, over time, percolated to the level of ruling a kingdom. This was one of the reasons for the Delhi Sultanate going through so many dynasties till it met its nemesis in the person of Babur the Mughal. However, as the kingdoms grew larger and the number of nobility who selected the next ruler increased, the process started to get overtly corrupted. Gradually a ruling king was able to bribe the nobles with wealth and positions to ensure that his favourite offspring would be selected to be the ruler after him. Thus the code of selecting the fittest for the role was derailed and replaced with heredity. Almost all successions in medieval Islamic Deccan was followed by the distribution of wealth and appointments of nobles to exalted titles by the in-coming ruler.

After establishing the kingdom, the Bahmanis battled with their Hindu rival kingdom of Vijayanagar occasionally and with indecisive results, although by and large a tacit peace prevailed most of the time. Along with the Bahmani kingdom's progress, the little known Marathas also started to become more prominent in local politics and moved towards a semi-autonomous status. The Bahmani rulers continued with the policy of religious persecution that had been instituted by the governors of the Delhi Sultanate who had brought Muslim rule to the Deccan. However, this policy was enacted more in the towns and other population centres, while the vast number of villages that formed the rural areas were left to their own devices. While contemporary chroniclers mention the religious persecution of the Bahmani rule in many of their accounts, modern day analysts have so far tended to soft-paddle it. The reason for this approach to the religious activities of the Bahmani rulers is unknown and inexplicable.

The Bahmani kings were essentially warlords, functioning at varying levels of success, and kept their kingdom on a war footing at all times. Minor skirmishes and border incidents were normal and continued unabated throughout the Bahmani rule. Viewed in a holistic manner, it is seen that the Bahmani rulers managed to hold on to power through an astutely applied combination of sly cleverness, continuous bribing of the more powerful nobles, instigating infighting within the nobility and a fair amount of ruthlessness. A number of the Bahmani kings were bigoted tyrants and did not consider the non-Muslim population of the kingdom, who were the majority, to be citizens of their kingdom—a factor that is also under-played in modern historical narratives.

Decline and Break Up

As the Bahmani dynasty continued its rule of the Deccan, the thirst for greater power and territorial expansion diminished in successive rulers. This was the result of the fact that succession to the throne was not a contested event anymore but bought through bribery and corruption. There was no need for an aspiring ruler to prove his fitness to rule or to win battles against contenders to ascend the throne. As it usually happens, the ease of accession led to the softening of the inner core calibre of leadership in the Bahmani house and led to a gradual, but perceptible, decline in the capability of successive rulers. After a dynasty is established in its rule, and successive rulers do not have the urge to expand their territorial holdings through military campaigns, there is always a tendency to move away from warfighting as a primary occupation to more cultural pursuits, especially in literature, the arts and architecture. Such a transformation can be seen in a number of cases and the Bahmanis were no exception.

Four reasons can be attributed for the breakup of the Bahmani kingdom. One, the declining personal capabilities and increasing incompetence of the rulers; two, the fact that there was no strong infrastructure to counter the decline since the polity of the kingdom was built around the person of the king/sultan that did not permit any alternative power base; three, the tarafdari system of administration, which gave almost complete independence to local governors who became powerful and could defy central administration; and four the division and animosity within the nobility between the phirangis and the Deccanis that tended to spin out of control at the slightest provocation. In the tarafdari administrative system that was established by the Bahmani dynasty, which was a copy of some other Muslim kingdoms, the weakness of a king/sultan could produce a rapid disintegration of central control with some regional governors able to even influence the royal courts and decisions. Invariably such a situation led to the balkanisation of the kingdom. The Bahmani dynasty faced such a situation by early 16th century, and by 1527 the kingdom had broken up into five independent states.

Much before the actual breakup, the nobles had become irrevocably divided in to the phirangi and Deccani factions that could never reconcile with each other. The factional division led to the weakening of the state power in the Deccan. The phirangi-Deccani divide was the lasting gift from the Bahmanis to the successor Deccani kingdoms. The two factions never managed to overcome the mutual animosity and the divide continued to be a detrimental factor that impinged on good governance and establishment of the rule of law.

Chroniclers also give a dubious distinction to the Bahmani rulers—uniformly each ruler has been recorded as having been ruthless towards anyone who could lay claim to the throne or stood in the way of his coming to the throne. It was common practice for the new king ascending the throne to blind and imprison all his siblings as a prerequisite to letting them live, which was also not ensured, since poisoning them while in prison was also a common practice.

The Bahmanis were a local Deccan dynasty. However, they continued to bring in Muslims from outside because of what can only be considered an inherent sense of inadequacy and thereby created the phirangi-Deccani schism that played a major role in the eventual breakup of the kingdom. In the more modern narratives a carefully orchestrated attempt at making the Bahmani rule look normal can be perceived. However, the fact remains that it is difficult to find a really benevolent and enlightened ruler amongst the list of the Bahmani kings, who could break the mould of bigotry, treachery, viciousness and deceit—the common character traits of Bahmani rulers. The people of the kingdom remained predominantly Hindus, even after nearly two centuries of concerted efforts at changing the demographic makeup of the region. The efforts to increase the number of Muslims in the kingdom took many forms—violent massacres that bordered on ethnic cleansing, forced conversions, and the import of foreign Muslims who were treated with extreme favoured partiality. More importantly, the common man remained miserable under the Bahmani rule with no effort being made to better their lot by the rulers.

When the tired Bahmani dynasty ceased to weild effective power, the Shahi dynasties usurped power from their different strongholds, declaring independence from the Bahmanis.

The Successor Shahi Kingdoms

The successor kingdoms to the Bahmani kingdom are called the Shahi kingdoms since the nobles who declared independence to create these truncated holdings, styled themselves with the title 'Shah'—presumably imitating the title of the great Shah of Persia, in an attempt to establish their 'royal' status and separateness to the other nobles. The process of the breakup was similar to the manner in which the Bahmani kingdom itself declared independence from the Delhi Sultanate. Regionally powerful warlords, who were appointed as tarafdars by the Bahmani rulers, were also opportunists to the core and declared independence when they observed the decline of central authority in Bidar. Ambitious provincial governors, disillusioned by the state of affairs in Bidar, declared independence one after the other, leading to the formation of five states.

The successor states that emerged were the Barid Shahis in Bidar, Adil Shahis in Bijapur, Nizam Shahis in Ahmadnagar, Qutb Shahis in Golconda, and Imad Shahis in Berar. Amongst these it could be stated that Bidar formed by default since it was the capital of the Bahmanis. Since the rebellions were all conducted by powerful governors in provincial capitals, the Prime Minister Qasim Barid took control of the capital and established the dynasty that carried his name. Bidar was territorially the smallest of the five kingdoms.

Bijapur, Ahmadnagar and Golconda were the more powerful kingdoms and has been studied in detail in this volume. The other two, Berar and Bidar, controlled only limited territories and exercised minimal influence in the further developments of the Deccan. Even so, they were more than of irritant value to the other three and continually engaged in behaviour that instigated animosity between the successor states. The five kingdoms would engage in continuous internecine wars and was also subject to incessant intrigue and betrayal. Paradoxically, although the relationship between the kingdoms was never on an even keel, they continued to create matrimonial and military alliances with each other, which were easily broken at the whim and fancy of any one party.

A study—as has been done in this book—clearly brings out the deplorable behaviour pattern of the rulers and their lack of integrity and 'character'. When viewed in an overarching manner, one is led to conclude that they did not deserve to be rulers but attained their positions because of their individualistic and opportunistic streak, which in turn made them successful warlords. The Shahi rulers as a whole became independent rulers by default with the founder of each dynasty being audacious and ambitious individuals. None of them produced worthy successors as such, although some of the rulers displayed better character traits and ability to rule than most of the others.

On Vijayanagar...

The fracturing of the Bahmani kingdom facilitated the further consolidation of the Vijayanagar kingdom, which then emerged as the most powerful in the Peninsula. Even at that time, Vijayanagar was cast as the bastion of Hindu culture, engaged in an endless fight against Muslim encroachment into the Deccan and South India. In actuality, there was a great deal of peaceful interaction between Vijayanagar and the Bahmanis as well as the Shahi kingdoms. In fact the powerful king Rama Raya of Vijayanagar exploited the rivalries between the Shahi kingdoms to his own benefit and had become the virtual king-maker for all of them. Upset with the overbearing behaviour of the Vijayanagar king, the Shahis formed a league, invaded the country and defeated its famed army. The Vijayanagar army was annihilated, Rama Raya summarily executed, the fabulous capital sacked and the kingdom effectively destroyed. Almost a century of relative peace and attendant prosperity ensued in the Deccan.

Even in this singular and important victory, the lack of astute thinking amongst the Shahi rulers is clearly visible. The fact that the great Vijayanagar kingdom could be defeated and brought to its knees by the combined Muslim forces of the Deccan did not make these petty rulers appreciate the fact that they were a powerful force when joined together. Immediately after the great victory, they lapsed into their normal behaviour of squabbling with each other and creating factions to control, undermine and stymy the growth of another. Any of the Shahi kingdoms that started to become more powerful were immediately brought to heel by the others who combined to curtail the rise. The inherent distrust and jealousies between the Shahis were potent factors in ensuring that each dynasty remained mediocre, although ruling wealthy kingdoms, throughout their existence.

Cosmopolitan Character

Even though all of them were keen to import foreign nobles, in a slightly surprising development, most of the Shahi kingdoms identified with the Deccani culture and the local nobles. Some, like the Adil Shahis, even went to the extent of embracing the memory of Deccan's ancient and illustrious dynasty—the Chalukyas. They placed Chalukya inscriptions and even Chalukya columns at the gateway to their capital in Bijapur. The Shahis were active patrons of art and also encouraged the cosmopolitan diversity of the people in this sphere. This stood in stark contrast to the almost fully homogeneous culture of the Muslim rule in North India, starting with the establishment of the Delhi Sultanate and flowing on to the Mughal rule. The royal courts of the Deccan were an interesting mixture of the foreign and local. By the 15th century they had managed to absorb Persian traditions that had been brought to the Deccan by the North Indian Muslims and also direct emigres from Central Asia. Simultaneously, the Deccani Muslims—born in the Deccan to foreigners and also local converts—continued to support the region's indigenous culture and traditions.

By the 16th and 17th century, the Deccanis were confidently assertive of their own culture and went on to create an early form of proto-Urdu language that came to called 'Dakhini'. By the end of the 16th century, even poems were being written in this language. Further, the Adil Shahis of Bijapur and the Qutb Shahi rulers of Golconda actively patronised the vernacular tradition—with both maintaining official records in the local language, Bijapur in Marathi and Golconda in Telugu. The three main kingdoms were fabulously wealthy and therefore, the rulers could engage in improving the major cities to cater for the growing population. In fact the quintessential Muslim city of Hyderabad was created as such an initiative by the Qutb Shahi rulers. The new city was centred on the Charminar (Four Minarets) but planned and built on the lines of Warangal, the old Kakatiya capital.

Adding to the cosmopolitan nature of the Deccan kingdoms was the active participation of the Hindu Brahmin community in the administration, unlike in North India. Brahmins were even appointed as governors of towns, diplomats and ministers while the cadre of lower level accountants were almost fully populated by them. For example, the entire revenue system in the Adil Shahi kingdom of Bijapur was run by Brahmins.

Peninsular India had flourishing ports on both the eastern and western coasts, which were trading hubs connected to South-East Asia and the Middle-East. It was obvious that certain amount of foreign influence would percolate into the region. The Deccan kings were eager to obtain warhorses for their armies, since they were almost always in a perennial state of war, and therefore attempted to attract trading partners to buy their rich textiles and other export items. From 1498, the Portuguese and in later centuries the Dutch, French and English, came to the Peninsula in the quest to establish trading monopolies. The Portuguese seizure of Goa from Bijapur was a significant event since it permitted the Portuguese to start the spread of Christianity through concerted proselytising in the conquered regions. The only advantage that accrued from the arrival of the Western powers was that it further emphasised the cosmopolitan nature of the Deccan kingdoms.

In a completely unprecedented manner for Islamic dynasties, the Deccan courts managed to absorb the influence of the past dynasties of the Deccan Plateau like the Chalukyas and the Kakatiyas and was also influenced by the Timurid dynasties, while being affected by the Central Asian, Habshi, Deccani, Maratha, Telugu, Hindu Brahmin and European cultures and traditions. The diversity of the influences that produced the complex culture of the Deccani kingdoms is unique not only in the multifarious history of the Indian sub-continent, but also across the entire world.

Rise of Other Communities

The Deccan Shahi kingdoms were involved in persistent and repetitive conflicts throughout the nearly two centuries of their existence. Therefore, the demand for quality military forces was always high. Accordingly, some communities who were more warlike than others, rose to prominence such as the East African military slaves, called Habshis. They were initially brought to the Deccan as slaves and then recruited for military purposes by the Bahmani kings and then by the Shahi rulers, particularly in Bijapur and Ahmadnagar. The proclivity of the Deccan Muslim rulers to import soldiers and commanders from Central Asia and to favour them over the local recruits in the military and administration was the root cause for the mutual distrust between the Westerners and the Deccanis (Phirangis and Deccanis). This mistrust in turn was one of the principle driving forces that created a perpetually unstable political environment.

The other community to gradually come to prominence, starting in the military field, was the Marathas. Both the Western Shahi kingdoms—Bijapur and Ahmadnagar—had large Maratha contingents in their army. Under the Shahi rulers, the Maratha 'Deshmukhs' continued their traditional role of collecting revenue and providing troops to the king, with many clans rising to prominence. Similarly in the Golconda kingdom, Telugu warriors called 'nayakwaris', who nurtured warrior traditions from the time of the Kakatiya kings, performed the same role as the Marathas. Both these groups were upwardly mobile and their increasing importance was enhanced by their service in the royal courts.

Decline and Eclipse

Founded on the failure of a much larger kingdom, by warlords of dubious individual capabilities, it is not surprising that the Successor Deccan Shahi kingdoms lasted less than two centuries, most of them vanishing within 150 years or so of their founding. The decline started with the two lesser Shahi kingdoms, Bidar and Berar, being engulfed by the larger ones, although this led to greater stability for a short period of time. Berar was taken over by the Nizam Shahis of Ahmadnagar and Bidar subsumed by the Adil Shahis of Bijapur. Even though it brought a sense of stability to the Deccan, the take-overs also came with a distinct disadvantage. With the take-over of Berar, the buffer to the north vanished and the Nizam Shahis now had to accept a common border with the great Mughals. The Mughals had by now consolidated North India and had started to move south earnestly.

The Mughal emperor Akbar had by now conquered and annexed Khandesh, a kingdom to the north of Berar that had been ruled by the Faruqi dynasty for nearly 250 years from their capital at Burhanpur. Further, the Mughals had already started to exert pressure on the Deccan kingdoms by this time. Ever since Babur had established the Mughal kingdom in 1526 after his victory at the Battle of Panipat, the Mughals had been consolidating their kingdom and had emerged as a behemoth swallowing everything in its wake. The metamorphism of the Mughal kingdom from a very precarious and fragile beginning to an all-consuming Empire was remarkable. However, the Deccan Shahi kingdoms and their rulers remained oblivious to the threat from the north.

The first to fall was Ahmadnagar. As soon as Malik Ambar, the Ethiopian born prime minister died, the kingdom could not survive the pressure from the north from the Mughals and the south from an expansionary Bijapur. On Ahmadnagar being annexed, Bijapur ruling in the south-west and Golconda ruling in the east acknowledged the Mughals as their overlords to ensure their own survival. Both these kingdoms continued in a state of autonomy till Aurangzeb's final onslaught. However, it did not take long for these two surviving kingdoms to follow the Nizam Shahi kingdom. Aurangzeb had twice been the Mughal governor for the Deccan and subsequently spent 26 years campaigning to bring the entire Plateau under Mughal control. By 1687, he had annexed both Bijapur and Golconda and both the Adil Shahis and Qutb Shahis had ceased to exist as ruling dynasties. From having direct Mughal influence, the kingdoms had transitioned to being Mughal provinces. By this time the Marathas had carved out a small but independent state for themselves. They went on to create an empire that stood up to the Mughal might.

An Analysis

Two developments standout in any analysis of the medieval Deccan kingdoms—the tradition of inducting the Habshi military slaves from North-East Africa who exercised enormous influence on the political developments; and the assimilation of the high-brow Persian culture into the South Indian ethos, producing a pleasing mixture in language and art that endures to date. The reason for the import of Habshis was the lack of stability in the region, which was also the primary cause of the final decline and downfall of the Shahi kingdoms. The inherent instability also led to unscrupulous nobles and contenders for the throne inviting external powers to intervene in domestic affairs. This tendency was also palpable during times of war between two of the successor states.

There were early signs of this malady—of inviting external entities to help—that would subsequently become the root cause for these kingdoms being extinguished. Right from the time of his arrival into the Indian sub-continent, Babur had been approached by the Shahi kings for assistance in subduing adversaries—other Shahi kings—even though he was a relatively new comer and not yet an established king as such. This aspect brings out uncomfortable questions with intangible answers. Did the long established 'Indian' Muslims suffer from an inferiority complex vis-à-vis the new arrivals from Central Asia? Was this inferiority a throwback to the perceived and dismissive inferiority of the 'Hindu', which may have diluted the 'spirit' of local Muslims since some amount of racial mingling was bound to have taken place over the years? There is no indication that the Shahi rulers had any information regarding the nascent power of the Mughals. In fact, the great power of the Mughals was built up after they established themselves in Delhi and subsequently in Agra. When Babur came to India, he was as good or as vulnerable as any other invader who had tread the Khyber Pass. Therefore, an appeal to him for assistance is an inexplicable turn of events.

The malady of believing in the exaggerated power of the foreigner is a real and very Indian challenge that persists in the Indian psyche till today. Elevating foreign capabilities above indigenous ones, as a tribe and as individuals, plagued security calculations in India then, and continues to do so even now.

The most noticeable factor in the fall of the Shahi dynasties was their lack of cooperation, even in the face of definitive annihilation. This could have been because of a lack of acumen to understand the extreme danger that they faced, since most of the unaffected rulers stood aside because of their vanity and the inherent pettiness to see an erstwhile adversary brought down. The same character flaw that afflicted the Hindu kings during the early days of the Islamic invasion, held sway with these worthless scions of once victorious warlords. Presenting a united front to a common enemy was an impossibility for the Deccan Shahi rulers. Further, even within this vexed situation the betrayal of trust between these kings was a common occurrence.

The blunder that led to the annihilation of the Nizam Shahi dynasty of Ahmadnagar was the invitation to the Mughal prince Murad to intervene by one of the factions fighting for the throne after the death of Burhan Nizam Shah II in 1595. In the Deccan the initial Western Muslim stock had mingled liberally with the locals and a distinctively Deccan nobility had emerged by the 12th century. By the time the Mughals had become serious about engulfing the Peninsula, the Deccan nobility was divided between the Phirangi and the Deccani

Introduction

factions and stand-offs and internecine wars were common. (This division has been covered in detail earlier.)

The political structures of the Muslim kingdoms in North India and in the Deccan were distinctly different. The rulers and nobility in North India revelled in their aristocratic pedigree traced back to Central Asia and Persia, becoming an entrenched hereditary aristocracy, and claiming racial superiority over the local population. The military slavery system that had created the slave dynasty in Delhi had been short-lived and in any case their last remnants were swept aside by the coming of the Mughals. The socio-political structure was entrenched with all power flowing from the person of the emperor downwards through nobles of different stature. On the other hand in the Deccan, military slavery as an institution continued to thrive. However, the Habshis did not, and could not, identify with the racial superiority that Iranian descendants arrogantly claimed. They also cultivated an ethical notion of loyalty with the freed slaves forming a patron-client relationship with their masters. These two systems came into direct conflict when Prince Murad moved to besiege Ahmadnagar, the northern most Shahi kingdom. The result was never in doubt.

There is an underplayed and under-analysed aspect to the Mughal conquest of the Deccan. It is true that the Mughals vanquished the entire lot and annexed the Deccan at the end of a long-drawn war. However, the same campaign brought about the beginning of the end of the 'greatness' of the Mughal Empire. It is not always acknowledged that the Shahis of Deccan played a prominent role in diminishing Mughal power that for centuries had stood unquestioned. One is tempted to speculate that had the Shahi rulers not weakened themselves through infighting and petty vanity, and faced the Mughals in a concerted resistance, the course of peninsular history may have been somewhat different.

Volume VI – Medieval Deccan Kingdoms

This volume of the series, *From Indus to Independence: A Trek Through Indian History*, starts with an overview of the Deccan and provides a detailed background of South India before the Islamic invasion. It also explains the spirited Hindu revival that took place before the entire Deccan was subsumed by the Islamic enterprise emanating from

North India. The book has been sub-divided into sections to facilitate better organisation of the narrative and also for ease of study. The first section could be considered a detailed prologue to the core subject of study in the book—the medieval kingdoms of the Deccan.

The second section deals with the history of the Bahmani dynasty; its tumultuous founding; the rule of various kings; and a detailed analysis of the breakup of the kingdom—the process, reasons and aftermath. The entire two-centuries of their non-productive rule is covered in great detail. This section is followed by three more sections that deal separately with the major successor kingdoms—Adil Shahis of Bijapur, Nizam Shahis of Ahmadnagar and Qutb Shahis of Golconda/Hyderabad. Welded equally into the three sections are the narratives of the Barid Shahis of Bidar and Imad Shahis of Berar. Their stories come out throughout the recounting of the history of the major Shahi kingdoms. An interesting point that comes out in the recounting of events after the Deccan had been conclusively converted to Islamic kingdoms is that, although all the dynasties put in place concerted attempts to increase the Muslim population of their kingdoms, the best that could be achieved was to have a maximum of ten percent of the total population adhere to the Islamic faith. However, the ethnic mix of the population, especially in the capitals and major towns, changed appreciably.

The last section of the book is a concluding analysis, in four chapters, of the impact and influence of the nearly four centuries of medieval Islamic rule of the Deccan Plateau. It becomes readily apparent that irrespective of the feelings of waste, ruthlessness and indulgence that a study of the rule of the Bahmanis and the successor dynasties create for the modern historian, the nearly four centuries of Islamic rule comprehensively changed the ethnic mix, socio-political norms and the practice of religion for all the peoples of the Deccan. The favourites of all ruling kings/sultans of the time, the foreign Muslims who were meant to stay 'unsullied' as separate entities, fell prey to the age-old Indian tradition—they mingled freely with the local population and became assimilated within the span of a few generations and centuries. In a broader context, the socio-economic-religious narrative of the Deccan is the story of India itself.

Introduction

Any migration into the sub-continent faced the same plight. Irrespective of their ethnicity, social customs and religious practices, the migrants were uniformly influenced in some way or the other, by the overriding ability of the sub-continental Hindu ethos of flexibility, adaptation and intermingling, which gradually created a new identity. In the Deccan, the phirangis, Habshis and the local population became mixed and created a new identity—the Deccanis.

Section I

THE DECCAN AND SOUTH INDIA
A PROLOGUE

The co-founders of Vijayanagar Empire realised very early the danger that Islam posed to the integrity of South India. They understood the need to present a combined Hindu resistance to the Muslim invasions from the north. This meant that the smaller Hindu states of the Deccan and South India could not be allowed to continue hostilities with their neighbours on a regular basis in pursuing the age-old Mandala theory of state security. Accordingly, the founders of Vijayanagar embarked on a conquering consolidation of the Deccan and South India, which would see the empire stretch across the Peninsula, from sea to sea.

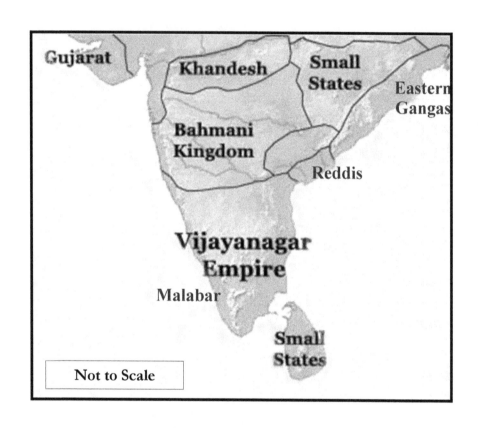

Map of South India – 1400 AD

Chapter 1

THE DECCAN – A BROAD OVERVIEW

The Deccan Plateau forms part of the Indian Peninsula bounded by the Vindhya Mountain Ranges and the River Godavari to the north and the Rivers Tungabhadra and Krishna to the south. The Eastern and Western Ghats, mountain ranges that skirt the sea coast on both sides of the peninsula serve as the eastern and western limits to the high lying plateau with elevations between 1000 and 2000 feet above mean sea level.

> **The Deccan – Deriving the Name**
>
> There are different opinions regarding the origin of the name 'Deccan' for the plateau that emerges south from the Vindhya Ranges. One is that it is derived from the word Dandaka, meaning forest, into which Lord Ram proceeded on exile. However, more probable is the argument that it is derived from the word 'Dakkin', which is the Prakrit version of the Sanskrit 'Dakshin' meaning the left or south.

Muhammad Qasim Firishta (died 1611), who lived in Bijapur for a number of years and is considered one of medieval India's foremost chroniclers, mapped the Peninsula in terms of the prevalent vernacular languages. He used a metaphor of kinship to explain the concept of such a division. He wrote that one of the four sons of India, 'Hind', was 'Dakan' who in turn had three sons called 'Marhar, Kanhar and Tiling'.

This meant the native speakers of Marathi, Kannada and Telugu and Firishta said that the combined territories populated by these three communities form the Deccan. Even today, in the 21st century, the Deccan consists of the linguistically defined states of Maharashtra, Karnataka and the un-divided Andhra Pradesh.

The Deccan was home to many rich and flourishing kingdoms, a fact that is confirmed through inscriptions, architectural remains, numismatics and the few records that have become available in the past few decades, which show the distribution of land grants. In the early days of the Delhi Sultanate, the new rulers did not have any knowledge of the country of Deccan and dismissed the region as being inhabited by 'pagan idolaters'. Consequently, till the end of the 13th century, the Muslims from North India did not venture south of the Vindhya Ranges. When the Islamic army finally marched south into the Peninsula, they did not face any serious or effective opposition and managed to reach almost to the southernmost point in the Peninsula without much ado. However, the Muslim armies were bent on plunder, not conquest and occupation. There was no permanent or lasting impact from the early incursions. The kingdoms of South India bent to the stormy arrival of the Northern Muslim army, but they did not break. As soon as the invaders had gathered their plunder and left, the Hindu kingdoms sprang back to independence.

The story in the Deccan was somewhat different. The Delhi Sultanate's army commander left a Muslim governor to rule at Devagiri (also spelt Deogiri in some books), which was renamed Daulatabad. However, the governor was not loyal to the Sultanate and did not maintain strong connections to the Delhi administration. In mid-14th century, when the oppression from Muhammad Tughluq started to become increasingly unbearable, the Devagiri governor along with his generals revolted. The Delhi sultan was immersed in controlling internal dissentions and was far too distant from Devagiri to mount any meaningful interference in order to subdue the nascent rebellion. This inability led to the establishment of an independent Muslim Kingdom in the Deccan, which was to last for more than 300 years.

The three centuries of the Delhi Sultanate's existence was a period of incessant wars, rebellions and civil strife. This is not surprising considering that an alien invading force was attempting to establish a kingdom in a land that had for centuries culturally and religiously absorbed the foreign invaders. The foreigners had always been gathered into the fold rather than being permitted to maintain a separate identity and/or create an independent kingdom. Even after three centuries of turbulence the final phase of the Sultanate was cataclysmic. It was akin to the death throes of a giant, wherein wars, revolts and dissention were ceaseless activities that led to the fragmentation of the northern part of the sub-continent into numerous kingdoms of varying size strength and stature; all of them at war with each other.

The stories of these fragmented states—many of them small, insignificant and even transient—are dreary tales of conflict, rebellion, and personal ambitions gone astray. The historical narrative is only a long list of kings and the battles they fought. Even the narratives vary in their accounts depending on the chronicler and his biases. Therefore, most of the accounts have to be discarded as being unreliable. No doubt, the self-perpetuating cycle of wars leading to fragmentation and then to further wars are important historic events. They mark a trend and a pattern that needs to be studied and analysed to draw tangible lessons from them. However, the actual events and descriptions of minor wars fought between small-time chieftains do not contribute in any meaningful manner to the understanding of the broader narrative. The events are common-place but the trends and evolving patterns and their impact on the socio-political and religious environments are critical factors to be noted.

The more notable successor kingdoms to the Delhi Sultanate were: Sind, Multan, the Rajput Principalities, Gujarat, Malwa, Khandesh, Jaunpur, Kashmir, Bengal, Orissa and Telangana. In the Deccan and South India the Bahmani Kingdom and the Vijayanagar Empire stood out as the most important states.

South India – 10th to 13th Century

The arrival of Islam as a military force to the Deccan and South India is a different tale. In order to understand the ease with which the Muslim forces raced through the Peninsula at the end of the 13th century, it is necessary to know the geo-political situation that was prevalent at the time in the Indian Peninsula.

After the fall of the Pallava dynasty in the early 10th century, the Cholas established themselves at Kanchi and exercised imperial sway and primacy over most of South India for the following 300 years and more. The glory of the Chola dynasty is recounted in the colonial empire that they built in Malaya and the 100-year naval war that they conducted against the Sailendra kings of Sumatra. *[Both these events have been covered in an earlier volume of this series of books and is not germane to the narrative in this book.]* The Cholas were inherently an expansionist dynasty. After he came to the throne, the illustrious king Rajaraja Chola expanded his territorial holdings by annexing Orissa and the territories to the River Tungabhadra. He has been given the sobriquet 'the Great' by many historians. Rajaraja's son, Rajendra Chola, annexed Ceylon (present day Sri Lanka), crossed the seas and after occupying Nicobar Island established Kadaram in the Malaya peninsula as indisputable Chola territory. Rajendra was also an innovative king. While continuing the expansionist pattern of his dynasty, Rajendra created a magnificent irrigation system, which ensured that the agricultural produce of his kingdom was surplus to requirements. The irrigation system that was built continued to function efficiently till the mid-19th century, proving the solidity and technical soundness of its construction.

In his effort to expand his kingdom further north in the Peninsula in pursuance of his continuous quest to annex new territories, Rajendra came into conflict with the Chalukya rulers of Maharashtra. The Cholas at this stage was strong and confident enough to involve themselves in two wars simultaneously—one a naval war overseas against the Sailendra kings and the other a land-centric conflict against the powerful Chalukyas. The might of the Cholas was displayed when they were victorious in both these wars. Kulothunga, one of the greatest among Chola monarchs, was able to bring peace and stability to the extended kingdom after the battlefield victories. Till mid-13th century the Cholas ruled in relative peace. All successful dynasties that create and nurture great empires finally come to a standstill and then decline through the rule of incompetent rulers who merely inherit the kingdom, without having had to fight to win it. The Cholas were no exception. They also suffered in the long-term from the incompetence of successive kings who weakened central authority. The Cholas vanished from the scene between 1250 and 1300, squeezed out by a belligerent Pandya dynasty in the south and an equally aggressive Hoysala kingdom in the north.

The Cholas reigned supreme with full authority over the entire South India for nearly four centuries. They were the first Indian dynasty to appreciate the importance of naval power in a peninsular context and instituted what could only be termed a cohesive maritime strategy. They controlled the entire Bay of Bengal and for nearly a century enforced imperial authority over Malaya; a century during which the Bay of Bengal could have been considered a 'Chola Lake'. The Chola reign was an extraordinary period of political, artistic and literary achievement. They were also builders of great temples that stand out even today for their artistic purity. The irrigation system that they put in place originated a new style that was 'widely adopted' by the British, with some modifications, successfully throughout their empire. In this context, it was the Cholas who conceived the idea of 'controlling a river at the head of its delta and thus securing the regular watering of lands'.

Malik Kafur's Incursion

By the end of the 13th century, the great Chola Empire had fully disintegrated and this was the time when Malik Kafur made his famous raid into South India. Since the power of the Cholas had been extinguished and there was yet to be a replacement power to step into the void, there was no real opposition to Malik Kafur's military prowess. He was able to move with impunity anywhere in the Peninsula that he preferred.

Earlier, at the demise of the once powerful Rashtrakuta empire, their territorial holdings had been carved into three independent kingdoms—the Yadavas ruling from Devagiri, the Kakatiyas from Warrangal in Middle Deccan, and the Hoysalas with their capital of Dwarasamudra in Karnataka. All three were rich and flourishing kingdoms ruled by renowned and generous monarchs. The kings were wise and just, known for their patronage of learning and art. By the time of Malik Kafur's invasion or raid, the Yadavas had already been conquered by the Delhi Sultanate and the Kakatiyas had been reduced to vassal status. The fact was that individually the three kingdoms were not strong enough to withstand the onslaught of Islam from the north. Malik Kafur's army was an irresistible force.

The Hoysalas were the remaining power in the Deccan and they had been in intermittent war with the Cholas during the latter's gradual and somewhat long-drawn decline. The eventual fall of the Cholas benefitted the Hoysalas the most. Under their most illustrious king Vira Ballala II (ruled for 47 years, 1173-1220), who was the son of a Pandyan princess, the Hoysalas became the preeminent power in South India, dominating the entire region. Their territory extended from the Madurai country to Mangalore in Malabar. The defeat of the Hoysalas by Malik Kafur is an important event in the history of South India. The fall of Dwarasamudra opened South India to Islamic invasion. At the time of Malik Kafur's invasion of Hoysala country, the Pandyas to the south were involved in a contentious succession struggle and did not offer any assistance to the Hoysala king. Kafur was very easily able to sack Madurai and return to Delhi, leaving behind complete chaos and a Muslim garrison as a token of his conquest.

At this juncture, as often happens in history, the ruler of a small and somewhat insignificant principality, but who was ambitious, capable and looking for opportunities to better his prospects came into the picture. Vira Ravivarman Kulasekhara was the ruler of the region around Quilon (modern Kollam in the state of Kerala). He seized the opportunity and expelled the Muslim garrison before it could establish itself. The he crowned himself at Kanchi as the new ruler of the remnants of the erstwhile Hoysala kingdom. The Muslims were not given an opportunity to establish themselves. Ravivarman's achievement should be counted as singularly critical to the further developments in South Indian history. It was the precursor to the vehement Hindu resistance to Islam in the Peninsula that lasted another three to four centuries. At this time South India north of Kanchi was in turmoil with the rapid withdrawal of the Islamic army of Delhi. There was no settled authority with the power to stabilise the region. The Yadavas of Devagiri were non-existent; and the Kakatiyas of Warrangal was in terminal decline after being repeatedly battered by Islamic invasions and already in a destroyed state.

River Tungabhadra became the rallying point for Hindu resistance, which very rapidly spread across the peninsula. Gradually it coalesced around the region with Warrangal as the centre. The initial rebellion was led by Prolaya Nayaka and Kapala Nayaka his cousin. Their strong movement of liberation led to the formation of the Reddi kingdoms of Addanki and Kondavidu. Simultaneously, Somadeva a scion of the imperial Chalukya dynasty, freed western Telugu country. The people of the Tungabhadra-Krishna Doab started a spontaneous and popular insurrection and threw off the Muslim yoke.

The unity of South India started to assert itself under two great leaders Harihara and Bukka. They started to organise a new state in 1336, known to history as the Vijayanagar Empire. The Vijayanagar rulers realised the necessity to consolidate control over South India at the River Tungabhadra line in order to defend it against foreign onslaught. Successors to Bukka expanded their holding south to Rameswaram and established control up to the River Krishna. Further northern expansion was checked by the rise of the Bahmani dynasty ruling in the Deccan.

The Bahmani Kingdom

Hasan alias Gangu Bahman Shah established a Muslim state between the Rivers Narmada and Krishna, in the heart of the Deccan in 1347, merely a decade after Vijayanagar was founded. He consolidated the territories north of the River Krishna. This kingdom became the embryo from which Muslim power in the Deccan was established and subsequently spread. This event was also fraught with great significance in South Indian history. The timing and context of its birth brought it almost immediately into conflict with Vijayanagar in the south and the Delhi Sultanate in the north. Boxed in by two powerful and warlike kingdoms on both sides, the rulers gradually became fully dependent on the majority Hindu population of the kingdom to function efficiently.

Conclusion

Peninsular India now entered state of unending struggle between Vijayanagar and the Bahmani kingdom that would last for centuries. Both the kingdoms, of necessity, were completely militarised states, never letting their guard down lest the other take advantage of the temporary weakness. The Vijayanagar emperors had added responsibility as the bulwark of Hindu religion. They were always reminded of their historic mission to defend Hinduism and South India from the depredations of a Muslim conquest. It is indeed true that if it had not been for a steadfast Vijayanagar, South India too would have easily fallen prey to the Islamic invasion in much the same fashion as the Gangetic Valley had succumbed. Vijayanagar denied the Islamic invaders any easy conquest for three long centuries.

Chapter 2

THE BRIDGE BETWEEN TWO ERAS

The geo-cultural axis, forged along the ancient trade routes that wound its way east through the Khyber and Bolan Passes, gradually became migratory corridors into North India. Subsequently they linked South Asia and the Iranian plateau by joining Lahore to Delhi. At Delhi the migratory route trifurcated—one led directly south to the Vindhya Ranges and beyond to the arid Deccan; a second continued the eastern journey towards Patna and Bengal; and the third took a tortuous way south-west through the deserts of Rajputana all the way to coastal Gujarat. This indelible axis that originated in Persia, or Iran, and traversed all the way to the Bay of Bengal and the Arakan mountain ranges carried with it Persian influence that, over a period of time, affected all aspects of Indian society. Persian influence spread into architecture, music, art, dress, technology, cuisine and all other areas of society. The Indo-Persian mingling of ideas spawned the hybrid language of Urdu, still in use in the sub-continent. It altered forever the socio-political organisation of the kingdoms of South Asia.

The three major kingdoms of Peninsular India, ruled by the Yadava, Kakatiya and Hoysala dynasties, were the last of the old order state system represented by the 'regional Hindu kingdoms'. In the second half of the 13th century, the Deccan and South India were on the cusp of a radical change to a system of kingdoms and monarchies represented by a transregional sultanate. The first chapter of the Delhi-Deccan migratory axis was starting to be written by early 14th century. Of the three kingdoms of the Deccan, the demise of the Kakatiya kingdom epitomises the rapid shift that was taking place in the socio-political ethos of the region. The troubles and tribulations of the last sovereign of the Kakatiya dynasty, Pratapa Rudra, is illustrative of the decline and fall of powerful kingdoms of South India. The alteration of the political system also had religious overtones and contained all the confusion that a clash of religions brings with it. In the Deccan, the arrival of the Delhi Muslim army heralded a forced transition—from an entrenched Hindu system to an Indo-Persian system based on rigid Islamic tenets. The new system that took hold lasted until the arrival of the British and the imposition of their socio-political system in late 18th century. Pratapa Rudra and his monarchy, the Kakatiya kingdom, stands silent witness to the violence and mesmerising speed with which the transition from regional Hindu kingdom to transregional Muslim sultanate took place.

Language, Territory and Culture

An abiding image of pre-colonial India is one of a static, tradition-bound, caste-ridden social order dominated by Brahminical Hinduism. The literature of Hinduism, written in Sanskrit, more often than not mentioned and elaborated on matters and events as they should have been, seldom attempting to explain them as they actually were. This picture of India—prominently portrayed as 'backward' in all aspects—was developed by the British as they started to colonise the sub-continent, in order to project and extol their own dynamism and progressive impetuses. They consciously defined India as stagnant and Indians as stubborn, being led by Brahmin ideologues sponsoring and steeped in Sanskrit texts. This interpretation of the Indian-Hindu society was far from the truth.

The true picture of pre-colonial India, especially in the Deccan and South India, emerges from the vernacular stone inscriptions that recorded day-to-day events and transactions relevant to the region. From these authentic records emerge the picture of a society and religious activities completely at odds with the British narrative, and to the descriptions in the classical texts. Further, the vernacular records are much more voluminous than the Sanskrit texts and provide details of not just the elite in society but also of the common people of the kingdom. They indicate a dynamism in the society that is completely ignored in the Brahminical texts written in Sanskrit. India may have been stubborn, but India, especially the South, was anything but static and stagnant.

In the Deccan, detailed inscriptions indicate the emergence of Andhra as a distinct cultural entity. As early as 1053, Telugu was known as 'Andhra Bhasa', the language of Andhra. This is perhaps the first instance of a language being mapped to a delineated territory, attributing and combining both culture and language to a people. By the 13th century, similar processes had separated both Maratha and Kannada territories. In the Deccan, language and territory conceptually fused to create a new cultural identity for the people. The next step in this development was a natural progression from the norms of the times wherein rulers were expected to advance and increase their territorial holdings. Chiefs, kings and monarchs started to map their political territory towards the regions where their language was dominant. The Deccan was now divided into three vernacular linguistic kingdoms, speaking Marathi, Telugu and Kannada.

In 1163, the chiefs of the Telugu-speaking Kakatiya clan declared independence from their imperial Chalukya overlords and created a kingdom with its capital in Warrangal. They initiated a new style of creating inscriptions in Telugu and gradually brought almost three-quarters of the undivided Andhra Pradesh of independent India under their banner. The kingdom was linguistic in its definition and rapidly transformed into a separate cultural territory. Across the Deccan similar processes were being enacted with warrior groups forming petty states throughout the 12th and 13th centuries. The championing of the local vernacular by all kinds of rulers, both powerful and of lesser capabilities, was a visible revolt against the pan-Indian superiority that Sanskrit had by then assumed.

In early 13th century, the Kakatiya kings annexed the rich Telugu-speaking coastal region between the Rivers Krishna and Godavari, thereby bringing all Telugu lands under their control. Around the same time, the Yadavas consolidated their authority over the Marathi-speaking population and the territories that they occupied. In Karnataka, the Hoysalas followed suit by expanding their hold over all Kannada speakers and their territorial holdings.

The rulers of these 'linguistic' kingdoms, the first of their kind in the sub-continent, connected the language to a distinct culture. They went on to legitimise the vernacular as the official language of the state, as opposed to the use of Sanskrit that had been so far prevalent. The results of this move were palpable. It crystallised local identity and assisted in community building where each individual had a sense of belonging to the whole. Perhaps more importantly, it established a direct connection between the ruling dynasty and the people through the shared linguistic identity. From here on it was easy to inculcate the sense of 'we and them' into the people, especially in times of danger to the state. Pride in their linguistically derived cultural identity is clearly evident in the inscriptions of the time.

The Kakatiya Kingdom

The Telugu kingdom ruled by the Kakatiya dynasty epitomises the character, psyche and ethos of the linguistic kingdoms of the Deccan. It also involuntarily became the bridge between the old and the on-coming new socio-political systems and is therefore studied in greater detail here. The inscriptions of the time provide a salutary indication of the dynamism of the Kakatiya kingdom.

The Deccan Plateau is semi-arid and extremely dry. As a result the interiors were sparsely populated. The landscape of Telangana, the Kakatiya heartland, is undulating with a large number of rain-fed streams that make it ideal territory to create reservoirs by building mud embankments to dam the streams. The Kakatiyas created hundreds of such reservoirs, called 'tanks', establishing a basic irrigation system and thereby opening the interior of the Deccan to wet and dry farming. The current estimate is that the Kakatiya kings, along with their vassal warrior chiefs, built nearly 5000 such tanks, a majority of which are still in use. The tanks gradually formed the basis of an economy that converted traditional nomadic herders into an established agrarian society.

Economy and the Temples

With an established irrigation system and the steady evolution towards a stable agricultural base, the economy became dynamic and the society started to change. As mentioned earlier, around 1230, the ruling king Ganapati (grandfather of Pratapa Rudra) had annexed the adjacent coastal region to the kingdom. This region already boasted a number of large temples, having been prosperous through agriculture for generations. Having become part of a much larger empire, these temples started to receive endowments from sources even far away—from merchants who wanted to ensure the extension of their network and from peasants wanting to establish their territorial right to cultivation and herding.

The temples started to play an important role in the development of the Kakatiya economy and society. Distinct from the great temples of the coast, numerous smaller temples were built in the interior of the Deccan, a trend that started only after the Kakatiya rule was established. Even though each of these temples were geographically limited in their influence, they became extremely vibrant stimuluses in expanding the agrarian society into the interior of the kingdom. Endowments from the local chiefs invariably came in the guise of building a tank in association with a temple that in turn turned arid land into cultivable fields. The intent of the king and the subordinate chiefs was two-fold—stabilising the economy through agriculture and ensuring the loyalty of the local population by controlling the tanks associated with the temple and their use in irrigation.

The temples also played a political role in the kingdom. The great coastal temples became agents for the integration of diverse people of the kingdom, although all of them spoke some variant dialect of Telugu. These temples became the focal points of the larger society, thereby inducing a sense of unity within the people. Similarly the smaller interior temples became the basis for forming vertical alliances between the local chief and the people. The temples and their associated tanks were normally built by the local chief, who was also the regional military leader subordinate to the Kakatiya king. They became central to the process of creating the pyramidal power base of the kingdom. The temple records of the time indicate the Telugu country to be a robust frontier society, expanding outwards, mainly based on increasing agrarian activities. This was achieved through maintaining and strengthening a clearly visible and extremely strong power hierarchy with the Kakatiya king at the apex and all power emanating from that single source.

There exists a dichotomy in explaining the connection between the kings and the temples, especially in South India. Accepted South Asian scholarship associates the temples of South India to the concept of kingship, kingdom and their connection to a divine and harmonious cosmos. This concept could have been derived from the extraordinary influence that temples had on the politico-economic development of the society. In a simpler manner, it has been explained away as a requirement for the king to be seen, and believed, to be directly associated with God. However, the concept of the 'divine right to rule' and claiming descent from celestial beings is a universal phenomenon and not restricted to either South India or the Deccan. Inexplicably, the South Indian kings have been singled out to be connected to their grandiose temples as catering to the need to establish and proclaim this divine connection to their subjects in order to establish their legitimacy.

The Kakatiya inscriptions provide a contrary view of having to proclaim the king's direct connection to the Gods. In these inscriptions, both temple and other general ones, the king is very seldom mentioned. When a king is mentioned in these records, it is almost never exalting his piety or connection to God but exuberant declarations of resounding battlefield victories that he brought to the kingdom. The theory of the connection of the king to the temple for divine legitimacy will have to be discarded, at least in the case of the kingdoms of the Deccan.

The Society

The Kakatiya society was typically imbued with the frontier ethos inculcating rapid change, in comparison to the more relaxed manner in which societies evolve. Therefore, it was more egalitarian and flexible, especially in the interior parts where the conversion from herders to cultivators was still taking place. The warrior-chiefs, controlling small territories, were called 'Nayaka' (a title that could be very broadly translated as 'leader'). This title could be obtained by anyone of adequate ability, regardless of his origin. Normally they were very generous in their donations to the temples, which indirectly benefitted the people at large. The egalitarianism of the society is further reinforced by the fact that no vernacular inscription mentions a birth-ascribed caste to any person mentioned in them.

The Kakatiya socio-religious environment was such that it was completely unaffected by Brahminical notions that governed traditional Hindu/Indian society. The warrior groups and their leadership did not claim to be Kshatriyas, the warrior 'caste' in normal Hindu society; they were content, in fact proud, to claim Sudra origin, which was placed one step lower than the Kshatriyas in traditional reckoning. Even the Kakatiya kings did not claim exalted status, happily embracing Sudra origins. It is therefore not surprising that jati and varna, the two defining birth-qualifications of a person in Brahminical Hinduism, does not find any mention in any of the Kakatiya inscriptions. The inscriptions only specify the occupation of individuals, such as Vedic Brahmin, Secular Brahmin, warrior-peasant, herdsman, Chief, military leader and so on. A large number of Kakatiya inscriptions that mention both father and son show different occupations for each, cementing the present-day understanding that in the medieval Telugu society, the practice of following the hereditary status was non-existent.

The openness of the Kakatiya society is clearly seen in the rise of officers of humble origin to higher ranks and posts, almost always at the expense of the traditional cadre culled from the established landed nobility. At the time that the dynasty was establishing itself, more than half the nobles and royal officers were from the hereditary, older and powerful families and only about 25 percent were from non-aristocratic background. When the dynasty was coming to an end, nearly three centuries later, the contribution towards the royal officialdom from the traditional nobility had been reduced to a mere 10 percent and the commoner-officers filled 50 percent of the positions. While this change in the distribution pattern demonstrates the move towards social equality, it also indicates another development – it showed the increasing autocratic power of the Kakatiya kings. They were able to break the entrenched power of the landed nobility without fear of rebellion. Similarly, the king was able to promote men of his own choice to positions of leadership with no concern regarding adverse consequences.

A Defensive Capital

The capital of the Kakatiya kingdom was Warrangal, today a provincial town that is not on the mainstream of modern India. In its heydays, it was a highly developed city with elaborate defensive structures. Its fortifications consisted of several concentric walls, still visible in a well-preserved manner today, interspersed with deep moats. The inner wall protected the primary citadel and was made of huge blocks of granite that stand around 20 feet in height. The blocks are irregular in shape, but fit together perfectly without the aid of any mortar. This wall is surrounded by a moat. The moat is then encircled with another earthen wall, once again surrounded by a moat.

The structure of the capital is such that it evokes a sense of a defensive crouch rather than the openness that would have indicated an offensive foreign policy and belief in the strength of the empire. This is paradoxical since the Kakatiya Empire suffered external attack only during the reign of the last king Pratapa Rudra. His predecessors had been left alone to rule. In fact, the earlier Kakatiya kings expanded the kingdom steadily till the entire Telugu-speaking Deccan territories were under their control. Warrangal was established in 1195 and successive kings built it into a perfectly defensible stronghold even though direct threats to the empire did not exist.

The Islamic Invasions and the Demise of the Kakatiyas

Although he was not the founder, the Kakatiya dynasty was firmly put on the map and consolidated by Ganapati. He was responsible for greatly expanding the territorial holdings. Ganapati regulated and increased commercial activities to take Kakatiya trade even beyond the sub-continent, across the seas. Ganapati had no sons and therefore placed his daughter, Rudrama Devi, on the throne. Unfortunately Rudrama also did not have any sons and on the advice of Ganapati, adopted one of her grandsons as her own son, who was anointed the heir apparent. This boy was Pratapa Rudra who ascended the throne in 1289. He ruled graciously for 20 years in a period that later historians have called the 'Golden Age' of the Kakatiyas.

Then came the storm that initially shook the foundations of the Kakatiya Empire, which subsequently brought it to its knees and then extinguished it. At this time the Delhi Sultanate had been in existence only for a relatively short period, but had already conquered the entire Gangetic plains. The Khilji Sultanate was without doubt the most powerful kingdom seen in the sub-continent till then. Ala ud-Din Khilji was a formidable general and an avaricious Sultan. He ordered his favourite slave general, Malik Kafur, to go south and invade the stable, peaceful and prosperous Kakatiya kingdom. In ordering the invasion, Ala ud-Din was not intent on annexation. He carefully instructed Kafur not to destroy the kingdom but to defeat the king and bring him, and his kingdom, into the growing fold of tributaries and vassal kingdoms that the Khilji Sultan was creating. This was based on an ancient Indian strategy of expanding the influence of the kingdom without assuming the direct responsibility of administering what could prove to be a rebellious new annexation.

In mid-February 1310, after two months of Warrangal being besieged, when the inner stone wall protecting the citadel was being invested by the Delhi forces, Pratapa Rudra sued for peace. Malik Kafur accepted the surrender and send a rich robe (*khil'at*) and subsequently a parasol (*chatr*) to Pratapa Rudra. These vestments symbolised Rudra's incorporation into the fold of Delhi's expanding circle of vassal kings. The parasol indicated that the Kakatiya king was now under the shadow of the Delhi Sultan. Pratapa Rudra was also required to don the robe and bow in the direction of Delhi from within his palace as a formal acceptance of Khilji supremacy. Even though all these actions—presentation of the robe and parasol, bowing towards Delhi—were ceremonial in nature it had an inherent effect of curtailing the freedom and independence that the vassal king had so far enjoyed. An annual tribute was imposed on Pratapa Rudra, which was paid for several years thereafter. Kafur returned to Delhi with immense wealth, there to be extravagantly feted by the Sultan.

With this one defeat, the political landscape of the Deccan changed forever. The Kakatiyas were no longer the dominant force they used to be and their southern Andhra vassals started to rebel, with some chiefs even declaring independence. The general perception in the Telugu country changed to the belief that Pratapa Rudra was now a lackey of Delhi. The perception was reinforced when the Kakatiya army assisted the Khilji invasion of the southern Pandya kingdom a year later. However, Pratapa Rudra shrewdly used the opportunity of the Khilji invasion of the far south to subdue the rebellions in the southern Andhra country. He personally led the Kakatiya army into the Tamil lands of the deep-south.

This military campaign must have created a belief in Pratapa Rudra's mind that he was now an 'ally' of Delhi rather than a vassal. He therefore stopped paying the annual tribute to Delhi in 1318. Obviously the Sultan in Delhi did not consider the Kakatiya an ally but a vassal, and therefore he send down General Khusrau Khan to chastise the errant king and to collect the overdue tribute. It is not an exaggeration to state that the Delhi army of the time was scientifically the most advanced, anywhere in the world. It was battle hardened, flexible and innovative in the application of its tactics. Once again Pratapa Rudra sued for peace, which was accepted with a huge increase in the annual tribute to be delivered to Delhi.

Once again the political ritual of accepting Delhi's suzerainty was enacted, but with one difference. This time, Pratapa Rudra was made to bow towards Delhi from the top of the ramparts of the Warrangal fort, while wearing the robe and carrying the parasol, in full view of the Kakatiya people. With this one act of subservience, Pratapa Rudra altered the socio-political situation of his kingdom. The Kakatiya king was perhaps unaware of this momentous change at that time.

In 1320, the Khiljis were replaced by the Tughluq dynasty in Delhi. There was obviously a period of confusion and uncertainty during this change over. Pratapa Rudra took advantage of this state of affairs in Delhi and once again stopped paying the annual tribute. A year later Ulugh Khan, the crown prince who was later to become Sultan Muhammad bin Tughluq, was send by his father to collect the tribute from the Kakatiya kingdom. He laid siege to Warrangal for six months and then withdrew to Devagiri when in-fighting broke out within his army. Devagiri was by this time fully conquered and annexed to the Delhi Sultanate, the rule of the Yadavas having been terminated by the Khiljis.

Ulugh Khan re-formed his army and returned to Kakatiya country within a year, now with a much strengthened army. This time, the third invasion, the Kakatiyas were given no quarter, the defences of Warrangal were breached and the city plundered and destroyed. By now the Delhi Sultanate had perfected the art of annexing the territory of Hindu kings by employing laid-down process. The process involved defeating the Hindu army in the battlefield; then desecrating the 'state temple', the temple that was important to the ruling king and dynasty since they derived legitimacy from the deity that was purported to protect the king; and then destroying this deity, which ensured that the Sultanate army visibly completed the annihilation of a dynasty. Ulugh Khan now enforced the same process. After Warrangal was put to the sword, plundered and raped, the Svayambhusive Temple of the Kakatiyas was destroyed and an enormous mosque built to the side of the temple's original location. *[In later years, the mosques would be built on the same spot, using the stones from the destroyed temple. At this time, Ulugh Khan may not have had the confidence to build on the site of the destroyed temple, fearing a rebellion and backlash from the people.]* He appointed a Muslim governor to rule and renamed Warrangal 'Sultanpur'. The Kakatiya kingdom came to an inglorious end, fully annexed and absorbed into the vast Delhi Sultanate.

Pratapa Rudra was captured and send to Delhi as a prisoner. On the journey north, pride and a sense of honour overtook the Kakatiya king and he opted to commit ritual suicide on the banks of the River Narmada, than be taken to Delhi as a prisoner.

Redefining Political Deccan

By the time the Kakatiya kingdom was obliterated by the Tughluqs, the Yadavas of Devagiri had long since become part of history. Therefore, what was different about the Kakatiya extinction? After the two defeats earlier, Pratapa Rudra had been presented ceremonial robes and had openly accepted Delhi suzerainty. Unlike in the case of the Yadavas, these were only the first two of a series of events that created a complete upheaval in the political structure of the Deccan. 13th century Deccan was home to kingdoms that were uniformly arranged to coincide with the linguistic territorial borders, which in turn brought about an unprecedented level of peace and stability to the region. In early 14th century, within a span of a few decades, the Islamic invasion shattered the tranquillity of the past few centuries and the shape of the region, without creating an alternative model. It was inevitable that successor kingdoms would emerge, particularly considering the waxing and waning of the power of the Delhi Sultanate. The Maratha and Telugu kingdoms and dynasties – the Yadavas and the Kakatiyas – were replaced by two emerging kingdoms, both multi-ethnic and transregional in character and ruled by self-proclaimed kings—the Bahmani kingdom and the Vijayanagar Empire. It would take another six centuries and the formation of an independent democratic India before the concept of linguistic territorial divisions would be attempted again.

Both the successor states in the Deccan clearly managed to severe all links to the Delhi Sultanate. However both derived a cultural system—political economy, dress, administration, organisation of military forces—from the one that had flowed from Iran/Persia into North India through the Turks who established the Delhi Sultanate in the sub-continent and subsequently invaded the Deccan and South India. Even though complete independence was assumed by both the successor kingdoms, institutional and ideological structures that were instrumental in the building of the Delhi Sultanate was a primary influence in establishing them. Other than these two major kingdoms, many other 'sultanates' of varying stature also sprang up in the Deccan and further south.

> ### The Concept of the Sultanate
>
> In the eastern Islamic world—meaning east of Baghdad and the Arab region—the Sultanate system took shape by the 10th century, deriving its cultural base from pre-Islamic Persia. By early 13th century, sultanates across the entire Islamic world were associated with the concept of mobile wealth, military slavery, and long-distance trade. These activities were built on a rigid hierarchy of royal officers and a court system that dispensed immediate and ruthless justice, both of which were loyal to the person of the sultan as practised in the earlier Persian Empire.
>
> The practice of military slavery, with slaves normally purchased in Central Asia, created the unintended effect of gradually diluting the importance of hereditary rank, replacing it with individual ability as the primary qualification for assured advance in the official hierarchy. The creation of the Slave dynasties in India and Egypt are astounding examples of this trend.

> Although religion played a convenient part in initiating military expeditions, it was detached from statecraft. Further, the culture, language and/or ethnicity of the people of a region were not considered limiting factors in advancing the political frontiers of the sultanate. By the time the Delhi Sultanate was established, the concept of the sultanate as an entity did not know any natural boundaries. The limit was defined only be the geographical extent to which revenue could be collected profitably.
>
> The sultanate armies were extremely mobile and technologically some of the most advanced that had so far been fielded in battle. They were well-versed in both rapid manoeuvre and siege warfare, equipped with the latest weapons and drilled in versatile techniques. The army provided the sultanate with the ability to mount trans-regional expeditions of plunder and conquest.

The Sultanate concept was propelled by two ideas, that of mobile wealth, most of which originated from plunder, and the practice of military slavery. In North India, a combination of the two ideas established a self-perpetuating cycle—wealth was plundered from non-believers and their temples as part of spreading the word of Islam; this wealth was then used to purchase/recruit more slaves from Central Asia who were in turn employed to perpetuate further plunder and conduct military expeditions against the wealthy, non-believing Hindus. The development and entrenchment of this cyclical process, it must be admitted, must have been the work of a devious genius.

The Iqta System

The Iqta was a unique system established by the Islamic rulers. The system was bedded on the concept of a military officer, considered to be of some calibre, being given a unit of land over which he had temporary right to collect revenue. The holder of an Iqta was called an Iqtadar (holder of an Iqta). In return for the temporary grant of the land, the Iqtadar was required to convert the revenue to cash, remit a laid down part to the central treasury and use the balance to raise, train and sustain a group of cavalry. The number of troops to be maintained depended on the decision of the Sultan and normally was based on the size of the land that was allocated.

The system had three inherent advantages. First, it provided the sultan with a fairly reliable army at short notice. Second, it provided the exchequer with funds and permitted the free movement of wealth; and third, it acted as tentacles that strengthened the political authority of the sultan even into faraway territories on the fringes of the sultanate. Further, some of the Iqtadars were hostile chiefs who had been subdued and then brought into the fold through the Iqta system. This ensured that they did not continue their hostile activities against the sultan once the central army had moved on after the initial subjugation. The Iqta system played a critical role in integrating the Deccan into the Delhi Sultanate, politically and economically.

Conclusion

Northern Deccan was annexed into the Delhi Sultanate in the span of a century through a series of calculated steps enforced in a gradual manner. The first step was the military defeat of the ruling monarchs after which they were made into subordinate or vassal rulers. This was accomplished by incorporating them into the Delhi 'circle' of tributaries through elaborate and pompous rituals and ceremonies. In the case of the Deccan kingdoms, they were merely brought into the 'shadow' of Delhi. The gift of the parasol to the defeated king testifies to this, a kind of hands-off approach. The second step was to again invade the kingdom based on some real or trumped up charges. After a second military defeat the kingdom was normally broken up and annexed to the territorial holdings of the Sultanate. The annexation was invariably accompanied by plunder and destruction, especially of the temples of the land, and then by the extinction of the ruling dynasty. This process may at times have taken more than two invasions as in the case of the Kakatiyas.

The third step was instituted after plunder and destruction of the capital and associated temples were accomplished. This was invariably followed by the construction of imposing mosques in the place where the 'state-temple' had existed, clearly indicating the end of a ruling dynasty and the entrenchment of another. If the kingdom was sufficiently large, it was parcelled into smaller provinces and Muslim governors appointed. The name of the Delhi Sultan was read out on every Friday during prayers at the mosque. In addition, at the grass root level the Iqta system subsumed the sovereignty of the defeated kingdom. The Kakatiyas, and earlier the Yadavas, were destroyed by this three-step system. Assimilation was comprehensive and complete when this system was applied.

The Kakatiya kingdom is the prime example of being the bridge between two eras in the Deccan. First, the stable regional kingdoms defined by linguistic territory, going through their 'golden ages' of prosperity. The Kakatiya kingdom, ruled by a dynasty that did not claim Kshatriya lineage and a society devoid of hereditary claims to nobility, greatness and power, epitomised this era. Early in the 14th century, another radically different polity—the trans-regional sultanate—with a completely different socio-political vision, challenged the status quo and overwhelmed the concept of linguistically defined regional kingdoms. Its unique three-step process of creating subordinate kings and then incorporating them into Delhi's imperial system was far too dynamic for the regional kingdoms to withstand. The Kakatiya kingdom and dynasty stand out as exemplar entities that fell to the more dynamic and unstoppable development of the socio-political and economic systems in the Indian sub-continent.

Chapter 3

A TALE OF THREE KINGDOMS

The once-great Chalukya Empire vanished at the end of 12th century, disintegrating into unrecognisable sub-states; and by early 13th century, the other great dynasty, the Cholas, were in terminal decline in a free fall. For the next century, the Deccan was dominated by the Yadavas in Devagiri and the Kakatiyas in Warrangal. Around the same time, in South India, the Pandyas were supreme in the Deep South and the Hoysalas to their north. The Yadavas were overwhelmed by repeated invasions by the Delhi Muslim army, and finally succumbed to the ferocity and viciousness of the attacks—initially becoming a vassal state and then being swallowed through annexation. That left only the three other kingdoms to control the remaining parts of the Deccan and the South.

Through most of the 13th century, there were no significant political developments in the region. An eerie peace prevailed—the calm before the storm. Since peace prevailed, however uncomfortable it may have been, there were conspicuous developments in trade and the arts in the Peninsula. The famous traveller-trader Marco Polo visited the region in 1292-93 and left a vivid description of the three kingdoms, their social and political structure, and the day-to-day life of the common people.

The Pandya king, Jatavarman Kulasekhara had suffered an ignoble defeat at the hands of Kulottunga III, the Chola king, in 1205. Kulasekhara was succeeded 10 years later by his younger brother Maravarman Sundara Pandya. Sundara was still smarting under the defeat his brother had suffered and almost immediately invaded Chola territory. Kulottunga, now wearied by age and caught unawares by the attack, found the might of the Pandya king unstoppable. Sundara Pandya sacked Uraiyur and Tanjore after which he drove Kulottunga and the crown prince Rajaraja III into exile. Sundara performed the Virabhishkha, a prayer-offering to celebrate the valour of the king in battle, in the Chola coronation hall and then proceeded to Chidambaram where he worshipped at the famous Nataraja temple. Then the Pandya army established camp at Pudukkottai.

The fleeing Kulottunga appealed to the Hoysala king Ballala II for assistance. A Hoysala army under prince Narasimha was send to help and started to intervene in the Pandya-Chola conflict. In the meanwhile Kulottunga met Sundara Pandya at his Pudukkottai camp and made a formal submission acknowledging the Pandya king as the suzerain, and agreeing to pay an annual tribute. The peace offer was accepted and the Chola kingdom was restored to Kulottunga. This point in history is considered the beginning of the second Pandya kingdom.

Decades of Confusion

Kulottunga III died soon after regaining his throne and was succeeded by Rajaraja III. Rajaraja proved to be an inept and incompetent ruler, a fact that accelerated the downward trajectory of the Chola kingdom. Internal revolts and rebellions increased in number and intensity across the Chola territories. A group of renegade Oriya soldiers raided the Chola kingdom from the north-east and reached Srirangam where they created grave disturbances. Only through the intervention of Sundara Pandya could they be dislodged and made to go back to their country. From the north-west, the Hoysalas had already reached Kanchi and were in conflict with the Telugu-chodas of Nellore, vassals to the Kakatiya dynasty.

The most debilitating blow to the integrity of the kingdom was dealt by the Kadava chief Kopperunjinga who had been a long-time vassal-tributary of the Cholas. With the decline of the Cholas, he had grown increasingly powerful and now allied with the Pandya king against Rajaraja Chola III. Rajaraja, already an ineffectual ruler, compounded his troubles by refusing to pay the annual tribute due to the Pandya king and even had the temerity to invade Pandya territory. Rajaraja magnified his character flaws by not being far-sighted and lacking the aptitude to have a clear appreciation of the developing situation.

Sundara Pandya easily repelled the Chola invasion, took the offensive and defeated Rajaraja, taking his chief queen captive. He once again conducted a Vijayabhishekha, a prayer-offering to celebrate victory, in Chola territory. Rajaraja who had fled on being defeated, attempted to join the Hoysala army but was intercepted on the way. In the ensuing battle at Tellaru, he was again defeated. This time he was captured by Kadava Kopperunjinga who imprisoned him in the fort at Sendamangalam.

Narasimha II, now the Hoysala king, assembled his army and came to the rescue of Rajaraja. He attacked the vassals of the Kadava chief and defeated the king of Magara, consisting of Salem and South Arcot, and marched towards Srirangam. He then despatched an army under two of his powerful and trusted generals with clear instructions to free and restore the Chola king to his throne and to destroy the Kadava power that had now reached its zenith. The generals were true to the orders of their king. They invaded Kadava territory, captured many places and won a decisive battle against the Kadava army at Perambalur. During this campaign they also defeated and punished a number of rebel Chola officers who had joined the Pandya-Kadava combine, as well as a prince of Ceylon who had joined the Pandya army. The Hoysala army reached Sendamangalam, where a besieged Kopperunjinga handed over the Chola king to the generals. Rajaraja was taken back to the Chola capital honourably and reinstated as king.

While his generals were reinstalling the Chola king to his throne, Narasimha himself had met Sundara Pandya in battle. At the Battle of Mahendramangalam on the banks of the River Kaveri, Sundara Pandya was defeated and forced to accept the restoration of the Chola kingdom to Rajaraja. Although greatly diminished in strength, the Kadava rebellion continued for some more years before it was completely subdued. By mid-1200s all three dynasties agreed on a peace that was sealed by inter-marriages between the three royal houses.

The Uneasy Peace

Rajaraja continued to rule for another 20 years after being restored to the throne by the Hoysala king and the territorial boundaries of the kingdom remained the same ad before even though he had suffered such reverses. However, he was only a nominal king. His power was greatly diminished and the kingdom was rife with treason, disorder and defiance to the orders of the king. Also, the Hoysala king influenced all internal matters, further diluting the status of the Chola. The Hoysala influence was also felt in the Pandya kingdom, although not as strongly as in Chola territory. For about three decades following 1220 or so, South India remained under Hoysala hegemony. This was the result of Somesvara, son and successor of Narasimha II, leveraging his father's battlefield successes and spending all his time expanding Hoysala influence into Tamil country. His own kingdom in the meantime was being administered efficiently by loyal ministers.

Rajendra III who came to the Chola throne after Rajaraja III was a more efficient and capable king. On assuming the throne he commenced a strenuous campaign to revive Chola power. He invaded the Pandya kingdom and defeated two princes of the realm in battle. Observing the rise of Chola power, Somesvara the Hoysala king and erstwhile Chola ally, joined the Pandya king to ensure that Chola power was contained before it was restored to the fullest extent. Rajendra was defeated in battle, after which an amicable peace was made.

> ### Choda Tikka of Nellore
>
> Choda Tikka, also called Gandagopala, was a minor king ruling territories to the north of the Chola kingdom and in an uneasy alliance with Rajendra Chola. In earlier times, Choda Tikka had been attacked, but not fully subdued by Somesvara. The Choda king was in continuous conflict with the Sambuvarayas and Kadavarayas, keeping them under check and thereby indirectly strengthening the Chola king, who would have otherwise had to expend energy to contain these rebellious clans.

> Choda Tikka was powerful enough to hold his own against the might of the Hoysala king, Somesvara, during the three-cornered contest and may have influenced the peace process on the Chola side of the deliberations. He was also bold enough to keep Kanchi for himself as a sort of compensation for his support to the Cholas. Choda Tikka was also allied with the Kakatiya Ganapti of Warrangal who was also an adversary of the Hoysalas. One can clearly see the employment of the Mandala Theory in the actions initiated by Choda Tikka Gandagopala in ensuring the security of his own kingdom.

Rising Pandya Power

Jatavarman Sundara Pandya

In 1251, Jatavarman Sundara Pandya, one of the most famous and celebrated warrior-kings of South India, came to the throne. He was a famed conqueror under whom the Pandya kingdom flourished and became the most powerful in the region. Through a mixture of coercion and persuasion he united the Pandya royal family, which was under normal circumstances prone to internecine conflict for all kinds of reasons, primarily regarding the power wielded by an individual prince/royal family member within the kingdom. The royal family remained completely loyal to him. Even at his ascension to power, he was viewed with such awe that instinctively the Hoysala and Chola kings—Somesvara and Rajendra—hastened to strengthen their mutual alliance.

The reaction of the Hoysala and Chola dynasties was not without reason. In the initial part of his reign, Sundara Pandya fought many wars and rapidly expanded the Pandya territory. He enveloped Nellore and further north and also captured some territory in Ceylon. The Ceylon king was forced to pay an enormous tribute. Kanchipuram was made the secondary capital of the Pandya kingdom and he effectively confined the Hoysala rule to the Mysore Plateau. He attacked and ravaged Malainadu, in Chera territory, and defeated the Chera king

Viraravi Udaya Marthandavarman. After this defeat, Kerala and a large part of Ceylon were directly administered by the Pandya king. After few minor skirmishes, Rajendra Chola was forced to accept Pandya suzerainty and thereafter continued to pay annual tribute to Sundara Pandya.

After consolidating his conquests, bringing under his control the more prominent minor kings and chieftains of the region, and subjugating the Chola king, Sundara went to war with the Hoysalas, for decades the predominant power in South India. The initial conflict was conducted in the region around the River Kaveri. There he captured the Kannanur Fort and forced Somesvara to retreat to the Mysore Plateau, which was the core of the Hoysala kingdom. Shortly thereafter Somesvara resumed hostilities with the Pandya king and was killed in battle by Sundara Pandya. After the defeat of the Hoysalas, the Pandya king moved against the Kadava chief Kopperunjinga and attacked Sendamangalam, his stronghold. The Kadava chief was forced to retreat and accept Pandya suzerainty. He was subsequently reinstalled to the throne as a vassal of the Pandyas. Sundara annexed the countries of Bana and Kongu from the Hoysalas and Kadvas. He proceeded to Chidambaram, where he paved the roof of the famous temple with gold and worshipped there in great splendour.

Sundara Pandya now ventured further north, killed Choda Tikka in battle and occupied Kanchi, which had been ruled by the Choda king for some years. He then defeated the Telugu army of Kakatiya Ganapati at Mudugur in Nellore district. Sundara conducted a Virabhishekham in Nellore to celebrate his victory. Carrying out the ceremonial rituals in different places and temples indicate that Sundara Pandya's victories were not transitory military triumphs, but that he won the battle and thereafter controlled the region in question, administering it back to stability where he could then comfortably carryout these traditional rites at his leisure without any hindrance.

Sundara Pandya carried out a second invasion of Ceylon on the invitation of a disgruntled minister. Parakramabahu II, who was the king during the first Pandya invasion, was still ruling Ceylon. On the Pandya invasion, he wisely left the northern part of his kingdom to be conquered without a contest. After a tumultuous and extremely successful 17-year rule, Sundara Pandya died in 1268. He was succeeded by Maravarman Kulasekhara Pandya I.

Maravarman Kulasekhara Pandya I

Kulasekhara was a worthy successor to Sundara and proved to be an accomplished king and great ruler. For long the Pandya kingdom had followed a unique system of a combined rule by a group of princes of whom one enjoyed primacy. The full details of this system is difficult to obtain. However, it is certain that such a system would have created some amount of internecine struggle within the dynasty, especially since a 'chief among equals' situation would have normally prevailed. This is confirmed by the fact that historians mention the dynastic loyalty that was given to Sundara Pandya as one of the remarkable achievements during his rule.

A little before his death in battle, Somesvara had divided the Hoysala kingdom into northern and southern parts between his two sons. The southern part encompassing the Tamil countries that the Hoysalas had overrun fell to the younger son Ramanatha, who then recovered the Kannanur fort and managed to fight off Sundara Pandya. Kulasekhara now decided to subdue Ramanatha who was also a close ally of Rajendra Chola III. In 1279, a fairly large battle took place with the Pandya king on one side and Ramanatha and the Cholas arraigned opposite. Kulasekhara Pandya emerged victorious and established Pandya rule over the entire Chola territory and the Tamil territories that the Hoysalas had been ruling over. Historically, this is the last time that there is a mention of Rajendra III, and more importantly, the Chola dynasty. This is one of those unfortunate instances in history when a celebrated and great dynasty that flowed majestically as a perennial river dries into a trickle that vanishes in an instant of weakness into nothingness. The Cholas were left as a footnote to history that indicate its glorious past, but a footnote nonetheless.

Kerala was still indirectly administered by the Pandya kingdom and rose up in revolt during the changeover of rulers. However, Kulsekhara easily putdown the rebellion. At this stage Ceylon came under the grip of a severe famine. Taking advantage of the situation, Kulasekhara Pandya attacked Ceylon and laid waste the countryside. He captured the fortress of Subhagiri and carried away the 'Tooth

Relic' (believed to be the tooth of Buddha) and considerable wealth. For the next 20 years or so, the entire kingdom of Ceylon was ruled by Pandya kings and could be considered yet another province of their kingdom. The next king, Parakramabahu III, went on a personal embassy to the court of Kulasekhara and persuaded the Pandya king to return the Tooth Relic.

Arrival of the Delhi Army

On Kulasekhara's death there emerged a war of succession between Sundara Pandya the heir apparent and Vira Pandya, the younger son of Kulasekhara through a favourite mistress. The civil war also coincided with the arrival of the first Islamic invasion of the Deep South by the Delhi Sultanate army, which was led by Malik Kafur. In the civil war, Sundara Pandya was defeated and immediately appealed to the Muslim general for help. Hereafter, the sequence as well as the exact happenings that took place during the events that unfolded are not clear. Some historians cite this appeal for help as the reason for Malik Kafur's foray into Tamil country. However, it is more probable that the Khilji dynasty's most famous general was already planning an expedition to South India as ordered by Ala ud-Din the Sultan in Delhi. Therefore, the request for help was only one more reason for Malik Kafur to go south and in any case the assistance he provided to Sundara remains uncertain. It is also certain that Sundara Pandya did not go to Delhi, as has been mentioned in some later-day writings, but approached Kafur when he was already in close proximity to South India.

Some later histories also state that Sundara was placed on the throne by Malik Kafur and that he left a Muslim garrison in Madurai to protect him. There is no shred of evidence to prove this turn of events. There is also no trace of Muslim power in South India after the departure of Malik Kafur. Epigraphic evidence conclusively prove that the Pandya brothers and their successors continued to rule the now-divided kingdom. What must be acknowledged is that the fratricidal succession war that left the country divided combined with the Muslim invasion undermined the strength of the Pandya dynasty, built by the great Sundara Pandya and his successor, the equally glorious Kulasekhara Pandya. The unusual system of 'group-ruling' that seemed to have been the norm of the Pandya kingdom played a critical role in diluting the greatness of the empire. The Pandya dynasty was now left with no solidarity within the royal house, which in turn provided the impetus for other powers to rise and contest the supremacy of the Pandyas. Once again, this development is not an unusual occurrence in history. When a once-great dynasty is beset with internal divisions, the smaller and ambitious tributaries will invariably start to pick at the body-politic of the kingdom.

The Travancore Interlude

The 13th century kings of Venadu, a component of later-day Travancore, claimed to belong to Yadukula that traced its descent from the Ay kings of the 8th century, who were in turn considered the descendants of Ay Andiran of the Tamil Sangam literature fame. Ravivarman Kulasekhara, ruling Travancore had styled himself the Chera 'emperor' when he came to power. He was an accomplished ruler with his capital at Kollam. The Cheras were the only dynasty in Peninsular India to have avoided being invaded by the Muslim army under Malik Kafur. This may have been because of the geographical barrier of the Western Ghats, which could have created great logistical challenges to the march of an army. In the last quarter of the 13th century, when the Pandya civil war was continuing without any tangible result, Ravivarman initially raided and then invaded Pandya territory. This was an opportunistic move by an extraordinarily ambitious king.

Ravivarman conquered Pandya lands up to Kanchipuram and Poonmallee and established authority over parts of both Pandya and Chola kingdoms. There is a mention in some records of his defeating a Vira Pandya, although further details are vague. Considering the time frame of the invasion, this Vira Pandya could have been the prince involved in the Pandya civil war. Around 1312-13, Ravivarman crowned himself on the banks of the River Vegavati in Madurai district.

Vira Pandya raised a force to regain lost territories from the Chera ruler. He managed to create an alliance with the Hoysala king Ballala III and also with Vira Udaya Marthandavarman, who was arrival to Ravivarman in Travancore. Marthandavarman now created a rebellion in Travancore that forced Ravivarman to retreat from the northern Pandya kingdom where he had established Chera control. The Pandya king regained this part of his territory, although Ravivarman continued to hold on to his conquests in the south of Pandya territories for some more years. After this brief intervention into mainstream politics of South India, the history of Travancore retreats to being fragmentary and obscure from the perspective of the broader narrative of the Deep South.

Decline of Pandya Power

At the time of the return of the Chera ing to his own country, the Pandya were involved in a five-cornered feud amongst the princes Vira, Sundara, Vikrama, Kulasekhara and Parakrama. At this stage Kakatiya forces under Muppidi Nayaka invaded Pandya territory. Facing almost certain annihilation, the feuding princes joined forces to defend their kingdom. By this time the Kakatiya king, Pratapa Rudra, had arrived to personally lead his army. The combined Pandya army of the five princes was comprehensively defeated, Kanchi captured and a Kakatiya governor installed there. This was a severe setback to the Pandya dynasty.

Even after this defeat, the Pandya kingdom continued to be debilitated by the system of co-regency that supported the joint rule by a number of princes, which almost always led to divisiveness and internecine conflicts of interest. At a time when the kingdom could only be saved by unified and concerted defensive action, these quarrels and in-fights diluted and limited the effort, which led to disastrous consequences. There was no prince of stature to bring order to the cacophony of dissent and the Pandya kingdom continued its downward slide. Taking advantage of the prevailing disunity and the complete lack of central authority, the more ambitious and powerful feudal chiefs and tributaries of the Pandya dynasty started to rebel and attempt to break away. Accordingly the Sambuvaraya scion Kulasekhara, declared independence. This was followed by Semapillai, son of Rajendra II and now in extremely reduced circumstances, declaring independence in the old Pudukottai state.

The Hoysalas, themselves in the throes of dynastic succession struggles, added to the confusion in the Pandya kingdom. The internal fight between the two Hoysala brothers, Ramanatha and Narasimha III continued unabated. Ballala III succeeded Narasimha to the rule of the majority Hoysala kingdom, while Ramanatha continued to rule a minor territory around Bangalore and the Kolar-Tumkur region.

On his death, Ramanatha was succeeded to the throne of this minor principality by his son Viswanatha. This was the end of this faction of the Hoysalas, which vanish from history. Ballala III was now once again the sole ruler of the Hoysala kingdom. He attempted to take advantage of the Pandya civil war and invaded their territory. At almost the same time, Malik Kafur was arriving at the northern borders of the Hoysala kingdom and Ballala was forced to abandon his attempts to capture lost territory from the Pandyas.

By about 1315, the Pandya Empire was completely broken up, insignificant territories being ruled by different princes. There is evidence of Sundara Pandya ruling to around 1320 and an inscription of Vira Pandya issuing an edict from Ramnad in 1341. During this period, Ulugh Khan the future Sultan Muhammad bin Tughluq, established Muslim rule in Madurai. Even so, this did not mean the end of Pandya rule in South India. Inscriptions in various places in the erstwhile Pandya kingdom attest to their scattered rule till about 1380.

The Scattered Rule of the Pandya Dynasty

Madurai was a Muslim enclave established by Ulugh Khan, but continued to be surrounded by the Pandya territories of Ramnad and Tanjore. There is epigraphic proof of these territories being ruled up to 1346 by Sundara Pandya's younger brother Maravarman Kulasekhara. The inscriptions also prove that his rule encompassed all the districts from Tirunelveli to Tanjore. Further, inscriptions of Jatavarman Parakrama Pandya indicate that there was an overlap of control of some Pandya territories since they state his rule till 1347 of Ramnad and surroundings as well as the Pudukottai state. Pudukottai had earlier been claimed by Semapillai, the Chola scion, but it is obvious that his control of the region was short-lived.

Vira Pandya, not the brother who was involved in the initial civil war that started the downward trajectory of the Pandya dynasty, has inscriptions that indicate his rule

> of some districts till 1380. Another Pandya, Parakrama, ruled in the far south at Nagercoil, in the extremity of the Peninsula till 1380.

During the latter-half of the 14th century, members of the Pandya dynasty continued to rule in small pockets all over South India but not as an identifiable single distinct entity. Essentially, the once-great Pandya Empire was bisected and then divided by different Pandya factions at odds with each other and incapable of defending themselves independently. The kingdom lost coherence and it did not take much effort for the emerging Hindu kingdom of Vijayanagar to sweep it aside in their march to glory.

Chapter 4

PROLOGUE TO HINDU REVIVAL

As in any number of cases in history before and after, there was an interim period of uncertainty and confusion following the overthrow of the Khilji dynasty by the Tughluqs. No doubt, the Tughluqs went on to establish one of the more significant dynasties of the Delhi Sultanate and also encroached into the Deccan and South India like the Khiljis. However, the kingdoms of the Deccan took this state of confusion as an opportunity to rebel and declare independence from the control of the Muslim Sultans of Delhi. Khilji militarism had completely dismembered the erstwhile kingdom of the Yadavas around the region around Devagiri, which therefore remained under the control of the Delhi Sultan. In effect the Yadava dynasty had ceased to exist. The lead to break away from Delhi was initiated by the other Deccan kingdom, the Kakatiyas, then ruled by King Pratapa Rudra.

While the Deccan was starting to get embroiled in rebellion, Ghiyas ud-Din Tughluq, after establishing his right to rule the northern Sultanate, resolved to do away with the Hindu kingdoms of the Peninsula. His ambition was to bring the entire sub-continent all the way to Cape Comorin the southern-most tip of the Indian Peninsula under the sway of Islam. The Tughluq's war against the Kakatiya dynasty and the eventual destruction of the Telugu kingdom was the initial part of this plan and has been covered in earlier chapters in this book. As a result of Tughluq incursions into the Deccan, at the time of Muhammad bin Tughluq's ascension to the throne, large parts of the Deccan and even some parts of South India acknowledged the sovereignty of the Delhi Sultanate. Both Devagiri and Warrangal, the strongholds of the Yadava and Kakatiya empires had been reduced to submission and the once flourishing regional kingdoms were under the effective control of officers of the Delhi Sultanate. Sultan Muhammad had also appointed a viceroy to rule the distant southern enclave in Ma'bar.

Only two prominent and independent Hindu states remained to offer resistance to the encroaching moves of the Delhi Sultanate—the kingdom centred on Kampili and the Hoysala kingdom with its capital at Dwarasamudra. More importantly, from religious and cultural viewpoints, they formed the bulwark against the rampant spread of Islam in the Peninsula.

The Fall of Kampili

The kingdom of Kampili was situated near the River Tungabhadra in the north-east of the current Indian state of Karnataka. It was ruled by a king, appropriately called Kampilideva, who was in regular feuds with both the Kakatiyas and Hoysalas. He was also a consistent and vehement opponent of Islam and in territorial dispute with the Delhi Sultanate after Devagiri had been conquered by the Muslim army. Kampilideva had managed, over a period of time, to extend the boundaries of his kingdom till it could have been considered a geographically large kingdom. It included the present day Anantpur, Chitaldurgh, Simoga, Raichur, Dharwar and Bellari districts. Kampili was separated from the Maratha province of the Delhi Sultanate, Daulatabad (old Devagiri) by the River Krishna in the north-west. Kampilideva was a shrewd diplomat and made overtures of friendship to Baha ud-Din Garshap, the Muslim governor of Sagar, near Gulbarga to counter the Daulatabad governor. Garshap was the cousin of Sultan Muhammad Tughluq and was in a running feud with the Sultan having laid claim to the throne of Delhi against him. After cultivating a sufficiently strong friendship with Garshap, the king of Kampili stopped paying the annual tribute to Delhi. At the same time, Garshap also decided to declare his independence and once again reiterated his claim to the Delhi throne.

Muhammad Tughluq deputed the governors of Gujarat and Daulatabad to deal with the upstart. In the ensuing battle on the banks of the River Godavari, Garshap was soundly defeated and was forced to flee to Kampili for refuge. Muhammad Tughluq now arrived personally at Daulatabad/Devagiri and took charge of the campaign. A number of battles and sieges ensued between the two armies, where in the initial phase victory alternated between both sides. Kampilideva withstood two attacks on his fortress at Kummata. However, in the third attack Muslim army, led by Malik Zada the governor of Gujarat, had overwhelming superiority over the Kampili forces. The odds made it impossible for the Hindu forces to defend the fort, which was overrun. Kampilideva made a strategic retreat to Hosadurgh which was also besieged by the Delhi Sultanate army. In 1327, when Kampilideva could no longer effectively withstand the siege, the ladies committed the rites of the (in)famous 'jauhar' and Kampilideva led his forces out to face the Delhi army on his last battle. The valiant king and his loyal troops were killed in battle. That the ladies of the kingdom of Kampili committed 'jauhar' at Hosadurgh, in keeping with ancient Hindu traditions, is confirmed by different sources and cannot be doubted. This episode is one of the few confirmed and corroborated instances of this 'ritual suicide process' having been carried out in South India.

Before embarking on his last battle, Kampilideva, ever the magnanimous king and mindful of his duties as a host, had send Garshap and his family to Dwarasamudra, the Hoysala capital, entrusting their safety to Ballala III. In earlier years Kampilideva had supported and saved the throne of Ballala III when t Hoysala king was attacked by king Ramadeva of the Yadava dynasty. This was before the time of the Khiljis destroying the Yadava dynasty. Kampilideva had relied on this fact when sending Garshap and his family to Ballala III to ensure their safety. However, unlike Kampilideva, the Hoysala king had no such exaggerated sense of honour or compunctions regarding the duty to protect guests who had sought refuge with him. On Kampilideva's defeat and battlefield death, Ballala surrendered Garshap and his entourage to Malik Zada, made peace with the Gujarat governor and acknowledged the supremacy of the Delhi Sultan. Malik Zada did not invade the Hoysala kingdom.

At this juncture, Muslim historians include the entire Deccan and South India as being part of the Tughluq Empire and some of the modern maps also depict this claim. They indicate that the Peninsula was divided into five provinces ruled by the Delhi Sultanate—

Devagiri, Tiling, Kampili, Dwarasamudra, and Ma'bar. While it is true that militarily these regions had been defeated, this assertion of Delhi rule over these provinces is factually incorrect. The exaggerated claim could be forgiven given the fact that the scribes were all beholden to the Delhi Sultan for their livelihood and in most cases also their physical well-being. The reality is that the Delhi Sultanate exercised only very tenuous control over these areas except for Devagiri. The rest of the areas had accepted Delhi suzerainty after being militarily defeated, but continued their autonomous rule and their connection to Delhi was almost non-existant. Muhammad Tughluq who had been camping at Devagiri during the campaign against Kampilideva left for Delhi in 1329.

The Wars of Liberation

Almost immediately on the Delhi Sultan leaving the Deccan, a concerted campaign to rid the Deccan and South India of Muslims commenced. It was obvious even to the casual observer that the people of the Peninsula had not taken kindly to Muslim rule and the imposition of a foreign set of religious and social rules that accompanied it. Simultaneously and perhaps also prodded by the forced imposition of Islam, there was a strong revival of Shaivism in the Peninsula. Underlying these developments was a sense of revulsion across the Peninsula at the widespread desecration and destruction of temples that usually followed the defeat of a Hindu king or chief. The Hindu population was unwilling to accept such behaviour without fighting back. *[This retaliation and push back against Islam is in sharp contrast to some of the current analysis being made, which depict the Hindus of the sub-continent, especially of South India, as being servile and easy to subjugate. Some modern historians have even propagated the concept that the Hindus 'welcomed' the imposition of Islam and thrived under the 'benevolent' rule of the Muslim kings/sultans. Nothing could be farther than the truth. A conscious attempt at making the Muslim rulers look 'presentable' in the eyes of the modern population is clearly apparent in these narratives that do not produce any shred of evidence to support the claims. A number of modern narratives of medieval Indian history are replete with such attempts. The reader would do well to be astute in his/her selection of readings for their study.]*

Shaivism that rose in the Deccan and South India was a strong and fanatical force that could be compared to militant Islam in some aspects. They were intolerant of even other forms of Hindu worship and cults. The role that this virulent form of Hinduism played in defeating Muhammad Tughluq's attempt to colonise and then Islamise the southern Peninsula is an under-studied and less understood part of South Indian history. Along with the militant stance of Shaivism, the inherent arrogance of the Muslim governors who were left behind to rule the conquered territories added to creating a severe back lash from the local population who were predominantly Hindus. (A major part of the liberation movement has been covered in detail in Chapter 1 of this volume.)

Somadeva, who claimed the position of scion of the ancient Chalukya dynasty, led a revolt by the Hindus of western Telangana against the governor of Kampili, Malik Muhammad. Ballala III, true to his nature, conveniently forgot his allegiance with the Delhi Sultanate and joined the rebellion at Kampili. The success of the rebellion that had the governor fleeing to North India, troubled the Delhi Sultan sufficiently for him to send two princes of the region who were captive in the Delhi court, Harihara and Bukka, to subdue it and restore order. These princes had a vague connection to the royal house of Kampilideva and their origins are the subject of some fanciful stories. (These stories, facts and fiction, have been covered in the second section of this book.) While these two princes embarked on their own journey, which was to lead to the creation of one of the most celebrated empires of South India, other equally momentous events that would change the political landscape of South India were gathering pace.

The Ascent of Hindu Kingdoms

Opposition to the heavy oppression by Muslim governors and officials in the conquered areas coalesced into a concerted movement for liberation in the Peninsula. This struggle for independence was led in the Deccan by Prolaya Nayaka and his cousin Kapaya Nayaka (mentioned in some Muslim chronicles as Kanhaya Nayaka). The uprising is confirmed by some inscriptions that also mention that as many as 75 minor nayakas, or chieftains, of the region joined or helped the cousins in their struggle. The rebellion was a great success and in a short span of two years the entire eastern coastal region from River Mahanadi to Nellore district was freed from Muslim overlordship. The

Hindu chiefs who took over power, rapidly restored *status quo ante* and reconstructed social, political and civic life in the old style.

Kapaya Nayaka, other than being a brave and successful general, was also a shrewd observer of the socio-political developments in the broader community. He instinctively appreciated that even though Islamic control of the region was broken, the scattered Muslim diaspora of amirs, slaves, merchants and local converts would be a direct hindrance to establishing complete and true Hindu rule. He entered into an alliance with Ballala Hoysala III, who was undoubtedly the most powerful Hindu king in the Peninsula at that time. Through a combined effort, Kapaya hoped to contain and then eliminate the Muslim pockets that were still existing in the region. Ballala who was busy improving the defences to the north of his kingdom to ward of an anticipated incursion by the Muslim governor of Devagiri/Daulatabad, send reinforcements to Kapaya to continue the task of overthrowing Muslim rule and rejecting the effects of Islamic occupation.

Kapaya Nayaka, now at the head of a much larger army, defeated the governor of Warangal, Malik Maqbool, who was forced to flee to Delhi. With this victory, the entire Telangana was made free of Muslim rule. Now Ballala and Kapaya started a joint campaign against Ma'bar, initially entering the region called Tondaimangalam adjacent to Madurai sultanate. They cleared the region of minor Muslim garrisons and reinstated the royal house of the Sambuvaraya dynasty who were the traditional rulers of the region. At this stage the entire territories of the old Kakatiya kingdom had been divested of Muslim rule. Further, other than the Maratha province around Devagiri that had been ruled by the Yadava dynasty, the whole of the Deccan was outside the influence of the Delhi Sultanate. In South India, the Madurai Sultan himself was a rebel against Delhi and more than half the Madurai territory had already been recovered from Muslim rule.

The Independence of Madurai

Jalal ud-Din Ahsan Shah, the Tughluq viceroy of Ma'bar had earlier declared independence and established the Sultanate of Madurai. He is said to have 'got rid of', a euphemism for murdering, officers loyal to the Delhi Sultan. Simultaneously the Hindu chiefs of the region also declared independence. As mentioned earlier, Ekambaranatha, the

Prologue to Hindu Revival

head of the Sambuvaraya clan, aided by Vira Ballala III and Kapaya Nayaka liberated the northern parts of South India from Muslim rule. Muhammad Tughluq was sufficiently alarmed by the developments in South India to start a march south from Delhi with a sizeable army to quell the rebellions in the incipient stage itself. However, the hapless Sultan was once again plagued by bad luck. (For details of Muhammad Tughluq's military campaigns, read *Volume V: The Delhi Sultanate*, of this series of books.) On the Delhi army reaching Warangal, there was an outbreak of an epidemic that decimated it, forcing the Sultan to return to Delhi without even having made contact with the rebels. This was the low-ebb in the prestige of the Delhi Muslim army in South India.

Ballala, the prime-mover in reinstating the Sambuvaraya dynasty to parts of Ma'bar, started a series of continuous skirmishes with the newly established Madurai Sultanate. Jalal ud-Din was assassinated after ruling for five years by one of his nobles, Ala ud-Din Udauji. The Sultanate of Madurai was at this time surrounded and hemmed in by Hindu kingdoms and fiefdoms. The break-up of the Pandya kingdom had resulted in most of the surrounding countryside being controlled by small but effective fiefdoms ruled by Pandya princes. The Madurai Sultan was forced to fight continuous, and at times simultaneous, battles with them to keep the sultanate intact. Udauji was a warlike noble and immediately on ascension planned an expedition against the Hoysala kingdom. In the ensuing battle at Tiruvannamalai, Udauji had the upper hand but was struck and killed by a stray arrow before he could claim victory. In the resultant confusion, Ballala managed to convert almost certain defeat into victory for the Hoysalas.

Udauji was replaced by his son-in-law Qutb ud-Din who was an incapable ruler. In true Islamic tradition he was murdered by the nobles after 40 days of rule. They brought Jalal ud-Din's son-in-law, Ghiyas ud-Din Muhammad Shah Damaghani to the throne. Madurai was in dire straits. Damaghani was a capable ruler but a violent and blood thirsty person. He became a ruthless ruler who killed people and carried out mass executions for pure pleasure. He started to practice unheard of cruelties on his Hindu subjects.

Buoyed by his earlier victory and spurred by the atrocities being committed against Hindus in Madurai, Ballala III now 80 years old, invaded Ma'bar, defeated the Muslim army and laid siege to the fort at Kannanur-Koppam. The siege continued for nearly 10 months before the besieged fort sued for peace. Ballala now committed an uncharacteristic error of judgement and permitted the commander of the fort to get in touch with Sultan Damaghani in Madurai. This was a strategic blunder. In an audacious move, Damaghani collected all available forces, which by some account were only 4000-strong, and force-marched to Kannanur and attacked the Hoysala camp. Ballala was taken by surprise, defeated and taken captive to Madurai. There he was first deprived of all the wealth of the Hoysalas and then killed, flayed, the skin stuffed with straw and the body hung outside the ramparts of the Madurai fort. Ibn Batuta reports seeing the body hung outside the Madurai walls. This was an ignoble end to a long-ruling king and a steadfast champion of Hinduism.

Damaghani died soon after this victory, reportedly of an overdose of aphrodisiac. His only son and wife had died earlier of cholera that was raging in Madurai and therefore his nephew Nasr ud-Din succeeded to the throne. Nasr ud-Din had earlier been a domestic servant in Delhi. His first act as sultan was to kill his cousin so that he could marry the widow who was Damghani's daughter. The detailed and coherent narrative of the Madurai sultanate finishes with this episode, since Ibn Batuta, who is the primary source for the information, left Madurai at this juncture. It is undoubtedly certain that around 1363-64, less than a decade after Nasr ud-Din came to power, Madurai was annexed by Bukka to the Vijayanagar Empire.

From the time of its foundation, the Madurai Sultanate was in the throes of a continual and prolonged war with its neighbouring and surrounding Hindu kingdoms. From various sources it can be gleaned that the war against the Muslim holding of Ma'bar was a series of battles that give the impression that it was a campaign that reduced the sultanate. The Madurai Sultanate was whittled down over time, rather than brought down as the result of one great battlefield defeat. Muslim power in the Peninsula was broken by 1370. There were feeble struggles for few more years after which it was completely extinguished. Madurai was an enclave geographically too far from the seat of Islamic power in North India to have survived for long. The fact that it survived for as long as it did, and not its eventual collapse, should come as a surprise to the historian.

Conclusion

Ballala III was succeeded to the throne by his son Virupaksha Ballala IV, of whom there is almost no information available. Nothing is known about him and the Hoysala kingdom was very soon overrun and annexed by the newly formed and rising Vijayanagar Empire. (The rise and dominance of Vijayanagar is covered in the next section in this book.)

The co-founders of Vijayanagar Empire realised very early the danger that Islam posed to the integrity of South India. They understood the need to present a combined Hindu resistance to the Muslim invasions from the north. This meant that the smaller Hindu states of the Deccan and South India could not be allowed to continue hostilities with their neighbours on a regular basis in pursuing the age-old Mandala theory of state security. Accordingly, the founders of Vijayanagar embarked on a conquering consolidation of the Deccan and South India, which would see the empire stretch across the Peninsula, from sea to sea.

Section II

THE BAHMANI DYNASTY

The surviving notes of observant foreign travellers provide the most accurate information from which the actual state of affairs in a kingdom can be inferred. In the case of the Bahmani dynasty, the Russian traveller Athanasius Nikitin, whose notes have survived the ravages of time, clearly states, '…the land is overstocked with people; those in the country are very miserable, while the nobles are extremely opulent and delight in luxury'.

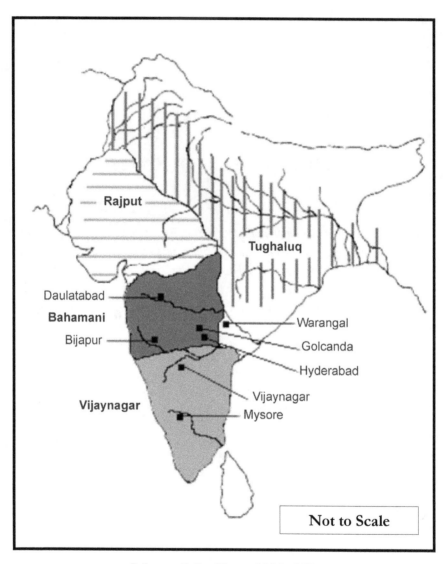

Map of India – 1400 AD

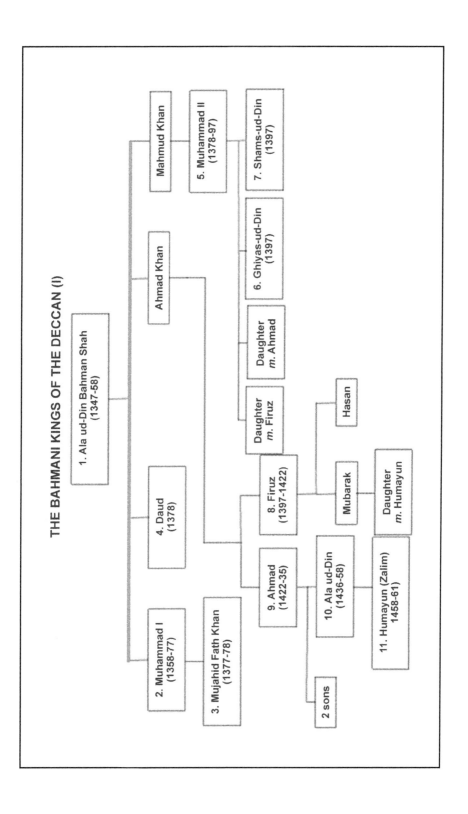

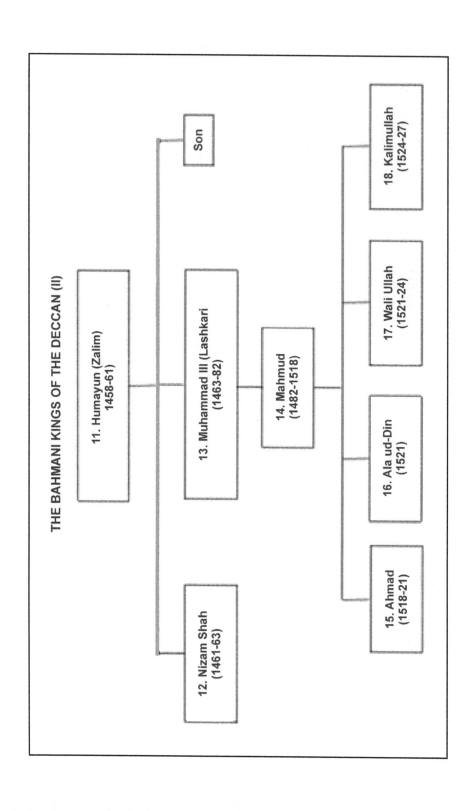

Chapter 5

ORIGINS

Background

While the Madurai Sultanate was being decimated by the regional kingdoms of South India, two brothers Harihara and Bukka, established the Vijayanagar Kingdom raising it on the broken foundations of the failing dynasties of the region. The early kings of this kingdom, which was to later attain exalted status, realised that if the insidious spread of Islam was to be combated in South India, they needed to combine and consolidate the power of the various Hindu states that were almost always at war with each other. There was an urgent need to end the prevalent and perpetual state of mutual hostility. The Vijayanagar kings took on this task. (The Vijayanagar Kingdom will be examined in detail in the chapters of the next section of this book.)

In 1347, another independent kingdom rose in the Deccan, the Muslim Sultanate that came to be called the Bahmani Kingdom. The coming to power of a Muslim dynasty in the Peninsula reemphasised the threat to Hindu religion and its associated culture and more immediate. It demonstrated the almost constant danger to the socio-political and religious *status quo* of the region. The story of Vijayanagar is the story of a medieval Hindu revival and domination of South India that kept Muslim influence away from the region for the next three centuries and more.

Sultan Muhammad bin Tughluq, reigning in Delhi, witnessed the self-destruction of his empire in front of his eyes. In the Deccan, the influential group of Muslim nobles, called Amiran-i-Sada by Muslim chroniclers, rebelled against the rule from Delhi. They set up their own independent kingdom with Daulatabad, erstwhile Devagiri, as the capital and Ismail Makh as the sultan in 1347. The story of how this development took place goes that when Muhammad Tughluq decided to shift the capital of the Delhi Sultanate to Daulatabad, he appointed Kuttulugh Khan as the governor. In turn Kuttulugh appointed a number of military officers as captains of the army. Within them was an adventurer named Hasan Gangu. Suspecting the loyalty of the nobles of the Deccan, Muhammad Tughluq asked Kuttulugh to send them to Broach, where he was camped at the time. In Broach, Muhammad had subdued a revolt by some nobles and thereafter executed them for their rebellion. During their journey to Broach, the Deccan nobles came to know of the treatment meted out to the nobles of Gujarat and suspected that the Delhi Sultan intended to murder them also.

The nobles turned back halfway through their journey, returned to Daulatabad and declared their independence under the rule of Ismail Makh, who was given the title Nasir ud-Din Ismail Shah. Muhammad Tughluq now attacked Daulatabad and imprisoned most of the nobles. Some nobles under the leadership of Hasan Gangu escaped to Gulbarga. Three months later Muhammad Tughluq had to go back to Gujarat to quell yet another rebellion. In the meantime, Hasan had been gathering an army with the aid of Kapaya Nayaka of Warrangal, and biding his time to initiate action. He considered the departure of Muhammad Tughluq from Daulatabad an opportune moment to make his move. Hasan attacked and defeated the Delhi army stationed in Daulatabad. The Delhi commander was slain, following which the Sultanate army dispersed and fled to Malwa.

Nasir ud-Din Ismail Shah, who had been placed on the throne by the rebel nobles before they were defeated by Muhammad Tughluq, was a peace-loving person and completely unfit to be the sultan of a newly formed kingdom. He willingly abdicated the throne in favour of Hasan who was a brave and warlike soldier. Hasan was unanimously elected by his confederates to be the sultan and crowned on 13 August 1347.

Thus was created the Bahmani Kingdom, which lasted in a unified state for nearly a century and a half. Thereafter it gradually declined in power and broke up into five independent kingdoms. Nominally however, the kingdom existed for 180 years with titular Bahmani kings ruling a small territory till 1527.

Ala ud-Din Bahman Shah

Hasan Gangu assumed the elaborate title of Ab'ul Muzaffar Ala ud-Din Bahman Shah on being crowned. There are two contradictory stories regarding Hasan's origins.

One. A Fascinating but Improbable Story

Hasan is said to have been born in 1290 in very humble circumstances. For the first 30 years of his life he worked as a simple farm labourer in the fields belonging to a Brahmin named Gangu. Since Hasan was an industrious and honest person, the Brahmin gave him a small piece of land and two oxen as a gift in appreciation of his hard work. One day while ploughing his land, Hasan struck a pot containing antique gold coins. He immediately took it to the Brahmin, who was greatly impressed with the poor labourer's honesty. Gangu, the Brahmin, was also one of the royal astrologers and therefore was able to inform the sultan of Hasan's probity.

The Sultan at that time was Ghiyas ud-Din Tughluq who rewarded Hasan by making him a captain in the army and placing him in-charge of a 100 horses in the cavalry. Gangu being an astrologer, and seeing the completely altered circumstances of his one-time servant, cast his horoscope, which revealed that Hasan would one day be king. Not holding this information back, Gangu told him the prediction and made Hasan promise that once he became king, he would adopt Gangu's name and also make him the finance minister of the kingdom that Hasan would rule in the future.

Hasan became Hasan Gangu, mentioned as 'Kangoh' by Muslim Chroniclers.

It is also mentioned in some chronicles that Shaikh Nizam ud-Din Aulia, the venerated saint of Delhi also predicted the good fortune awaiting Hasan. Some other sources provide a less romantic version regarding the origins of Hasan, which connect Hasan's ancestry to the ancient Persian king Bahman. Ferishta discounts the reports regarding the Persian connection and endorses the 'Brahmin' story. He insists that the appellation Bahman was adopted by Hasan to honour the promise that he had made to his old master since 'Brahmin' was, and even today is, often pronounced as 'Bahman'. Ferishta insists that Hasan was a low-born Afghan.

> **Two. The Persian Connection**
>
> According to Iswari Prasad, an acknowledged authority on medieval Indian history, modern research has undoubtedly established that Hasan was indeed one of the descendants of Bahman Shah, the king of Persia. The story about his connection to the Brahmin astrologer is purely a myth. The author of the authoritative chronicle, *Burhan-i-Masir*, is considered by historians to be a more reliable authority regarding the narrative of events in medieval Deccan than Ferishta. He states that Hasan traced his origins from Bahman bin Isfandiyar and does not mention the connection to a Brahmin master even once.
>
> Hasan's connection to the Persian ruling dynasty is supported by Nizam ud-Din Ahmed, the author of *Tabkat-i-Akbari*; Ahmad bin Razi, the author of *Haft-Iqlim*; and by Haji ud-Dabir who wrote the famous and authoritative history of Gujarat. These three authors are highly respected authorities regarding medieval Islamic history of India. Further, Hasan's claims to royal Persian ancestry have also been corroborated by contemporary inscriptions.
>
> Even so, there are few facts that do not find satisfactory explanations regarding Hasan's early life. For example, Yahya, an earlier authority than the authors mentioned above, refers to Hasan as Sultan Hasan Kanku. The title 'Kanku' does not find any clear explanation and could

> be considered a version of 'Gangu'. Considering this, Ferishta's claim that Hasan was a low-born Afghan cannot be completely discounted off-hand. However, the story of Hasan's servitude and the discovery of the pot of gold that changed his life will have to be considered embellishments to a success story.

It is safer to leave the origin of Hasan Gangu 'Bahman Shah' open to debate since no conclusive proof exists to either discount or accept one or the other version. Similarly, in the larger scheme of the history of the Deccan, the real reason for Hasan adopting the title 'Bahman' that led to the dynasty he founded being called 'Bahmani' does not merit greater examination and is only of superficial interest. The fact remains that for some unverifiable and obviously obscure reason, Hasan adopted the title Bahman Shah from which the dynasty derived its name. It is also certain that Hasan began life in humble circumstances and came to the throne on his own merit. It can be surmised with reasonable accuracy that Hasan's thirst for adventure brought him to Daulatabad, since the Deccan was the 'El Dorado' in North Indian Muslim imagination.

Bahman Shah Reigns

Bahman Shah ruled for 11 years and the title is found in many inscriptions in the Gulbarga mosque as well as on coins of the dynasty. Soon after assuming the throne in Daulatabad, Bahman Shah shifted the capital of the kingdom to Gulbarga. This may have been a calculated move to put more distance between Delhi and the capital of the fledgling kingdom. It could also have been for sentimental reasons, since Hasan Gangu derived his strength from the army that he built at Gulbarga. Gulbarga continued to be the capital of the Bahmani kingdom till 1425, when the capital was shifted to Bidar.

Bahman Shah spent most of his reign waging war subduing refractory and recalcitrant chieftains in the immediate neighbourhood of the capital, expanding his territorial holdings, and exacting tribute from smaller principalities. In conducting negotiations to expand the territory of the kingdom, Hasan did not spare even his old ally Kapaya Nayaka. Nayaka was forced to cede control of the fort at Kaulas and also to pay an annual tribute to the Gulbarga ruler. The first major expedition of the newly anointed king was towards the Nasik region during which the remnants of the Delhi army was conclusively driven out of the Deccan. He then subjugated the Hindu principalities around Baglana. The chiefs who accepted Bahmani suzerainty were permitted to continue to rule their fiefdoms while those who opposed Hasan were summarily executed and their territories annexed.

Throughout its existence as a viable entity, the Bahmani kingdom was in perennial conflict with the Vijayanagar Empire that had been established a mere decade earlier in South India. This power struggle started in the second year of Bahman Shah's reign, and the first conflict did not yield any decisive results for either of the kingdoms, although the Muslim records insist that Bahman Shah was able to capture and annex Karaichur. Five years later a second conflict followed in which the Bahmani kingdom was allied with the Madurai Sultanate. There are conflicting versions of the result of this conflict. The Muslim chronicles declare a Bahmani victory whereas the Hindu sources claim that Harihara I ruling Vijayanagar achieved a resounding and decisive victory. It can be surmised that the end-result of the conflict was once again indecisive.

Irrespective of the indecisiveness of both the conflicts with the rising power of the Vijayanagar kingdom, by the end of Bahman Shah's reign, his kingdom was territorially extensive. It extended to the Arabian Sea in the west and included the ports of Goa and Dabhol; the eastern limit was marked by Bhongir; and the Rivers Penganga and Krishna bounded the northern and southern borders. It covered parts of the Marathi, Telugu and Kannada speaking linguistic regions. With the establishment of the Bahmani kingdom, the era of the trans-regional states had firmly arrived in Peninsular India.

Bahman Shah considered further conquest, very clearly indicated by the coinage of the time describing him as 'A Second Alexander'. The assumption of such a title shows the vaulting ambition of the new king, fed by his having achieved minor military victories over the small-time Hindu chieftains. Unfortunately for him, the greater ambitions of military conquest were cut short by ill-health brought on by the extreme exertions that he had been undertaking for a number of years.

Hasan Gangu was not merely an adventurous soldier of fortune who happened to be at the 'right place at the right time'. Once having achieved the throne, he proved to be a devoted king, fervently dedicated to the administration of his kingdom. Further, he was successful in extending the borders of his infant kingdom not only through military actions but also shrewd bargaining and coercion. These two points alone perhaps tends to tilt the argument regarding his origins towards accepting his ancestral connections to the royal house of Persia. In medieval times a mere labourer, if he was indeed born into such a low status, was highly unlikely to have the inherent acumen to carryout successful military campaigns and be able to negotiate with kings and chieftains of long standing.

Bahman Shah divided the kingdoms into tarafs, or provinces, and assigned each to amirs who had rendered good service to him during the military expeditions before and after he came to power. These amirs had to maintain a specified number of retainers who were to be send to the king, when required, for military service. In the case of Bahman Shah this meant that the provincial soldiers were almost continuously under his command since the king was almost always at war.

Further proof of the possibility of his royal pedigree and connections is given by the fact almost immediately on assuming the throne, Bahman Shah insisted and demanded on the courtiers maintaining the dignity of the court with decorum. He created a hierarchical aristocracy, grading each noble according to the power and influence that an individual wielded, a judgement that the king alone made. By doing so Bahman Shah kept the nobles, who had been instrumental in his gaining the throne but were also prone to rebellion, under check and loyal to him. He appointed several officials to the court and palace, clearly demarcating the duties and responsibilities of each, which facilitated in maintaining the decorum of the palace as well as the offices that were essential for a smooth administration.

Ala ud-Din Bahman Shah, the founder of the Bahmani kingdom in Western Deccan died in 1358 at the age of 67 after prolonged illness that had almost incapacitated him. He was succeeded by his son Muhammad Shah I.

Chapter 6

THE GULBARGA SULTANS

On his death bed, Bahman Shah nominated Prince Muhammad as his heir and exhorted all other princes and nobles to be loyal to him. Muhammad came to the throne with no opposition and celebrated his coronation with great pomp and ceremony, assuming the title Muhammad Shah. The huge expenses for the coronation was a great drain on the treasury. So much so that the new Sultan had no option but to set out on a conquering march to bring wealth to the coffers, much like what his father had endeavoured to do earlier.

Muhammad Shah I

On Muhammad coming to the throne, Kapaya ruling Telangana from Warangal and Bukka ruling the fledgling Vijayanagar kingdom, send demands to the new Sultan to return the territories of Kaula to Warangal and the Raichur Doab to Vijayanagar. Both these territories had been conquered and annexed by Muhammad's father Ala ud-Din during his reign. Muhammad in turn demanded that both Kapaya and Bukka pay tribute to him, as was his due as the new Bahmani Sultan. A Telugu army under the command of Kapaya's son Vinayak Deo that was send to reconquer Kaula was decisively beaten back by the Bahmani forces. Buoyed by this victory, Muhammad took the offensive and decided to invade both Telangana and Vijayanagar. Considering the parlous state of his treasury and that he had only been anointed king recently, this decision was a brave move demonstrating the self-confidence that Muhammad had in his own capability. It is obvious that he harboured ambitions to better his father's record of conquests.

Even though the Bahmani kingdom, from its very inception, had been at odds with Vijayanagar, the invasion by Muhammad Shah could be considered the real beginning of the long-drawn war between the two newly formed states in the Deccan and South India. It is also noteworthy that these two kingdoms were the successors of the regional linguistic states that had co-existed in relative peace for nearly three centuries.

The first invasion of Warangal has been reported by the Bahmani court chroniclers as a 'great' success, while it is also mentioned that the Hindu forces fought with tenacious bravery and courage. The two statements are dichotomous, considering that it was written by the court scribes, who never missed an opportunity to relegate Hindu kings and their forces to the status of cowards. It has to be surmised that the invasion was only a part-success, although Muhammad managed to collect a great deal of wealth from his minor victory. There were a number of battles thereafter, in which Muhammad repeatedly had the upper hand, even though no outright victory was achieved. In one of the battles, the crown prince Vinayak Deo was captured by the Muslim forces and executed. This changed the complexion of the contest.

Enraged by the execution of his son, Kapaya approached Firuz Shah, the Delhi Sultan for assistance against the Bahmani kingdom. In the meantime, Muhammad Shah attacked Warangal in force and Kapaya was unable to withstand the onslaught. He sued for peace and was forced to surrender the Fort of Golconda to the Bahmani Sultan. The Telangana chieftain also surrendered a turquoise and gold throne to Muhammad Shah, which was installed in the Hall of Audience in Gulbarga. The accounts of these battles and the Bahmani victory is obtained purely from the account written by Ferishta who was obviously biased to singing the praises of his king, Muhammad Shah. An impartial assessment of Ferishta's recounting of Bahmani history shows that no setback of the Bahmani Sultan receives a mention in them. Therefore, Ferishta's accounts cannot be taken at face value. He states that Muhammad now wanted to conquer the whole of Telangana but accepted a treaty of peace after Golconda was ceded. This statement is also difficult to believe in its entirety, considering Muhammad's ambition and position of advantage, as described. The fact, not mentioned by Ferishta, is that Telangana was not the easy conquest as has been described, but a stubborn and resolute state that held its own at all times, and after the initial setback, successfully blocked further Bahmani advances.

According to the peace deal, Golconda was fixed as the permanent border between the two kingdoms. Considering the peace deal, however uneasy it may have been, and the fixing of a permanent boundary line, it is more likely that the Bahmani conflict with Telangana was defensive in nature and also that it did not yield any clear victor or unambiguous victory to either side. At best it can be stated that Muhammad Shah emerged in a slightly better position than when he entered the conflict.

Conflict with Vijayanagar

Ferishta also mentions, in great and glorified detail, Muhammad's victories over the kingdom of Vijayanagar. Once again the reports are suspect and needs to be watered down. It could be presumed that the Bahmani kingdom did not suffer any outright defeat, or that they did not lose the war as such. There is also a statement that Vijayanagar imposed several strictures on Muhammad, one of which was to not kill any Hindus, after the Bahmani Sultan is supposed to have achieved a battlefield victory. Again, this is a contrary report, since it is highly unlikely that a defeated opponent could pass a stricture on the king of the victorious forces. This 'victory' of the Bahmani Sultan was certainly only an indecisively concluded battle, ending in a negotiated settlement.

Ferishta then goes on to claim that Muhammad and the following Bahmani Sultans thereafter adhered to the pact and did not kill any more Hindus. This also not borne out by actual facts. In medieval times, pillage and plunder of enemy towns and killing ordinary citizens of the adversary kingdom was normal, across the world. More so during times of conflict. The Indian wars were no exception. Acts that are seen as atrocities within today's concept of morality, were common place, and in this instance, practised by both Muslim and Hindu forces with equal ferocity.

Irrespective of the hyped up and embellished reports, the conflict with Vijayanagar went to assume epic and formidable proportions. Muhammad Shah had already set his mind on invading Vijayanagar.

The immediate catalyst to do so, other than Bukka's demand for the Raichur Doab to be handed over, was the humiliation of a Bahmani messenger in the Vijayanagar court who had been send by Muhammad demanding that the king of Vijayanagar pay tribute to the Bahmani Sultan. As the war drums began to beat, Bukka crossed the River Tungabhadra and seized Mudgal. Almost immediately, Muhammad Shah counterattacked and recaptured Mudgal. The Muslim army made exemplary use of artillery and cavalry in the successful recapture, whereas the Hindu artillery was employed late and ineffectually. This is one of the first confirmed use of guns in the Deccan. The artillery contingent on both sides were officered by Europeans and Turks.

After this battle, Bukka resorted to a combination of guerrilla tactics and direct action, resorting to pitched battles only when he was certain of victory. After a series of battles and skirmishes, both sides agreed to accept River Krishna as the boundary between the kingdoms.

By reconciling River Krishna as the border, Bukka essentially won the Raichur Doab, which lies between the River Tungabhadra and Krishna, which was his original claim and the core reason for the conflict. This fact is reason to believe that Muhammad Shah was not very successful in his attempt to 'punish' Vijayanagar for its temerity in asking for the return of its conquered territory. Although Muslim chronicles proclaim a great victory for the Bahmani Sultan, facts on the ground point towards an unsuccessful campaign, if not an outright defeat. The truce with Vijayanagar was not one-sided, but definitely weighed in favour of the Hindu kingdom. Repeated embellishment of the narrative that are not corroborated by actual facts on the ground, continually undermine the veracity of the reports filed by the Muslim chroniclers throughout the history of the Bahmani dynasty.

Domestic Rebellions

While the truce with Vijayanagar was being enacted, the governor of Daulatabad Bahram Khan Mazandarani who was also a son-in-law of Bahman Shah the founder of the dynasty, rebelled. He was also in conflict with another son of Ala ud-Din, Muhammad's brother. Muhammad easily suppressed the revolt and banished Mazandarani from the kingdom. During this campaign, Muhammad was assisted by the Maratha chief Kombha Deo, then ruling Berar. For his troubles, Kombha appropriated revenue of the region for himself. This independent act of the Maratha chief indicates that Muhammad Shah was not as powerful as it is made out to be in his court chronicles.

> ### The Marathas
>
> This is perhaps the first direct reference to the Marathas, as a separate and distinctive race or entity, in the narrative of the Deccan. The Muslim chronicles mention them as occupying the area called 'Mharat', obviously a corruption of the Hindu name Maharashtra, which encompassed the strip of country lying between Gujarat in the north and Pune in the south, bounded by the Konkan coast in the west and the Deccan in the east. The territory is a narrow hilly tract, full of inaccessible valleys and wooded hills. The terrain is difficult to traverse and both inhospitable and hostile.

An Efficient Sultan – Prone to 'Indulgence'

Muhammad Shah was ruthless in enforcing his will, especially in domestic matters. He was the ultimate champion of orthodox Islamic faith and therefore gets fulsome praise for all his actions from Muslim chroniclers of the time. Enforcing the rules of orthodox Islam was considered the epitome of being an exemplary ruler and Muhammad stuck to the script as none of the Bahmani rulers had done so far.

Medieval Deccan Kingdoms

> With the usual exaggeration that typifies his writings, Ferishta reports the aftermath of the conflict with Vijayanagar: '...five hundred thousand unbelievers fell by the swords of his warriors in defence of the faith of Islam, by which the districts of the Carnatic were so laid waste that they did not recover their natural population for several decades.'
>
> Ferishta,
>
> As quoted in *History of the Deccan* – Volume I, by J. D. B. Gribble, p. 46.
>
> (First published 1896)
>
> *[An interesting observation has to be made regarding the quote above. The author states that the massacre of the unbelievers (read Hindus) was carried out in the 'defence' of Islam. It is difficult to understand how Islam was being 'defended' when the invasion was perpetuated by the Muslim kingdom on a predominantly Hindu kingdom. Such religiously couched justifications for offensive actions of extreme brutality abound in the Muslim chronicles in the sub-continent.]*

True to form, like many other Sultans, Muhammad was also a hypocrite. While enforcing strict religiosity on his subjects and nobles, he himself led a life of complete 'indulgence' according to a number of other corroborated reports. In fact it is believed that he died of excessive drinking in 1375, after ruling for 17 years.

On the other hand, Muhammad Shah was a diligent and efficient administrator. He established a council of ministers and created the position of Peshwa, a tradition that was continued into later-day kingdoms in the Deccan. He also created a decentralised administration. This was a great forward looking reform, which is a great concept when the king is strong and able to enforce his will easily. However, if the central control is weak, the very same concept tends to break up the kingdom. Muhammad paid particular attention to commerce understanding it to be fundamental to the prosperity of the kingdom. In order to facilitate easy trade he suppressed the prevalent state of common highway robbery. He is reported to have executed more than 20,000 brigands and thieves. He is also credited with building the great mosque of Gulbarga.

While he did have his positive side, particularly in administering the kingdom, Muhammad was a passionate and impulsive king. He was easily offended and given to venting his wrath, ever ready to avenge even the slightest perceived offence to his dignity. His personal bravery was never in question and he was not averse to undertaking military campaigns, personally leading small forces against numerically large opponents. It is obvious that Muhammad Shah was a talented military commander.

The Weak Successors

Muhammad Shah was followed to the throne by his son Ala ud-Din Mujahid Shah. Ala ud-Din was a handsome man of great physical prowess that earned him the sobriquet of 'balwant' or 'the strong'. He had a short reign of about three years, the main event during which was a war with Vijayanagar provoked by the Sultan. He demanded the return of the territories that had been ceded to Vijayanagar in earlier times and on being refused, invaded Vijayanagar. By now Vijayanagar was a powerful kingdom commanding the allegiance of a number of dependent princes of South India. Gradually the kingdom had also taken on the mantle of being the bulwark against Muslim invasions and the insidious spread of the Islamic faith towards South India from their stronghold in the Deccan.

Bukka still ruling Vijayanagar and consolidating his kingdom avoided pitched battles and harried the invading forces constantly. He wore down the invading army through hit and run tactics while luring them deeper into his own territory. When the Bahmani forces reached close to the capital, they were decisively defeated and had to flee back. At the same time a nine-month siege of Adoni by the Bahmani forces also ended in abject failure. Mujahid blamed his uncle Daud Khan, who was the commander of the Bahmani forces during the expedition, for its overall failure. Stung by the accusation, Daud Khan retaliated by murdering Mujahid on 15 April 1378 and claiming the throne for himself. The kingdom descended into chaos brought about by fratricidal conflicts.

During his reign Mujahid promoted Persians and Turks to higher positions in the administration in preference to the local Deccani Muslims. Thus he perpetuated the division between the Deccani and foreign Muslims and sowed the seeds of jealousy that exacerbated an already tense relationship between the two. This was one of the fundamental reasons for the intrigue, plots and assassinations that plagued the Bahmani kingdom throughout its existence. The division contributed a great deal to its ultimate collapse and dismemberment.

Within a month of usurping the throne, Daud was also murdered by a hired assassin on the orders of Mujahid's stepsister, Ruh Parwar Agha. Daud Khan's son Sanjar was blinded to ensure that he did not make any claim to the throne. Muhammad Shah II, the son of the youngest son of Ala ud-Din was proclaimed sultan.

Muhammad Shah II

Muhammad Shah was a man of peace, entirely devoted to religion and poetry. The internal turmoil following the Bahmani defeat was exploited by Vijayanagar who took advantage of the situation and annexed a large slice of land in the West Coast that included the port of Goa. Muhammad II established an uneasy peace with Vijayanagar. He also managed to contain the palace and court intrigues that was becoming commonplace. The regicidal atmosphere prevalent in the capital was contained. Having re-established some semblance of stability, Muhammad devoted himself to his primary interest of pursuing poetry, literature and scientific learning. He established educational institutions, monasteries and a number of mosques. Muhammad also enforced the 'holy law' across the entire kingdom. This would have meant unnecessary and at times unbearable pressure on the majority Hindu population of the kingdom. However, medieval Indian sultans were not in the habit of considering Hindus either their subjects or even as normal people—they were sub-human in the eyes of Muslim Sultans.

Persian Poet Hafiz

Muhammad Shah II was renowned as a patron of poetry and learning. He had invited the Persian poet Hafiz to grace his court. However, Hafiz faced a severe storm at sea after he had embarked for India and turned back to his home port, vowing never to venture out to sea again. He wrote an ode and send it to the Sultan which was received with great pleasure.

Hafiz's ode, translated to English reads:
For the wealth of the world I will not exchange
The wind of my garden which softly blows;
My friends may rebuke me, but I will not range:
I will stop here at home with the bulbul and the rose;

Enticing no doubt, is your beautiful crown,
With costliest gems in a fair golden bed;
But through perils and risks that ominous frown,
I might win it, perhaps, but then have no head.

When I thought of your pearls, it seemed then to me
To risk a short voyage would not be too bold;
But now I am sure, one wave of the sea
Can *not* be repaid by treasures of gold.

What care I for pearls or for gems rich and rare
When friendship and love at home both are mine?
All the gilding or art can never compare
With the pleasure derived from generous wine!

> Let Hafiz retire from the cares of the world,
>
> Contented with only few pieces of gold;
>
> In the lap of repose here let him lie curled,
>
> Far removed from the sea and its dangers untold!
>
> As translated in *History of the Deccan* – Volume I, by J. D. B. Gribble, p. 53.
>
> (First published 1896, reprinted 2002)

Although Muhammad Shah was a person of simple habits, he had an exalted concept of the kingly office. He followed a very modern doctrine where the king was supposed to be only a trustee of divine wealth and not the owner. Along with practising this concept, he was also very interested in the welfare of his subjects. Of course, in this case, 'subjects' were only followers of the Islamic faith, the Hindus who made up the majority of his subjects were not considered worthy of being given the status of being a Bahmani citizen. This division was clearly seen when the Sultan organised relief during a famine in the kingdom between 1387-95, when succour was given only to Muslims and an unaccounted number of 'infidels and non-believers' died of starvation.

Muhammad's last years were beset with the conspiracy of his sons to usurp the throne. He died in April 1397. Malik Saif ud-Din Ghuri, a powerful and competent minister who had rendered distinguished service to the Bahmani dynasty since its founding days also died immediately after the death of Muhammad Shah II. This further destabilised the kingdom. Muhammad was followed on the throne by his eldest son Ghiyas ud-Din, a headstrong and indiscreet prince. Within two months he was dethroned and blinded by the chief of the Turkish slaves, Tugalchin, who brought Shams ud-Din Daud – a minor and Ghiya's half-brother – to the throne. Tugalchin assumed the role of the regent and appropriated all power himself.

Two grandsons of Ala ud-Din I, Firuz and his brother Ahmad, who were also sons-in-law of Muhammad Shah II took it on themselves to remove the Turkish slave from power. They overpowered Tugalchin, blinded the child-Sultan and took over the kingdom. Firuz was crowned Sultan in November 1397 with the title Taj ud-Din Firuz Shah with his brother and co-conspirator, Ahmad, becoming the Chief Minister of the kingdom.

Firuz Shah

Firuz reigned for an eventful 25 years, which could be considered the most engaging period in the annals of the Bahmani kingdom. He proved to be a vigorous king—sagacious, enterprising and with a keen mind. Contemporary Muslim chroniclers extol his virtues as being a 'good, just and generous king' and as a ruler 'without equal observing practices of his religions with strictness'. These are obviously exaggerated estimates of a definitely good king. Indeed Firuz was a cultured, talented and liberal monarch, while also being a linguist and a calligrapher of renown. He was a keen student of astronomy and built a major observatory in Daulatabad. Equally obvious is the fact that without a doubt he drank excessively, was very fond of music, and maintained a large harem populated by women of different nationalities. Firuz was no religious recluse.

Firuz was a good administrator who did not baulk at employing competent Brahmins to high positions. His reign was marked by three distinct campaigns against Vijayanagar. For the three decades following Muhammad Shah's unsuccessful invasion of Vijayanagar, the Bahmani dynasty was completely immersed in its own domestic squabbles to undertake any external adventures. Therefore, during that period there were no major conflicts between the two kingdoms.

First Vijayanagar Campaign – 1398

Harihara II of Vijayanagar invaded the Raichur Doab with a massive army of 30,000 cavalry and 900,000 infantry in early 1398. Simultaneously there was a Hindu rebellion on the north bank of River Krishna, which was almost immediately crushed by the Bahmani forces. The Vijayanagar forces deployed on the southern bank of River Krishna and prepared for battle. It is reported by Muslim chroniclers that the army covered an area of 27 kilometre square, which is obviously an exaggeration of a later time, since the outcome of the battle against such a large enemy supports the claim of the 'greatness' of Muslim forces. Firuz's army is reported to have been only 12,000, once again the numbers definitely reduced to emphasise the magnificence of the reported victory. However, it must be admitted that the Bahmani forces were numerically inferior to those arrayed by the Vijayanagar kingdom.

Firuz, arriving on the northern bank, appreciated the difficulty in crossing the river against a numerically superior force and resorted to subterfuge. He send some soldiers disguised as travelling minstrels to infiltrate the Vijayanagar camp and gain the trust of the enemy soldiers. This group used to perform every night in the enemy camp. On a predetermined night, during the usual performance, they fell upon the prince and killed him and his bodyguards. Confusion reigned in the Vijayanagar camp and taking advantage of this diversion, Firuz crossed the river unopposed.

Harihara was in no position to offer battle and withdrew to his capital with his son's body. Firuz pursued the withdrawing forces for a while, harassing the rear, till Harihara purchased peace by paying a substantial indemnity. Firuz returned to his kingdom after appointing a military governor to rule the Raichur Doab.

Second Vijayanagar Campaign – 1406

Harihara II had died in 1404 and been succeeded by his son Devaraya I. There is a romantic love episode attached to the second campaign.

The Thwarted Romance of a King

The story goes that Devaraya was besotted by the beautiful daughter, Parthal, of a goldsmith in the village of Mudgal in the Raichur Doab. However, the girl had refused to marry the king. In order to win her over, the king attempted to capture the village. In order to escape the king's wrath Parthal and her father fled north. In retaliation, the Vijayanagar troops laid waste the countryside surrounding

> Mudgal. Subsequently Parthal was married to Firuz's son Hasan Khan. This story is recounted only by Ferishta and is not corroborated by any other source. It has to be discounted as a fanciful and untrue tale recounted to discredit the character of the Vijayanagar king.

The fact remains that Devaraya invaded the Raichur Doab, maybe to avenge his father's probable defeat few years back and/or to take revenge for his brother's murder. Firuz could not accept this move and declaring the invasion an aggression of his kingdom, which technically it was, he attacked Vijayanagar. In this instance Firuz and the Bahmani forces suffered a decisive defeat. Firuz himself was wounded in the battle and withdrew to a hastily constructed fortified camp, close to Vijayanagar territory. Although defeated, Firuz was able to ravage to countryside around his camp. The suffering of his people made Devaraya ask for peace. He gave one of his daughters in marriage to Firuz along with the district of Bankpur as dowry. Even though the marriage was conducted with great pomp and ceremony, the kings parted in anger.

Third Vijayanagar Campaign – 1417

The fort at Pangal that belonged to the Bahmani kingdom had earlier been captured by Vijayanagar. In 1417, Firuz Shah decided to recapture it. From its very inception the expedition was a disaster. The fort was besieged and could not be overrun for nearly two years. The static nature of the siege brought disease into the Bahmani ranks which was decimated over a period of few months. In 1420, Firuz was defeated and retreated to his kingdom. Vijayanagar forces captured the southern and eastern provinces of the Bahmani kingdom. Firuz was completely shaken by this emphatic defeat and loss of territory and withdrew from the affairs of state immediately on his return to the capital.

Other Military Adventures

After the first Vijayanagar campaign, which is claimed as a victory in Bahmani records, Firuz led an expedition against the Gond Raja Narsingh ruling Kherla about four miles north of Betul in modern

Madhya Pradesh. Narsingh is reported to have invaded Berar at the instigation of the Vijayanagar king and the support of the Muslim rulers of Malwa and Khandesh. When the Bahmani forces took on Narsingh, the instigators of the original invasion did not come to the aid of the embattled ruler. The Gond forces offered stiff resistance, although in the end Narsingh was forced to sue for peace.

Between the second and the final Vijayanagar expedition, the Gond governor of Mahur rebelled. Firuz marched to the region, but returned without putting down the revolt. No reason is given for this inaction by a warlike king. At this stage, Telangana was on the verge of a civil war between two factions—the Vemas and Velamas—for succession. The Vemas were supported by Vijayanagar and obviously Firuz had to support the Velamas. The Bahmani forces had limited success in some minor skirmishes in the early days of the struggle. However, they were forced to retreat when Kataya Vema's lieutenant, Allada Reddy, defeated the Bahmani army that was being commanded by Ali Khan.

These setbacks should have warned Firuz that his army was not as powerful as he thought it to be and prudence would have dictated that he not go to war with Vijayanagar. This was specially so since Vijayanagar was on the rise and becoming more powerful by the day. A pragmatic assessment of the performance of the Bahmani army in minor skirmishes would have indicated the actual state of affairs, and perhaps Firuz would have been spared the ignominy of the defeat and his subsequent withdrawal from public life.

End of Firuz's Rule

Towards the time of the third Vijayanagar campaign, Firuz started to suspect his brother Ahmad of plotting against him. The suspicion was furthered by a prediction made a while ago by a saint, Khwaja Gisu Darag, that Ahmed would be the next sultan instead of Firuz's eldest son and favourite, Hasan Khan. At the same time, two slaves had inveigled themselves into the Sultan's favour. The slaves, Hosiar Ain-ul-Mulk and Bedar Nizam-ul-Mulk were moderately successful military commanders, having achieved some minor victories in the battlefield. After his defeat at the fort of Pangal, Firuz left the running of the kingdom to these two slaves.

Ahmad realised the Sultan's animosity and it became obvious that his position in Gulbarga had become untenable. Therefore, he fled from the capital with a small entourage. The group accompanying him also had within it a rich merchant of Basra called Khalaf Hasan. In some reports of the events that followed Ahmad's flight from Gulbarga it is mentioned that this Hasan used his considerable wealth to win over the Bahmani army to support Ahmad. There are three variations in the narrative after this, each of them equally feasible.

The first is that a contingent of the army was sent in pursuit to capture Ahmad. However, they were defeated by Ahmad and fled back to the capital with Ahmad in pursuit. On Ahmad arriving at Gulbarga, the royal army deserted Firuz and joined Ahmad. Ahmad took charge of the capital, captured Firuz's sons and had the ailing Sultan either strangled or poisoned. The second narrative states that even before Ahmad could flee, an attempt was made to capture and imprisoned him. However, the army, swayed by the prediction of the saint and no doubt induced by the wealth of the merchant from Basra, switched to Ahmad's side. Ahmad now laid siege to the capital. Firuz, by now a sick man, was carried to the battlefield by the troops who had stayed loyal to him. He fainted and the citadel then surrendered to Ahmad. Firuz abdicated in favour of his brother and died within a few weeks of the incident. He was obviously 'done away' with, either by being poisoned or strangled.

The third version states that after fleeing the capital, Ahmad 'persuaded' the Habshi slaves in the royal army to join him – the persuasion obviously made possible by the spread of money by the wealthy merchant. Ahmad then marched back to the capital after making elaborate preparations for a major battle. A vicious battle ensued with death of many on both sides. Firuz realised that he could not win the battle and that he could not continue to rule without the support of the army. Therefore, he asked his son Hasan Khan to submit to Ahmad. Ahmad was then declared Sultan.

Irrespective of the correctness in terms of the detail of the events as they unfolded, the salient facts are that the royal army decided to join Ahmad, in all probabilities induced by the bribes that were passed out, and Firuz abdicated in Ahmad's favour. It is also clear that Firuz was subsequently killed.

Firuz Shah – The Individual

By all accounts Firuz was an enlightened ruler. He was not a rigid Muslim and could be considered a nominal Sunni Muslim who was religiously very tolerant. He was found of wine and music and also held regular and erudite discussions with philosophers, poets and historians. As mentioned earlier, he also built an observatory at Daulatabad and encouraged the study of astronomy. Firuz was an accomplished linguist and calligrapher. It is mentioned that he had ladies from different parts of the world in his harem and that he could converse with each of them in their own language.

Firuz was interested in improving commerce and paid careful attention to the two ports of the kingdom—Chaul and Dabhol. These ports serviced the trade from the Red Sea, the Persian Gulf and Europe. It is obvious that Firuz understood the importance of trade to the prosperity of the nation and therefore took measures to improve that aspect of governance. Although an accomplished king, Firuz could not understand the weaknesses of his administration, which finally brought him down from the throne.

Chapter 7

THE BIDAR SULTANS

Ahmad Shah Bahmani

After Firuz abdicated, Ahmad Shah ascended the throne without any opposition. His minister and other supporters advised him to kill Hasan Khan, Firuz's son, since they felt that he would be a threat to the new Sultan; even if not immediately but definitely in later times. This was wisdom founded on experience since an aspirant to the throne who had been set aside invariably formed a coterie of his own and rebelled to reclaim the throne, often leading the kingdom to civil war and associated chaos. Wholesale fratricidal killings when there was a change of sultans were therefore common in the medieval Indian context. However, in this case Ahmad refused to put to death his nephew or even blind him, as was the usual practice. Instead, he bestowed the jagir of Firuzabad on Hasan. The prince was completely devoid of any political ambition and accepted the jagir with gratitude. He then went on to fritter away his time in an almost single-minded pursuit of earthly pleasure.

Ahmad was very unlike his suave and worldly brother. He was crude in his outlook and behaviour, and revelled at being considered a 'saint'. The common people referred to him with the title Vali, meaning saint. It is obvious that Ahmad took the title rather seriously since he was prone to displaying his saintly powers to his subjects.

> ### Ahmad Shah 'the Saint'
>
> It is reported that when the kingdom was in the grip of a long and terrible draught he took it on himself to appeal for divine intervention. In full view of a large number of people, he reverentially climbed to the top of a significant hill. There in front of his subjects who had gathered to see their Sultan work a miracle, he began to pray for rain. Rain clouds are supposed to have gathered soon, as if on call, leading to heavy rains and an end to the draught.
>
> The story is not corroborated with any certainty or verifiable evidence, and is probably a tale indicative of the belief that people had regarding the piety of the Sultan.

After ruling the kingdom from Gulbarga for a few years, Ahmad shifted the capital to Bidar. The rest of the narrative of the Bahmani kingdom is usually referred to as the Bidar Period. From a strategic point of view, Bidar was better suited to be the capital, considering that the kingdom had by now expanded substantially to the east. Further, the three linguistic regions of the kingdom converged on Bidar making it an obvious choice as the administrative headquarters. The crowning characteristic that made the Sultan decide on the shift may have been the more salubrious climate of Bidar.

Vijayanagar Campaign

Although outwardly saintly in his normal disposition, Ahmad Shah was an aggressive and brutal army commander. He was able to wage successful campaigns against all his neighbours. He fought Gujarat, Malwa and obviously Vijayanagar. Ahmad's first campaign was mounted against Vijayanagar almost immediately after he came to the throne. The only reason was the obvious need to avenge the inglorious defeat that his brother had suffered, which had led to Ahmad becoming the Sultan of the Bahmani kingdom. Vijayanagar was ruled by Devaraya II who, on coming to know of the Bahmani intention to invade his kingdom, appealed to the Warangal king for help. Although help was promised and a contingent was send to Vijayanagar, the Telangana forces deserted on the eve of battle much to the discomfiture of Devaraya.

The opposing armies were arraigned on the north and south banks of River Tungabhadra and battle ensued on the banks of this dividing river. The Bahmani forces numbered around 40,000 and some estimates put the Vijayanagar forces at more than a million. While this estimate is obviously an exaggeration, it is certain that the Vijayanagar army was numerically superior to the Bahmani forces, even though they were reduced in number by the withdrawal of the Telangana contingent.

Faced with a numerically superior force, Ahmad made a detachment cross the river to the south bank at night, some distance upstream from the main camp. This small force attacked the Vijayanagar camp from the rear, achieving complete surprise and throwing the Hindu army into confusion. While Vijayanagar was in disarray, the main Bahmani force managed to cross the river. In the ensuing battle, Vijayanagar forces were routed. Devaraya was forced to withdraw to his fort in Vijayanagar and take up a defensive position. Ahmad Shah now displayed his ruthless streak by mercilessly laying waste the countryside; indiscriminate slaughter and enslavement of the civilian population; and wholesale and arbitrary destruction of temples.

The Sultan's Lucky Escape

The Vijayanagar expedition was long-drawn and Ahmad Shah was in the habit of going out hunting for recreation. During one such outing, the Sultan was separated from his bodyguards but spotted by a foraging Vijayanagar cavalry contingent. They launched an attack on the Sultan who took refuge in a mud enclosure, where he was surrounded by his pursuers.

Although the situation soon became very precarious, the Sultan was saved by the last-minute arrival of a detachment of his own bodyguards under the command of a faithful officer, Abdul Qadir. This contingent consisted of foreign mounted archers, who subsequently went on to become a prominent part of the Bahmani army in later years.

After his providential escape, Ahmad continued his advance on Vijayanagar, stepping up the carnage and leaving a trail of wanton destruction in his wake. In order to alleviate the suffering of his subjects who could not be protected from the wrath of the Bahmani Sultan, Devaraya II purchased peace by paying a substantial tribute. Since the Bahmani forces were already deep inside Vijayanagar territory, Ahmad insisted on being escorted out of the kingdom by the crown prince. This action was intended to humiliate the dynasty, an objective that seems to have been achieved. Ahmad Shah did not wage war against Vijayanagar for the remainder of his term.

Other Campaigns

In 1424, Ahmad Shah marched into Warangal, defeated the Raja fairly easily and annexed the entire kingdom to Bahmani holdings. Warangal was not a 'small' kingdom and therefore, the rapidity of the conquest is somewhat perplexing and difficult to understand. The annexation of Warangal resulted in a substantial eastward spread of Bahmani territory. With this defeat, Warangal finally ceased to exist as an independent entity.

The success of the first two expeditions—against Vijayanagar and then Telangana—spurred Ahmad to undertake more military expeditions. In 1425, he marched against the rebellious Raja of Mahur who was enticed to surrender and then put to death. Ahmad then raided Gondwana and spent more than a year at Ellichpur, rebuilding the forts at Gawligarh and Narnala. These forts thereafter defined the northern frontier of the Bahmani kingdom.

Earlier during Firuz's reign, Timur had nominally granted the title of both Gujarat and Malwa to the Bahmani Sultan. *[The only claim Timur had to make such a grant was that he had invaded the sub-continent and defeated the Delhi Sultan, after which he went on a marauding trip through North India before returning to his kingdom in Afghanistan.]* Ahmad Shah decided to stake his claim and turned his attention to these two independent kingdoms. In order to foster trouble in the region, Ahmad entered into an alliance with the ruler of Khandesh, which was a small but independent kingdom claimed by both Gujarat and Malwa. Malwa was ruled by Hushang Shah. He had earlier compelled Narsingh of Kherla (today's Kurla?) who was a vassal of the Bahmani kings, to change allegiance and swear fealty to Malwa. In 1428, when Hushang Shah laid siege to Kherla to collect the tribute due to him, Narsingh appealed to Ahmad Shah for help. Taking this opportunity to force a face-off with Malwa, Ahmad marched to Ellichpur.

Ahmad's religious feelings now came in the way of following through with his promise of assistance to Narsingh. He was assailed by doubts regarding the 'correctness' of fighting a fellow Muslim ruler to assist and defend an infidel king. This made Ahmad initially hesitate to attack and subsequently he decided to withdraw from the area without giving battle. On the Bahmani forces withdrawing, Hushang made a strategic miscalculation. He surmised, wrongly as it turned out, that the withdrawal was a sign of weakness and cowardice and pursued Ahmad with a considerable force. At this affront, Ahmad set aside his religious misgivings and turned back. Hushang Shah was decisively defeated in a battle fought on the banks of River Tapti. Narsingh had also joined the fray on the Bahmani side and chased Hushang all the way into Malwa. He then returned and ceremoniously entertained Ahmad Shah in Kherla.

On his way back to his capital, Ahmad Shah made camp in Bidar. He was taken in by the climate and strategic position of the city and decided to shift his capital to Bidar. The actual shift took place in 1429, when the township was renamed Ahmadabad Bidar. In later years the name was once again changed to Muhammadabad Bidar, as it is known today.

Bidar of Antiquity

Bidar is an ancient Hindu city, possibly Vidarbha. It is considered the scene of the adventures of King Nala and his Queen Damayanti of antiquity, mentioned in the broader story narrated in the Mahabharata and also immortalised as an epic poem by the great Kalidasa. Irrespective of the veracity of the story of Nala and his consort Damayanti having lived in the city, it is certain that Bidar was a metropolis of a great and ancient Hindu kingdom in its early days.

During Ahmad's sojourn in Bidar, his eldest son Ala ud-Din Ahmad was married to the daughter of Nasir Khan of Khandesh as part of an emerging alliance. Ahmad now divided the governance of his empire between his four sons and a favourite noble. Ala ud-Din, the heir apparent and eldest son was kept in Bidar, with the youngest son Muhammad as his companion; Muhammad Khan was made the governor of Berar; Daulat Khan was given the Telangana region; and the noble Malik-ul-Tijar was awarded Daulatabad. The last appointment is questionable since Daulatabad was a bone of contention with the Delhi Sultanate as well as the Maratha rebels in the region. That province had never been fully under Bahmani control, which was tenuous at the best of times.

Soon after the defeat of the Malwa forces, Ahmad Shah ordered a wanton attack on Mahim—which stood on the site that is today the island of Mumbai—that was within the territory of the Gujarat Sultan, Ahmad I. This action obviously precipitated a drawn-out conflict. Unlike the religious scruples that he displayed at the initial stages of the conflict with Malwa, Ahmad this time supported a Hindu chief who was rebelling against the Gujarat Sultan. Obviously piety and scruples were thrown to the wind and sacrificed at the altar of pragmatism and opportunism. The Bahmani army led by its general was conclusively defeated by the Gujarat forces – not once, but twice – suffering great losses in the bargain. At this stage Ahmad Shah personally took over the reins of the expedition and obstinately persisted with attacks on the southern borders of the Gujarat kingdom. Other than substantial losses to the Bahmani forces, these attempts did not achieve anything.

The last few years of Ahmad Shah's rule was replete with conflicts, battles and skirmishes. He behaved like a dervish, whirling around and fighting with all he came into contact with, and anyone who came in his way. From a Bahmani point of view, none of these conflicts or encounters were particularly successful and some were even humiliating defeats. The defeats invariably led to Ahmad Shah accepting one-sided terms for peace, which others foisted on him. The Gujarat war and its follow-on conflicts exhausted the Bahmani Sultan personally and also the kingdom's treasury. Hushang Shah smarting under the defeat he had suffered watched from a distance the draining of both the physical and resource power of the Bahmani Sultan. At an opportune moment he attacked and captured Kherla, putting the ruler Narsingh to death. Ahmad, in his depleted condition, attempted to march to Kherla but was dissuaded from doing so by Nasir Khan. Nasir Khan organised a peace with Malwa, the conditions of which were unfavourable to Ahmad and the Bahmani kingdom. Kherla was permanently annexed to Malwa.

Before his death in 1435, Ahmad Shah attempted to mount an unsuccessful expedition against a rebellion in the Telangana region. This was the last of the military adventures of the Bahmani Sultan who considered himself a saint. At his death, he was aged around 64 and had retired from public life after placing his eldest son on the throne. The Bahmani kingdom was at this stage bounded by Malwa in the north; Gujarat in the north-west; extended all the way to Goa in the south; and reached Masulipatnam on the Coromandal coast to the east. The northern hill country was still held by minor Maratha chieftains.

Ahmad Shah's Rule – Entrenchment of a Schism

As an individual, Ahmad Shah was a brutal bigot and a cruel tyrant. He was a superstitious and fanatical Muslim who used the veneer of religion for conveniently pursuing his purposes as seen in the opportunistic manner in which religion was twisted to facilitate his military campaigns. This aspect of his character is in sharp contrast to that of his brother Firuz, who was educated enough to have been sceptical about religion and life itself in general. It is also possible that Ahmad displayed some superficial soft corner for the poets and other learned people to create an impression of being somewhat like his more sophisticated brother and predecessor and to be following his footsteps. He commissioned the writing of the *Bahman-nama*, a versified history of the infant Bahmani dynasty by the poet Azari or Isfarayin of Khurasan. This was a poor imitation of the *Shah-nama*. The *Bahman-nama* has been lost to history, but since it would have been laudatory in nature, is unlikely to have provided any more actual details about the dynasty than what is available now.

The most important development that took place during Ahmad Shah's reign was the divisions that got entrenched in the Muslim community of the Deccan, which played a major part in the subsequent demise of the dynasty. Ahmad Shah regularly employed Turks, Arabs, Mongols and Persians, who were mainly Shias, in both the military and civil administration in various levels of the hierarchy. This incursion by foreigners into the officialdom of the kingdom was resented by the local Deccani Muslims who were supported by the African Negroes as well as the off springs of the African officials and Indian mothers. The majority of this group were Sunni Muslims and a surreptitious rivalry started.

This rivalry came out in the open when the foreign military officers blamed the local Deccani Muslims for the defeat suffered during the Gujarat campaign, accusing them of cowardice. *[This deprecating opinion about the local (Indian) Muslims, held by the 'foreign' Muslims gradually became entrenched and continued throughout the 'Islamic period' in the history of India. Sadly, the religion that touts equality of all before the Almighty, still practises this discrimination, clearly visible in the treatment meted out to the Muslims from the Indian sub-continent, who are considered as decidedly inferior, in the kingdoms of the Middle-East, where they form the bulk of the migrant work force.]*

Ala ud-Din II

On accession to the throne, Ala ud-Din promised the dawn of a glorious reign. Adhering to the promise that he had made to his father, he treated his youngest brother Muhammad, who had been left as his companion, with gracious fraternal generosity. This was unusual for the times, when any potential rival to the throne was either blinded or summarily executed on a prince assuming power in order to avoid future challenges. Muhammad however did not reciprocate the feelings.

He was misled by the anti-Ala ud-Din faction and contested the throne, demanding that the kingdom be divided between himself and Ala ud-Din. He collected a force, rebelled openly and seized the Raichur Doab, Bijapur and some other districts. He also appealed to Vijayanagar for assistance, despite that kingdom being the traditional foe of his own kingdom for generations. Ala ud-Din personally met the rebel forces on the battlefield and, although there was heavy slaughter on both sides, successfully put down the rebellion. The defeated rebel army scattered and Muhammad implored forgiveness, which was gladly granted by Ala ud-Din. This action was also an act of extraordinary magnanimity on the part of Ala ud-Din, who also assigned the Raichur

Doab as a jagir for the young prince. Muhammad lived in peace in his jagir for the rest of his life, never once breaking his allegiance to his elder brother.

This episode is noteworthy since it is an exception to the normal flow of events during the medieval Muslim occupation of the Indian sub-continent. While the actions of Muhammad sticks to the script, Ala ud-Din's treatment of his youngest brother is an aberration of kindness in an otherwise sordid, but popularly condoned set of actions that were normally practised. In an indirect and somewhat vitriolic manner, Muhammad's rebellion legitimises the Islamic practice of kings killing or blinding all siblings and near relatives and imprisoning them so that there would be no royal leaders with pretentions to the throne available to start rebellions against the newly installed king. It can be observed that the splendour and power inherent in the Indian throne possessed a fatal attraction to those of whom the accident of birth placed near it. By sheer experience the incumbent kings had realised that the only way to consolidate their rule and avoid civil war was to get rid of any possible competition and pretenders to the throne, immediately on assuming power. Ala ud-Din's behaviour is perhaps the only notable exception to this norm, at least in the history of a major dynasty.

Ahmad Shah Vali's Tomb

Ala ud-Din built a magnificent dome over his father's grave in the outskirts of Bidar. The ceiling and walls of the dome were decorated with calligraphy and floral designs and the colours of the designs, especially the ones towards the top of the dome, still remains fresh and bright today. The paintings are beautiful and elegant and is unique in the Indian sub-continent. An inscription on the dome provides the exact date of the death of Ahmad Shah as 17 April 1436.

There is an interesting practice connected to the tomb. Even today an annual fair is held by the Lingayat sect to honour the Vali at his tomb. Legend has it that this is a continuation of the celebrations that took place when the tomb was constructed and sanctified.

(The Lingayat sect emerged as reactionary force against Hinduism in the 12th century. While it rejected most of the broad Hindu traditions, it also assimilated aspects of it. The sect wanted to be considered a separate religion—this demand for status as an independent religion continues to percolate even today in modern India.)

Military Exploits

In 1436, Ala ud-Din conquered parts of the Konkan and the Raja of Sangamewar was forced to give his daughter in marriage to him. The princess was known as 'pari-chehra' or 'fairy-face' and immediately became the Sultan's favourite, much to the annoyance and subsequent jealousy of the first queen. These feelings were further embittered by the fact that the new princess was an infidel. Nasir Khan, the first queen's father, felt offended by Ala ud-Din's change of preference and invaded Berar. At this juncture the division between the foreigners and the Deccanis in the royal court came out in the open. True to their style, the Deccanis advised caution in dealing with Nasir Khan, whereas the ever brash and adventurous foreign contingent went into battle under the command of Malik-ul-Tijar.

The Bahmani forces won a grand victory and therefore became the favourite faction of the Sultan. They were allowed to sit on the right side of the Sultan in court, the place of honour. Even so this was not the end of the rivalry between the two factions, which continued unabated. The rivalry bubbled along, degenerating into internecine conflict at times, with definitive detrimental effect to the efficiency of the military and general administration of the kingdom.

War with Vijayanagar

The conflict between the Bahmani and Vijayanagar kingdoms continued unabated with the usual savagery during the entire period of Ala ud-Din's rule. Ferishta, always erring on the side of exaggeration, writes that Ala ud-Din cautioned Devaraya II, his contemporary ruler of Vijayanagar against executing two Muslim officers of the Bahmani army who had been captured, stating that it was the rule of his family, '...to slay a 100,000 Hindus in revenge for the death of a single Muslim'.

Around 1442-43, Devaraya II, an astute student of military history and tactics, constituted a council to discuss the reasons for repeated Bahmani victories in the battlefield, at times even against numerically superior forces. The council reported back that the two fundamental strengths of the Muslim army were—the Muslim expertise in employing and manoeuvring their cavalry; and the skilled archery contingents that were employed with devastating efficiency. Accordingly, Devaraya revised his policies of recruitment to the army and also the religious rules of the kingdom. He started to recruit Muslims to the army, in an effort to improve the cavalry regiments and permitted the building of mosques in the country for these soldiers to worship.

Once he felt confident about the competency of his army, Devaraya invaded the Raichur Doab, captured Mudgal and besieged Raichur and Bankapur. At the same time the Vijayanagar army laid waste to the countryside of Bijapur and Sagar. In response the Bahmani army took to the field. It is certain that three major battles were fought and a number of smaller clashes and skirmishes also took place. However, none of them were decisive. There is an uncorroborated report that in the third battle Devaraya's son was killed, which is highly improbable since no other source confirms the fact. Mudgal, the captured fort was besieged for months by the Bahmani forces without any decisive outcome. Devaraya bought peace by agreeing to pay a stipulated tribute. This turn of events could indicate some amount of discomfiture on the Vijayanagar side, especially of the continuing siege. Essentially, status quo was maintained as far as territorial control was concerned.

The Battles of the Waning Years

The last years of Ala ud-Din's reign was marked by a number of rebellions, one flowing from the other. It started with Ala ud-Din's brother-in-law and governor of Telangana, Jalal Khan, proclaiming independence as the ruler of Telangana. Ala ud-Din personally marched to put down the revolt and punish the rebel. On hearing this, Jalal send his son Sikandar to Malwa seeking help of Mahmud still ruling there, although he had ben soundly defeated by the Bahmani forces earlier. After sending out the appeal for help, Jalal Khan shut himself up in the fort at Nalgonda. At this time Ala ud-Din had been confined to his palace because of an injury to his foot, which was misrepresented by Sikandar to Mahmud of Malwa as Ala ud-Din being dead and the Bahmani kingdom being in chaos. Buoyed by this news Mahmud joined the rebellion.

On realising that Bahmani army was being led personally by Ala ud-Din, Mahmud retreated to his kingdom, breaking away from the rebel group. Ala ud-Din left the siege of Nalgonda in the hands of one his ministers, Mahmud Gawan and pursued Mahmud into his kingdom. Jalal Khan and his son were defeated by the Bahmani forces, but were pardoned by Ala ud-Din on the recommendation of Mahmud Gawan. Incidentally, this is the first mention of Mahmud Gawan—who was to become one of the great personalities of medieval India—in the historical narrative of the Deccan.

Last days and Death

Ala ud-Din died around 1457-58 at the end of a bloody and strenuous career after having designated his son Humayun as his successor. Ala ud-Din had been mercurial in his policies and action and his personal character was an unholy and unpredictable mix of benevolence and tyranny. He was totally contemptuous of court formalities and ruled within his own whims and fancies. For example, it was a contemporary norm for the king to hold a public audience every day. He stopped this practice, and at one time held an audience only after a five-month break. The regularity of the king's audiences became once every three or four months.

He spent inordinately long periods of time in his harem and drank wine to excess in private. However, he presented to the public a visage of a sternly orthodox Muslim, even punishing his subjects suspected of having consumed wine. Hypocrisy, that was to be the central character trait of Muslim rulers in India, was openly visible in the conduct of Ala ud-Din, both in his public and personal life. While exhibiting the persona of an orthodox Muslim to his subjects, Ala ud-Din was not overly religious in his personal observation of the faith. He followed this with the passing of edicts that made it compulsory, on pain of exacting punishment, for the common people to observe the religious norms in their strictest form. Within this complex character, he considered himself a just ruler, giving himself the title Al-adil, meaning 'The Just'. He built a number of mosques with attached public schools. He is known to have built a large hospital in Bidar, which was thrown open for the treatment of the sick and poor.

Chapter 8

LAST DAYS AND BREAK-UP

The Divisions in Court

The Tarafdari system that was instituted by Hasan did not take long to become entrenched in the socio-political structure of the kingdom. Gradually, the tarafdars, the governors of the tarafs or provinces, started to acquire local prestige. This trend invariably led to greater separatist tendencies that became increasingly more difficult for the Sultan to control. These separatist forces continued to gain momentum till mid-15th century. At this time, the subterranean division that had been percolating amongst the elite nobles supporting the ruling dynasty came out in the open, clearly dividing them into two rival groups – the Deccanis who were the local Muslims and the Pardesis, meaning foreigners.

The Deccanis were domiciled Muslims of the region. No doubt a majority of them traced their origins outside the Deccan, but a few of the nobles of high standing were either direct converts or the offspring of converts. The outsiders, over a period of long stay in the Deccan had inter-married with the locals, changed their way of life vis-à-vis customs, eating habits, dress and social life style. A number of them were also of darker complexion than the Arabs and other foreigners, on account of the lineage from local marriages. Even foreign officers initially employed by Hasan had gradually become 'Deccanised' over a century and were considered to be 'local'. In addition, a number of Africans – mostly Abyssinians – had also mingled with the local population and this mixed population was also counted amongst the Deccanis. They were dark-skinned and often were lesser educated and cultured, therefore treated with contempt by the Pardesis, the pure foreigners.

The Deccanis also contained Hindu converts. Two exemplary models were: Fathullah Imad Shah the founder of the Imad Shahi dynasty in Berar; and Ahmad Nizam Shah, who founded the Nizam Shahi dynasty in Ahmadnangar. Both these noblemen were originally Brahmin Hindus. The Deccanis looked upon the native land as their territory and were suspicious of any foreigner attempting to obtain a foothold, territorially or as officials in the royal court. These foreigners automatically became rivals in the mind of the Deccanis.

The Pardesis, as the name implies, were outsiders who were mostly first generation immigrants. The Bahmani kings employed them freely and this created a large flow of these foreigners into the country—their numbers increasing with each passing year. They came from all parts of the larger Islamic world outside the sub-continent – Persia, Turkey, Central Asia, Arabia and Afghanistan. The common trait that bound them was that they were all adventurers of reasonable military and administrative capabilities. The Deccan at that time was considered a land of adventure and opportunity where an individual's valour was recognised and statesmanship rewarded without any questions being asked about his antecedents. The only qualification needed was to be a Muslim!

From the beginning of this process, the Pardesis exercised considerable influence in the kingdom's politics as well as in the decision-making at court. However, in the initial days, the Deccanis did not feel the competition since the Pardesis were few in numbers and therefore their influence was negligible. There was another reason for the Deccanis not having considered them a threat to their hegemony. The Pardesis were few and therefore intermarriage with the locals was common, which in turn led to assimilation into the Deccani group. The creation of a separate identity for the Pardesis came with increased numbers in their immigration and the perpetuation of a Pardesi community that stood away from the local Muslims, the Deccanis. It was not long before two distinct factions were formed at court—the Pardesis and Deccanis.

The Pardesis were more active and energetic and therefore more successful than the Deccanis. The reasons are obvious. They had to work hard to prove themselves in an alien land and against the odds of not being liked by the locals. It was also not surprising that they considered the Deccanis inferior. The rivalry became entrenched and intense, often leading to riots and skirmishes. The division was exacerbated by the religious difference between the two factions, with the Pardesis being majority Shia and the Deccanis being of the Sunni persuasion.

By the end of the 14th century, the Deccanis had been pushed to the fringes of the court and almost completely displaced from power. However, during the reign of Ahmad Shah Vali, the Deccanis managed to insinuate themselves back into the Sultan's favour at the cost of the Pardesis. In 1430-31 the Bahmani army was soundly defeated by the Gujarat forces three times in a row. The Pardesi Amir in-charge of the Bahmani forces attributed the defeat squarely to the cowardice of the Deccanis. However, the Deccanis managed to convince the Sultan that the debacle was the result of the bad advice rendered by the Pardesi officers. The rivalry finally led to the massacre of a large number of Pardesi nobles at a place called Chakan. The Deccanis had organised the ambush after getting the Sultan's approval to do so, obtained through convincing him of a false story. The Sultan subsequently came to know of this deceit by the Deccanis and relegated them to subsidiary status. However, the rivalry continued and contributed directly to the weakening and subsequent fall of the Bahmani dynasty.

Humayun Shah

On Ala ud-Din's death some nobles set on the throne Hasan, Humayun's younger brother. However, Humayun was the late Sultan's choice for the position and he had no trouble setting aside the young upstart and assuming the throne. The nobles who had supported Hasan were either killed, imprisoned or fled the country in fear. Hasan was captured, blinded and imprisoned. Humayun was already known for his cruelty and this evil reputation was confirmed by his actions on assuming the throne. The savagery of his deeds earned him the title 'Zalim' or 'Cruel Tyrant'. His cruelty was such that some historians compare him to the Roman emperors Nero and/or Caligula. It is interesting that contemporary Muslim chroniclers praise his wit, learning and eloquence while at the same time mentioning his 'fierce disposition'. The description of his character as 'fierce' is nothing but a euphemism for savage cruelty, since they could not have mentioned anything more derogatory than this vague statement as death would have been meted out to them without doubt. Similarly, praise for his learning and wit was undoubtedly inserted to soften the reference to his cruel character.

Humayun favoured the Pardesis or foreigners above the Deccanis, whom he relegated to the background. He secured the services of an exceptionally able minister, Najm ud-Din Mahmud bin Muhammad Gawan Gilani who became known to history as Mahmud Gawan, and made him the lieutenant or Malik Naib, bestowing the governorship of Bijapur on him.

> **Mahmud Gawan**
>
> There is an authoritative biography of Mahmud Gawan written by Abdul Karim Hamdani from which details of his life and times can be understood.
>
> Mahmud was a native of Qawan in Iran where his ancestors were Viziers, or ministers, of Shah Gilan. Mahmud himself was a trader who came to the Deccan in 1453 when he was 42 years old, with the sole purpose of enhancing his trading activities. Noticing his administrative capabilities, Ala ud-Din made him an Amir (noble) in his court.
>
> Humayun conferred the title of Malik-ul-Tajjar on him, raised him to First Minister and entrusted important duties to him. This is perhaps the only commendable act that was done by Humayun Shah during his reign.
>
> Mahmud Gawan was an exceptionally gifted administrator and was prudent to a fault. He went on to serve four successive Bahmani sultans, most creditably and loyally for over three decades. He was a stabilising influence in the Bahmani kingdom during a period of extreme political turbulence and internecine conflicts that was debilitating the kingdom.

Humayun Shah ruled only for a short period of time – his reign marred by a series of rebellions and unrest. The major events recalled regarding his regime are neither military conquest nor expeditions nor administrative reform but the hideous cruelty that he perpetuated with savage brutality.

There were two major rebellions during Humayun Shah's reign. The first was in Telangana by Sikandar Khan and his father Jalal Khan. The other was in the capital Bidar when Humayun and his trusted minister Mahmud Gawan were in Telangana putting down the rebellion there. True to form, Humayun put down both the rebellions with maniacal ferocity. The rebellion in the capital was instigated by the supporters of Hasan, the blinded and imprisoned prince. The rebels were captured by the then governor of Bijapur Siraj Khan, Mahmud Gawan having relinquished the governor's post to be the First Minister in court, and handed over to Humayun Khan.

Hasan was thrown in front of a ferocious tiger in the presence of Humayun Khan and was devoured. Every single person connected to the rebellion in even very minor ways such as being the cook of a rebel, or seen to have assisted the rebellion in some way, were tortured and killed. The cruelty was such that it exceeded all bounds of normalcy, making even the court chroniclers describe the savagery in detail. Even though he had the king's ear, Mahmud Gawan was unable to reign in Humayun's spiteful and ferocious cruelty. Further, the talented queen Makhdumah Jahan also attempted to intervene to stop these acts but was unable to reason with the blood-thirsty Humayun. Humayun Shah was murdered in September 1461, reportedly by an African maid servant, who was 'tired of his inhuman cruelty'.

Universal Joy at the Death of Humayun Shah

The poet Nazir composed a chronogram that expressed the universal joy felt by his subjects at his death. It indirectly provides the date of his death. It goes:

> 'Humayun Shah has passed away from the world.
>
> God Almighty, what a blessing was the death of Humayun!
>
> On the date of his death, the world was full of delight.
>
> So 'delight of the world' gives the date of his death.'
>
> The Persian words, which are the equivalent of 'delight of the world' are 'Zauq-i-Jahan. The numerical values of the letters of that term comes to 865, the Hijra year of Humayun's death.

Nizam Shah

Since he was murdered very early in his reign, Humayun Shah had not yet nominated any successor. Therefore, the three most powerful people in the court—the queen Makhdumah Jahan, the first minister Mahmud Gawan and Malik Shah Turk known by his title Khwaja Jahan—brought Humayun's 8-year old son Nizam Shah to the throne. Some neighbours, Orissa and Warangal in particular, considered the boy-Sultan's accession as an opportunity to make territorial inroads into the Bahmani kingdom, but were repulsed.

At the same time the Sultan of Malwa, Mahmud Khilji, marched towards Bidar and advanced almost unopposed. Mahmud Gawan and Khwaja Jahan assembled a force and marched to oppose the Malwa army. The Bahmani forces were routed in the battle that ensued, suffering a great defeat, and fled the field. Khilji now continued his advance, laid waste the countryside and occupied Bidar. Nizam Shah had been removed to Firuzabad on the River Bhima prior to the arrival of the Malwa forces. In complete distress at the turn of events, Mahmud Gawan appealed to the Sultan of Gujarat, Mahmud Begarha, for assistance. Begarha entered the Deccan with a large force, because of which the Malwa forces withdrew to their own territories. Khilji attempted another invasion the next year, but the coalition forces of Bahmani and Gujarat kingdoms frightened him and he returned to Malwa without engaging in battle.

> ### The Dowager Queen – Makhdumah Jahan
>
> Humayun Shah's wife, Makhdumah Jahan, who was a granddaughter of Sultan Firuz Shah, was one of the most remarkable women to have appeared in the Deccan Plateau.
>
> She aided Mahmud Gawan energetically in all activities of the court after her son Nizam Shah was brought to the throne. She was instrumental in rapidly dismantling the evil set up of her husband's misrule. She ensured that all innocent persons who had been incarcerated without reason were freed and reinstated all servants who had been dismissed without cause. She took active part in reinvigorating the moribund administration. The Queen was almost single-handedly responsible for repelling the Orissa-Telangana combine that invaded Bahmani in the first year of Nizam Shah's rule.

Unfortunately, Nizam Shah died suddenly on 30 July 1463, the day set for his marriage, after a brief rule of only two years.

Muhammad Shah III

Even though Nizam Shah's death was unanticipated, the Council of Regency – the queen-mother, Mahmud Gawan and Khwaja Jahan – that had guided the kingdom during his short rule was sufficiently entrenched to effect a seamless transfer of power. They raised Nizam's younger brother to the throne with the title Muhammad Shah III. However, the Khwaja Jahan had become ambitious and started to sideline the queen-mother from the decision-making process. The young Sultan, denounced Khwaja in the open court and had him murdered, also in the open. Mahmud Gawan was made Vakil-us-Sultanate, the deputy of the Sultanate, effectively becoming the Prime Minister. He continued in this position till 1481 when he was murdered.

Mahmud Gawan now had unlimited power, but conducted himself with considerable moderation and single-minded devotion to ensure the kingdom's welfare. He fought a number of successful wars against the neighbours of the Bahmani kingdom, increasing its spread to the greatest extent ever. At its height, the Bahmani kingdom spread from Goa to Orissa, covering the entire breadth of the Peninsula. Goa was the best port of the Vijayanagar kingdom and its capture is particularly significant. The capture of Goa was not only a military victory over the hereditary enemy of the Bahmani dynasty, but brought the entire west coast trade under their control.

Gawan's most important military exploit was the conquest of Hubli, Belgaum and Bagalkot that brought the full Bombay-Karnataka belt under Bahmani sway and consolidated control of the long Konkan coast. The young Sultan also participated in the military expeditions, earning him the title 'Lashkari', meaning warrior. There was a war of succession in Orissa, in which the Bahmani army intervened successfully that further increased the status of the kingdom. The new conquests also enriched the kingdom. A Russian traveller of the time, Athanasius Nikitin visited Bidar and wrote that it was 'the chief town of the whole Muhammadan Hindustan'.

Expedition to Kanchi

A military raid on Kanchi or Kanchipuram is considered the most remarkable exploit of Muhammad Shah. Kanchi was extremely sacred to the Hindus and housed several temples that were immensely wealthy. In 1481, Mahmud Shah force-marched to Kanchi and defeated the Hindu forces. However, the Muslim chroniclers mention that the Hindu army fought valiantly and ferociously to defend the temple-town. This is high praise coming from the Muslim writers who habitually belittled the Hindu armies. The Hindu army must have been of exemplary quality to gain such praise. The chronicles go on to state that the city was razed to the ground along with all its temples. It is obvious that Kanchi was plundered and many atrocities committed in the name of victory, which were also religiously motivated. However, the claim of the entire city being razed is an exaggeration. The Bahmani army collected immense booty and returned. On Muhammad turning 15 years of age, the queen-mother, one of the most sagacious ladies to honour the position, retired and died soon after.

The Story of Mahmud Gawan

The Bahmani kingdom was traditionally divided into four 'tarafs' or provinces and ruled by centrally appointed governors called tarafdars, essentially provincial governors. Since factionalism—between the Pardesis and Deccanis—was rampant in the kingdom, the tarafs were equally divided between them. The Pardesi nobles ruled Gulbarga with Bijapur under Mahmud Gawan and Daultabad under Yusuf Adil Khan; and the Deccanis ruled Telangana through Malik Hasan and Berar under Fathullah Imad-ul-Mulk.

Administrative Reforms

Mahmud Gawan was relatively not involved in factional politics and the Sultan reposed complete faith in him. With the support of the Sultan he commenced administrative reforms aimed at improving the kingdom's position and consolidating central control. Gawan divided each of the four tarafs into two and appointed new governors for the newly created provinces. Further, of the resulting eight tarafs, he kept several under central control so that the revenues from them could be used exclusively by the Sultan. This curtailed the enormous power so far wielded by the tarafdars. In addition Gawan appointed district collectors who were directly responsible to the royal court of the Sultan in Bidar. Only one fort in each taraf was left to the governor with the rest being manned by officers appointed by the king and directly responsible to him. These moves effectively curtailed all possibilities of rebellion against the Sultan.

Mahmud Gawan strictly enforced the reforms. He also enforced the collection of revenue and was extremely strict in ensuring that allowances were provided in a timely manner for the maintenance of the stipulated number of troops by all governors. Needless to state, these measures meant for the betterment of the administration was unpopular with the governors who had so far enjoyed unlimited freedom and power.

Gawan's Murder

As mentioned earlier, Mahmud Gawan was a Persian by birth and therefore nominally belonged to the Pardesi faction, although he was personally not biased either way. He held the highest position in court and obviously had precedence over the Deccani faction, which was led by the tarafdar of Telangana, Malik Hasan Nizam-ul-Mulk Bahri. The administrative reforms that Gawan had instituted while improving the efficiency of the central control over the kingdom, also curtailed the uninhibited power that the tarafdars had so far enjoyed. It is no wonder that the reforms were unpopular amongst the nobles and that there was growing and widespread resentment against Mahmud Gawan.

The Deccanis led by Hasan decided to put an end to Gawan and resorted to deceit to achieve their nefarious purpose. They bribed the keeper of Mahmud's personal seals, forged a letter purporting to invite the king of Orissa to invade the Bahmani kingdom on which the seals were affixed and produced it in front of the Sultan as proof of Mahmud Gawan's disloyalty. Prior to this act, the Deccanis had poisoned the Sultan's ears with many imagined tales of Gawan's duplicitousness and acts of betrayal of the Sultan. On receiving the forged letter, the Sultan already biased against Gawan, flew into a rage and called Mahmud Gawan into his private chamber. There he had him summarily executed without even giving the loyal minister a chance to explain himself. The date was 5 April 1481 and Gawan was 78 years old.

> 'Thus perished by the ignoble hand of the assassin a veteran public servant, who had a glorious record of military triumphs and administrative achievements to his credit. The besotted Sultan discovered afterwards that he had been tricked by the fallen minister's enemies, but the injury that he had done to himself and the state was irreparable.'
>
> Ishwari Prasad,
> *History of Medieval India*, p. 371.

The only councillor of the Bahmani kings who combined loyalty and ability in equal measure and which raised him to the status of a statesman, who had served the dynasty for 35 years with unstinting devotion, was eliminated in a fit of misplaced rage by the impetus Muhammad Shah. Not only was this a great crime but it led to the almost immediate dissolution of the Bahmani kingdom. Mahmud Gawan was the glue that had so far held the state together.

Mahmud Gawan – The Statesman

Mahmud Gawan deserves high praise as one of the foremost, if not the greatest, statesmen of the Deccan in medieval times. His entire career was about unswerving loyalty and devotion to the Bahmani kingdom and dynasty, being completely focused on the concepts of territorial expansion and administrative reform. In his private life, Gawan was simple, generous, charitable, learned and of a blameless character. It is even conceivable that he could have healed the widening rift between the Pardesis and the Deccanis had it not been for the habitual rancour of Malik Hasan who finally brought him down.

> 'Simplicity of living, courage and determination in times of difficulty, generosity and magnanimity of temper, love of justice and benevolence, a character that defied temptations so common in a state despotically governed, a lofty conception of morality in an age when the grossest vices were condoned or connived at—all these are traits attributed to him by the unanimous testimony of Muslim historians.'
>
> Ishwari Prasad,
> *History of Medieval India*, p. 372.

Mahmud Gawan was not the paragon of virtues as he is made out to be by contemporary Muslim chroniclers. There was a complete downside to his character. Gawan was single-mindedly relentless in his pursuit of non-Muslims, showing absolutely no mercy on anyone not of the Islamic faith. He was intolerant to the extreme while also being a devout and fully observing Muslim in his private life. More than any of his predecessors, Mahmud Gawan was responsible for the subjugation of the Hindus in the Deccan, through acts of commission and omission that ground the non-Muslim population continually into the dust.

It is recorded that Mahmud Gawan subordinated all personal considerations to carry out his public responsibilities. His murder was the death knell of the Bahmani dynasty.

The Curtain Falls on the Bahmani Kingdom

When Mahmud Gawan was murdered, the Pardesi amirs left the capital for their provinces without seeking the permission of the Sultan as was customary. Even though Malik Hasan became the Prime Minister, some of the Deccani nobles, the more even-handed ones, also disapproved of the treacherous murder of Gawan. Having realised his mistake, Muhammad Shah was full of remorse and took to heavy drinking. He died within a year of his illustrious minister's murder.

Some chroniclers opine that amongst the Bahmani Sultans, Muhammad Shah was next to Firuz Shah in learning. He was also an energetic ruler and a good soldier. His undoing was the fact that he was unduly fond of wine and made a number of brash and dubious decisions while in an inebriated state. The execution of Mahmud Gawan was one such. Muhammad is the last king of the Bahmani dynasty worth mentioning separately. He was followed on the throne by five more 'Sultans' who were mere puppets in the hands of unscrupulous nobles.

Muhammad Shah III was followed on the throne by his 12-year old son Mahmud, while all power was wielded by Malik Hasan. The boy-king attempted to have Hasan assassinated but the plot failed and resulted in Mahmud being placed under stricter control, becoming a helpless virtual prisoner. Very rapidly the authority of the Sultan, wielded by Malik Hasan, started to be questioned by the nobles. Most of the governors of the provinces started to disobey royal orders. Yusuf Adil Khan, now the leader of the Pardesi faction, instigated revolts in Goa and Chakan, while in the east the governor of Telangana rebelled.

The boy-king Mahmud, managed to have Malik Hasan caught and strangled while the latter was proceeding to capture the royal treasury. To make matters worse, Mahmud on reaching maturity, proved to be an imbecile, preferring the company of buffoons and others of the same ilk; indulging himself in debauchery and idleness. The Deccanis now attempted to dethrone Mahmud, but was stopped by the intervention of the Pardesis. This led to the massacre of the Deccani and African factions by the Pardesis that is reported to have continued for three consecutive days and nights. After this episode, the balkanisation of the Bahmani kingdom gathered pace.

In 1490 Yusuf Adil Khan declared independence in Bijapur and Fathullah Imad-ul-Mulk did the same in Berar, with both assuming royal titles. There was no attempt from the Sultan to bring the rebels under control. Two decades later Qutb-ul-Mulk declared independence in Golconda and Barid ul-Mulk did the same in the capital Bidar itself. Prior to this declaration of independence, Amir Barid had been in full control as the Prime Minister after the murder of Malik Hasan. Barid had kept Mahmud the Sultan in humiliating conditions before his death in 1518. This could be considered the virtual end of the dynasty.

The four sons of Mahmud Shah were brought to the throne one-by-one as mere figureheads and done away with at the whim and fancy of Amir Barid. Even though the Bahmani princes were nominally ruling in Bidar during this period, it will not be incorrect to put 1490 as the date for the rise of the Barid Shahi dynasty that ruled from Bidar. The life and times of the four sons of Mahmud who 'adorned' the throne for about a decade is not worth a mention in the history of the Bahmani kingdom. The last of these princes, Kalimullah, appealed to Babur for assistance after which he fled to Bijapur and then to Ahmadnagar where he died. With this death the Bahmani dynasty officially came to an end. An inglorious end to an inglorious dynasty.

This is the story of the Bahmani kingdom, not an edifying tale. The Bahmani dynasty did not by any means write an attractive chapter in the annals of Indian history, quite the contrary.

The Bahmani Dynasty – An Assessment

Of the 18 kings/sultans who ruled the Bahmani kingdom, only very few were not debauched drunkards. Further, all of them were religious bigots—their bigotry varying only in the brutality of their treatment of non-believers—who had absolutely no sympathy for their majority Hindu subjects. The Bahmani kings wholeheartedly supported forced conversion. The sultans lived in self-created bubble of factionalism and often tended to make blunders and calamitous decisions.

Even though marriage to local women were encouraged and was common place, the Muslims did not exceed a mere 15 per cent of the total population of the kingdom at any time. However, the sultans were evenly blood-thirsty, ferocious and cruel, who gloried in the persecution of Hindus, from the time of the founding Sultan Hasan Bahmani. The reports of the Bahmani kings being patrons of learning has to be understood within the limits that was placed by the Sultans themselves. They built many mosques and imparted religious education to the Muslim population and treated the Hindus as second class citizens with no benefits given in return for their contribution to the betterment of the state. Thus the sultan felt responsible for only 15 per cent of the entire population that he ruled. Contrary to the reports of contemporary Muslim chronicles and even some modern day historical analysts who praise their rule, the Bahmani Sultans come across as being inhuman oppressors, sucking the land dry to live their own lives in exaggerated luxury.

An unbiased analysis of the recorded annals of the Bahmani kingdom shows that they are replete with instances of organised murders and massacres of the predominantly Hindu population; desecration of countless temples, primarily to loot the wealth stored in them; and disgraceful orgies conducted in the court and which went on for days at a time. The Bahmani army, much praised by both Muslim chroniclers of the time and some modern day historians, was nothing but a rampaging rabble that was a law unto itself. The huge armies that were maintained were little better than armed mobs who were extremely inefficient in actual battle. The only redeeming factor in this sordid tale of butchery and intolerance, if there can be one, is that all this took place in medieval times and therefore could in some ways be considered 'normal' for the era. In Europe during these times, the tactics of burning so-called heretics at the stake and using the rack to obtain confessions and punish dissidence, was normal.

Whatever the reasons given to make the Bahmani rule look normal, it is certain that none of the Bahmani Sultans were enlightened rulers. Each one of them revelled at being deceitful, treacherous and bigoted, holding on to power by any and all means at their disposal. Self-aggrandisement, the forced spread of Islam, and ensuring a rapid shift in the cultural milieu of the Indian sub-continent were their primary aims.

The Bahmani kingdom was split between five succeeding dynasties—the Imad Shahi in Berar; Nizam Shahi in Ahmadnagar; Adil Shahi in Bijapur; Qutub Shahi in Golconda; and Barid Shahi in Bidar. Thus ended the rule of the Bahmani dynasty, not going down in a flourish of trumpets, but drowning in their own ignoble deeds with not a single person sorry to see their unholy demise.

Chapter 9

THE BAHMANIS – CONCLUDING DEDUCTIONS

By late 15th century, domestic frictions, internecine conflicts, and incessant rebellions had become regular features within the Bahmani kingdom. The final break-up therefore could not have come as a surprise to even casual observers of the downward spiral the kingdom had been on for the previous few decades. The early 1500s were chaotic years—the kingdoms that succeeded the Bahmani kingdom in the Deccan were involved in an endless round of wars and skirmishes, within an ever-shifting melee of alliances and hostilities. In this confusion, religion hardly played a role. The manoeuvrings and conflicts were purely political in nature. In the dance for power and position, Muslim kingdoms aligned with the Hindu Vijayanagar kingdom against other Muslim states and factions within Vijayanagar sough the assistance of Muslim kingdoms against the central Hindu ruler.

In this ever-increasing spiral of conflict, one major battle stands out as being of great significance. In an act not repeated before or thereafter, four of the five successor states of the fragmented Bahmani kingdom—Bijapur, Ahmednagar, Golconda and Berar—came together with a unity of purpose not commonly seen during that period. In the Battle of Talikota in January 1565, the Muslim combine delivered a deathblow to the Hindu Vijayanagar kingdom from which it never fully recovered. This great victory however did not stop the Muslim kingdoms from continuing their individual fights amongst themselves even later. The infighting between the kingdoms of the

Deccan continued unabated for another two centuries till the Mughals finally obliterated any signs of these petty Muslim kingdoms of the Peninsular Deccan.

The Character of the Bahmani Dynasty

The character of a dynasty as a whole and the nature of its achievements must be carefully considered to establish their position and status in the broader scheme of history, especially in the complex, and at times convoluted, historical narrative of the Indian sub-continent.

The pure factual narrative of the Bahmani dynasty reads as an extremely bloody chronicle. Of the 18 sultans who sat on the Bahmani throne between 1347 and 1518, four were murdered and two were deposed, blinded and imprisoned. Other than the fifth Sultan who was peace-loving, all the others who attained majority and maturity were blood-thirsty religious fanatics and several were drunken debauches. More indicative of their lack of fineness than these statistics is the fact that no narrative written even by the sycophantic Muslim chroniclers of the time, which provide a favourable and positive image of his character, exists about any member of the royal family. Only Mahmud Gawan is worthy of some praise, although he did not belong to the Bahmani dynasty. However, even this scrupulous minister was a fanatical and bigoted Muslim without a trace of kindness towards non-believers.

It is true that the dynasty initiated minor irrigation works that peripherally benefited the common farmers. Even so the fact remains that these works were meant to ensure an improved revenue for the crown, no kindness was intended for the poor farmers. Even the marginal credit that accrues to the dynasty because of the irrigation works is completely wiped out by the 'wholesale devastation wrought by the wars, massacres and burnings' that was commonplace in the Bahmani kingdom. A historian finds it extremely difficult, even after painstaking research, to find a single benefit that was conferred on the Indian sub-continent by this bedevilled dynasty.

Another yardstick to estimate the character of a dynasty is to measure the collective effect of their rule on the common people of the kingdom. This assessment should not be based on inferences drawn from the conspicuous events of the time as reported by the biased and self-serving court chroniclers whose accounts are, unfortunately, the ones that normally survive. The surviving notes of observant foreign travellers provide more accurate information from which the actual state of affairs in a kingdom can be inferred. In the case of the Bahmani dynasty, the Russian traveller Athanasius Nikitin, whose notes have survived the ravages of time, clearly states, '...the land is overstocked with people; those in the country are very miserable, while the nobles are extremely opulent and delight in luxury'.

From researching the Bahmani dynasty it becomes clear that the primary aim of the Bahmani sultans was to exterminate the population of the Hindu states against whom they fought continuous and vicious battles. Failing this, the objective was to drive the Hindus to convert to Islam. They made a concerted attempt to achieve these aims, sparing no cost or effort in this quest. True, they succeeded in killing unaccounted hundreds of thousands of Hindus and also in converting a considerable number. However, the population of the Bahmani kingdom remained predominantly Hindu, despite the two centuries of violent effort to alter the demographic balance.

Arrival of the Europeans

One event of critical importance that had long-lasting impact on Indian history happened during the Bahmani rule – the arrival of European naval fleets in the Indian seas. In 1498, three decades before the invasion of North India by Babur the Mughal, a Portuguese fleet under the command of Vasco da Gama arrived in Calicut a northern Kerala port. Over the next few decades the Portuguese entrenched themselves in a few coastal enclaves. Since their main interest was overseas trade, they immediately came into conflict with the Arabs who had so far held the monopoly on seaborne trade with India. A series of naval encounters ensued in which the Portuguese broke the Arab domination of the Indian trade. Arab sea power was also vanquished in a series of skirmishes. The monopoly now rested with the Portuguese.

It became imperative for the coastal kingdoms of the Peninsula to maintain good relations with the Portuguese since they controlled the sea lanes for trade. External trade was also critical for the peninsular armies to obtain horses from the Middle East and Central Asia—the dependence on seaborne trade was vital to the security of the kingdoms. This was the signal for the Portuguese to start influencing local politics and playing minor roles to improve their position. They also commenced missionary work, converting some Hindu families to Christianity and also making some Syrian Christians to shift allegiance to the Roman Catholic Church. They also made one attempt to loot a Hindu temple located in Vijayanagar territory. In response, Rama Raya the ruling king of Vijayanagar, attacked Goa, which had become a Portuguese holding, looted it and also overran San Thome. The Portuguese were chastised and did not make any further attempts to invade the Hindu kingdoms; neither did they manage to make any further territorial gains.

As the Portuguese power in Europe waned, so did their politico-economic role in India. They got sidelined in the broader movement of events and associated sub-events in the Indian sub-continent.

The Phirangi – Deccani Divide

The Bahmani kingdom was established by rebels who threw off the yoke of the Delhi Sultanate in order to create an independent sovereign kingdom in the Deccan. This rebellion was ably supported by the local nobles. These nobles were 'Deccanis', a term that denoted the descendants of the Muslims who had migrated from North India to the Deccan, starting from the early 1300s. They were of part-Turkish ancestry and their origins can be traced to the Central Asian region, from where they had marched in conquest to the northern plains of the Indian sub-continent. Contextually therefore, the term 'Deccani', at least in the initial stages, referred to North Indian immigrants who had opposed the Tughluq regime in Delhi, while stationed at the extremity of the Delhi Sultanate—in Daulatabad and further south.

By early 16th century, a mere two centuries after their initial arrival in the Deccan, these immigrants were fully rooted in the Deccan society. They had acquired the local languages—Marathi, Telugu and Kannada—and also developed a distinct vernacular of their own that came to be called Deccani Urdu, which is still in use. In political terms, the mantle of rebels and rebellion was removed from these people, they were not anti-Tughluq insurgents any more. They had become

'Deccanis', a group that was distinctly different to the 'Hindustanis' of North India. They formed a distinct political and socio-cultural group within the Deccan kingdoms, practising their own customs and traditions and growing strong as an active power-base within the broader structure and hierarchy of the kingdoms.

If a dividing line was to be drawn to denote the timeframe when the delineation of the Deccanis from other groups—both from North India and from outside India— took place, as well as to indicate the evolution of the rebels into a more defined group, it would have to be drawn the time when the Bahmani kingdom's capital was shifted from Gulbarga to Bidar. The date of this event, around mid-15th century, would best indicate the nuanced shift in the socio-political standing of the Deccanis from being rebels to becoming an independent group with its own ethos and power base.

The Bahmani kingdom, and more so the dynasty, suffered from an inferiority complex of being the backwaters in terms of Islamic culture since they lacked the sophistication and refinement of the Persianised court ethos that was splendidly on display in Delhi. North India continued to be infused regularly by new migration from the Central Asian region through the Khyber and Bolan Passes, which helped it to constantly update cultural aspects of the kingdom in line with the greater Islamic world centred on the Ottoman Empire. Since the Bahmani kingdom in the Deccan had been hewed off in a rebellion, there was no cultural or commercial contact with North India. This enforced division meant that the Bahmani region was starved of impetus, and wherewithal, to continue the Persianisation that was considered essential to maintain the façade of cultural and civilisational elegance and superiority. Hence, the Bahmani kings were always on the look out to induct 'talent' into the administration through appointing to important positions persons from outside India, who had Persianised attributes and were of aristocratic descent.

The quest to bring men of letters and presumed 'refinement' from the West reached its zenith when two consecutive Bahmani kings used to send a ship each year to the Persian world to induce and recruit 'better' educated people to migrate to the Deccan with the promise of wealth, prestige and guaranteed senior official positions. Through this process was brought to Bidar the family of Shah Nimat Allah Wali from Kirman, a famous religious scholar of the Islamic world. The elite corps of the Bahmani army, consisting of 3000 horse-mounted archers, was also imported from the Khurasan region. The ships also brought back the famed Arab horses for service in the Deccan army.

> ### The Arab Warhorse in the Deccan
>
> Throughout the medieval times, heavy warhorses were in great demand in the Indian sub-continent, mainly for service in the armies of the different kingdoms. In fact heavy cavalry forces, capable of rapid manoeuvre and able to strike extremely damaging blows to the adversary, were the ultimate expression of state power. The kingdoms of the Deccan were no exception and each one maintained carefully developed and prized cavalry forces. However, the agricultural produce of the region was not conducive to the breeding and raising of heavy warhorses. The Deccan cavalry was dependent on imported warhorses.
>
> With the Bahmani rebellion and the creation of a new kingdom in the Deccan putting an end to trade with North India, there rose a strategic need to source warhorses from some other regions. So far, warhorses had followed the land route from Central Asia to the northern part of the Indian sub-continent from where they moved south to meet the demands of the Deccan.
>
> In order to overcome the dearth of warhorses, the Deccan kingdoms opened the trade route to the Arabian Peninsula across the seas, thereby avoiding the reliance on the land route through North India. The Arab warhorses played an important role in the warfare of medieval Deccan kingdoms.

The 'imported', and more importantly, Persianised men were originally called 'gharbians' – meaning Westerners, people who came from lands to the west of the Indian sub-continent – in the Deccan. Subsequently they came to be generally referred to as 'Phirangis', a common term that was evolved by the Deccanis to depict all foreigners. The word is still used with the same meaning. However, there was a derogatory tinge associated with this word, especially in medieval Deccan. The Deccanis disliked the Phirangis because they were given preference for appointment to important positions in the administration and military by the Bahmani kings as well as by the rulers of its successor states.

All the Phirangis were immigrants from the Persian speaking world—Khurasan, Afghanistan, Central Asia and Iran—and were not all people of calibre as they claimed to be, although invariably they were appointed to senior positions. This exacerbated the ill-feeling towards them. These Phirangis, were of a separate ethnicity and originally reached the Indian shores as merchants, scholars, administrators and soldiers. Their only qualifying trait was that they were uniformly fully Persianised. Since they were a minority in the Deccan, they tended to remain together as a group bound to each other through a shared language and culture. Further, it was inescapable that they inter-married; and over a period of time created a recognisable bloc that was not only ethnically distinctive, but also stood out from the local Deccanis as a conspicuously different political, cultural and social group.

Since the local nobles, the Deccanis, did not come from abroad—in the sense that they were migrants from the north of the sub-continent who had assimilated with the local population—they resented the favouritism being shown to the Phirangis. However, it was inevitable that the two groups would go on to become the principal components of the socio-political order of the Deccan kingdoms. The antagonism between the two groups started early in history and coalesced into vicious and deadly conflicts over a period of centuries. The polarisation between the Phirangis and the Deccanis that finally led to the dismemberment of the Bahmani kingdom was bound to happen for two reasons. First is the inherent human tendency to be jealous of a more successful or favoured group, especially when there is an inherent feeling of one's own worth not being recognised. The Deccanis felt disenfranchised by the actions of the kings who preferred the Phirangis to the locals. Second, the Deccan kings were adept at dividing their nobles to stem any rebellion and therefore found it beneficial to play one group against the other. In a climate where succession struggles and palace revolts were common place, this tactic ensured the longevity of the dynasty. However, in the long term it proved to be a major factor in the undoing of centralised power, a tenet on which the stability of the kingdom rested.

The two groups developed into separate power centres across all the kingdoms of the Deccan. The groups created a sort of de facto apartheid system that waxed and waned in favour of one or the other dependent on the whims and fancies of the reigning monarch that determined the ascendancy of one or the other group. The power of a group was directly connected to the preference of the king and the favours that he bestowed. Intrigue was all-pervasive in such an atmosphere. The death of the most dedicated and capable prime minister of the Bahmani kingdom, Mahmud Gawan, was the result of the phirangi-Deccani rivalry.

The Deccan kingdoms had enormous natural resources within their territories and therefore should have been strong and the dynasties long-lived. However, they remained weak and unable to defend themselves from any concerted external attack, because of the internal divisions between the two power blocs, which were created by the kings themselves out of a false sense of inferiority. The Muslim Deccan kingdoms did not produce a single visionary king who could righted this imbalance and succumbed into obscurity as soon as a powerful external authority, the Mughals, appeared on the scene.

Section III

THE SUCCESSOR KINGDOMS OF THE DECCAN

THE ADIL SHAHIS OF BIJAPUR

It is to the credit of the Adil Shahis, that they were instrumental in creating a composite and secular culture in Bijapur. Being immigrants from Iran, the Adil Shahis brought the culture and traditions of the Middle-East to Bijapur. After gaining power, they insisted on following the customs, rituals and court culture of Persia, thereby influencing the ceremonies, etiquette, art and even architectural developments of the Bijapur kingdom.

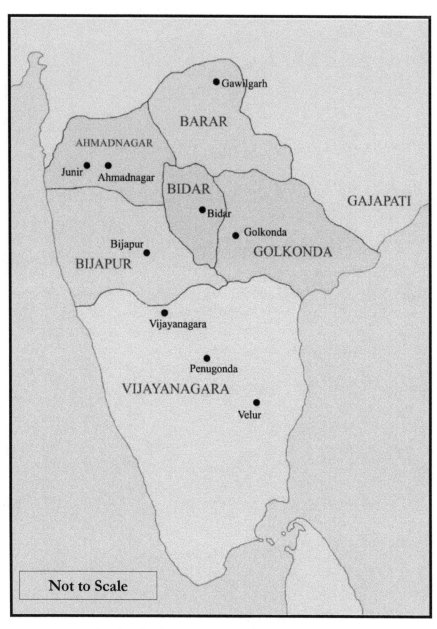

Major States in Southern India c. 1485
showing of autonomous Deccan Sultanates

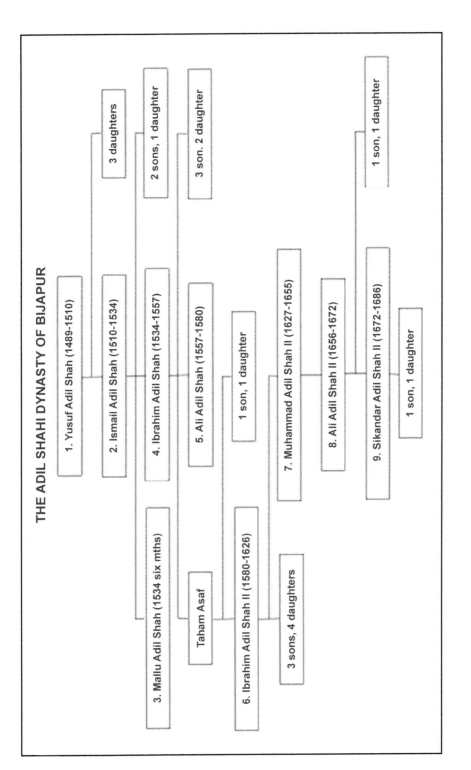

Chapter 10

YUSUF ADIL SHAH ESTABLISHES A KINGDOM

The death of Muhammad Shah in 1482 was the virtual end of the Bahmani dynasty, although a few more Bahmani sultans nominally ruled from Bidar. On Muhammad Shah's death, Mahmud Shah his 12-year old (only eight years old according to some reports) son was placed on the throne. He was rapidly followed by three more child kings, who were mere puppets. After the first few years of this rule by proxy, the kingdom was plunged into a series of power struggles and intrigue. Effective governance came to an end in the Bahmani kingdom. From the time of Sultan Muhammad, the Bahmani kingdom of was fully consumed by internecine wars and its power was at the lowest ebb. Understanding the weakness at the centre, a number of powerful and opportunistic nobles started to declare independence.

Taking advantage of the prevailing confusion, Yusuf Adil Khan declared independence. He assumed the title of Shah, made Bijapur the capital of his fledgling kingdom and started to rule under the title Yusuf Adil Shah. By early 16th century, five nobles had divided the erstwhile Bahmani kingdom amongst themselves and established five Muslim kingdoms in the Deccan.

Yusuf Adil Shah

The story of Yusuf's birth and later adventures is a highly romantic tale. It appears that he was born to Sultan Murad II of Turkey in 1443. When Murad died in 1450-51, his eldest son Muhammad succeeded to the throne. In conformity with the accepted wisdom and custom of the times, Muhammad immediately ordered the execution of all his male siblings, as well as other royal male children, in order to prevent the possibility of a later-day rebellion from someone with even a remote claim to the throne. When the executioners came to collect the seven-year old Yusuf to be put to death, his mother bribed them sufficiently for them to accept a substitute for Yusuf who looked reasonably similar and who was then put to death.

The queen/princess entrusted Yusuf to the care of a Persian merchant, having given him a large sum of money to ensure the safety and upkeep of the prince. The Persian merchant—Khawaja Imad ud-Din—took the prince initially to Ardebeel where he was tutored by Sheikh Suffee, who was the founder of the Suffee royal family. Thereafter, Yusuf was moved to Saweh where he was educated with the merchant's own children. Yusuf's mother kept in touch and also provided additional funds when required. Yusuf remained in Saweh till he was 16 years old and so derived the surname 'Sewai' in later years.

At this time, Yusuf decided to try his fortune in Hindustan, as a number of ambitious Persian youth were inclined to do, and arrived at the port of Dabul, to the south of Goa, in 1458. From Dabul he made his way to Bidar, the capital of the Bahmani kingdom, where another benefactor introduced him to the royal family as one of his Turkish slaves. Yusuf was diligent and hardworking and was placed under Nizam-ul-Mulk Turk who was the 'master of the house'. Nizam was the officer who had murdered the Khawaja Jehan in open court on the orders of the boy Sultan Muhammad and was therefore in great favour with the Sultan. Nizam-ul-Mulk treated Yusuf as a brother, an attachment that was wholeheartedly returned, with Yusuf remaining loyal to Nizam till the latter's death.

In 1467, the Sultan ordered Nizam-ul-Mulk to capture the fort at Kherla, then a tributary and part of the kingdom of Malwa. Yusuf, by now having earned the title Adil Khan, accompanied Nizam on the expedition. The fort was captured after prolonged fighting and at great cost. However, two Rajput warriors, seeking to avenge the extraordinary abuses that were heaped on the defeated Hindu population of the fort, murdered Nizam-ul-Mulk in a suicide mission. Yusuf and another Turk, Dariya Khan, took charge of the army and returned to Bidar with Nizam's body and a large amount of plunder from the expedition.

The Sultan was happy with the performance of the young officers and promoted both of them. The captured fort at Kherla was given to Yusuf Adil Khan as his 'jagir'. However, the Bahmani Sultan soon signed a peace treaty with Malwa, according to which Kherla reverted to the control of Malwa.

Yusuf Adil Khan now attached himself to Mahmud Gawan, the rising star in the Bahmani kingdom. Mahmud Gawan held Yusuf in great esteem and styled him as his adopted son, formalising the relationship a few years later. Mahmud Gawan appointed Yusuf the governor of Daulatabad. Yusuf assumed the role with gusto and fairly quickly recovered some border forts that had been lost to Malwa in earlier times. Yusuf also managed to subdue two Maratha chieftains operating in the fringes of the Daulatabad governorate, which brought a great amount of booty. In an astute move, Yusuf Adil Khan returned to Bidar with this immense wealth and presented it to the Sultan. This move entrenched the position of Mahmud Gawan, his mentor, as well as his own position with the Sultan. Together, father and adopted son became the Sultan's favourites and the toast of the capital.

The Sultan of Bijapur

When Yusuf declared independence, the fledgling kingdom of Bijapur extended from Sholapur and Gulbarga in the north to Goa in the south. In the east it shared a border with the Vijayanagar kingdom along the River Krishna. The forts at Raichur and Mudgal were under the control of the Bijapur kingdom, while the Doab between the Rivers Tungabhadra and Krishna remained contested between Bijapur and Vijayanagar.

Bijapur, from now on ruled by the Adil Shahi dynasty, endured as a kingdom for a little more than the next two centuries. This period also coincided with an era of great restlessness and of momentous events in the history of the Peninsula. Of the successor Muslim kingdoms to the Bahmani kingdom that sprang up in the Deccan on its break-up, Bijapur was the greatest and last but one to succumb to the Mughal onslaught. The power of the Muslim rulers were limited at this juncture when one kingdom was being pulverised and from its ashes five kingdoms were being forged. Taking advantage of this relative weakness, the Vijayanagar kingdom rose to great power. This rise was further profited by the successor kingdoms also being weak in their initial period of formulation. The partitioning of the Bahmani kingdom and the formation of the successor kingdoms culminated in the rise of the Vijayanagar Empire to the zenith of its power and glory. A less conspicuous development was that the same period bore witness to the commencement of the development of Maratha power—an event of great import at a later stage in Indian history.

Muslim power in the Peninsula was continually waning, a downward slide that was speeded on by the arrival of the Europeans. The Portuguese had established a foothold on the western coast, their power centred on the port of Goa, which had for all practical purposes been taken over by them. The partitioning of the Bahmani kingdom also made it easier for the Mughals to destroy the successor states one-by-one, in a development that was to take place almost two centuries later.

> ### Bijapur – The Capital of the Adil Shahi Dynasty
>
> Bijapur stands on the site of an ancient Hindu village called Bichkhanhalli and five surrounding villages. Even today, inscriptions from the 11th and 12th centuries and some broken down Hindu victory towers are visible in Bijapur. In its Hindu identity, the city was called Vijaypur or the city of victory, which is corroborated by the ruins of the victory towers.
>
> Bijapur had been the seat of a governor of the Bahmani kingdom for a period of time before Yusuf Adil Shah took over control.

Yusuf Shah improved the existing buildings as well as the citadel and commenced building protective city walls, which took almost his entire reign to complete.

As was to be expected, on Yusuf declaring independence, Qasim Barid, the powerful minister in Bidar who was actually ruling the crumbling Bahmani kingdom although proclaimed as the regent nominally ruling on behalf of a puppet Sultan, decided to put down the rebel. Barid incited the Vijayanagar king to join him in declaring war against Bijapur and the upstart Yusuf Adil Shah. However, Adil Shah easily defeated the combined attack and thereafter peace prevailed for a few years.

After consolidating his position in Bijapur, Yusuf attacked and captured the Raichur fort. Repeated attempts by Vijayanagar to recapture the fort were repelled and defeated. In this victory, Adil Shah obtained immense wealth as plunder, which he very wisely used to further establish his own kingdom. He gave generous gifts to the nobles who had followed him, thus further binding them to his own fortunes.

A Token Gesture

Although established fully as an independent kingdom, in a surprise move, Adil Shah sent two robes and a gold-studded horse to Sultan Mahmud nominally ruling in Bidar, as a token acknowledgement of Bahmani supremacy. The Adil Shahi kings continued this practice of acknowledging the supremacy of the Bahmani Sultans for some more time to come.

Sultan Mahmud Bahmani also visited Bijapur, where he was lavishly entertained. The story goes that the Sultan refused to take the presents that were given to him on his departure, stating that if he took them with him, his Minister Qasim Barid would confiscate them on his arrival in Bidar. This demonstrated the real state of affairs in the crumbling Bahmani kingdom.

This action of Yusuf Adil Shah, of acknowledging Bahmani supremacy has never been rationally explained since he did not need the blessings or approval of the Bahmani Sultan to continue ruling his newly founded kingdom. Adil Shah had by then accrued sufficient power to withstand an attack or invasion by any of his neighbours. In any case the Bahmani Sultan did not possess any semblance of power to act on his own. An unexplained quirk in the character of Yusuf, otherwise a bold and charismatic leader!

The Gulbarga Revolt

The Peninsula, especially the Deccan, was going through tumultuous times. In 1495, the governor of Gulbarga, Dastur Dinar, revolted and declared independence. Qasim Barid, ruling in Bidar, requested Adil Shah's assistance to put down the rebellion. Dastur was easily defeated by the joint forces and taken prisoner. Barid wanted to put him to death, but Adil Shah prevailed in preventing the execution and also restored Gulbarga to Dastur. Adil Shah had cultivated a personal friendship with the nominal Bahmani Sultan, Mahmud, and now conspired with him to cut off Qasim Barid from his estates. Barid became alarmed by this development and after collecting a large army, attacked Adil Shah. Yusuf was victorious in the ensuing battle fought near Kinjooty in 1497.

After this battle, which could be considered the proverbial last nail in the coffin of the Bahmani kingdom, the five emerging Muslim kingdoms partitioned the Deccan between them. Yusuf Adil Shah was given the provinces that Dastur Dinar had been ruling, including Gulbarga. The Bahmani Sultan remained the only nominal king with no territory to rule other than the capital Bidar, which was also ruled by his minister in reality. Even the minister did not have the wherewithal to capture any territory to increase his holdings. By the time of this partition, Qasim Barid had been replaced by his son Ameer Barid who had inherited his father's position. Ameer Barid instigated Dastur Dinar to rebel again and attempt to regain possession of his provinces, sending him some Abyssinian forces as assistance. In a fierce battle on the banks of the River Bhima, Yusuf Shah defeated the rebel forces and Dastur was killed in battle. Yusuf Adil Shah's adopted brother who was instrumental in ensuring Bijapur victory also succumbed to injuries sustained in this battle. This decisive victory firmly established the status of Yusuf Adil Shah as an independent king and also increased his already considerable prestige. Gulbarga now became an indelible part of the Adil Shahi kingdom.

Change of Religion

During his sojourn in Persia, Yusuf Shah had 'imbibed' the basics of Shia doctrine from the Royal House of Suffee, by now governing Persia. In 1502, he changed the religious affiliation of his newly founded kingdom from Sunni to Shia. The introduction of this somewhat drastic change was done with great moderation and pre-calculated temperance. Usually, new religious converts and also the people who could be considered 'born-again', tend to be bigoted zealots of the new religion that they have adopted. In the case of Yusuf, he remained extremely tolerant and was careful to let his subjects know beforehand that he would not interfere in their individual religious beliefs or practices. He went to the extent of promulgating a royal decree that no one was to be coerced to renounce his or her faith and that no forced conversions were to be attempted. This show of extreme tolerance resulted in most of the nobles and officers of the state remaining loyal to Yusuf Adil Shah.

The change of the official religion of the Adil Shahi kingdom in Bijapur however created great animosity from the other four sultans ruling the Deccan kingdoms. They formed a league against Yusuf and declared what has, in later days, come to be called 'the holy war of the four brothers' against Bijapur. They decided to attack Bijapur. The two armies facing each other were in complete contrast to each other in their capabilities and characteristics. Yusuf Shah's forces were numerically smaller, but extremely well-trained; whereas the opposing force of the alliance was large, but disorganised hordes of individual soldiers. Even so, Yusuf Shah decided to be cautious in engaging the enemy forces arrayed against him and resorted to an astute guerrilla campaign. Through well-calculated moves, Yusuf managed to draw the bulk of the opposing forces into the territory of Imad-ul-Mulk ruling in Berar and an ally and mentor of Yusuf.

Imad had sufficient influence on Yusuf to persuade him to restore Sunni practices in his kingdom, which somewhat pacified the other sultans. Further, Imad-ul-Mulk wrote to the other sultans that they were being used by Ameer Barid for his own purposes. Ameer was one of the principal instigators of the military action against Bijapur. Imad let it be known to the other sultans that Ameer wanted to annex Bijapur for himself and the religious angle was only a ploy to achieve this objective. On considering this missive, the sultans of Ahmadnagar and Golconda returned to their kingdoms, leaving Barid isolated. Once Barid was isolated, Yusuf Shah confronted him and defeated him in battle. Then he returned to Bijapur in triumph, since he had been away from his capital ever since the 'holy war' had been initiated against him. The entire episode took place in a span of a mere three months. The rest of Yusuf Adil Shah's reign was peaceful from a domestic perspective. The people and the administration were devoted to creating a stable and prosperous kingdom.

The Portuguese Interlude

On 26 August 1498, the Portuguese naval commander Vasco da Gama effected a landing on the island of Anjidiv in south Kanara. This was an event with enormous consequences for the Indian sub-continent, although at that time no king, sultan or chief of any consequence attached much importance to it. Vasco da Gama then landed on the mainland Peninsula near the mouth of the River Kalinadi. Yusuf Adil Shah send an expedition under the command of a Muslim Jew to evict the foreigners. However, the expedition was defeated by the Portuguese and the commander captured. He was subsequently taken to Portugal, converted to Christianity and was given the name Gasper da Gama.

From 1498 onwards, every year increasing number of Portuguese ships started to arrive on the west coast of the Peninsula. In 1509, they captured Goa. Goa was a favourite seaside retreat of Yusuf Shah and he personally led the forces send to liberate the port. Goa was recovered but Yusuf Adil Shah died a few months later. Taking this opportunity, the Portuguese re-captured Goa. The Portuguese chronicles are silent about this see-saw control of the port, mentioning only the 're-capture'. However, it is obvious that a re-capture can only take place if it had been taken away in the first place. Therefore, it is obvious that Yusuf Shah's expedition had been successful. Yusuf Adil Shah died in 1510 and was succeeded by his son Ismail Adil Shah who was only 14 years old at the time of coming to the throne.

Yusuf Adil Shah – The Person

In any analysis of the times, Yusuf Adil Shah comes out as one of the most remarkable medieval rulers in the Deccan. He was a fearless warrior, a great general and also an astute statesman. He was highly educated, humane and tolerant in all aspects of governance. He wrote poetry, put the poems to music and sang them himself. In a clear departure from the normal, there are no reports of bigotry during the entire period of his rule. Considering that bigotry and religious zealotry are the dual stains that mar the reputation of almost all other Deccan Muslim rulers, this is no small achievement. Even the temporary change of the official faith of the kingdom from Sunni to Shia was effected with singular care, moderation and extreme tolerance.

Yusuf was a patron of art, literature and learning. He spent liberally on buildings and public works, a trend that was followed through by his successors. The Adil Shahi kings left noble memorials behind, more than any of the other Muslim kingdoms of the Deccan with the exception of the Qutb Shahi rulers of Golconda. Yusuf's private life was without blemish. He did not maintain a harem, as was the standard practice of sultans of the age, and also did not spend any of the royal treasure on personal pleasure. He had only one wife, a Hindu Maratha princess, daughter of a chieftain called Mukund Rao. Yusuf Adil Shah was a temperate and virtuous human being. He could be considered an aberration in an age of debauchery and indulgence by sultans and nobles.

The queen was given the title Boobooji Khanun and Yusuf's religious tolerance is partly attributed to her direct influence on his religious thought process. Khanun was a lady of great ability and political acumen with a strong character. The king had three daughters and a son. The daughters were married to the sultans of Berar, Ahmadnagar and Bidar—with the family ties strengthening the unity of the Muslim kingdoms.

Throughout the reign of Yusuf Adil Shah, Hindus were given offices in the state administration, based purely on merit with no preference or bias being bestowed on account of an individual's religious persuasion. Similarly, credit and promotion to officials were bestowed on pure merit. Religion was relegated to the back when recruitment to public employment was being undertaken, a novelty in the Deccan of the time. Equality of all people in front of the state administration was a concept far ahead of its time when Yusuf Adil Shah instituted it in a decidedly Muslim kingdom.

Chapter 11

ENTRENCHING THE DYNASTY

When Yusuf Shah died, his son Ismail Shah was only 13 or 14 years old (some reports state his age as 9 years). On his deathbed, Yusuf appointed a trusted noble, Kamal Khan to be the guardian of the young prince and also the regent till Ismail achieved majority. He also made the other nobles promise to adhere by his decision and to obey Kamal Khan in all matters of state. For the first few years after assuming the regency, Kamal Khan governed well and wisely, and was popular with both the nobles and the common people. He ensured that Bijapur remained friendly and on amicable terms with all its neighbours. He also concluded a treaty with the Portuguese, confirming their possession of Goa, and made sure that both parties adhered to the terms of the treaty.

As the young Sultan was close to reaching majority, Kamal Khan succumbed to the obtrusive intoxication of power and started to entertain ambitions of usurping the throne for himself. As an example to follow he had the action of Qasim Barid who had been the minister for the last few Bahmani kings and then had usurped power. Qasim had thereafter founded a dynasty ruling from Bidar, even though the territory that they controlled was not large. Kamal Khan now initiated decisive action to fulfil his ambitions. He formed an alliance with Amir Barid, son and successor of Qasim, and then incarcerated the young Sultan and his mother Boobaji Khanun in the Bijapur fort. Kamal Khan then went on to lay siege to Sholapur, which was reduced after three months. He then returned to Bijapur in triumph to claim the throne. However, on the advice of few astrologers, he postponed the actual date of the coronation.

Ismail Adil Shah

While the usurper, Kamal Khan, was dithering about the date for his assumption of the throne, the Queen-mother decided to take action and strike back. She colluded with a female slave and Yusuf Turk, a nobleman who had continued to be loyal to Yusuf Shah and was also the foster father of the young Sultan, and had Kamal Khan murdered. For a few weeks confusion prevailed and Kamal Khan's son, Sufder Khan, made an attempt to capture the palace. He was repulsed by a small group of palace guards who had remained loyal and faithful to Boobaji Khanun. The young Sultan took an active part in the defence and is reported to have been instrumental in killing Sufder Khan, the leader of the revolt. Ismail Shah, now around 17 years old, once again became the Sultan of Bijapur, now in his w right.

During this short period of confusion, Amir Barid had laid siege to Gulbarga. On hearing of the murder of Kamal Khan and the defeat and death of his son in the uprising, Amir discontinued the siege and returned to Bidar. At the same time, the Vijayanagar king, Krishna Deva Raya had attacked Raichur and successfully annexed the fort. Capturing Raichur was only a prelude to a long and successful career for Krishna Deva Raya, who went on to be a victorious and illustrious king of his dynasty.

Military Exploits

Even though he had managed to put down the nascent uprising and assumed the throne, Ismail Shah's military troubles and adventures continued unabated. Amir Barid who had withdrawn from the siege of Gulbarga was still smarting under the 'loss of face' that he had suffered because of his unilateral about-face. Ever the conspirator, he made friends with the kings of Berar, Golconda and Ahmadnagar. These kings were also envious of the large territorial holding and the enhanced prestige that it brought to the Adil Shahis of Bijapur. They agreed to wage a combined war against Bijapur to capture its territory and reduce its stature. Accordingly the four other Muslim kingdoms of the Deccan assembled a large army and marched against Bijapur.

Ismail Adil Shah, although young and fairly inexperienced, marched out of his capital at the head of a force of 12,000 cavalry to meet the advancing forces. He pinpointed Amir Barid's forces and carried out a vigorous attack on them. The Bidar forces fled the field under this unrelenting attack. Although the Barid's were ruling Bidar and the surrounding countryside, they had continued to maintain the Bahmani Sultan as the nominal head of the kingdom. When the Bidar forces fled the field, they had abandoned their nominal Sultan, Muhammad, who along with his son Ahmad was captured by the Bijapur forces.

Ismail Shah treated the Sultan and his son with great courtesy and also got his own daughter married to Ahmad. *[The fact that Ismail at this time was only in his late teens makes this claim of his daughter being married off to the Bahmani prince suspicious and is a bit of a non-starter. There is no further mention of this marriage alliance and could be discarded as fanciful reportage of court chroniclers.]* In any case Muhammad, his son and entourage were send back to Bidar with a 5000-horse cavalry escort, as befitting the status of a ruler. On this escorted return of the Bahmani heir, Amir Barid took fright regarding the intention of Ismail Shah and escaped from Bidar. Muhammad became, temporarily, the actual Sultan of Bidar. Having escorted the Sultan to his home, the Bijapur forces departed for their own kingdom. Immediately, Amir Barid returned and Muhammad reverted to his old, and accustomed, puppet role in an abject state of subjugation. Few years of peace prevailed in Bijapur. During this interlude, Ismail received an embassy from the Persian monarch, an explicit acceptance by the Persian king of the independent status of the Adil Shahi dynasty.

Around 1520, Ismail made an unsuccessful attempt to recapture Raichur and Mudgal. The expedition failed because of a tactical blunder committed by Ismail Shah himself. He attempted to cross a flooded River Krishna, the decision for this action being taken while Ismail was under the influence of liquor, after excessive consumption of wine. During the crossing the Sultan himself was almost killed, very narrowly escaping drowning. Ismail then went on to wage war against the other kingdoms—individually and even when they formed coalitions against Bijapur. Amir Barid was staunchly anti-Bijapur and always joined one or the other kingdoms fighting against Bijapur and also against each other. However, even though Barid was almost always the instigator, he did not assume the lead in any of the battles, being content to be in the periphery of the conflict. He thrived on intrigue against everyone else, continually keeping the cauldron of the Deccan bubbling. Even with alliances arrayed against him, Ismail Shah was moderately successful in his military expeditions.

Ismail Shah continued with his father's policy of creating matrimonial alliances with the other kingdoms. Accordingly he gave two of his sisters in marriage to the sultans of Berar and Ahmadnagar. Honouring these very loosely formed alliances, Ismail Shah send a large contingent of troops and money to assist the Nizam Shahi ruler of Ahmadnagar when that kingdom was attacked by the Sultan of Gujarat, around 1529. The invasion was repelled without much damage being inflicted on Ahmadnagar. Amir Barid had also joined the alliance against Gujarat. On the withdrawal of the Gujarat forces, he attempted to corrupt the Bijapur forces against their Sultan before they started their return home. By now Ismail Shah's patience was running out with the continuous needling of Amir Barid and he decided to put an end to the intrigues once and for all. With direct assistance from the Imad Shahi ruler of Berar, Ismail Shah attacked and laid siege to Bidar. Amir Barid fled to Golconda and brought reinforcements from there to assist him. In the ensuing battle Ismail Shah defeated the combined Bidar-Golconda army, and captured Amir Barid.

Amir Barid was subsequently ransomed by his sons, who were permitted to leave Bidar with their father and the extended Barid families. Surprisingly, there is no information regarding the fate of the real Sultan—the scion of the Bahmani dynasty. It is presumed that the Barids took him and his family along with them when they were exiled by Ismail Shah. The Adil Shahi dynasty now controlled Bidar and its territories. Ismail went on to distribute a great amount of wealth to the Berar Sultan who had helped him and also to the prominent nobles in his court. An intervention by Imad Shah ruling Berar made Ismail pardon Amir Barid for his activities against Bijapur. Ismail Shah then went on to invade the Raichur Doab, compelling Amir Barid to assist him in the campaign and fight alongside Bijapur forces. The Bijapur army captured Raichur after a three-month siege. After being under Vijayanagar rule for 17 years, Raichur now formed part of the Adil Shahi territories.

After the successful campaign to retrieve Raichur, Ismail Shah reinstated Amir Barid as ruler of Bidar after Amir swore an oath of loyalty to Ismail Shah. The oath did not have any effect on the fundamental nature of Amir Barid, who continued to intrigue against all and anyone who he perceived to be inimical to his personal interests.

A state of internecine conflicts continued unabated in the Deccan, with the kingdoms fighting each other; creating alliances, fighting battles, and then breaking up old alliances to create newer ones—in an ever-changing kaleidoscope of intrigue and wars fought to a standstill with no clear victors and peace brokered at the end of indecisive battles.

Ismail Shah's last campaign was against the Qutb Shahis of Golconda. From the time that the Telengana forces had aided Amir Barid, Ismail had harboured a distaste for their actions. Mounting a military expedition to punish them was therefore almost inevitable from his point of view. However, before the expedition could be put in motion, Ismail Shah took ill and died in 1534. The siege of Golconda that had started was immediately lifted by the commander-in-chief of the Bijapur army, Assud Khan. The General returned to Bijapur with the Sultan's body along with the two young princes, Mallu and Ibrahim, who had accompanied their father for the campaign.

Ismail Adil Shah – A Synopsis

Ismail Adil Shah has been described as having been 'prudent, patient and generous'. It is said that he was always ready to forgive the transgressions of his nobles and the people, so much so that even while this character trait was considered a virtue, people took advantage of the Sultan's forgiving nature to get out of tricky situations. Ismail was artistic by nature, being a poet and musician in his own right. He was also a skilled saddler. Ismail Khan was extremely polished in his manners, much more so than the Deccani nobles, since he was trained in Turkish and Persian etiquettes, customs and habits.

After establishing his rule over Bijapur, Ismail Shah was acknowledged as the principal Muslim king of the Deccan, a position reinforced by the arrival of the Persian embassy towards the mid-term of his rule. It is also obvious that the other kings of the region accepted the pre-eminent position of the Adil Shahis, even if it was with reservations that were never openly expressed. However, Ismail Shah could not make any headway against the powerful Hindu kingdom of Vijayanagar throughout his 25-year rule. This 'failure' must have rankled in the mind of the Sultan during his reign.

The Short Interlude of Mallu Shah

Assud Khan was Ismail Shah's trusted and able minister as well as a brave and strong commander of the Bijapur forces. After completing the rituals of burial of the late Sultan, he crowned the eldest prince of the dynasty, Mallu, as the Sultan. Mallu Adil Shah was a licentious young man and an incompetent administrator. Many nobles had expressed their opposition to making him the Sultan. In fact, Assud Khan himself had misgivings regarding Mallu's suitability to be an effective Sultan. However, the loyal General was honour-bound to carry out the last command of his master and therefore dutifully placed Mallu on the throne. Since Mallu was technically still a minor, Assud Khan the devoted and loyal minister, was now the most powerful man in the Bijapur kingdom. At this critical juncture and throughout the rest of his life, Assud Khan proved himself to be a statesman of great integrity and unquestionable loyalty to the Adil Shahi dynasty; rare qualities in those times.

After assuming the throne, Mallu gave himself up to reckless debauchery. Further, he also started to display his inherent vicious nature that had so far been kept carefully hidden. Disgusted by the young Sultan's behaviour Assud Khan gave up his official positions and retired to his private estates in Belgaum. Mallu continued his immoral and profligate ways and in a short span of about six months had managed to antagonise all the nobles, even the ones that had initially supported his claim to the throne. The kingdom was charging headlong into a crisis. According to a story, the crisis was precipitated by Mallu asking a high ranking and respected noble, Yusuf Khan, to send his young son to the court for Mallu to sodomise him. Obviously Yusuf Khan refused and moved away to his personal estates. Mallu Shah send a contingent of soldiers in pursuit tasked with capturing and beheading Yusuf Khan. However, Yusuf's personal bodyguards were able to easily beat back the royal forces who fled back to the capital.

At this low point in the affairs of the kingdom, Mallu Shah's Grandmother Booboojee Khanun, now the grand old matriarch of the Adil Shahis, decided that the decline of the dynasty must be stopped and took action. She asked the venerated noble Yusuf Khan for assistance in deposing the king. Yusuf, ever loyal to the Adil Shahi dynasty, first asked Assud's permission to take action and obtained the cooperation of the erstwhile minister to do so. Yusuf Khan then gathered a large force and entered the capital, encountering no opposition. Mallu Shah, along with his youngest brother and companion was seized, blinded and imprisoned. Mallu's younger brother Ibrahim was proclaimed king as Ibrahim Adil Shah.

Ibrahim Adil Shah

The first official decree that Ibrahim proclaimed was to change the religion of the kingdom back to Sunni Islam. Ever since his father Ismail had changed it to the Shia creed and later recanted for political reasons, the kingdom had informally favoured the Shia. This practice was officially ended by this proclamation. The second act of the new king was to dismiss all foreigners from royal service. Turks, Persians, Mongols and a miscellany of other nationalities in royal service were relieved of their duties and asked to fend for themselves elsewhere. However, Ibrahim kept a 400-strong special force of foreigners as his personal bodyguard. The dismissed foreigners were replaced by Deccanis and Abyssinians. *[It is interesting to note that throughout the medieval history of the Deccan, Abyssinians were never considered 'foreigners' and always sided with the Deccanis in the power struggle against the foreigners that bubbled along below the placid surface of the Adil Shahi court. It is also clarified here that the term 'Deccani' was used exclusively to indicate the descendants of the first Muslims and some converts to have settled in the Deccan following Ala ud-Din Khilji's initial foray south of the Vidhya Mountains. The term did not include the Hindus and their nobles who were the majority in the region.]*

The large-scale summary dismissal of the foreigners from royal service was detrimental to the kingdom in two distinct ways. First, the foreigners had so far formed the hard core of the Bijapur army, which was almost immediately gutted on their precipitous departure. Second, the Vijayanagar king was quick to take advantage of the sudden availability of a large number of well-trained and hardy soldiers. He immediately employed them, providing them money and even building a mosque in the capital for their worship. . Vijayanagar went on to create a 3000-strong Muslim force, which proved invaluable in later years.

> ### The Vijayanagar Episode
>
> When Ibrahim assumed the throne, Vijayanagar was embroiled in a succession struggle. (This part of Vijayanagar history will be covered in detail in the next volume of this series that covers the history of that kingdom.) The ruling king Rama Raja was on an expedition to the south in order to bring in line the refractory kings of Malabar and Madurai. He had left the capital in the charge of a 'trusted' noble—Hoji Perumal Rao. Some discontented nobles had been planning a rebellion and took the absence of the king from the capital as an opportunity to put their plan into action.
>
> The rebel nobles, who were in majority by now, induced Perumal to support them in placing a child king on the throne and to becoming the regent. Within a few months, Perumal had the child king strangled and assumed the throne. Rama Raja was out of power for some time and having collected a strong enough force, started his return to the capital to reclaim his throne.
>
> Perumal realised that he did not have the military strength to withstand the assault being planned by Rama Raja. He invited Ibrahim Adil Shah, his northern neighbour, to assist in the approaching battle, offering him a large subsidy. The subsidy that was promised is reported to have been the equivalent of 40,000 pound sterling at that time's value. Ibrahim agreed and reached Vijayanagar with a large force and was received with great pomp and ceremony.
>
> The arrival of the Adil Shahi king and the assumption by Ibrahim of a controlling role in the matters of state in Vijayanagar thereafter was disliked by the nobles in court.

Entrenching The Dynasty

> Further, an alliance with a Muslim king was something that the staunchly Hindu nobles and minor kings, who supported Perumal, was unwilling to countenance. They asked that Ibrahim be send back, a condition they insisted on being fulfilled in return for their continued support for Perumal to remain king. Accordingly, Perumal gave a huge sum of money to Ibrahim and requested him to return to Bijapur. Ibrahim acquiesced and returned to his kingdom a great deal richer than when he had set out—without having done anything to earn the wealth.
>
> Rama Raja returned and reclaimed his throne with ease. Hoji Perumal Rao, the short-term king, committed suicide.

Changing Fortunes

After returning from Vijayanagar a much wealthier person than when he set out, Ibrahim send an army under Assud Khan to capture the fort at Adoni. The attack was repelled by the Vijayanagar forces under Rama Raja's brother Venkatadri. A peace acceptable to both sides was arrived at after Assud Khan managed to capture the family on Venkatadri in a surprise raid on the Vijayanagar camp.

Even since Ibrahim came to power, Assud Khan's power in court had been steadily increasing. He was the most important noble in court. This led to other nobles concocting jealous intrigues against him and making assiduous attempts at poisoning the Sultan's mind. They obviously succeeded, because Ibrahim ordered Assud Khan to come to Bijapur with the undeclared intention of executing him summarily for perceived treason. Assud became aware of the plot and instead of returning to Bijapur, once again retired to his estate in Belgaum.

Such internal strife led to a slow bleeding of power in Bijapur. Three other Deccan kingdoms—Bidar, Ahmadnagar and Golconda—took advantage of the situation and joined together to invade Bijapur territory. They invested Sholapur and then marched to Belgaum where they forced Assud Khan to join them against Ibrahim's army. In an astute disinformation move the coalition army used Assud Khan's name and stature to garner support for their invasion into the Bijapur territory. The people of the Adil Shahi kingdom still held Assud Khan in great esteem because of his unwavering loyalty to the Adil Shahi dynasty. Even as he was forced to join the invading forces, he invited the Imad Shahi ruler of Berar to assist Bijapur in this time of its extreme threat. Once this was achieved Assud Khan himself joined the combined forces of Berar and Bijapur. The invading forces could not stand up to the combined army with Assud Khan also joining them and decided to retreat from the invasion. The change of scenario was unanticipated and therefore the invading army had not planned it as a contingency. During the retreat, Amir Barid of Bidar died on his way to his capital. The alliance was forced to return Sholapur and promise to not invade Bijapur again. As usual such promises were not worth the paper it was written on. An uneasy peace prevailed for a few months before conflict broke out again.

The very next year there was a three-pronged attack on Bijapur. Ali Barid who had succeeded his father in Bidar, the Nizam Shahi king of Ahmadnagar and the king of Vijayanagar attacked the Bijapur kingdom simultaneously. Assud Khan, once again reconciled with the king, took the lead in repelling the invaders. He craftily made individual peace with both the Vijayanagar king and Nizam Shah and then defeated the Bidar army in the field. Even with this victory, Bijapur was not able to stabilise the situation. The next year, the anti-Bijapur trio attacked again and were again defeated. This time Ibrahim Shah personally led the Bijapur army and fought at its head with great bravery. This victory and the role that he had played as a military commander combined to make Ibrahim arrogant. He ill-treated the ambassadors that Nizam Shah of Ahmadabad had send to the Bijapur court—reason enough for war to breakout afresh.

During this war fortunes that had for many years favoured Bijapur, changed. Ibrahim was soundly defeated in battle twice within a short span of six months. Although he was more than willing to take the credit for victories, Ibrahim was unwilling to accept the responsibility for the repeated defeats of his army. He blamed the Hindu officials in his service and had a number of them publicly executed. The extreme cruelty with which the Hindu nobles were treated disgusted

Assud Khan who, as was his wont in similar circumstances, once again retreated to his estate in Belgaum.

With the departure of Assud Khan from active participation in matters of state, Ibrahim's power was considerably reduced. Taking advantage of these circumstances, Ibrahim's brother Abdullah made an attempt at usurping the throne. On the palace coup being unsuccessful, Abdullah fled to the Portuguese territory of Goa and took refuge there. The Portuguese attempted to create an alliance to place Abdullah on the throne of Bijapur. They also attempted to get Assud Khan on-side to help with the plan. However, the ever faithful Assud Khan refused to be part of this attempt. The importance of this incident is not the fact that an attempt was made to replace the ruling king, but the fact that this was the first time that a European power had made an attempt at directly interfering with and trying to influence local politics.

Assud Khan died soon after he thwarted the first Portuguese attempt at influencing the course of events in an Indian kingdom. Ibrahim Shah was now left with no capable, trustworthy or loyal advisor. Wars, conflicts and skirmishes continued in the Deccan without a break; and alliances were made, broken and new ones formed. The Vijayanagar kingdom continued to make inroads into the territories of the Deccan kingdoms and also kept them divided by intervening in their internecine conflicts in an opportunistic manner. By siding astutely with one or the other of the Shahi kingdoms, Vijayanagar managed to keep them disunited.

In one of these battles, Ibrahim Shah was defeated in the battlefield because of some tactical blunders that he himself has committed. However, as was usual for him, Ibrahim immediately blamed his defeat on his commanding general, Ain-ul-Mulk. Fearing retribution, the general retired to his estate, pursued by Ibrahim's forces. Ain-ul-Mulk defeated the forces send to capture him. At this juncture, Ibrahim asked the Vijayanagar king for assistance in bringing the, now rebel, general to book. The Hindu forces surprised Ain-ul-Mulk and on being defeated in the battlefield, he fled to Ahmadnagar. Unfortunately he was assassinated in Ahmadnagar. Once again the interference of Vijayanagar to create divisions within the Deccan Muslim kingdoms is seen to have borne fruit.

Even though victorious in an oblique manner, Ibrahim Shah could not countenance the fact that he had been defeated in battle and that his prestige thereafter had been re-instated by his arch enemy, monarch of Vijayanagar. To add to the embarrassment, the monarch was the central pillar of the Hindu religion, holding the spread of Islam at bay. Devoid of any sage and sane advice after the death of Assud Khan, Ibrahim gave himself up to debauchery and fell ill soon after. Although a team of doctors started to look after him, he ill-treated the doctors who could not bring any relief, even having some of them executed in public. The rest of the palace medical team fled from the capital. With no treatment available, his medical condition deteriorated rapidly. Ibrahim Shah died in 1557 after ruling the Bijapur kingdom for 24 years.

Conclusion

Although Ibrahim Adil Shah was a passionate ruler, he was also headstrong and impulsive. Assud Khan had managed to give him sagely advice and kept him on track, ensuring a prosperous rule for a long time. However, Assud's death turned Ibrahim into a licentious tyrant, very similar to his elder brother who he had replaced. Ibrahim was almost constantly at war, barring few brief spells of respite. However, he did not possess noticeable military talent to ensure that the wars went in his favour. He did display personal bravery in some battles, but even that character trait was not a constant and rose and fell with his moods. Personal bravery was not always on show in Ibrahim. Therefore, the battlefield victories that he has claimed as his personal victories have to be credited to the capable generals in his service. In fact the final military debacle that led to his debauchery and eventual death was brought on by his own tactical incompetence.

Throughout Ibrahim's rule the Muslim kingdoms of the Deccan remained in complete disharmony. Vijayanagar took full advantage of the situation and kept them divided while increasing its own power, territorial hold and influence. Ibrahim instituted three important changes in the administration and rule of the kingdom that had long-lasting impact on the Deccan as a whole. First, he employed Hindus to the clerical positions in the administration, especially in the revenue and accounts branches. Gradually they managed to get an unbreakable stranglehold on the finances of the kingdom. Second, he started to use the vernacular, instead of the foreign Persian language, in keeping the royal records. This made the records easily accessible to the broader population that in turn also produced contradictory records, making it easier for later-day historians to better understand the progress of past events. The embellishments that court historians made to the actual events and the 'white-washing' of despicable deeds of the king and/or the battlefield debacles that took place became more difficult to achieve.

The third change was of the greatest consequence. He started to recruit the 'bergees', a derisive term used to indicate the Maratha, into the military forces. A majority of them belonged to the Bijapur and Ahmedabad region and almost all of them were mercenaries, providing their own horses and equipment. The Marathas were more 'gentlemen soldiers' rather than the generic rank and file soldiers. These soldiers, who were also tactically well-schooled and thinking men, brought with them a new style of warfare that was perfected in later days by their illustrious king Shivaji. Their favoured method for the conduct of a campaign was to avoid standing battle against another army in traditional combat by eluding the enemy as far as possible while continually harassing them in every way possible while they were on the march. The Marathas excelled in cutting the enemy's supply lines and in following a scorched earth policy as soon as the enemy moved forward into their territory. They conducted what in modern times would come to be called Guerrilla War or Irregular War.

Ibrahim Shah brought about changes in the Adil Shahi religious policy, declaring the Sunni or the Shia sects as the state religion alternating them at regular intervals. Although these changes seem to have been made at the whim of the Sultan, some good came out of it. This policy ensured that the kingdom started to entrench a sense tolerance between the two sects, which gradually percolated also to the treatment of the Hindus. This made the Bijapur kingdom better religiously integrated in relative terms with the other Muslim kingdoms.

Chapter 12

GROWING STRENGTH

On Ibrahim Adil Shah's death, even though the succession was trouble free, the Bijapur kingdom was thrown into a brief period of confusion. Taking advantage of this limited time of uncertainty the ruler of Ahmadnagar, Hussein Nizam Shah invaded Bijapur. He was assisted by the Qutb Shahi ruler of Golconda.

Ali Adil Shah

Ali Adil Shah succeeded his father easily, without any serious contenders laying claim to the throne. He decided to avenge the unprovoked attack by the Ahmadnagar king and also wanted to regain Sholapur and Kalyan that had been captured by the Nizam Shahis earlier. Ali Shah formed an alliance with the Vijayanagar king Rama Raja and also induced the Golconda king to abandon Hussein Shah and join the Bijapur combine. The Imad Shahi ruler of Berar, traditionally supporters of the Bijapur state, was cajoled by Hussein Shah to join his alliance. This realignment if forces is a classic demonstration of the fluid geo-strategic situation that prevailed in the Deccan.

> ### The Value of Friendship with Vijayanagar
>
> The contemporary narratives of the time, including those of different court chroniclers, indicate that friendship with Vijayanagar was highly prized by the Muslim kingdoms of the Deccan because of the former's power and military strength.

> Around the time that Ahmadnagar and its allies were preparing to invade Bijapur, a son of Rama Raja then ruling Vijayanagar died. Ali Shah took the extraordinary step of paying a condolence visit to the king in his capital, accompanied only by a 100 followers. This action of a king going almost unprotected into the territory and capital of a sometime rival king was unprecedented. The voluntary action of the Bijapur king clearly indicates the importance of nurturing friendship with Vijayanagar.
>
> Ali Shah was received in Vijayanagar with great hospitality. Further, the Queen adopted him as a son, sort of cementing the relationship between the two countries.

After paying his condolences, Ali Adil Shah returned to Bijapur. Although a great deal of comradery was exhibited in Vijayanagar between the two monarchs, the reality was somewhat different. Rama Raja was at this stage almost 90 years old and had, over time, become arrogant in his behaviour. He had made Ali Shah feel like a supplicant by his overbearing and haughty behaviour. Ali Shah had felt slighted by this behaviour but did not show any signs of discomfiture or anger while in Vijayanagar. However, he returned home bearing a grudge against the old king.

The turn of events now moved along in similar lines to what had transpired about 150 years ago between Firuz Shah Bahmani and Deva Raya, then ruling Vijayanagar. A year into Ali Shah's rule the anticipated invasion by Hussein Nizam Shah of Ahmadnagar and his allies took place. True to his promise, Rama Raja send a large army to assist Ali Shah. On the arrival of the Vijayanagar army, Hussein Shah was abandoned by his allies and in the ensuing battle the Ahmadnagar forces were routed. The Sultan fled to his capital and shut himself in the fort, while the entire country was ravaged by the victorious forces. From here on, a progression of events started that was later to have serious consequences for the Vijayanagar kingdom. This point in history could be identified as the time that the seed that finally led to the decline and final fall of that magnificent empire was planted.

The Hindu forces of Vijayanagar, now buoyed by an easy victory, avenged the number of massacres that they had suffered at the hands of Muslim forces in earlier campaigns by committing similar atrocities on the Muslim population of the Ahmadnagar kingdom. The long oppressed local Hindus also joined the fray, making the massacres, rape and plunder take on the shade of a divisive and sectarian civil war. More than the immediate massacre and looting that followed the defeat of the Nizam Shahi forces, there was another factor, perhaps more important, at play. Rama Raja, by now an old, but extremely vain and authoritative king had become extremely arrogant regarding his own power and the stature of his empire. During this campaign he habitually treated the Muslim kings of the Deccan as his vassal supplicants. It is reported by both Muslim and Hindu chroniclers that he would make the Muslim kings walk considerable distances within his entourage before permitting them to mount and ride alongside him. If this is indeed a true depiction of his behaviour, it demonstrates a degree of arrogance far surpassing that displayed by any other monarch of Vijayanagar. It is not surprising that the Muslim kings were disgusted by the king's attitude and the treatment meted out to them.

In the meantime, Ahmadnagar defied all attempts at subduing the fort and at the approach of the monsoons, the siege had to be lifted. An uneasy peace was declared. At the end of the war, Rama Raja made all the Muslim kingdoms cede at least two districts each to Vijayanagar control. Ali Adil Shah who had invited the Vijayanagar king to intervene on his side took stock of the situation. He realised that Sholapur had not been retaken; Ahmadnagar still continued to be an independent kingdom ruled by the same king who had invaded his country; and on top of this humiliation, he had lost two districts to the Vijayanagar Empire. Adding to his discomfiture, he also felt that he had been disgraced by Rama Raja—the epitome of a Hindu monarch—in front of the other Muslim kings and nobles. In an unbiased overall assessment Ali Adil shah realised that he had not gained anything and had instead suffered a loss of prestige, dignity and territory. Most importantly, Ali Shah realised the growing power of Vijayanagar, which permitted it to treat all the Muslim kingdoms with disdain and roughshod over them at will. It opened his eyes to the danger that Vijayanagar posed to the sovereignty of the Deccan Muslim kingdoms. He was astute enough to realise that the situation eventuated because the Muslim kingdoms were perpetually at odds with one another, constantly chipping away at each other's power base. Ali Shah established this as one of the primary reasons for the ascendancy of Vijayanagar.

Alliance against Vijayanagar – Sound of the Death Knell

After deep consideration, Ali Adil Shah conceived the idea of creating a league of the Muslim kingdoms to attack and break its powerful stranglehold over the region that the Hindu kingdom exercised, which was overshadowing all of them. He first convinced the Qutb Shahi king of Golconda regarding the need to defeat the king of Vijayanagar. Once this was achieved, he undertook serious negotiations with the other Muslim kings. A trusted noble of the Qutb Shahi dynasty, Mustafa Khan, was send to Ahmadnagar to persuade Hussein Nizam Shah to come into the fold. Although Hussein and his kingdom had been subjected to a great amount of abuse during the recently concluded war, he accepted the invitation to join the league. The extent of animosity felt by the Muslim kings against the Hindu king can be understood by this one event alone. It is obvious that all the Muslim kings were smarting under the shabby treatment meted out to them by Rama Raja and that they harboured great hatred against him for his high-handed behaviour.

During these negotiations within the three more powerful Shahi kingdoms, Hussein Nizam Shah, the king of Ahmadnagar was persuaded to give his daughter Chand Bibi in marriage to Ali Adil Shah and gift Sholapur to him as dowry. In return, Ali Shah gave his daughter in marriage to Hussein's eldest son, Murtaza. (The description of the influence that Chand Bibi exerted on the history of the Deccan will be provided later in this volume. At this stage it is only necessary to mention that Chand Bibi belonged to a long list of heroine queens who adorn the historical narrative of the Indian sub-continent.)

This 'holy' league being formed against Vijayanagar was joined by The Barid Shahi ruler of Bidar with alacrity. Barid Shahi rulers habitually were inclined to join and even instigate all kinds of intrigue, against any kingdom or ruler who they felt were standing against the Barids' self-interest. For some inexplicable reason the Imad Shahi sultan of Berar was not invited to join the anti-Vijayanagar league. The reasons for this omission could be speculated. It could either be because it was felt that the Imad Shahis were not powerful enough to contribute meaningfully to the forces that the league was putting together, which was indeed true; or it could be because the Berar rulers were known to be fickle in their allegiances and changed sides according to their contextual convenience. In fact, it could actually have been a combination of both these factors. Whatever the real reason(s) for its exclusion, it is clear that Berar was not part of the league.

In 1565, the armies of the four Muslim Deccan kingdoms came together on the plains of Bijapur and marched to Tellikota on the banks of River Krishna. The Battle of Tellikota that ensued is one of the most important battles, a momentous event and a major turning point in Indian Peninsular history. In the battle, the Raja of Vijayanagar was conclusively defeated, marking the beginning of the rapid decline and final end of a magnificent Empire—the last standing evidence of great Hindu power not only in South India, but the whole sub-continent. *[The Battle of Tellikota is covered in great detail in the section that covers the history of the Vijayanagar Empire, since the consequences of the outcome of the battle was felt almost exclusively in the Hindu Empire rather than in the Muslim Deccan kingdoms.]*

Continuing Rivalry in the Deccan

Even though they combined effectively to break the power of Vijayanagar, as soon as that objective was achieved, the Deccan kingdoms returned to their old ways of infighting and intrigue against each other. Each kingdom undertook activities aimed at preventing any of the others from increasing their power and becoming strong. The only ambition of each of the kingdoms seemed to be to bring each of the others aspiring for power to heel. Almost immediately after Vijayanagar was defeated, Ali Shah invaded parts of the kingdom with the intention of annexing territory. Rama Raja's brother Vekatadri appealed to Hussein Nizam Shah in Ahmadnagar for assistance, which was promptly provided. Facing this combined force, the Bijapur troops were forced to withdraw. In the ensuing peace, the Deccan kingdoms agreed between themselves that no one would invade Vijayanagar without the mutual approval of all the others. This agreement was typical of the disunity that prevailed amongst the Deccan kingdoms and reinforced the inherent distrust that existed between the Shahi dynasties.

Soon after, the two Muslim armies that had recently faced each other, marched together against Berar where the Prime Minister Tufal Khan had deposed the Imad Shahi king and usurped the throne. The army ravaged the countryside of Berar in this invasion. During this joint invasion of Berar, Ali Adil Shah made a surreptitious attempt to usurp Ahmadnagar from the young Murtaza Nizam Shah who had inherited the throne from his father, Hussein. However, this attempt proved to be unsuccessful and Ali Shah returned to Bijapur. Even so, this attempt at deposing Murtaza led to three years of continual conflict between Bijapur and Ahmadnagar.

In 1569, a large Bijapur army under the command of General Kishwar Khan invaded Ahmadnagar territory. Murtaza Nizam Shah and the Queen-mother, who was acting as the Regent and was for all practical purposes the de-facto ruler during the young prince's minority, marched out to meet the Bijapur forces. Murtaza had by this time attained majority and was not only more mature, but also impatient of being controlled by a woman Regent, even though the lady was his own mother. He asserted his independence with the help of some nobles and imprisoned the Queen, removing her from the exalted position she had so far assumed. Murtaza went on to attack the Bijapur army at the head of his own forces and besieged and captured the fort at Dharur, where Kishwar Khan was killed in battle.

Murtaza was assisted in this battle by the Qutb Shahi king of Golconda. However, the combined army could not take advantage of this victory over the Bijapur forces. They were unable to follow through with an attack on Bijapur territory because of disunity and distrust between the two armies. Ali Adil Shah shrewdly concluded a peace treaty with the Nizam Shahis, thereby averting further damage to his prestige and also protecting his territorial integrity. According to this treaty, Ali Shah was permitted to conquer as much of Vijayanagar territory as he could and Murtaza Shah was permitted to annex Berar to his kingdom.

Ali Adil Shah now embarked on a conquering march into Vijayanagar territory to the south of his kingdom. He conducted an effective siege and starved into submission the fort at Adoni, which had so far been considered impregnable. After this spectacular success, he moved further into the Carnatic, the core home territory of Vijayanagar. He captured Dharwar, Binkapore and Gandikota, reaching River

Pennar in relatively quick time. The capture of 'territory' mentioned in the chronicles of the Deccan kingdoms followed a particular pattern, which was true of all Muslim conquests in the peninsula. The military forces would fight for and capture the forts and other strongholds of the adversary, while the countryside was normally left untouched. The forts would either be destroyed or garrisoned by Muslim soldiers. The peasants in the countryside continued to live the same life, oppressed by a new master, and paying taxes to a Muslim landlord instead of a Hindu chief.

In these battles and victories only the royal families faced any change in circumstances, since they were forced to retreat or even flee from their territories on being defeated. Artisans, traders and craftsmen continued to ply their craft and trade, paying taxes to the victor. Nothing changed for them. Some Hindu landlords were also permitted to stay on, paying a fixed rent to the Muslim government. Muslim governors, residing in the captured forts and backed by a small contingent of soldiers, kept order within the 'conquered' territory. The large, and majority, Hindu population remained in situ as an integral part of the kingdom while also being separate from the ruling entity and the religious persuasions that were officially practised. The entire system worked the other way too, the situation being the same for the minority Muslim populations who resided in Hindu kingdoms. In the Deccan, the general population continued to practice their own religious rites and age-old customs and traditions. It is true that temples were desecrated and even destroyed during war, but this was done as much for looting the wealth of the temples as for religious bigotry. The situation returned to normal during times of peace and in many instances the destroyed temples were even re-built.

The Changing Face of the Deccan Army

From the end of the 15th and through the 16th centuries, a subtle change took place in the demographic constitution of the Deccan Shahi armies. Three major but gradual changes contributed to and entrenched this alteration in the constitution of these armies. First, many Hindu zamindars, meaning nobles and landlords, changed their loyalty and became aligned to the Muslim rulers. In order to demonstrate their faithfulness to the new rulers, they contributed Hindu retainers to the Sultan's army, making amalgamation a necessity. Second, the constant feud between the foreign and the Deccani Muslims was coming to a head during this time, with the foreigners being pushed out of favour. This increased the Deccani, or local, influence within the army. Third, the foreigners, who normally came from the north-west were now attracted to the larger and more opulent army of the Mughals in Delhi. In turn, this reduced the number of foreign adventurers wanting to travel to the hot, humid and sultry peninsula to join the armies of the Deccan Shahi kingdoms.

It was not surprising that gradually the Deccan armies became predominantly manned by Hindu 'warlike' tribes and groups—mainly the Marathas, Rajputs and also the Beydars. However, they were still mainly officered by Muslims. There were also exclusive Muslim battalions who were a mix of Arabs, Abyssinians and other foreigners. By the end of the 16 century, the armies had become predominantly Hindu in composition, which in turn brought about changes in the basic tactics that were employed and altered the warfighting style itself. There is also opinions expressed by some analysts that the religious mix and mercenary nature of the armies of the Deccan also contributed to a gradual decline in their fighting efficiency. In effect it was though that the army had been 'weakened'. However, there is no evidence to substantiate this claim. The Deccan armies remained as good or as bad as in previous years.

The Rise of the Marathas

The Marathas first came into prominence as soldiers when they distinguished themselves as superb irregular cavalry during the rule of the Bahmani kings. They were especially adept at warfare in the hilly and jungle terrain, whereas the majority Muslim forces of the Deccan kingdoms were not very good in conducting warfare in this terrain and/or in an irregular mode. The Muslim forces excelled in set-piece battles in the plains where the employment of freewheeling cavalry was their forte. However, when it came to having to innovate in unconventional battles conducted in harsh and inhospitable terrain, they were no match for the intrepid Maratha warriors. This fact was to be proven repeatedly in later days.

The mixing of Muslims and Hindus in the Deccan armies brought into focus and emphasised a clear difference between the nobles of the two religions. In the Deccan Shahi kingdoms, the Muslim nobles and

Growing Strength

other prominent citizens chose to be granted 'jagirs', or land grants, in the plains close to the capital. They did not reside in their estates far away from the seat of power, but preferred to stay close to the luxury of the capital so that they were able to indulge in the intrigues, which were almost always percolating in the royal court. The outlying provinces, the hilly parts of the Deccan, were largely left to the Hindu zamindars who provided retainers to the Shahi armies. Gradually there emerged a cadre of tough and hardy Hindu soldiers, mostly Marathas from the region who were brought up in their own faith, customs and traditions but were also well-versed in the Muslim art of warfighting.

Inevitably this development paved the way for revolt and rebellion as these soldiers and their leadership started their quest for more freedom and ultimately independence itself. The minor rebellions and other developments in the Deccan could, in some ways, be identified as the planting of the seed that became the beginning of the Maratha nation, which subsequently grew in later days to lay claim not only to the Deccan but to the sovereignty of the entire Indian sub-continent.

The Maratha Revolt

Around 1578, a number of Maratha chiefs owing allegiance to the Adil Shahi dynasty rebelled in the outer reaches of the kingdom. Ali Shah send an army to subdue them. However, the army consisted of 'plains' soldiers and could not make any headway against the tough Maratha irregular forces of the hills. The army returned after a year of fruitless campaigning without achieving any success and having suffered considerable losses. Ali Shah's minister, Mustafa Khan, then devised a devious plan, which was to lure the Maratha chiefs to Bijapur with promises of gifts and by declaring a truce, after which they would be slaughtered. Accordingly a Brahmin, Vasuji Pant, was send to invite the chiefs to Bijapur. A number of them accepted and were subsequently assassinated in Bijapur, according to the plan.

The principal chief of the Marathas, Hanumanta Naik, had refused the invitation suspecting planned foul play and had rapidly withdrawn with his followers to his stronghold of Bilkonda. This act of extreme treachery by the Adil Shahi king and his minister had serious consequences that influenced future events. First is that this action does not merit even a single mention in the chronicles written by the Muslim court historians of the time. Since the event has been confirmed by other sources as having taken place but is not mentioned by the 'official' historians, it throws into doubt the authenticity of the entire chronicles and also lends the narrative to the question as to how many other incidents that would have brought out the ruling dynasty in bad light have been consciously omitted. The art of 're-writing' history is obviously not new.

Second, the treachery that was perpetuated lived on in the collective Maratha memory and gradually became a factor in inculcating a long-lasting race hatred towards the Muslims in the region. The followers of Islam were considered untrustworthy in an overarching manner. On the positive side, this hatred also proved to be a uniting factor, bringing the Marathas together against a common 'foreign', mainly Muslim, enemy, who was considered an invader. Third, this act of treachery was a turning point in the Hindu-Muslim relationship in the Deccan. Till this act, a certain amount of amicability was prevalent in the relationship between the religions in the Deccan. With the perpetuation of the Bijapur massacre, there emerged a clear estrangement between the two religious communities that never healed thereafter.

Soon after the Bijapur massacre, in 1580, Ali Adil Shah was assassinated by one of his favourite eunuchs, apparently for some offence that Ali Shah had given him. He was succeeded on the throne by his nine-year old nephew.

Ali Adil Shah presided over a kingdom that was almost constantly at war. He was also continually engaged in the political intrigues involved in making and breaking alliances, which seemed to have been a common practice amongst the Deccan Shahi kingdoms. Ali Shah was also a builder, with the Jumma mosque and some waterworks in the capital Bijapur being attributed to him. Perhaps the most important event of his reign was the arrival of a Mughal embassy in Bijapur, where the ambassador stayed for a period of time. This was the first foray of the Mughals into the Deccan.

Chapter 13

THE ZENITH

At the time of Ali Adil Shah's death, the most popular and prominent person in the kingdom was his wife, Chand Bibi, who was also the sister of the ruling Nizam Shahi king of Ahmadnagar. She was a level-headed woman of great intellect, energy and sagacity.

The Story of Chand Bibi – Part I

While Ali Shah was the reigning king, his intrepid Queen, Chand Bibi, had accompanied her husband on many military expeditions, at times even taking to the battlefield alongside the Bijapur forces in action. In times of relative peace and also when Ali Shah was away from the capital on expeditions, Chand Bibi conducted the affairs of state with aplomb and also gave public audiences in open court. She was just and firm in her dealings and was therefore revered by the common people of the kingdom. Ali Adil Shah died without having sired any sons. He had two nephews—Ibrahim and Ismael who were in the line of probable succession. Chand Bibi took the lead in deciding the succession and was instrumental in crowning Ali Shah's nephew, the minor Ibrahim Adil Shah II, as the new king. After the crowning of the young prince, Chand Bibi took over the running of the kingdom's affairs, ably assisted by a senior noble, Kamil Khan Deccani.

Although Chand Bibi was the power behind the throne, she ensured that she was not mistaken to be ruling as the queen, making sure that the young, nine-year old king Ibrahim Adil Shah was always seated on the throne in the public hall of justice whenever the court was in session and judgements were passed. She scrupulously maintained her role as the regent and nothing more. Gradually, Kamil Khan, her co-regent started to usurp disproportionate power and Chand Bibi fell out with him on this account. She brought in Kishawar Khan, one of the old and trusted generals as the co-regent, dismissing Kamil Khan from the post. Kamil Khan was killed while fleeing from Bijapur.

It was not long before Kishawar Khan also started to display his proclivity to be high-handed and to bypass the queen-regent in taking decisions on matters of state. He was also rude to some of the nobles and considered them to be his vassals rather than of equal status. The nobles therefore advised Chand Bibi to remove Kishawar Khan from the position that he occupied and to bring in Mustafa Khan, then the governor of Binkapur, as the co-regent. *[The need for the queen, powerful, capable and liked by the people, to have a noble as the co-regent is indicative of the social system prevalent in the Muslim community of the time, where a woman, even though she was the queen, was not considered capable enough to rule the kingdom effectively without the assistance of a 'man'. The noble appointed co-regent was supposed to be the lead in the duo that was ruling on behalf of the young prince. This perception of the weakness of women had, by this time in the development of the religion, further developed into subjugation of women in the Muslim society. Even in the 21st century, Muslim women are subjected to ridiculously callous treatment as 'belonging to' either the father or the husband. In contrast, Hindu women in ancient and medieval times were completely free. However, the Muslim influence on the Indian society gradually made them observe the social etiquettes that were imposed on Muslim women and also became unfairly subjugated by the male members of their families. This retrograde move is more observable in the Northern parts of the sub-continent, where Muslim influence has been observed to be the greatest and played out for the longest time.]* Kishawar Khan got wind of the plan to relieve him of his regency and had Mustafa, his likely successor murdered by a lower level jagirdar in Binkapur, before he could start his journey to the capital.

At this stage, the power struggle between the queen and Kishawar Khan took an ominous turn. Kishawar Khan physically took the young prince into his custody and confined Chand Bibi in the fort at Satara. He provided a reason and/or pretext for this action by accusing her of conspiring with and inciting her brother—the Nizam Shahi king ruling Ahmadnagar—to invade Bijapur. It was obvious to all that this was a blatant lie and that the charges were trumped up.

Chand Bibi's conduct as a just and fair regent had made her a well-liked sovereign. Kishawar Khan had not bargained for the loyalty she evoked within the army and also amongst the general population. On he being incarcerated, the soldiers garrisoned outside Bijapur started to march to the capital in order to depose Kishawar who had become a tyrant by this time. Kishawar realised the turning tide against him and fled from Bijapur, seeking asylum in Ahmadnagar. It was obvious that the Ahmadabad king would refuse any request for refuge since his sister was the one that had been imprisoned. Kishawar fled further to Golconda, seeking sanctuary. In Golconda, a relative of Mustafa Khan murdered him in revenge.

Chand Bibi was brought back from imprisonment and resumed the role of the Regent and appointed Ekhlas Khan as the new minister and co-regent. Ekhlas was an Abyssinian with a violent temper and personality. Till this time the Abyssinians had always sided with and been considered part of the Deccani faction amongst the nobles at court, especially in their fight against the Phirangis, the foreigners. *[Being considered part of the Deccani faction could perhaps be attributed to their physical appearance of being black because of their African origin, whereas the Arabs and others who constituted the Phirangi faction were fair-skinned and with distinctly different facial features. The current obsession that Indian's have with 'fair skin' goes back not only to the medieval times but can be traced to ancient times!]* With Ekhlas appointed to the high position as the senior minister, the Abyssinians now separated from the Deccanis, forming a third faction amongst the nobles in the Deccan kingdoms. The factious fights within the Bijapur kingdom continued unabated and was intensified because of the Abyssinians. It gradually took on the hue of a civil war. The kingdom was in turmoil.

Taking advantage of the domestic upheaval in Bijapur, the kings of Berar, Bidar and Golconda formed an alliance, invaded the country and surrounded the capital. Ekhlas Khan, even though impetuous and inclined to violent outbursts, was extremely loyal to the Adil Shahi dynasty while also being an able soldier and a determined military commander. Further, the dowager queen-regent, Chand Bibi, herself joined the defending force accompanied by the young king. This act of exemplary courage greatly improved the morale of the Bijapur forces and they held out despite the fact that the siege was imposed with great severity. At one stage of the siege, the invaders blew a 20-foot breach in the defending walls but the Bijapur forces managed to hold the invading forces back. It is said that Chand Bibi personally led the forces that guarded the breach while it was being repaired.

At this time of extreme danger, the Abyssinians, who were the primary cause of the division within the kingdom, 'surrendered' to the indomitable queen. Chand Bibi appointed a new minister and continued with the defence of the kingdom. Her army now numbered around 20,000 loyal soldiers—led by a mix of Deccanis, Phirangis and Abyssinians. After more than a year, being unsuccessful in conclusively defeating the Adil Shahis, the invading forces lifted the siege of Bijapur. The Queen-Regent had almost single-handedly redeemed the kingdom, by sheer will power and open demonstration of personal example and steadfast courage. The Bijapur forces had achieved victory of sorts, if not succumbing to an extended siege could be classified as a victory. Chand Bibi had expected to bring peace and stabilise the turmoil within the kingdom after this victory. However, it was not to be.

During the conflict with the invading force, one of the military commanders, Dilawar Khan, had shown exemplary courage and leadership. He had gradually risen to the position of the senior most military commander of the kingdom. At the end of the external invasion, after the invading forces had withdrawn, Dilawar blinded the new minister who had replaced Ekhlas Khan and took over the role himself. He then went on to commit many atrocities, all aimed at curtailing the queen's power and influence in the affairs of state. Gradually the queen-regent was reduced to running the royal palace and educating the young king, while Dilawar Khan became the de facto ruler of the kingdom. Despite his inherent cruelty, which was regularly displayed, Dilawar was an able administrator. He improved the governance of the kingdom and ensured that the court and its rulings were respected.

During this time when Dilawar Khan had taken over the reins of the kingdom, the Kingdom of Ahmadnagar was convulsed by patricide and factional conflict to claim the throne. (The events that transpired in Ahmadnagar will be described in a later chapter.) Chand Bibi, whose brother was the ruling king in Ahmadnagar was physically there, on a visit to her brother and as a princess of the Nizam Shahi dynasty. She had undertaken the journey since her ward, Ibrahim, was

The Zenith

maturing and coming of age. In this growing confusion, the Bijapur army intervened in Ahmadnagar and concluded a peace. Chand Bibi returned to Bijapur with the returning army. She was now devoid of all power in her country.

On her return, Chand Bibi realised that the Bijapur that she had come back to was very different to the one that she had left. Bijapur had changed a lot during her absence. The political situation had altered considerably, with the young king Ibrahim Adil Shah having taken over the public conduct of all royal business. However, Ibrahim received his aunt with great affection, welcoming her home with pomp and ceremony. Even the common people celebrated her return, since she was held in great affection by them. Chand Bibi was shrewd enough to understand and judge the altered circumstances and gracefully retired from public life, giving advice only when asked for by the young ruler. She lived in peace, administering locally when the king was out of Bijapur, but only on his explicit request to do so.

Chand Bibi was a contemporary of Queen Elizabeth I of England. She was a woman of equal ability, political talent, education and accomplishment as the English monarch. Further, Chand Bibi's realm was in no way inferior to the one that Elizabeth ruled—it was as large, as populous and as rich as England was at that time.

> '…a woman who, surrounded by jealous enemies, preserved by her own personal valour and endurance her kingdom from destruction and partition; who through all temptations and exercise of absolute power, was at once simple, generous, frank, and merciful as she was chaste, virtuous, religious and charitable—one who, among all the women of India, stands out as a jewel without flaw and beyond price.'
>
> Colonel Meadow Taylor in *The Noble Queen*,
> Quoted in J. D. B. Gribble,
> *History of the Deccan*, pp. 221-22.

(The story of Chand Bibi does not end here; the second part of her biography will be continued in a later chapter.)

Ibrahim Adil Shah II

Ibrahim Adil Shah had grown up to be a young man of considerable talent and ability under the meticulous tutelage of his aunt, the redoubtable queen Chand Bibi. On achieving majority, he assumed full powers in the running of the kingdom, while his aunt, the regent, was away visiting her brother in Ahmadnagar. At this stage the Nizam Shahi kingdom was going through internal strife because of an intense succession struggle. Ibrahim's first action as king was to advance with a large army to Ahmadnagar with the intent of placing his brother-in-law Meeran Hussein on the throne. During the march, he came to know that Meeran had killed his own father. In a rare case of a medieval monarch displaying ethics and morality as opposed to grabbing the opportunity to better his own situation, Ibrahim withdrew support for Meeran and returned with his army to Bijapur.

When Meeran Hussein was subsequently murdered by a rival faction, Ibrahim once again attempted to advance on Ahmadnagar. However, the campaign was not successful because of the rivalry between the two commanding generals—Dilawar Khan who was also the chief minister and Bulleel Khan who had been brought back by Ibrahim from a campaign he had been leading in Malabar. In the process of marching towards Ahmadnagar, Dilawar Khan managed to capture and blind Bulleel Khan, through intrigue. Ibrahim Shah was incensed at this wanton act of Dilawar, but could not act against the all-powerful minister at that time. He wowed to get rid of the minister when an appropriate opportunity arose.

In Ahmadnagar, Dilawar Khan now at the head of the Bijapur forces was almost defeated and barely managed to retreat and rejoin Ibrahim Shah's camp. At this stage Ibrahim, although the nominal king, was a virtual prisoner of Dilawar Khan and his cronies. However, Ibrahim managed to escape from the camp one night. Assessing that he may not any longer be able to control the king, Dilawar took fright and sought refuge in Ahmadnagar. Burhan Nizam Shah, now ruling Ahmadnagar, gave asylum to Dilawar Khan forgetting the assistance that he had received from the Bijapur king in an earlier crisis.

The Zenith

Not content with receiving asylum and treatment befitting his earlier position in Bijapur as the chief minister, Dilawar precipitated another war between Ahmadnagar and Bijapur. He was now fighting on behalf of the Ahmadabad king against his own country. Obviously it was acceptable in the medieval Deccan to change loyalty and forget the human quality of integrity to fit the evolving circumstances and one's own personal situation. Dilawar leading the Ahmadnagar army, first attempted to reduce and annex Sholapur, a fort that had long been the bone of contention between the two kingdoms.

Ibrahim Shah permitted the invading Nizam Shahi forces and Dilawar's army to advance well inside Bijapur territory, pretending that he was too weak to resist the invasion. When the adversary forces reached the River Bhima, on the banks of which they started to build fortifications, Ibrahim invited Dilawar Khan to come back to Bijapur and resume his old employment as chief minister. Lulled by the obviously weak situation of the Bijapur king, Dilawar went to Bijapur expecting to be reinstalled as the minister and to once again assume control of both kingdom and king. Instead he was taken prisoner, blinded and locked up in the fort at Satara, where he remained till his death.

Ibrahim Adil Shah now marched against the invading force, forcing Burhan Nizam Shah to retreat and then sue for peace. The Adil Shahi king granted peace on the condition that the fortifications that the Nizam Shahi forces had built on the banks of River Bhima would be razed to the ground by the Ahmadnagar forces themselves. This was agreed to, and Burhan was forced to initiate the process by ritually removing the first stone from the fortifications. The Ahmadnagar forces returned to their kingdom—a much chastised king and army. Following the retreat of the Nizam Shahi army, peace and stability prevailed in Bijapur for a few years. Ibrahim Shah send an army under Munjum Khan to bring few recalcitrant Hindu kings of Malabar under control, in order to stabilise the kingdom. Munjum advanced towards Malabar, first capturing a fort at Mysore. However, before the Malabar kings could be subdued, rebellion broke out in the Bijapur kingdom, and Munjum was recalled by Ibrahim.

A Brother's Rebellion

Ismael, Ibrahim's younger brother, had been made governor of Belgaum but was kept within great constraints. His governorship was nothing more than a glorified and honourable confinement. It is not surprising that Ismael was unhappy about the situation. Over a period of time he managed to get the support of a number of nobles and in 1593, he rebelled, declaring independence from the Bijapur kingdom. The chief minister of Bijapur at this time was Eyn-ul-Mulk and he too was disgruntled with the lack of stature and power given to him by Ibrahim. This situation made him only minimally influential in the affairs of state. He felt that Ismael would be a more malleable king and therefore supported him. The open support of the minister for the younger brother resulted in fomenting a general revolt across the countryside.

Burhan Nizam Shah, smarting under the humiliation of the earlier defeat by Ibrahim Shah, moved against Bijapur with an army to support Ismael. In addition, spying an opportunity, the vassal Hindu rajas of Bijapur also rose in rebellion. The Portuguese in Goa, always on the lookout for any opportunity to interfere in local politics, also send some forces to assist Ismael. These developments placed Ibrahim Shah under enormous pressure. In this time of critical danger to his continued rule and also to the integrity of the kingdom, Ibrahim turned to his aunt Chand Bibi for advice and assistance. As usual her advice was sagacious and well-thought through.

Chand Bibi advised Ibrahim to deal with his adversaries one at a time, individually and in isolation before they could effectively combine to form a joint force; an advice that Ibrahim followed to the letter. Accordingly, he send his senior commander Humeed Khan to meet Eyn-ul-Mulk who had by this time openly joined the Belgaum forces of Ismael. Humeed Khan pretended to have abandoned Ibrahim's Bijapur forces and enticed Eyn-ul-Mulk to come outside the Belgaum fort. At this juncture, the Nizam Shahi forces of Ahmadnagar were only a few days march away from Belgaum. However, Eyn-ul-Mulk did not wait for these forces to join up and went out to parlay with Humeed Khan. Moving out of the safety of the Belgaum fort was a tactical blunder. Eyn-ul-Mulk may have wanted to end the rebellion with the help of Humeed Khan and also may not have wanted to take the assistance of Ahmadnagar in placing Ismael on the throne. If he managed the usurpation on his own, his influence on Ismael would have been increased. In any case, this decision led to a debacle.

In this instance, when Eyn-ul-Mulk came to meet Humeed Khan, Humeed Khan charged him and cut off his head and took the young prince Ismael prisoner. On knowing this development, the rebel army scattered in panic and confusion. Seeing the major part of the rebel force disintegrate, Burhan Nizam Shah withdrew to his kingdom, his ambition to avenge the earlier defeat once again put on hold. Thus ended the ill-fated rebellion led by Ismail, but instigated by older nobles who had their own grievances to redress.

The Ahmadnagar Episode

On returning to Ahmadnagar, Burhan Shah took ill and died soon after. The kingdom was already suffering from multiple dissentions ever since Burhan had come to power. These, till now simmering under the surface of stability, now broke out into the open. Burhan was succeeded by his son Ibrahim Nizam Shah, who was haughty by nature. He ill-treated and was rude to the Bijapur Ambassador in his court, who decided that it would better for him to return to Bijapur, rather than suffer further indignities.

Ibrahim Adil Shah set out with an army to avenge the direct insult to his ambassador, which was obviously indirectly aimed at himself. The ensuing battle against Ahmadnagar was hotly contested with the advantage swinging both ways and the result hanging in the balance for a while. As was his wont, Ibrahim Nizam Shah rashly advanced into the periphery of the Bijapur army with only a small retinue of guards and then plunged into the thick of the battle. A small contingent of Bijapur cavalry surprised the Ahmadnagar group guarding the king during his foray deep into the Bijapur forces. In the ensuing melee, a stray arrow struck Ibrahim Nizam Shah who was killed instantly. On the death of their king, the Ahmadnagar army fled the battlefield in disarray.

The death of Ibrahim Nizam Shah plunged Ahmadnagar into a succession struggle and into further chaos. Chand Bibi, who was a princess of Ahmadnagar, was requested to become the regent for an infant prince who was raised to the throne at the end of the succession struggle. (The detailed narrative of this part of Chand Bibi's contribution to the Deccan Muslim kingdoms will be given in the next chapter.) It is sufficient here to state that during her regency in Ahmadnagar, Chand Bibi received unrestrained support from her nephew, Ibrahim Adil Shah, whenever she faced any trouble.

Chand Bibi's regency in Ahmadnagar—till her death and the annexation of the Nizam Shahi kingdom by the Mughals—is intimately connected to the history of Bijapur. The annexation of Ahmadnagar by the Mughal forces was a debilitating blow to Ibrahim Adil Shah. He withdrew into his capital after the catastrophe that befell Ahmadnagar, which was followed by desultory inactivity within the Deccan. Ibrahim did make some attempt at regaining his status by making overtures to Akbar, the ruling Mughal Emperor of the time. An alliance was agreed upon, which also included a Bijapur princess being given in marriage to Akbar's son. At this time, Bijapur was at the height of its splendour and magnificence. Asad Beg, a noble from the Mughal court who was send to escort the Bijapur princess to Delhi, provides an unbiased report of Bijapur.

Asad Beg's Description of Bijapur

'That palace, which they call Hajjah, was so arranged that each house in it had a double court. ... All round the gate of my residence were lofty buildings with houses and porticos; the situation was very airy and healthy. It lies in an open space in the city. Its northern portico is to the east of a *bazaar* of great extent, as much as thirty yards wide and two *kos* [four miles] long. Before each shop was a beautiful green tree, and the whole bazaar was extremely clean and pure.

...the whole bazaar was filled with wine and beauty, dancers, perfumes, jewels of all sorts, palaces and viands.

> In one street were a thousand people….; none quarrelled or disputed with another, and this state of things were perpetual. Perhaps no place in the wide world could present a more wonderful spectacle to the eye of the traveller.'
>
> H.M. Elliot & John Dowson,
> *The History of India: as told by its own historians, The Muhammadan Period*, Vol VI, p. 163
> Also quoted in J. D. R. Gribble,
> *The History of the Deccan*, variously pp. 245-47.

Conclusion

Ibrahim Adil Shah's rule is considered the zenith of the power of the Adil Shahis of Bijapur. He died in 1626 after a long and eventful reign. Ibrahim was a great patron of architecture and during his reign was built some of the finest buildings to be seen in Bijapur. His tomb, the construction of which was begun immediately on his assuming the throne, took 36 years to complete and is a spectacular group of splendid buildings, called 'Ibrahim Roza'. This group of buildings is considered to be the most brilliantly and elaborately adorned of all the Muslim structures in the entire Indian sub-continent. The tradition of commencing the construction of one's own tomb on accession to the throne was practised by various dynasties, across the world, in medieval times. The custom could have been adopted to provide a stark reminder to the king of the ultimate fate of all human beings, irrespective of the person's brilliance, bravery, power or the splendour of his/her achievements. Death was, and continues to be, a great equaliser. The significance of this philosophy and the reasons for its adoption by many dynasties, which crosses the boundaries of race, religion and location of the dynasties concerned, would form a fascinating study.

Ibrahim Adil Shah was a man of learning and refined taste. On his death he left behind a kingdom that was extremely wealthy, guarded by a large and powerful army. He is considered to have been the best of the Adil Shahi kings. Perhaps the ultimate testimony to the greatness of Ibrahim, as a ruler and a human being, is the fact that throughout his life he was extremely devoted to his aunt, who had brought him up with love as her own son and had taught him the ways of a good king. Such gratitude and affection were uncommon traits for a monarch to display during the times that he ruled.

Chapter 14

THE FINAL COLLAPSE

The fall of Daulatabad and end of Malik Amber's rule also heralded the beginning of the end of the Deccani Muslim kingdoms. (Malik Amber's foray into the Deccan and his eventful rule is described in a later chapter in the section dealing with the Nizam Shahi kingdom of Ahmadnagar.) By the 1630s, the Nizam Shahi dynasty had ceased to exist, despite the heroic efforts of some loyal generals and ministers to keep the dynasty alive by proclaiming as king a distant relative of the last Nizam Shahi king. By 1635, only Bijapur and Golconda remained independent amongst the five Deccan Shahi kingdoms, which had replaced the Bahamani kingdom in the Peninsula. Berar and Bidar could be discounted in this calculation since throughout the history of the successor dynasties of the Deccan, both of them had remained insignificant entities of limited or even no influence in the broader flow of the geo-political events that were taking place.

By early 17th century, even Golconda and Bijapur had started to receive ambassadors from the Mughal court in Delhi, instructing them to pay tribute to the emperor and also stipulating the amount that was to be paid annually. They were also instructed to read the weekly 'qutba' in the name of the Delhi Emperor, signifying that both the Adil Shahi and Qutb Shahi kings in Bijapur and Golconda respectively were not independent rulers anymore. They had been subsumed into the greater empire, been reduced in status to vassal states and ruled at the pleasure of the Mughal Emperor. However, they had not been defeated in battle or been conquered, therefore nominally both the kingdoms remained independent.

The Delhi court also appointed officers to reside in the capital of both the kingdoms, who informed the emperor of all activities in them and also interfered in the affairs of state, giving guidance to the rulers whenever they felt it necessary. *[This could have been the model that the British adopted when they instituted the concept of 'Residents' in a faraway time after they had assumed control over most of the sub-continent.]* The power and stature of the Mughal Residents can be understood by the fact that both the Adil Shahi and Qutb Shahi kings went out of their capital to meet and escort the accredited officers to their courts. The Delhi Residents were representatives of the great emperor and could not be treated as mere nobles, even by kings. The reduced stature of the Deccan kings is also noticed in the manner in which the Delhi chroniclers of the time referred to them. From the time of the collapse of the Ahmadnagar kingdom, the Delhi scribes/historians refer to the Bijapur and Golconda kings as Adil Khan and Qutb-ul-Mulk, having done away with the title of Shah, which was customarily given to independent king.

Mahmud Adil Shah

Mahmud Adil Shah had succeeded his father to the throne in 1626. Bijapur continued to show outwardly that it was submissive to the orders of the great Mughal emperor, while surreptitiously assisting the Maratha chief, Shahaji, to continue with his acts of rebellion. This double-dealing led to the Mughals launching a punitive expedition against Bijapur. The Mughal army, laid waste to the countryside and ravaged the farmlands, although the actual fighting between the two forces were desultory at best. There were no decisive battles fought and a state of flux prevailed. However, Mahmud Adil Shah sued for peace, which was conditionally granted. The Bijapur king was to pay a tribute of 20,00,000 worth local currency in gold and jewellery to Delhi and also had to promise to reign in the Maratha chief. If Adil Shah failed to control the Marathas, then he would have to join the Mughals in fighting and defeating the Maratha forces. At this juncture the Mughal Emperor Shah Jahan was physically in the Deccan. On this one-sided peace being settled with Bijapur, he returned to Delhi. The emperor's return to Delhi relieved the Deccan of the enormous financial strain of supporting the large imperial camp, which was a moving city by itself.

The Final Collapse

Since Shahaji did not stop his acts of rebellion, the Mughal forces, along with a coerced Bijapur army, mounted a combined offensive against his strongholds. The Maratha chief put up a strong opposition but was unable to withstand the might of the two armies. He was comprehensively defeated and forced to enter Bijapur service. Almost immediately Adil Shah send Shahaji to campaign in the Carnatic region, where the Maratha commander proved himself to be a powerful and victorious commander.

During the Carnatic campaign, Shahaji, the Maratha chief, had reduced Mysore, Arcot and the entire Tanjore region all the way to the River Cauvery. In appreciation, Mahmud Shah gifted the Tanjore region as a personal jagir, or fiefdom, to Shahaji. Although he reigned for 30 years, Mahmud Shah was not successful in holding back the imperial army of the Mughals from encroaching his territories in the north. Almost as if in compensation, he extended his dominion to the south and south-east, well into the Carnatic. During these southern invasions and defensive actions against the Mughal army, Mahmud Shah did not take to the battlefield to lead his forces, preferring instead to stay in his capital and depute his generals to command the battles. He indulged in his passion for architecture and construction, building many handsome structures in Bijapur, including the celebrated Gol Gumbaz.

The Gol Gumbaz

The Gol Gumbaz is one of the most remarkable buildings in the world. The dome is built in 'pendatives' – an architectural process by which a square is gradually contracted into a circle. The Gol Gumbaz dome is bigger than that of the Pantheon in Rome and covers an area of 18,225 square feet. The structure was also used to house the tomb of Mahmud Adil Shah after his death. It is reported that the Gol Gumbaz took 10 years to build.

The Gol Gumbaz is a landmark building, visible from more than 25 miles distance. The only criticism of the building, mostly from modern architects, is that the entire structure lacks sufficient height to make it a truly grandiose and aesthetically great building.

Mahmud Adil Shah died in 1656. Although he achieved territorial expansion towards the Carnatic in the south, he was also forced to acquiesce to being a vassal of the great Mughal Emperor ruling in Delhi, becoming the first Adil Shahi ruler to accept this diminished status. Mahmud's rule was the beginning of the end of the dynasty, although the crumbling of the edifice on which the Bijapur kingdom was built could not be noticed because of the outward stability of his reign.

It is certain that Mahmud was aware of the gradual decline in his status and therefore continued the clandestine support to the Marathas. Towards the end of Mahmud's reign, the Marathas were led by Shahaji's son, Shivaji, who was much more able than his father and also of a more volatile temperament. Shivaji increased the Maratha power in the Deccan and led an open rebellion against the Mughal power. He also revolted against his nominal sovereign, the Adil Shahi king of Bijapur who had been served by his father. (The rise and subsequent decline of Maratha power is covered in a separate volume that is forthcoming.)

Ali Adil Shah II

Mahmud was succeeded by his son, 19-year old Ali Adil Shah, to the kingship of Bijapur. At the time of his accession to the throne, the Mughal prince Aurangzeb was on his second tenure as the viceroy of the Deccan. Almost immediately on Ali Shah assuming the throne, Aurangzeb mounted an expedition against Bijapur. Contemporary and even few modern historians provide two reasons that were put forward by the Mughal prince for undertaking this unprovoked invasion. The first was that the Adil Shahi king was unable to control the rebellious activity of the Maratha Chief, Shivaji, which was the responsibility of the Adil Shah as per the peace treaty that had been enacted earlier between the Mughals and Bijapur. To some extent this was a true allegation. However, the Mughal should have devised a plan with the Bijapur king to subdue the arrogant Maratha chief, rather than invade the Adil Shahi kingdom.

The second reason provided could also have been true, but the evidence is a bit more tenuous. Mahmud Adil Shah did not have any children and therefore the queen had adopted an orphan into the royal family and brought him up as her son and the heir apparent. In fact, during the initial phase of Ali Shah's rule, the queen acted as the Regent. The Muslim records of the time do not mention the adoption, but provides oblique references to the fact that the queen could not bear children. *[This is once again a questionable reference and wrong in all probabilities, since the Islamic religion permitted multiple marriages and nothing could have stopped the king from marrying again, especially when he was not able to have children with his first queen. Medieval kings, irrespective of their religion married many princesses and had multiple sons from different queens to ensure the progression of the dynasty.]* The adoption of Ali Shah is only confirmed by the reports of two European travellers, Tavenier and Thevenot, who visited Bijapur during this time and left accounts of the socio-political situation in the Adil Shahi kingdom. There is no need to doubt the words of these two Europeans, since the adoption was also given as the reason by Aurangzeb for his invasion. According to Muslim law, adopted children were not recognised as the lawful heirs to the father's property. Aurangzeb claimed that in the absence of a natural heir, the Bijapur kingdom lapsed to the Mughal Empire, since it was a vassal state.

Aurangzeb laid siege to Bijapur with a large army, refusing all offers for peace provided by Ali Shah. Even though peace overtures were being made, the Adil Shahi kingdom offered stiff and obstinate defence. While the siege was in progress, information was received that the Mughal Emperor Shah Jahan had fallen ill making it necessary for Aurangzeb to proceed to Delhi in haste. He accepted a rapidly concluded peace treaty that gave him an enormous tribute, lifted the siege and started his march back to Delhi with a large, powerful and rich army, which was personally loyal to him.

The Afzal Khan Episode

As soon as Aurangzeb departed from the Deccan, Shivaji who had been lying low for some time, took the opportunity to carry out a series of raids into imperial Mughal, as well as Bijapur, territories. Irritated by this affront, Ali Shah decided to crush the Marathas for good. He gathered a large army and placed it under the command of Afzal Khan, an experienced and trusted general, giving him explicit instructions to defeat and eliminate Shivaji. In 1659, Afzal Khan set out with the huge army consisting of 5000 cavalry, 7000 specially-trained infantry and a large artillery force. The specially trained force was meant to cater for the hilly terrain at the core of the Maratha territory and to neutralise the guerrilla tactics that Shivaji habitually employed.

As the Bijapur army advanced ponderously, Shivaji kept retreating while carrying out hit and run raids at random. The large army was enticed to enter the Mahabaleshwar hills, bringing them close to the Maratha stronghold at the fort of Pratapgarh. Here, Shivaji proposed a one-on-one meeting with Afzal Khan to discuss terms to arrive at an amicable peace, giving the impression that he was overwhelmed by the strength displayed by the Bijapur general and his powerful army. Sure of his superior strength, Afzal Khan agreed to the meeting without any aides. Arriving alone at the designated meeting area, Shivaji surprised the Bijapur general by attacking him with two daggers. Although Afzal Khan attempted to retaliate, he succumbed to his injuries. Earlier Shivaji had instructed his forces to surreptitiously surround the Bijapur army. While the attack on the person of the general was being carried out, the Maratha forces simultaneously attacked the Bijapur army. Leaderless, the Bijapur army fled in confusion, with a large number of them being killed in the melee.

Following this defeat of the Bijapur army, Shivaji plundered the kingdom, reaching to the wall of the capital itself. Ali Adil Shah could not countenance this brazen act of the Maratha chief and raised another army to bring him to heel. He entrusted the command of the army to Fazl Khan, son of the slain Afzal Khan, who was also a reputed general. However, this time the king accompanied the army in its march into Maratha territory. Shivaji once again adopted his usual guerrilla tactics and withdrew from the plains of Bijapur into the hilly, Maratha country. His intent was to draw the Bijapur forces far away from their home base and then prolong the war indefinitely in order to logistically wear out the Adil Shahi army. However, in the few unavoidable pitched battles that had to be fought during the retreat, the Bijapur forces were decisively victorious.

Once the Marathas were ensconced in their own territory, they emerged out of the hills and carried out successful hit-and-run raids into the fringes of the Bijapur forces at will, repeatedly harrying the Muslim army. Even though Fazl Khan fought with great bravery and tactical skill, he was unable to bring the campaign to a successful conclusion. After a drawn out campaign in which no one was gaining

The Final Collapse

any recognisable edge, a sort of peace was concluded in 1662, with a two-way bargain being arrived at after negotiations. It was decided that Shivaji would acknowledge Ali Shah as his suzerain in return for which he would be permitted to retain all his conquests as Maratha territory. The territory ceded encompassed the entire Konkan coast from Kalyan to Goa as well as the region above the Sahaydri mountain ranges starting from the River Bhima all the way to River Varna, a strip of land about 130 miles long and 100 miles wide. From the terms of the peace it is obvious that the Maratha chief was able to dominate the negotiations. It was also an indication of the waning power of the Adil Shahi dynasty.

The peace lasted for about six years during which Bijapur showed some signs of rejuvenation. However, this was a deceptive indicator. In reality, the kingdom was gradually decaying from the inside while retaining an external illusion of strength and domination.

Traveller's Tales

Few European travellers visited Bijapur around 1648-50 and left fairly accurate descriptions of the capital and the kingdom. Descriptions of Bijapur so far had always included ecstatic descriptions of the beauty and magnificence of the architectural splendours that is supposed to have abounded around the capital. It is noteworthy that mid-17th century write-ups of Bijapur does not mention its architectural wonders, but only mentions the large number of goldsmiths and jewellers who plied their trade in the market. This change in the description has to be interpreted as the decline in the wealth available at the treasury for the king to indulge in building great monuments. It is certain that the Adil Shahis were already on the path of decline and eventual fall.

The Dutch traveller Baldoeus visited Bijapur in 1660, or thereabouts. He estimated the size of the kingdom to be about 250 leagues long and 150 leagues wide. (One league can be approximately assumed to be three miles, although

> the exact measurement vary in different places between three and 3.45 miles) However, even Baldoeus does not mention any particular building or public works as being of particular interest. This absence of any mention of building works of note indicate the gradual decline of the dynasty's capacity to expend wealth on the beautification of the capital and their inability to undertake welfare activities because of lack of resources.
>
> It is obvious that by the mid-17th century, the Adil Shahi king was merely clinging to power and that storms were battering the dynasty.

The Mughal Interlude

In 1666, a Mughal force under the Rajput general Jai Singh marched into Bijapur, ostensibly to collect the arrears in tribute to the Mughal Emperor that had remained unpaid by the Adil Shahis. Ali Shah recognised the threat and offered to pay the entire amount due, but Jai Singh refused to accept the offer. Left with no choice but to fight, Ali Shah raised a large force to face-off with the Mughal forces. It is highly likely that Shivaji, always at odds with the Mughals whom he considered to be foreigners, also contributed to the Bijapur army. Bijapur still had some of the old spark left and put up a strong and spirited defence. During the ensuing battle and siege, the Mughal army was hit by a plague that decimated their ranks. Jai Singh was defeated and was forced to retire to Kirkee, renamed Aurangabad since it had been Aurangzeb's headquarters while he was on his second tour as viceroy of the Deccan. Some narratives also mention the township as Daulatabad, although the authenticity of this claim is suspect.

Even though the Mughal forces withdrew from Bijapur, Ali Shah could not take advantage of the victory. The kingdom was far too weak to undertake any offensive action against the retreating adversary. Ali Shah could not even enforce his will. Although Bijapur had been saved, the 'victory' came at a high price. Ali Shah had first to make major concessions to Shivaji for his assistance and also agree to pay a yearly tribute to the Maratha chief. The tables had been clearly turned by the vassal against the master. The annual tribute was intended to stop Shivaji from enforcing a levy, called chouth, over Bijapur territory. Ali Adil Shah had lost control over his kingdom. Bijapur was now at the mercy of the Maratha chief and open to invasions by the Mughal forces.

> ### 'Chouth'
>
> Chouth was a levy, which was the equivalent of one quarter of the total revenue that was produced. The Marathas levied this tax over all the territories that they controlled, even temporarily, and also on territories that they raided. By paying 'chouth', the districts, even if they were not ruled or even under the control of the Marathas, avoided debilitating raids that they mounted on territories that did not comply.
>
> It is a fact that over a century later, the Marathas in the zenith of their power, was able to levy chouth over the greater part of the entire sub-continent—from the River Cauvery in the south to the River Ganga and the foothills of the Himalayan ranges in the north.

Soon after repelling the Mughals, in 1672, Ali Adil Shah died. He was succeeded to the throne by his 5-year old son, Sikandar Adil Shah. This accession was immediately followed by a bitter civil war initiated by rival factions vying for power. A senior noble, Khawas Khan had assumed the role of the Regent to the infant-king and was initially supported by two other powerful ministers—Abdul Karim and Muzafar Khan.

A Second Mughal Intervention

Not long after placing Sikandar Shah on the throne, the ministers and the Regent fell out with each other, starting a bitter rivalry. It is reported in some chronicles that the quarrel between the ministers was instigated by some Brahmin agents owing allegiance to Shivaji. However, this cannot be verified. Khawas, unable to control the feuding ministers, appealed to the Mughal Emperor for assistance and promised the hand of a Bijapur princess in marriage to one of the emperor's sons. The emperor send an army under the command of Khan Jahan, ostensibly to assist the Regent and then to escort the princess to Delhi, but in reality with the express order to annex Bijapur to the empire.

Before the Mughal army could reach Bijapur, the people came to know of the Regent's approach to the Mughal Emperor that was considered treachery and rose up in indignant revolt. They murdered Khawas Khan and replaced him with Abdul Karim as the Regent. The new Regent and the people of Bijapur got together and started preparations to oppose the Mughal army. Popular support for Abdul Karim's preparations for the defence of the kingdom was overwhelming. In the ensuing battle for Bijapur, the Mughal army was defeated and forced to move out of Adil Shahi territory.

Aurangzeb, now the emperor in Delhi, attempted diplomatic measures to seize control of Bijapur, He send an agent to the Adil Shahi court, nominally an overture as a mark of friendship, but in reality with a clear mission to subvert the loyalty of the nobles and to divide them. A period of confusion and danger for the Bijapur kingdom ensued. Never one to pass an opportunity to enhance his own position, Shivaji who had already declared himself Raja in 1674, rapidly consolidated the jagir of Tanjore and Gingee that had been granted to his father earlier by Mahmud Adil Shah.

Capture of Tanjore – The Truth

Many accounts in Indian historical narrative mention that Tanjore (Thanjavur) was captured by the Marathas under the leadership of Shivaji. This is incorrect. Tanjore and the supposedly impregnable fort at Gingee were captured by Bijapur forces despatched by Mahmud Adil Shah in 1637. The invasion of the Carnatic was an attempt by the Adil Shah to increase his territorial holdings as compensation for the loss of territory in the north.

This Bijapur expedition to the south was commanded by Shahaji, the Maratha chief and Shivaji's father, who had

> been forced to join the service of the Adil Shahi king after a long career as a rebel commander. Since he was an extremely successful military commander, he was subsequently given Tanjore and Gingee as a personal jagir by Mahmud Adil Shah. Therefore, the region remained Bijapur territory and was not 'conquered' by the Marathas.

The Maratha Intrigue

While Shahaji was still serving as a vassal to the Bijapur king, his son Shivaji had risen in revolt in the traditional Maratha territories. In response, the Adil Shahi king imprisoned Shahaji for a period of time hoping to subdue his troublesome son and when this attempt failed, had send a force under Shahaji himself to quell the rebellion. Nothing much was achieved by this expedition. By this time Bijapur had weakened as an independent state and Shivaji continued his 'independent' rule of the territories that he controlled. He now took over the territories that had been granted as jagir to his father—Tanjore and Gingee—added Vellore to the holdings and placed his step-brother Venkoji in charge. Venkoji was placed as Shivaji's deputy and not of Adil Shah, the Bijapur king.

There was a bit of a scuffle between the brothers for control of this territory with Venkoji claiming independent control of the entire jagir, which Shivaji opposed and managed to stop. Thereafter, Venkoji ruled as the deputy to Shivaji. This episode of the disagreement between the two brothers is beyond the scope of this narrative and will be described in a later volume that narrates the history of the Marathas. Here it is only necessary to assert that the Carnatic Maratha kingdom was not the result of Maratha conquest, but created by Maratha enterprise made possible by the decline and weakness of the Adil Shahi dynasty. Venkoji went on to become the founder of the Tanjore Maratha dynasty that lasted till the last decade of the 19th century. Of course, like most other Indian dynasties of the time, the later day kings of the dynasty were only nominal kings whose rule was restricted to small territorial holdings. Thus the southern territories of the Adil Shahi kingdom passed on to the Marathas.

After establishing control of his holdings in the Carnatic, Shivaji went on to create an alliance with the Qutb Shahi king of Golconda with the aim of annexing Bijapur and dividing it between them.

The Third Mughal Attempt

When the Bijapur Regent came to know of the Maratha-Qutb Shahi plan to annex Bijapur, he sought the assistance of the Mughal general in the region. Together, the Bijapur-Mughal combine mounted a pre-emptive attack on Golconda. Although the Bijapur army had repeatedly shown their mettle in the defence of their capital, a number of extraneous factors intervened to make this invasion of Golconda a bitter defeat. On the retreat, the Bijapur army, which had not been paid for some months, mutinied. At this ignoble moment in the once powerful Bijapur army, the Abyssinian governor of Adoni, Masud Khan, stepped in to take opportunistic control. He paid off some elements of the army and disbanded the rest, and proclaimed himself the senior minster.

Aurangzeb was not happy with this arrangement and demanded that Bijapur pay the arrears of tribute that was due and also fulfil the terms of the treaty, which had stipulated sending a Bijapur princess to Delhi to cement a matrimonial alliance. Masud Khan rejected the demand and refused to either pay tribute or send a reluctant princess to Delhi. As was the normal flow of events, a Mughal army under Dilawar Khan was despatched and laid siege to Bijapur. It is reported as an aside that the designated Bijapur princess, even though she was not happy with being given away to a Mughal prince, voluntarily went over to the Mughal amp to avoid Bijapur being brought under siege. However, the Mughal commander refused to lift the siege of the capital.

With the siege becoming desperate, Masud Khan turned to Shivaji for help. In return he promised to hand over the Raichur Doab to the Marathas. Shivaji led his forces in assistance and ravaged the rear of the Mughal army all the way to their base in Aurangabad. However, Dilawar Khan proved to be obstinate and continued with the siege of Bijapur. True to the promise that he had given the Adil Shahi Regent, Shivaji now turned around and attacked the rear of the Mughal army surrounding Bijapur and started to cut their supply lines. Unable to create a breach to defeat the defending Bijapur forces and harried by the interdiction in the rear by the very capable Maratha forces, Dilawar was forced to lift the siege and retire to Mughal territory. Bijapur had been saved again by a slender thread and at a very high cost. The transfer of the Raichur Doab to the Marathas for their help reduced the once grand kingdom to a minor province enclosed within the expanding Maratha territory.

The Beginning of the End

The people of Bijapur were unhappy with the turn of events and the complete reduction in status and power of the kingdom. On popular demand, Masud Khan the architect of the dubious victory, was forced to step down and two other nobles, Shirza Khan and Syed Makhtum, were elevated to the senior ministers' role. In this interim period Shivaji died and had been succeeded by his son Sambaji to the leadership of the Marathas. The new ministers of Bijapur now made an error of judgement that was to prove fatal for the Adil Shahi dynasty.

The ministers, perceiving—wrongly as it turned out—that with the death of Shivaji, the Maratha power was waning, demanded the return of the territory granted to the Maratha king, from his son Sambaji. The demand was refused and the Bijapur kingdom did not have the military might to retake the territories by force. Although the status quo prevailed without any military confrontation, the demand managed to alienate the Marathas who had so far maintained a reasonably benign relationship with the Adil Shahi kings. With this one intemperate act of the new and inexperienced ministers of Bijapur, the Adil Shahis lost the only reliable ally who could have come to their assistance to hold back the repeated attempts of the Mughals to annex their kingdom. The Adil Shahis and the Marathas had shared an intimate relationship that oscillated between friendship and indifference under different circumstances. The rupture of this connection with the Marathas spelt the beginning of the end of the Bijapur kingdom as an independent entity. The end was now not only inevitable, but also very near.

The Final Collapse

Bijapur now went through a few years of relative peace, for the last time in its eventful history of the Adil Shahis. The Mughal Emperor,

Aurangzeb, never gave up his intention to subdue and annex the Deccan, more for religious reasons than any ambition to increase the territorial holdings of his empire. He was a bigoted religious fanatic who held the Deccan Muslim kingdoms in equal and utter contempt as he did the Marathas. Aurangzeb considered the Marathas infidels who were accursed heathens and 'vile dogs'. The Muslim kingdoms of the Deccan he considered to be detestable heretics. His ire was particularly directed at Bijapur and Golconda, the two surviving kingdoms that also happened to follow the Shia persuasion in their religion. Further, these kingdoms also permitted infidels to thrive in their territories; for example, the chief minister of Golconda was a Hindu; and both states practised a policy of tolerance towards Christians.

Aurangzeb had also noticed, during his extended stay in the Deccan, that a number of Hindu practices and even superstitions had crept into the daily religious rituals of the Deccan Muslim community. In the 300 years of 'independent' practice of the Islamic faith in the peninsula, a great intimacy had developed between the races and religions that mingled together more harmoniously than anywhere else in the sub-continent. There was not only mutual tolerance, but a strong affection had developed between the Muslim rulers and their Hindu subjects in the kingdoms of Bijapur and Golconda. This robust link was weakened only by the decline of the Adil Shahi power. For these reasons, the religious fanaticism of the Mughal Emperor made him abhor the Deccan Muslims as much as he hated the heathen Hindus.

In 1683, Aurangzeb gathered a large army and started his final assault on the Deccan, which was to last for the next 24 years and from which the emperor would not return to his capital in Delhi. The army that moved out of Delhi was so large that it fell upon all in its way like an avalanche in slow-motion, grinding everything in its path to powder and sweeping away all obstructions that sprang up before it in its own ponderous manner. By 1685, Sholapur had fallen to the Mughals and Bijapur was firmly sighted in Mughal eyes. By the time Mughal advance outposts reached the vicinity of the River Bhima, Bijapur forces and the population had rallied behind their ruler as in earlier times, and put forward a cohesive defence. They achieved some initial success against the advance parties of the Mughal army. Gradually, and inexorably, the

The Final Collapse

Mughal commanders kept tightening the net around Bijapur, closing in without any let up.

The Adil Shahi forces were well-officered and efficient. But the might of the Mughal army was such that they had to continually fall back. The odds against them were very heavy. Even so, the defence of Bijapur was extremely well conducted. Bijapur is situated in the middle of a vast wasteland that is almost a desert. The Mughal forces unable to live off the land, suffered great privation through the lack of adequate provisions and were unable to make an impression on the defenders. As the siege dragged on, Aurangzeb personally took charge of the operation. Even then the defence of Bijapur continued with great gusto. Finally, the garrison of indomitable fighters succumbed to hunger, rather than the military might of the Mughals, and capitulated on 15 October 1686.

Sikandar Adil Shah, the last of the Adil Shahi kings, was imprisoned in his own capital and poisoned to death a year later on Aurangzeb's direct orders. Bijapur was annexed as a Mughal province—a once great kingdom reduced to vassalage and the dynasty made extinct on account of the religious intolerance by the last emperor of yet another magnificent Muslim dynasty.

Chapter 15

A CONCLUDING EVALUATION

The Adil Shahi kingdom of Bijapur was centred on modern Bijapur district in Karnataka, in the western region of the Deccan Plateau. Earlier it had been a province of the more extensive Bahmani kingdom. The Bijapur kingdom was established in 1489 and ceased to exist as an independent entity on its annexation by the Mughal Empire on 12 September 1686. The founder of the Adil Shahi dynasty, Yusuf Adil Shah, started his career as a Bahmani sultan-appointed governor of the province. In fact even though he declared independence during his governorship, he and his son continued to title themselves as 'Adil Khan'. Khan, meaning Chief in Mongolian and later adapted to Persian, conferred a lesser status than Shah which indicated royal rank and title. It was only Yusuf Khan's grandson who first used the title Shah after which the term Adil Shah started to be used commonly to indicate the ruling monarch of the Bijapur kingdom.

The kingdom's borders varied throughout its two centuries of existence, although the northern boundary remained relatively stable. After the initial stabilisation, the kingdom expanded southwards into the Carnatic, and also encompassed the Raichur Doab after the defeat of the Vijayanagar Empire in the Battle of Telikotta in 1564. Later campaigns by kings of the 17th century extended the formal borders of the kingdom and at its greatest extend, Bijapur exercised control over the region as far south as Bangalore. The kingdom was bound in the west by the Portuguese colony of Ga and in the east by the kingdom of Golconda.

From its inception, Bijapur was immersed in the instability and chaos of regional politics resulting from the collapse of the Bahmani dynasty. Being constantly in conflict with the other successor kingdoms to the Bahmani kingdom curtailed its ability to develop to its full potential, even during times of relative peace. However, the greatest threat to the Adil Shahi kingdom's security started in late 16th century, from the Mughal encroachment into the Deccan. As the most powerful of the Deccan Muslim kingdoms, Bijapur was specially targeted by the Mughal emperors and their generals. Even though it was Mughal power that finally eclipsed the Adil Shahi dynasty, the decline actually started and was accelerated by the continual rebellion by the Marathas who occupied the hilly tracts to the north-west of the kingdom. The Marathas were responsible for weakening the kingdom, which made it relatively easy for the Mughals to impose various treaties that subsequently forced the Adil Shahi's to initially accept Mughal suzerainty, and fifty years later to its outright annexation as a Mughal province.

The Arrival of the Marathas

From the inception of the kingdom, the Adil Shahis occupied vast tracts of land in the Konkan, which were inhabited by Marathi-speaking peoples. Historically, the first Maratha chief to be gifted a 'jagir' by the Adil Shahi king of Bijapur was Shahaji. According to the prevalent medieval custom, a jagir was to be controlled and used by the person it was granted to, while the king continued to own the land that was gifted. Even though control rested with the 'jagirdar', the person who obtained the jagir, the forts in the region remained under the direct control of the king, who garrisoned it with his own forces. This system ensured that a jagirdar did not become too powerful or usurp the land. Shivaji, Shahji's son and successor, declared independence from the Adil Shahi suzerainty by taking over the forts in his area of influence—much larger than the jagir given to his father—and also by capturing some forts even outside his territorial control. During this period of conquest, Shivaji captured the forts at Rohida, Sinhgad, Purandar and Torana. He also defeated the Mores clan who were loyal to the Adil Shahis and were in possession of Javali.

The Marathas and the ruling Muslim nobility traditionally shared cordial relations. Ibrahim Adil Shah was partial to the Marathas, giving

A Concluding Evaluation

them important positions in the military as well as in civil administration. During his reign and for some time thereafter, official documents were written in both Arabic/Persian and Marathi. Many official documents of Bijapur that survive to this day starts with an invocation to Saraswati, the Hindu goddess of learning. Muhammad Adil Shah changed this policy of tolerance and cordiality with the Marathas and attempted to drive a wedge between the Maratha chief and other minor chieftains who were courtiers in his court and therefore, loyal to him. However, he seems to have overestimated the loyalty of the minor Maratha chieftains in his court, because the attempt to divide the Marathas did not achieve any success.

Muhammad's son, Ali Adil Shah took a somewhat more conciliatory stance, perhaps because of the fact that Adil Shahi power was waning and there were continuous internal dissentions, some of which were already out of control. The dynasty's power was further eroded when Shivaji killed Afzal Khan, one of the most powerful and effective military commanders of Bijapur. When a common enemy in the form of Shaistha Khan arrived on the horizon, the Marathas and the Adil Shahis were forced to reconcile and put up a combined front. Shaistha Khan was a Mughal general who had been send by the Delhi emperor with a large army to conquer the Adil Shahis and subdue the rebellious Marathas. Both the quarrelling groups understood the need to contain the Mughal ambition to establish roots in the Deccan. By this time, the Nizam Shahis of Ahmadnagar had been destroyed and their kingdom annexed to the Mughal Empire. Neither the Marathas, nor the Adil Shahis, wanted a re-enactment of the Mughal conquest of Ahmadnagar. The need to reconcile, led to a pact between the two antagonists.

This treaty of 1667 not only perpetuated the alliance between the Adil Shahis and the Marathas, but also gave Shivaji independent rule of all the territories that he controlled. Even though Shivaji was only nominally responsible to the Bijapur king for the past few years, this treaty made him independent and removed the 'vassal' status from him. His earlier proclamation of being a 'king' was now finally vindicated. His status as an independent ruler was further established by Shivaji sending a Maratha envoy, Babaji Naik Punde, to be stationed permanently in the court at Bijapur. Maratha power had finally arrived on the scene as an independent entity. Shivaji was formally anointed and crowned King of the Marathas in 1674, which not only enhanced his prestige and stature but also awarded him the prerogative to negotiate independently with other kings in a credible manner.

The fundamental principle on which Shivaji built his Deccan policy was the need to maintain internal unity in the Deccan in order to ensure that the Mughals were not permitted to gain a foothold in the region. Therefore, he strived continually to ensure the strength of the Deccan as a whole in facing the Mughal incursions. He made concerted attempts to contain the incessant in-fighting and mutual hostilities of the Deccan Shahi kingdoms, especially after the death of Ali Adil Shah. After being crowned King, Shivaji entered into an alliance with the Golconda king, Abu Hassan Qutb Shah. The Bijapur kingdom was at a very low ebb at this time and Shivaji and his ally the Qutb Shahi king felt that Bijapur needed to be 'rescued' from foreign invasion and occupation. Accordingly they hatched a plan to partition Bijapur territory between them, although it never came to fruition.

Shivaji – The Regionalist

In the proposed carving up of Bijapur, the coastal region between Rivers Tungabhadra and Kavery were to become Maratha territory. Gingi, later to play an important role in Maratha history, became the centre of Maratha power in the Peninsula. Even though Shivaji was the prominent leader of the Marathas, they were also riddled by internal rivalries. One of the major groups, the Gorpade clan, had been introduced to the Adil Shahi dynasty by Shahaji, during the reign of Ibrahim Adil Shah. They entered Adil Shahi service and remained loyal to the Adil Shahis, even playing a major role in the capture of Shahaji himself. There was an underlying animosity then onwards between the Gorpade and Bhonsle clans.

There was also division within the house of Shivaji itself. The relationship with his step-brother, Venkoji had not traversed a smooth path and had degenerated into battles and occasional conflicts. In battle, Hambirao Mohite the commander of Shivaji's forces, defeated Venkoji. However, being the younger brother, Shivaji pardoned him and restored him to the control of the Maratha jagir in the Carnatic that had been granted to their father Shahaji. The correspondence between the brothers indicate that Shivaji had demanded half the territory of the jagir that their father had bestowed on Venkoji. This demand seems to have been amicably resolved.

In creating the alliance with the Qutb Shahi king, Shivaji persuaded other Maratha chiefs, including Maloji Gorpade the powerful head of the Gorpade clan to join the alliance. He also made Venkoji, controlling the southern Maratha territories from Tanjore, nominally as a vassal of Bijapur, join the alliance. At this stage, the Muslim kingdoms of the Deccan was divided between the long-feuding Phirangi and Deccani factions of the nobility. In Bijapur, the successor to Ali Adil Shah was his minor son and therefore Bijapur was ruled by the Phirangi noble Bahlol Khan. The alliance was primarily directed against this Adil Shahi regent.

In Bijapur, Bahlol Khan ruling as supreme authority succumbed to selfish ambition, and sought an alliance with the Mughal commander in order to usurp power for himself to be declared king of the Adil Shahi kingdom. The Deccani noble faction, under the leadership of Sarja Khan, opposed this move and defeated Bahlol Khan and his supporters in 1677. Bahlol Khan died a few months after this defeat. Shivaji had been steadfast in supporting the minor king, Sikandar Adil Shah, assisting the Deccani faction with troops and money as well as himself harassing the Mughal forces that were encroaching the Bijapur kingdom. After Bahlol's defeat the Mughal forces withdrew, prompting Shivaji to claim, in one of his letters, that he had averted the danger to Bijapur and protected the Adil Shahi dynasty from extinction.

In gratitude for the assistance, Sikandar Adil Shah granted Shivaji a large tract of land in the south. He also permitted Venkoji to stop paying the annual tribute due for the jagir, effectively giving away the Carnatic territory around Tanjore. In many authenticated documents, Shivaji reiterates his policy of opposition to rule by the Phirangi faction, steadfastly supporting the Deccani nobles as the true rulers. As mentioned earlier, Shivaji was totally focused on protecting the Deccan from Mughal invasion. He was consistent in attempting to get the Phirangi faction out of the Deccan, since these nobles instinctively sided with outsiders like the Mughals who invaded the Deccan.

At this stage in the development of Maratha political power, Shivaji was a focused regionalist rather than a religiously motivated clan leader. His priority was in maintaining the independence of the Deccan and not ensuring the continued 'independence' of Hinduism as a religion. This attitude is demonstrated by the fact that although he could have easily dethroned the Adil Shahi dynasty after the defeat of Bahlol Khan and the Mughal army, he chose not to, leaving the boy-king as the legitimate ruler. He did not consider the Shahi dynasties of the Deccan, especially the Adil and Qutb Shahis, as foreigners and maintained amicable relations with them. He definitely formed the concept of the Deccan being a separate entity from the territories north of the Vindhya ranges and also conceived of it being a single entity, not divided into different kingdoms. From this belief developed the Maratha concept of a pan-Indian kingdom.

Bijapur – The Metropolis of the Deccan

From mid-16th century, when the Adil Shahi dynasty made it their capital, Bijapur became a prominent city in India. It gradually became a celebrated centre of culture, trade, commerce, education and learning. At its zenith, Bijapur was the epicentre of a confluence of different communities, religions and races. In some records, Bijapur is depicted as surpassing the grandeur of Delhi and Agra, the great cities of the Mughal Empire.

Even before the Adil Shahis adopted Bijapur as their capital, the town was the Khilji governor's seat. The Bahamani Prime Minster, Mahmud Gawan created a separate province with Bijapur as the capital and also had his own property in the city. A number of mausoleums and other edifices were built in Bijapur during the Bahamani rule. Thus Bijapur was already a fairly large and important town even before the Adil Shahi dynasty took it over and made it their capital. Since the battlefield victories of the Adil Shahis, especially the victory over the Vijayanagar kingdom, brought in enormous wealth, the kings spend lavishly in the beautification of the capital. Three consecutive kings—Ali, Ibrahim, and Muhammad Adil Shahs—created many monuments, palaces and other structures in the city. The rule of these three monarchs, lasting almost a century (approximately 1560 to 1650 or so) could well be considered the golden age of Bijapur.

The Adil Shahis were secular in their outlook and liberal in their patronage of art and education. Therefore, Bijapur attracted scholars, poets, painters, dancers, Sufi saints and other men of art and literature from all parts of the world, belonging to all races and religions. In the 17th century, Bijapur was known by the epithet 'Palmyra of the Deccan'. At the absolute height of its glory, the population of Bijapur is supposed to have been in excess of 980,000, a huge number for the times. Around 1604-05, the Mughal Emperor Akbar despatched a noble from his court, Mirza Asad Beg, to carry out a diplomatic mission in Bijapur. Asad Beg had seen both Agra and Delhi in their greatness and wrote an account of Bijapur in his travelogue, Wakiat-e-Asad Beg. The description of Bijapur compares it favourably with the two cities of the Mughal Empire. His graphic description of the city gives an authentic account of the prosperity and richness of this flourishing city.

On Education and Learning

Bijapur had been a centre of learning in South India, much before the advent of Muslim rule in the Deccan. This is confirmed by the bi-lingual, Marathi-Sanskrit, inscriptions that are visible under the Persian epigraph in the Karimuddin mosque (16th century vintage) in the city of Bijapur. It is reported that Karim ud-Din was the Khilji governor of Bijapur and found the educational and learning effort in the city to be at par with the efforts seen at Benares in North India. Hence he named Bijapur the 'Benares of the South'. During the Bahamani rule, Bijapur continued its academic excellence.

One of the most learned Sufi master of India, Ain ud-Din Junnaidi who authored more than 120 books, lived in Bijapur from 1371 until his death in 1390. His disciples and other Sufis continued to keep the master's work and traditions alive in Bijapur for a long time. The academic excellence that emanated from Bijapur was such that it was considered the 'Second Baghdad' in the output of scholarly works and activities, especially in the Islamic world. Most of the kings of the Adil Shahi dynasty were men of learning, being well-versed in religion, logic, grammar and the sciences. They also patronised teachers and scholars, encouraging and facilitating discussion and debate amongst them.

Bijapur boasted a Royal Library under the control of one Sesh Waman Pandit who had more than 60 calligraphers, gilders of books and illuminators working permanently under his supervision. Further, a noted scholar Shah Zayn Muqbil is reputed to have owned more than eight hundred manuscripts of which he had himself authored three hundred. As a result of royal patronage, a large amount of literature in Arabic, Persian and Deccani Urdu had been written during the Adil Shahi rule. In addition, local languages like Marathi, Kannada and Sanskrit also flourished. In fact Kannada was the official language in the southern part of the Bijapur kingdom with all official transactions being done in this language.

Conclusion

The Adil Shahis could be considered to have been the leading house amongst the five Deccan Shahi kingdoms for most of their existence. This is a dubious honour since they were also the instigators of rivalries and conflicts, although the kings of the regime cannot truthfully be added to the list of perennial trouble makers for all neighbours who allied with other kingdoms and changed sides without any scruples. To the contrary, some of the Adil Shahi kings were steadfast in their loyalty to their allies.

It is to the credit of the Adil Shahis, that they were instrumental in creating a composite and secular culture in Bijapur. Being immigrants from Iran, the Adil Shahis brought the culture and traditions of the Middle-East to Bijapur. After gaining power, they insisted on following the customs, rituals and court culture of Persia, thereby influencing the ceremonies, etiquette, art and even architectural developments of the Bijapur kingdom. Gradually this led to a synthesis of this foreign 'culture' with local sensibilities that in turn was heavily influenced by the majority Hindu culture. The splendour of Bijapur at the zenith of its glory demonstrates this secular mindset of the Adil Shahi dynasty.

Section IV

THE SUCCESSOR KINGDOMS OF THE DECCAN

THE NIZAM SHAHIS OF AHMADNAGAR

The events that unfolded for in Ahmadnagar, towards the end of the Nizam Shahi rule, are common embodiments of the long history of the sub-continent, both past and into the future—an initial succession struggle in a kingdom followed by the weaker faction seeking assistance from an external power base, normally a more powerful kingdom; the external agency attacking and defeating the legitimate rulers of the kingdom; and the kingdom itself thereafter being annexed by the external power.

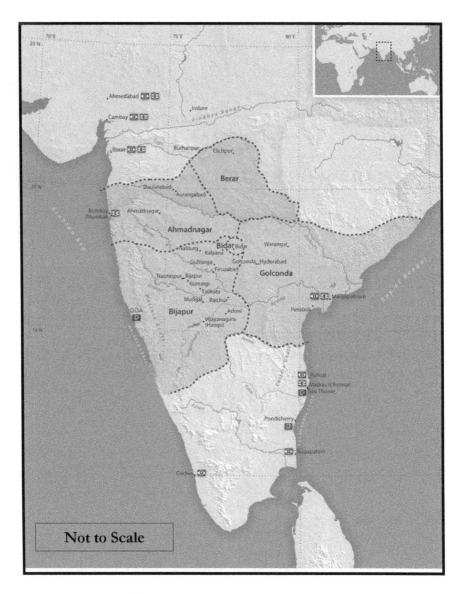

The Deccan in the 17th Century

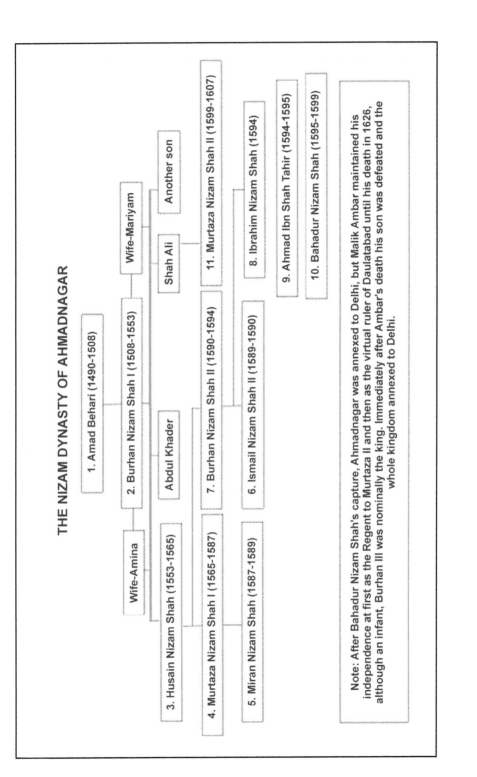

Chapter 16

THE FOUNDING OF A KINGDOM

During one of his frequent wars, Ahmad Shah Bahmani took a Brahmin boy captive and converted him to Islam, renaming him Malik Hussein. The boy proved to be extremely intelligent and endowed with considerable all-round ability. The Sultan had him educated along with his eldest son and heir apparent, Muhammad. Hussein therefore became well-versed in Persian and Arabic. Muhammad became Sultan in 1462 and almost immediately promoted his 'studying-companion' to the rank of 'One-Thousand', placing him in-charge of a thousand soldiers. Hussein was subsequently made the royal falconer, from which appointment he assumed the surname of Bahri (falcon was called beher in Persian, Arabic and Urdu). Since he was a capable and loyal officer, he was subsequently conferred with the governorship of the Telangana province.

In the internecine conflict between the Phirangi and Deccani nobles that wracked the Bahmani kingdom in its declining years, Hussein played an important part in getting the king to slay Mahmud Gawan on trumped up charges. The killing of Mahmud Gawan by the conspiracy of the Deccani nobles was one of the last nails in the coffin of the Bahmani kingdom, although it may not have been apparent at that time to the perpetrators. Hussein became the Prime Minister after the removal of Mahmud Gawan and started to wield unlimited powers across the kingdom. The Sultan honoured him with the title Nizam-ul-Mulk. Hussein now despatched his son, Malik Ahmad who was a chip of the old block, as capable and intelligent as his father, to the Konkan coast where some minor chiefs were concocting a rebellion.

Malik Ahmad conducted an extremely successful campaign in the Konkan, subduing a number of hill-country chieftains, reducing a number of forts and collecting a great deal of wealth in the bargain. He was able to gain effective control of the entire coastal region. In acknowledgement of this achievement, Hussein appointed Ahmad as the governor of Junair.

> ### Mahmud Gawan's Warning
>
> Malik Ahmad was married to a princess of the Bahmani dynasty. While totally believable and a number of contemporary chronicles mention this fact, there is no proof available to confirm this fact. Mahmud Gawan had observed the extraordinary ability of Malik Hussein and also seen that Hussein's son, Malik Ahmad, had grown up to not only be a competent military commander but also an able administrator. Gawan, ever the faithful minister of the Bahmani rulers, had felt that the father-son duo would become a threat to the declining Bahmani dynasty. Further Mahmud Gawan was suspicious of the loyalty of Malik Hussein towards the Bahmani Sultan, knowing that he supported the Deccani faction of the nobles. Therefore, Mahmud Gawan had advised the Sultan to keep the father and son separated at all times. However, Gawan's murder by the Sultan himself was proof that his advice was obviously not heeded.

After placing his son as the governor, Hussein now felt that he was powerful enough to depose the Bahmani Sultan and claim the throne. Accordingly, around 1486, he rebelled and seized control of Bidar after declaring independence from the Bahmani dynasty. He also asked his son to come to Bidar and join forces to strengthen their position. However, the best laid plans go awry even at the best of times and the country was at best turbulent. The rebellion went awfully wrong. Muhammad Shah, Hussein's old friend and the nominal Bahmani Sultan, could not countenance his rebellion and had Hussein strangled to death. There were sufficient number of nobles who were willing to commit this act since jealousy of Malik Hussein's power was rife in the court. In committing the murder, Muhammad was assisted by Pasand Khan, one noble opposed to the meteoric rise of Hussein.

When Hussein was murdered in Bidar, his son Malik Ahmad was half-way through his trip to join his father. On hearing of the assassination, he turned around and retired to his governorship, making camp at the township of Khiber. He assumed the titles of his father and called himself Ahmad Nizam-ul-Mulk Bahri. He established Khiber as the seat of his government and commenced to rule independent of the Bahmani Sultan. Although he started his rule as Ahmad Nizam-ul-Mulk, a few years later he assumed the royal title of Ahmad Nizam Shah. However, his rebellion was not going to be accepted without any action by the Bahmani ruler, although it was already the twilight of the dynasty.

Bidar Retaliates

By this time, Kasim Barid was in control of Bidar as well as the Bahmani Sultan and the broken remnants of the erstwhile kingdom. He knew that Ahmad had to be brought under control if the Bahmani kingdom was not to implode fully. Therefore, he send a large army under the command of Nadir-ul-Human to subdue Ahmad Nizam-ul-Mulk. Ahmad was an able soldier and a brave commander. He adopted the Maratha tactic of conducting guerrilla warfare against the numerically superior adversary to great effect. After whittling down the Bidar army through asymmetric means, Ahmad conclusively defeated them with the commander Human being killed in the battle.

Kasim Barid now send an even larger force under the combined command of 18 Bahmani nobles to destroy Ahmad Nizam-ul-Mulk. The army is reported to have been over 18,000 in strength. Fully aware of the superiority of the invading force, Ahmad eluded the main force and did not fight any pitched battles. Through astute manoeuvring, he managed to arrive at the rear of the main Bidar force with a small force of about 3,000 elite cavalry, attacked and entered Bidar. After entering Bidar, Ahmad displayed his superior tact. First he freed all the relations of his father who had been imprisoned after Hussein was murdered. Thereafter he imprisoned the families of the nobles who were leading the army against him and carried them away as hostages. However, he treated them honourably at all times.

Bidar retaliated by changing the commanders of their forces, removing the 18 nobles and placing Jahangir Khan, the governor of Telangana at the head of the army. Jahangir had a considered and well-deserved reputation as an able commander. Ahmad, outnumbered and aware of Jahangir Khan's capabilities, retreated to the hills of the Konkan. He moved from Junair to Paithan where he received further reinforcements from his own minister. Jahangir Khan besieged the town. When monsoon broke out, Jahangir let down his guard presuming that Ahmad's forces would also stand down. Grabbing this opportunity, Ahmad Shah carried out a surprise attack at night on the Bidar forces. He found most of the force to be intoxicated and was able to put a majority, including Jahangir Khan, to the sword. The Bidar army was conclusively defeated and fled in confusion. Ahmad laid out a grand garden and built a palace where this victory was achieved and called it Bagh-i-Nizam. This battle conducted in 1489 itself came to be referred to as the Battle of the Bagh in later days.

After this victory, Ahmad Nizam-ul-Mulk declared complete independence, and on the advice of the Adil Shah of Bijapur, took the title of Shah and assumed other trappings of royalty, including the white umbrella, normally reserved for ruling monarchs. There were some objections from the nobles to Ahmad assuming the white umbrella, which were duly pacified.

The White Umbrella in the Deccan

When Ahmad Shah assumed the white umbrella, signifying his royal status as a king, most of his nobles took exception. Till this time, Ahmad had been content with the title Nizam-ul-Mulk and was considered equal to all of them although he was the leader of the group—a sort of chief among equals. In order to placate this embryonic rebellion, Ahmad explained that he had taken the umbrella to shield himself from the sun and not as a sign of royalty. The nobles reluctantly accepted this explanation with the caveat that they were also permitted to carry white umbrellas, as could all subjects of his territory. Ahmad, having adopted the title of Shah, had no choice but to accept this condition.

From this time forward, in Ahmad Shah's kingdom, the king and the beggar carried the same umbrella. In order to recognise the king, a red cloth was attached to his umbrella, while all others carried purely white umbrellas. Gradually the custom spread across all the kingdoms of the Deccan. This custom, smacking of egalitarianism, was completely contrary to the custom of the Mughals where only the emperor was permitted to carry any kind of umbrella. *[The Indian concept of 'Chatrapati', the ruler under whose umbrella the kingdom prospered, may have been the origin of the concept of carrying an ornate umbrella amongst the kings of the sub-continent. This term indicated the security, peace and stability that was prevalent under the virtual umbrella of the ruling king, indicating the spread of his control.]*

With the declaration of independence by Ahmad Nizam Shah and the unsuccessful attempts by Kasim Barid, now the de facto ruler of Bidar, to bring him under control, the dismemberment of the Bahmani kingdom was complete. Different parts of the kingdom were held by powerful nobles, who were busy consolidating their positions. Out of this chaos emerged five independent kingdoms—generically referred to as the Shahi kingdoms—that are being discussed in this narrative. The five rulers believed that by establishing independent kingdoms they would bring about peace and prosperity to the Deccan and contain the debilitating situation that prevailed towards the end of the Bahmani rule. However, this belief turned out to be a pipe dream. For the next two centuries, these five kingdoms were constantly at war with one another, forming and breaking alliances against each other, at times for nothing other than pure jealousy. Two centuries of contests for supremacy and inability to cooperate against external aggression drove all of them in the path to oblivion.

Although two centuries could be considered a relatively small period in the broad spectrum of Indian history that spread across millennia, the Shahi kingdoms of the Deccan left behind a clearly noticeable legacy that influenced the religious development of the Peninsula. Further, they also had a long-lasting influence on the literary, art and architectural development of the region.

Complex Intrigues

Ahmad Shah was an enlightened ruler and did away with the concept of ruling through tyranny and oppression. He brought in values of justice and equality into hid domain, which in turn added to the loyalty of the nobles and thereby strengthened the fledgling kingdom. In addition, he reorganised the army on new lines. Since the strength of a country in medieval times was founded on the strength and efficacy of its army, this initiative also contributed directly to enhancing the status and stability of the new kingdom.

At the time of Ahmad Shah creating his new kingdom, Daulatabad was under the possession of two brothers, Maliks Wojah and Ashraf. They had formerly been in the service of Mahmud Gawan and later been given independent charge of the township by Malik Hussein. They were efficient administrators and in firm control of the town. Malik Wojah was married to Ahmad Shah's sister. When a son was borne to Wojah, Ashraf felt vulnerable fearing that he would be dispossessed of his position as co-ruler. He therefore murdered both his brother and nephew. At this act, Ahmad Shah's sister Bibi Zainab, sought her brother's assistance in bringing the perpetrator of her husband's murder to justice.

Ahmad Shah assembled his army and advanced towards Daulatabad. During the march, he provided assistance to Kasim Barid who was besieged in Bidar by Yusuf Adil Shah. Ahmad intervened and lifted the siege, although the Adil Shahi king had earlier been a mentor to him. The fundamental policy of all the Deccan Muslim kings was to ensure a balance of power that was palatable to all. Therefore, whenever one king or the alliance of two or more started to display a proclivity towards becoming more powerful than the others, instinctively the others joined forces to bring them down. While this attitude may have ensured that each kingdom maintained some semblance of

The Founding of a Kingdom

sovereignty, it also ensured that each kingdom individually remained weak and open to intervention by external forces. This lack of unity was the Achilles' heel that finally brought down the Muslim kingdoms of the Deccan. The result of this informal policy was that the five main kingdoms made, broke and then reformed alliances of convenience, which lasted only to deal with a particular emergent situation. These alliances could be summed up as the ultimate expression of selfish motivation and lasted for the entire duration of the existence of the five Shahi kingdoms.

Having raised the siege of Bidar, pushing back the Adil Shahi forces and restoring Kasim Barid, Ahmad Shah proceeded towards Daulatabad, the city of his original intent. However, the fort proved far too strong to be subdued by direct assault, even by the superior Nizam Shahi forces. Ahmad Shah then resorted to surrounding the fort and prepared for a long drawn siege. Even the siege was initially not effective and Ahmad Shah started to enforce a scorched earth policy by laying waste the farmland around the fort at harvest time in order to deny the besieged population recourse to food and other resources. Further, he started to build a town near to Daulatabad, at a village called Bhingar, to act as the headquarters that controlled the siege activities. This was the township that stood near the River Sina, between Juna and Daultabad, which Ahmad Shah named after himself – Ahmadabad. The construction of the new town was completed rapidly in two years.

The siege of Daulatabad continued for seven years and the fort was only taken by Ahmad Shah around 1500, after the death of the indomitable Malik Ashraf. From that date onwards, Daulatabad remained in the possession of the Nizam Shahi kings, till such times as the extinction of the dynasty.

Other Minor Actions in a Complex Scenario

In 1495, the Bahmani governor of Telangana, Qutb-ul-Mulk Deccani died. The Bahmani Sultan took advantage of this unforeseen vacancy in the ruling hierarchy to attempt once again to re-establish some vestige of power for the dynasty and appointed Dastur Dinar as the governor. After a few months, Dastur was asked to vacate the position in favour of Qutb-ul-Mulk Hamdani, who was appointed as a reward for loyal service to the Bahmani kingdom. This unprovoked dismissal greatly offended Dastur Dinar, who was obviously rankled. He decided to rebel and seek autonomy by not handing over the province to the newly appointed governor. He also requested Ahmad Shah for assistance in maintaining his autonomy. Accordingly, Ahmad Shah send a contingent under one of his generals to Telangana. The forces of Dastur and the Nizam Shahi contingent together managed to capture some amount of territory to add to the existing holding.

The Bahmani Sultan, now at the end of his own resources, sought Yusuf Adil Shah's assistance to suppress the rebellion and bring Dastur to heel. In response to the request, Yusuf Shah send a large army to Telangana. In the ensuing Battle at Mahendri, the combined Nizam Shahi-Dastur army was comprehensively defeated; Dastur himself was captured, produced before the Bahmani Sultan, and condemned to be beheaded. However, he was later pardoned, reinstated and his old jagir restored. The reinstatement was not liked by Yusuf Adil Shah who had coveted Dastur Dinar's jagir and had hoped to annex it as 'payment' for the assistance delivered to the Bahmani Sultan. He therefore attacked the hapless Dastur, who fled to the protection of Ahmad Shah. Unable to come to a compromise and not individually powerful enough to defeat the other in battle, the Adil and Nizam Shahi kings appealed to the Bahmani Sultan to settle the dispute. This shows that even when the Bahmani kingdom was in a fairly powerless state, the Sultan held sufficient moral power for the breakaway kingdoms to appeal to him for arbitration regarding disputes between them. The Sultan ordered Yusuf Adil Shah to desist from proceeding against Dastur Dinar, an order that was reluctantly obeyed. Thereby the crisis was resolved.

The pursuit of self-interests was vividly demonstrated by the dealings between the Adil Shahis of Bijapur and the Nizam Shahis of Ahmadnagar. Ahmad Shah acted as a check against the growing power and stature of Yusuf Adil Shah. Yusuf Shah on his part was always attempting to annex the truncated parts of the floundering Bahmani kingdom, looking out to increase his territorial holdings. Ahmad Shah was shrewd enough to join the Adil Shah in this pursuit of partitioning the remnants of the decaying Bahmani kingdom. This opportunistic act had a dual purpose. First, it paved the way to ensuring that his own territorial holdings continued to increase; and second, that Yusuf Shah was not only monitored, but also kept under check. Such duplicitous behaviour was common amongst the successor kingdoms in the Deccan.

The League against Bijapur

In 1504, Yusuf Adil Shah proclaimed Shia Islam as the official religion of his kingdom. This declaration was followed by a certain amount of confusion within the Adil Shahi kingdom. More importantly, the proclamation was considered heretical by the other Muslim kingdom, who continued to adhere to Sunni Islam tenets. Ali Barid, controlling Bidar the erstwhile Bahmani capital and also ruling the remnants of the Bahmani kingdom on behalf of the puppet Sultan, took the initiative and created a League to oppose the 'heretic' Yusuf Shah. The League consisted of all the other Sunni kingdoms of the Deccan.

The League initiated action with Ali Barid capturing some territory from Bijapur around Gangawati and with Ahmad Nizam Shah demanding that Yusuf Shah surrender certain territory that the Nizam Shahi claimed as their own. Yusuf Shah retaliated by recapturing the territories from Ali Barid and 'respectfully' declining Ahmad Shah's demand. The refusal of Ahmad Shah's demand led to the Nizam Shahi forces, by some reports with as many as 10,000 cavalry, invading Bijapur territory. Once again Yusuf Adil Shah responded by overrunning Ahmadnagar territory and laying waste the countryside. Subsequently the Adil Shahi forces entered Berar, where the ruling Imad Shahi king Ala ud-Din joined them. Yusuf Shah thus re-established his primacy in the Deccan. At this turn of events Ahmad Nizam Shah prudently withdrew from the League and returned to his capital.

Other Setbacks

Ahmad Shah was ambitious and considered the actions against Bijapur to have damaged his standing and stature as an independent king. In fact, the fiasco of the League against Bijapur annoyed him. He was keen to reclaim and even enhance his prestige. An opportunity arose when there was a succession struggle in the minor kingdom of Khandesh and one of the claimants to the throne, took refuge in Ahmadnagar. Ahmad Shah decided to attack Khandesh and ensure that the claimant he supported was placed on the throne.

> ## Khandesh
>
> Khandesh was a small principality situated in the valley of the River Tapti. It was bounded on the north by the Vindhya and Satpura Ranges, in the south by the Deccan Plateau, west by Gujarat and in the east by Berar. It was part of the Tughluq Empire at the height of its territorial spread and thereafter continued as a feudatory of the Delhi Sultanate, but as a semi-autonomous territory. At some stage during this existence in a somewhat vague status, it had become embroiled in a conflict with Gujarat. However, peace had been established, which led to stability and relative prosperity.

Khandesh was now ruled by Daud Khan. The Nizam Shahi forces encountered not only the forces of Daud Khan, but an army that had been buttressed by the forces of Malwa. The combined army of Khandesh and Malwa, put Ahmad Nizam Shah's forces to flight. Once again Ahmad Shah had to be content with a withdrawal to his capital without achieving his objective.

On the death of Daud Khan, succession struggle re-erupted in Khandesh. Ahmad Shah decided once again to intervene in the domestic affairs of Khandesh to support his protégé. However this time, he had cobbled an alliance with Ala ud-Din Imad Shah of Berar and together they proclaimed the Nizam Shahi proxy as the king of Khandesh. Ahmad Shah entered Khandesh and placed his proxy on the throne. However, Ahmad Shah had not contented with another claimant to the throne supported by the Sultan of Gujarat, Muhammad Shah. The Gujarat Sultan advanced into Khandesh and Ahmad Shah returned to his kingdom, leaving a small contingent as a token protection force for his proxy on the throne. Muhammad Shah easily removed this person from the throne and placed his own protégé as the ruler. Thereafter he returned to Gujarat, not having faced any serious opposition during this campaign. Before returning to his own kingdom, Muhammad Shah chastised Ahmad Shah in public, humiliating him by calling him the son of a slave, who should never have attempted to become a king. Ahmad Shah had no recourse to counter this humiliation and re-establish his credibility.

Ahmad Shah's final days as king were despondent. In 1508, his trusted minister and valiant general, Nasir-ul-Mulk Gujarati, died, leaving the king with no loyal and reliable advisor. Gujarati had been the mainstay for the kingdom's administration while the king pursued his ambitious activities. His death put an end to Ahmad's ambition and his restless quest for glory, recognition and stature. Ahmad Nizam Shah never recovered from the sudden demise of his wise, faithful and trustworthy minister. He died in 1509-10, leaving behind a seven-year old son to succeed him. Before his death, Ahmad Shah made all the nobles take an oath of allegiance to the child-king.

Ahmad Shah's Personality

Ahmad Shah had a well-deserved reputation for being a person with great ability. His father had ensured that he received a comprehensive and excellent education. As a minor, he was devoted to literary and cultural pursuits and as a teenager he had become proficient in the art of warfare. As a result, Ahmad Shah was renowned for being highly virtuous and for practising enormous self-control. Stories of the greatness of his virtues and his exemplary character abound in accounts by contemporary writers. He was generous and forgiving to a fault, encouraging less capable officers to strive harder to achieve better results, rather than meting out punishment for incompetence. This trait made the nobles devoted to him, assuring complete loyalty.

The Introduction of Duelling

Ahmad Shah was upset by the endless feuds that his nobles brought to him for arbitration and settlement. He therefore introduced the concept of duelling to settle differences between nobles, which were brought to his notice. The idea was for the contending persons to enter into a duel, with the first to inflict a wound on the opponent being declared the winner. The entire process was very tightly regulated, with Ahmad Shah himself monitoring the activities. Further, blood feuds emanating from duelling deaths were prohibited to ensure that the nobles did not form adversarial groups.

A strategic analysis of Ahmad Shah's activities clearly indicate a flaw in his character that led to personal dissatisfaction for the king. All initiatives that he undertook was intended to improve his position as a newly established king. However, he was not a good judge of character and despite his extensive education, he was not adept at understanding the geo-political developments around his kingdom. The combination of these two factors almost always led to all his initiatives developing into setbacks and humiliations. Even the good counsel of his minister, Gujarati, could not hold back the debacles that Ahmad Shah created on his own.

He continually underestimated the power of the Gujarat Sultan and also the influence of the two factions of nobles at home—the Phirangis and the Deccanis—not being able to judge and select the group that he should support fully. The divisions between the nobles always interfered with the progress of any initiative that he wanted to advance. Even though driving ambition made him extremely restless, he was unable to realise any of his dreams, repeatedly being defeated by more powerful kings and/or alliances in the neighbourhood. His only achievement was to have been able to carve out an independent, but minor, kingdom to the south of Pune, stretching from the west coast of the Peninsula to the borders of the kingdom of Khandesh.

Chapter 17

CONSOLIDATION
BURHAN NIZAM SHAH I

Burhan Nizam Shah was only seven years old when his father, Ahmad Nizam Shah the founder of the dynasty, died. Ahmad had elicited an oath of allegiance towards the young prince from his nobles. They were true to the oath and the business of governance was undertaken by nobles loyal to Ahmad Shah. These nobles were led by Mukammal Khan and his son Mian Jamal ud-Din, who was conferred the title Aziz-ul-Mulk. The combination of ambition and perceived opportunities to achieve them have the capacity to lead astray even strong-willed and loyal people and Mukammal Khan was no exception. In short order he started to behave as an independent king rather than a benign Regent to a minor king, which irritated the 'phirangi' faction of nobles. In addition, Jamal ud-Din was vain and insolent, treating everyone with disdain and harshness.

In order to bring down Mukammal Khan and his son, the opposing nobles formed a group and plotted to remove Burhan from the throne with the intention of replacing him by his brother Rajaji. This proposed coup failed and the phirangi group fled to Berar, where they were provided shelter by Ala ud-Din Imad Shah then ruling that country. This group, resident in Berar under the leadership of Rumi Khan, continued to stir trouble in Ahmadnagar. They cited a number of reasons and instigated Ala ud-Din, then only titled Imad-ul-Mulk not having assumed the more exalted and royal title of Shah, to invade Ahmadnagar. On the advance of the Berar forces, Regent Mukammal

Khan marched out to meet the invaders who were encamped near Ranubari. In the ensuing battle the Berar army was soundly defeated.

On the army being defeated, the phirangi group abandoned Ala ud-Din who then fled the battlefield and was forced to seek refuge with Adil Khan Faruqi III, then ruling the kingdom of Khandesh. Faruqi negotiated a peace between Berar and Ahmadnagar, facilitating the reinstatement of Ala ud-Din to his throne in Berar.

Burhan's Early Years

The Regent Mukammal, although harbouring great ambition, ensured that the young king was properly educated and from an early age was well-versed with the 'duties of a king'. Therefore, Burhan was aware of the events taking place within his kingdom and also in the neighbourhood. At a very early age he had started to take a keen interest in the geo-political developments in the Deccan.

Immediately after the Ahmadnagar-Berar clash, Ali Barid the Regent ruling Bidar on behalf of the Bahmani prince, attacked the Adil Shahi kingdom of Bijapur. Ali Barid was comprehensively defeated by the Ismail Adil Shah and his powerful army. Burhan made his first foray into diplomacy at this stage, negotiating with the Adil Shahi king and ensuring that Ali Barid was reinstated to the regency to continue to control both the capital Bidar and the hapless Bahmani prince/nominal sultan. At this stage, the Bahmani dynasty existed only in name, since the sultan was retained on the throne as a puppet by the Barids to provide legitimacy for their de facto rule of the last remnant part of the once extensive Bahmani kingdom. Unhappy with his condition the Bahmani Sultan, Mahmud Shah, displayed some vigour and escaped to Berar. In the acrimony that ensued, Burhan sided with Ali Barid, while the Deccan was rapidly marching towards yet another self-defeating conflict. Before conflict could actually break out, Mahmud Shah rejoined the Barids. The Bahmani Sultan's rebellion against the Barids was stillborn.

Watching this fiasco unfold, Ala ud-Din Imad-ul-Mulk realised that the real strength behind the Barid clan was the Nizam Shahis, with the young Burhan starting to flex his muscles and influence the complex and flexible political scenario. Ala ud-Din therefore felt the need to cut the young prince of Ahmadnagar down to size. As a result two battles ensued between Berar and Ahmadnagar—one at Boregaon and the other on the banks of the River Deonati—which were both indecisive. Young Burhan now mounted a vigorous invasion of Berar, forcing Imad-ul-Mulk to flee and seek sanctuary in Gujarat. Considering this a sort of victory, Burhan initiated negotiations to annex the district of Pathri from Berar, reportedly on the request of the local inhabitants. To be fair, he offered one of his own districts producing equal revenue in exchange for Pathri. Although in an inferior position, the Berar king refused the deal. Therefore, Burhan laid siege to Pathri and even though the Berar forces defended the fort strenuously, the fort and the district were annexed to Ahmadnagar.

Fall and Rise Again

During this time Burhan fell in love with a dancing girl, Ameena, and was besotted by her. He married her and made her the principal queen. More importantly, he started to spend all his time with her, neglecting his kingly duties and gradually fell to debauchery. Mukammal Khan, his chief minister, who was already fairly old attempted to bring the king back to his senses by asking him permission to retire. He requested Burhan to assume responsibility of the administration and retired to his estate, where he died soon after. Instead of realising the mistake he was making and taking charge of the administration, Burhan appointed Mukammal's son, Aziz-ul-Mulk, as the prime minister and continued his profligate lifestyle.

Jamal ud-Din Aziz-ul-Mulk was tyrannical in his behaviour and cruel and unjust in his dealings. He gathered all power in his hands and, as was usual in such circumstances, started to entertain ambitions of becoming an independent ruler, and of supplanting the Nizam Shahi dynasty. Accordingly, he succeeded in gradually isolating Burhan from all his attendants, permitting only old nurses to look after him. Thereafter Aziz-ul-Mulk attempted to poison the king, which was thwarted by one of Burhan's old wet nurses. This episode made Burhan appreciate the threat to his own safety and to his dynastic rule. He and some loyal nobles wanted to get rid of Aziz, but realised that they were not strong enough to do so, since all power now lay with Aziz-ul-Mulk. Burhan therefore recruited the governor of Antur, Jai Singh Ji, to help him get rid of Jamal ud-Din. A plan was hatched to lure Aziz-ul-Mulk to Antur by Jai Singh who pretended to have rebelled against Ahmadnagar. This would in turn make it necessary for Jamal to march to Antur. However, Jamal ud-Din send troops under the command of his brother to quell the rebellion.

Burhan and Jai Singh's forces in Antur defeated the Ahmadnagar forces and after having captured the commander, insulted him, cut off his nose and sent him back to Ahmadnagar. This act angered the Aziz-ul-Mulk who personally marched to Antur. On the way he was waylaid by Burhan, who captured and blinded him. Burhan Nizam Shah then assumed full administrative responsibilities of the kingdom personally and appointed a pious and learned man, Mir Rukn ud-Din, as the chief minister. However, piousness is not an anti-dote to ambition when power is thrust on a person and Rukn ud-Din became arrogant and egotistical, forcing Burhan to remove him from the post on the appeal of the people.

The Story of Shah Tahir

Shah Tahir was a descendent of the Fatimid Caliphs of Egypt and was an unrivalled genius, learned and skilled in statesmanship. His ancestral home was in Khurd, a village in the Qazim district of Persia at the border of Gilan. He reached a very high degree of spiritual and secular attainment and became famous across Persia and also the greater Islamic world for his knowledge, attracting students from far and wide, especially from Egypt and Bokhara.

He followed the Shia sect and therefore a large number of his students also converted to the Shia sect. Gradually his fame came to the attention the Shah of Persia, Ismail Safvi, who invited Tahir to the royal court. Tahir became a courtier of the inner circle, becoming extremely popular and influential in court. His influence and fame reached a level where the Shah himself was irritated with the rapid rise of Tahir's stature. In order to reduce his direct influence and keep him away from the capital, the Shah appointed him the principal of the school at Kashan.

Such was the reputation of Tahir that students now flocked to Kashan, which was soon turned into a great centre of learning. Shah Tahir continued to rise in prominence and therefor elicited the jealousy of local nobles and other officials, even though Tahir was personally not an ambitious man. Lesser men becoming jealous of the achievements of genuinely great personages is a recurrent theme in history. In order to damage Tahir's reputation the nobles of Kashan wrote to the Shah alleging that Tahir was engaging in the propagation of the Ismailia faith, which was abhorrent to both the Shias and the Sunnis. Further, they accused Tahir of corresponding with the kings of the neighbourhood to instigate them to rebel against the Shah of Persia. On receiving these missives and without verifying the correctness of the accusations, the Shah ordered Tahir's execution.

The Diwan (Prime Minister) at the court of the Shah was Tahir's friend and send him an early warning regarding the impending execution. This facilitated Tahir's hurried departure from Kashan in mid-winter, leaving all his wealth behind. He sailed across the Arabian Sea reaching Goa on 19 April 1520. From Goa he proceeded to Bijapur, but could not find favour with Ismail Adil Shah. Tahir then went on the Haj to Mecca and returned to settle in Parenda under the patronage of Makhdum Khwaja Jahan.

The wheels of fortune turn in inexplicable ways. While Tahir was resident in Parenda, a nobleman from Ahmadnagar visited Khwaja Jahan and was very impressed by Tahir's learning and erudite lectures. On returning to Ahmadnagar, he explained to Burhan Shah the excellence of Tahir's learning and the effectiveness of his religious discourses. Burhan in turn invited Tahir to his court and was also deeply impressed by his learning. He settled Tahir in Ahmadnagar and appointed him to give discourses in the Jami-Masjid.

Relationship with Other Deccan Kingdoms

The last Bahmani Sultan, Kalimullah Bahmani, continued to harbour ambition to regain the old status of his once powerful dynasty. Since he did not have the wherewithal to achieve this objective, he surreptitiously approached the Mughal king Babur, freshly enthroned in Delhi after defeating the last Lodi emperor, for assistance in regaining his balkanised kingdom. In return he promised to cede to Babur the districts of Berar and Daulatabad. Unfortunately for Kalimullah, this correspondence leaked out and in the acrimony that followed, he was forced to flee the country. The Adil Shahi ruler in Bijapur refused him sanctuary, whereas Burhan Nizam Shah offered to provide shelter. However, Shah Tahir advised Burhan against giving refuge to the hapless Bahmani Sultan and accordingly he was banished from Ahmadnagar. This event, where Burhan was considered an alternative to the Adil Shahis and his banishment of the Bahmani Sultan, could be considered the real declaration of the Nizam Shahi kingdom's independence.

Almost immediately after the final eclipse of the Bahmani kingdom, Bijapur initiated actions to form an alliance to fight the growing power of the Hindu Vijayanagar Empire. Ismail Adil Shah send Ahmad Haravi as the envoy to fashion what was an uneasy peace with Ahmadnagar as a prelude to mounting a war against the Raja of Vijayanagar. Ismail also gave his sister, Bibi Maryam, in marriage to Burhan Shah to seal the peace treaty. Burhan had demanded Sholapur as dowry for the marriage which was not forthcoming, which led to some misunderstanding that threatened to turn ugly and break the peace initiative. Tahir intervened again and persuaded Burhan to drop the demand for Sholapur to be handed over. The situation was controlled. However, thereafter Sholapur became the bone of contention between Bijapur and Ahmadnagar.

In Ahmadnagar, Ameena gave birth to a boy, named Muhammad Hussein. With the arrival of a son who was presumed to be the heir apparent, Ameena was celebrated as the 'would be queen-mother'. She and the other wives started to ill-treat Bibi Maryam, who in turn complained about her treatment to her brother, ruling in Bijapur. Ismail Shah remonstrated with Burhan and also abused and insulted the Ahmadnagar ambassador in his court. Tensions between the two kingdoms continued to mount and war became inevitable.

Burhan Shah's Wars

Understanding that war with Bijapur was certain, Burhan solicited the assistance of Ali Barid in Bidar and Ala ud-Din Imad-ul-Mulk in Berar and decided to take the initiative. The combined army of the three kingdoms advanced into Bijapur territory, initially to wrest Sholapur from Ismail Adil Shah. In turn, the Bijapur army moved to protect its territory. In the ensuing battle, Asad Khan Lari, the Bijapur commander, opposed and defeated the Imad-ul-Mulk who left the battlefield and retreated to Berar. On the Berar army leaving the field, Burhan Shah also withdrew from the battle, leaving a large booty that was captured by the Bijapur forces. Ismail Adil Shah now forced Ala ud-Din to join him against Burhan Shah and their joint forces captured Pathri. Almost immediately, Burhan joined hands with Ali Barid and recovered Pathri.

The Nizam Shahi–Barid combine now marched against Berar forcing Al ud-Din Imad-ul-Mulk to flee his kingdom and take refuge with Muhammad Shah I, then ruling Khandesh. In turn now, the Khandesh and Berar armies jointly attacked Burhan but was defeated by the Nizam Shahi–Barid armies. Sometime during this continuous series of battles and skirmishes, Ala ud-Din proclaimed himself equal to the other rulers and took for himself the title of 'Shah', becoming known as Ala ud-Din Imad Shah. Obviously, the trappings of royalty was an important part of establishing the stature of the king. To avenge the defeat at the hands of his erstwhile ally, Ala ud-Din appealed to Bahadur Shah, the Sultan of Gujarat, for assistance. This provided the Gujarat Sultan with an excuse to interfere in the Deccan, which had been his long time ambition. The internal squabbles of the Deccan now assumed a different hue.

The Gujarat Sultan Invades the Deccan

In 1528, Bahadur Shah I, the Sultan of Gujarat marched into the Deccan. On his way he was met by Ala ud-Din Imad Shah's son who escorted him to Daulatabad. Bahadur Shah's army consisted of 100,000 cavalry and 900 elephants. It is obvious that he had come with a different objective than to purely assist the Imad Shahi king. Burhan send a military contingent to assist the Daulatabad garrison, but they were easily defeated by the Gujarat forces. Since the fort could not be easily overrun, Bahadur Shah laid siege to Daulatabad. Burhan played for time, repeatedly requesting audience with Bahadur Shah and then delaying the meeting citing different reasons. Daulatabad was not an easy fort to capture and failing to bring the siege to a successful conclusion in a reasonable time, Bahadur Shah started to march towards Bidar.

During this march, Bahadur Shah was approached by envoys from Burhan Shah, Ismail Adil Shah and Ali Barid bearing presents, pleading with the Sultan to establish peace in the Deccan. The ulterior motive was also to convince him that the real culprit in creating the current chaos in the Deccan was Ala ud-Din Imad Shah, and that he was the real aggressor. These initiatives confirm three facts: first, the Gujarat Sultan was far more powerful than any of the Deccan kings, individually or in combination; second, the Deccan kings were aware that the Sultan was not in the Deccan for altruistic purposes but harboured ulterior motives to conquer and annex at least some parts of the Deccan for himself; and third, the Shahi kings were incapable of presenting a combined front even in the face of a common and powerful enemy. In the event, Bahadur Shah established peace between Berar and Ahmadnagar, accepted the token subservience of the other two kingdoms and returned to Gujarat. The real reason for this benign return to his own country could have been the fear of being away from his country for far too long, when the newly established Mughal Empire in the north was rapidly growing in strength and ambition.

Peace in the Deccan did not last long. The very next year Jafar Khan, son of Ala ud-Din Imad Shah, was back in Gujarat, complaining to Bahadur Shah that Burhan Nizam Shah had breached the peace conditions that had been established the previous year. He requested another Gujarat expedition to the Deccan. Accordingly, Bahadur Shah embarked again to pacify the Deccan and was joined on the way by the king of Khandesh with his forces. Other minor kings along the route submitted meekly to the powerful Gujarat army lumbering towards the Deccan. As they approached Ahmadnagar, Burhan became alarmed at the immense size of the Gujrat army and started to request assistance from his neighbours and friends. He asked for help from both Bijapur and Golconda and even wrote to Babur in Delhi for aid. However, the

Mughal had his hands full establishing his kingdom and battling local opposition, and therefore did not have the spare capacity to involve himself in the Deccan, even if he had wanted to. The opportunity was being offered to him at too early a stage in his Indian adventure. Similarly Golconda was preoccupied with the struggle inside Telangana and declined to assist the Nizam Shahi king.

Both Ismail Adil Shah and Ali Barid however, realised the full import and the possible cascading effects of letting Bahadur Shah overthrow Burhan Shah and provided full assistance. The Gujarat army easily expelled Burhan from the areas he had annexed from Berar—the districts of Mahur and Pathri—and then proceeded deeper into Ahmadnagar territory. During this march, Ali Barid came across a Gujarat contingent that had become separated from the main body and defeated it, also putting to flight a rescue party that had been send to bail out the original contingent. However, a larger Berar force, under Ala ud-Din Imad Shah fighting alongside the Gujarat army, forced Burhan Shah to retreat further into Ahmadnagar territory.

Bahadur Shah reached Ahmadnagar, occupied the Nizam Shahi palace for 40 days and then proceeded to Daulatabad, leaving Ala ud-Din to complete the capture of Ahmadnagar. Burhan attempted to defend Daulatabad and was defeated in a battle near the town, although he had also been joined by Ali Barid's forces. Even after this battlefield defeat, the siege of Daulatabad continued, since the commander of the fort was a resourceful and active soldier, who managed to hold the Gujarat forces at bay. At this juncture, Ali Barid the ever self-centred noble, switched allegiance from Burhan to the Gujarat Sultan and also made peace with Ala ud-Din Imad Shah. While the siege of Daulatabad was continuing, the Gujarat forces continued its winning march, laying siege to Pathri that had been recaptured by Burhan. Pathri was a strong fort and the fighting continued unabated.

The Deccan kings were, if anything, astute in their calculations of the geo-political developments. Burhan now started to send out peace overtures to Bahadur Shah, while also opening a conversation with Ala ud-Din Imad Shah. Ala ud-Din and Burhan had already realised that Bahadur Shah's ultimate intention was to annex both their independent kingdoms to the Gujarat Empire. To thwart this ambition, when the lull in the fighting at the onset of the monsoon season took place, Imad Shah took the opportunity to withdraw from the campaign and went back to his capital. Bahadur Shah was also a canny ruler and immediately realised the precariousness of his own situation—far away from his power base and with an extremely stretched logistical supply line that passed through enemy territory. He hastily concluded peace with Burhan on advantageous terms and returned to Gujarat. Burhan reclaimed Mahur and Pathri, which remained Ahmadnagar territory thereafter.

The Gujarat – Ahmadnagar Alliance

Burhan Nizam Shah was by now grown into an experienced statesman, having shed his irresponsible behaviour of his younger days. He carefully used the sagacity, learning and diplomatic skills of Shah Tahir to inveigle himself into the good graces of Bahadur Shah. In the interim period, Bahadur Shah had become even more powerful by defeating his long-standing adversary Malwa, and annexing it to the expanding Gujarat Empire.

A Far-fetched Report

An unsubstantiated report regarding Shah Tahir's mission to Gujarat states that he managed to get the Gujarat Sultan to pronounce Burhan with the title 'Shah', changing his title from Nizam-ul-Mulk to Nizam Shah. If this is true, the event would have to be considered the official establishment of the Nizam Shahi kingdom. This report is difficult to believe and would have to be discarded as incorrect.

The embassy of Tahir to Gujarat took place in 1531-32. It is reliably learned that the Nizam Shahi rulers assumed all the trappings of independence including royal titles as early as 1490. Further, the Gujarat Sultan was only a neighbouring sultan of equal status, at least nominally, albeit more powerful. Burhan would not have approached an equal to bestow royal titles to the Ahmadabad king. It is obvious that this claim was an embellishment added to the report in later days to establish the importance of Shah Tahir's diplomatic mission.

Bahadur Shah was by this time was cognisant of the political changes taking place in North India and also extremely aware that with the annexation of Malwa, he shared a common border with the fledgling Mughal kingdom. He could foresee the on-coming competition with the Mughals and therefore wanted as many allies as possible to stand by his side to withstand the oncoming storm of the future. He therefore welcomed the move by the Nizam Shahis to cement their relationship.

In creating an avowed friendship and alliance between the two kingdoms, both the kings had their own ulterior motives. Creation of alliances, throughout history and even in modern times, has always been done with carefully calculated advantages that accrue to each of the parties. *[There are no instances of a nation, especially if it is powerful and independent, entering into an alliance with another country purely on altruistic reasoning. In the modern day, some of the more developed nations have a minority of people believing that material aid being provided to a less developed nation should be without any caveats. This belief is naïve at best and foolish at worst. Aid is the precursor to the creation of alliances. Alliances are made, and aid provided only if they bring some political, geo-strategic or trade advantages to the more powerful of the participating nations.]* In this instance, Bahadur Shah, ever the ambitious and active Sultan, wanted assistance from Ahmadnagar to subsequently confront the Mughals in the north and drive them out of the sub-continent. The annexation of Malwa had sharpened Bahadur's vaulting ambition. He envisaged a possibility to become the ruler of the entire north and western part of the sub-continent.

Burhan Nizam Shah, by now a proficient king, harboured his own designs regarding the alliance with Gujarat. He wanted to make use of the alliance and, if necessary the powerful Gujarat military machine, to reduce his rival Deccan kings to servitude. He would then become the undisputed power in the Deccan. It is clear that ambition underpinned the basis of the alliance. On the creation of the alliance it also became clear to the other Deccan kingdoms that Burhan was on an equal standing with Bahadur Shah, who had so far dominated the Deccan kings at will. Ahmadnagar and Berar had become sort of vassal states to Gujarat during the Gujarat campaigns of the previous decade, unable to stand up to the overwhelming power that Bahadur Shah was able to bring to bear. Both Burhan and Ala ud-Din now threw away the yoke that had been imposed on them during the two consecutive

Gujarat campaigns into the north-western Deccan. Essentially, both the Shahi kingdoms had bent in the Gujarat storm, but had not been broken.

> ### The Fall of Gujarat – An Aside
>
> Bahadur Shah was a Sultan of restless ambition, although this was not without cause; after all he had managed to annex Malwa, with whom Gujarat had harboured a long-standing rivalry. After the annexation of Malwa, it was inevitable that Gujarat would come into confrontation with the Mughal kingdom that had been established to the north of Malwa and with whom they now shared a common border.
>
> Although Burhan Nizam Shah was in an alliance treaty with Bahadur Shah, he instigated the Mughal king, Humayun, to attack Gujarat. Humayun first drove Bahadur Shah out of Malwa and then defeated and expelled him from Gujarat itself. (The details of this confrontation will be provided in a later volume in this series, which deals with the Mughal Empire.) While he was engaged in these battles of survival, Bahadur Shah had sought assistance from his 'allies' in the Deccan. Both Burhan and Ala ud-Din had refused to help, which obviously hastened the fall of Bahadur Shah. Both the Deccan kings did not have the foresight to visualise that a similar fate would befall them at a later time. Bahadur Shah, from being a powerful Sultan became a fugitive. Gujarat came under Mughal control and was never again able to interfere or dictate terms to the kingdoms of the Deccan as an independent entity.

The Deccan Shahi kingdoms fell back into their usual routine of—fighting internecine wars that did not amount to any lasting victory or defeat; creating alliances between themselves that the kings felt no compunction in breaking at will even within months of them being formed; being completely self-absorbed in all actions that they initiated; and all the while carefully ensuring that no one individual king became powerful enough to establish a hegemony.

Dealings with Vijayanagar

The internecine wars and rebellions in the Deccan led to a situation wherein the rebel nobles in one country took refuge in another one inimical to the first. In these manoeuvrings, invariably the Nizam Shahis and Adil Shahis in Bijapur almost always found themselves in opposing sides, supporting adversarial groups. However, all these conflicts remained indecisive, and therefore festered along with no obvious conclusion. The times were uncertain and the Deccan kings were paranoid regarding any one of them becoming relatively more powerful either own their own or through external alliances.

In such a geo-political climate, it was not surprising that in 1552, Burhan entered into an alliance with the powerful Hindu king Sadashiva Raya ruling Vijayanagar. The alliance was meant for mutual assistance in two independent enterprises. Ahmadnagar would deploy its army alongside that of Vijayanagar to assist Sadashiva Raya in recapturing Raichur and then the combined armies would help Burhan take Sholapur, both from the Adil Shahi kingdom of Bijapur, then ruled by Ibrahim Adil Shah. Although the alliance was not as smooth as was expected because of mutual mistrust between the two rulers, they managed to achieve their individual objectives of enlarging their own territories as planned.

Buoyed by the success of their enterprise, the combined army now proceeded to lay siege to Bijapur itself. At the very beginning of the siege, Ibrahim Adil Shah fled to the safety of another fortress at Panhai. While the Bijapur siege was underway, Burhan Shah took ill and on the advice of his court physicians, returned to Ahmadnagar. When he was informed of this development, Sadashiva Raya lifted the siege and retired to his capital. Thus the attempt by one Deccan kingdom to subsume another remained 'half-baked' without reaching successful completion.

A Religious Struggle

At the height of his power, Burhan Nizam Shah changed the official religion of his kingdom to the Shia sect. Some reports suggest that this was done under the influence of Shah Tahir who adhered to and propagated the Shia persuasion of Islam. In any event, Burhan's decision was opposed by a large number of his subjects led by Maulana Pir Muhammad, who had been his tutor for some time when he was a young boy. The Maulana led his followers in rebellion and also started to correspond with some army officers, instigating them to revolt against the king.

The Maulana and his followers then went on to surround Tahir's house, accusing him of being the root cause for the king's actions. Burhan was encouraged by his nobles to act against the rebels but hesitated to initiate any drastic action, stating that he had vowed not to injure his own teacher, the Maulana. Finally under pressure from the nobles to control an emerging chaotic situation, the Nizam Shahi army was send to attack the rebels. On the arrival of the army, the Maulana was deserted by his followers. He was captured and was to be executed, but his life was spared on the intervention of Shah Tahir. Further, he was released from prison after four years and permitted to leave the Nizam Shahi country. The Maulana is reported to have entered into the service of Bairam Khan, the regent ruling the Mughal Empire on behalf of the child-king Akbar and to have been the king's tutor for a brief period of time.

Even though the incipient revolt against the imposition of the Shia sect was stamped out quickly, the unilateral change of religion brought Burhan Shah into conflict with the rest of the Deccan kingdoms. These kingdoms started to organise and anti-Nizam Shahi confederation. Surrounded by adversarial neighbours, Burhan made an attempt to appeal to Humayun in the north for assistance. Once again no help was forthcoming from the Mughal, who was at that time engaged in a life and death struggle with Sher Khan (later Sher Shah Suri) for the throne of Delhi. Realising that military resistance to the combined might of the other kingdoms would be futile, Burhan resorted to diplomacy. He managed to win over the Sultan of Gujarat, the most powerful member of the anti-Nizam Shahi confederacy. In the meantime he was strengthening his army. Having split the confederacy, Burhan went on to defeat Ibrahim Adil Shah in battle, thus ending the confederacy against Ahamadnagar. Around the same time, the Persian Sultan, Shah Ismail Safavi, heard of the Nizam Shahi conversion to the Shia sect and send an embassy to Ahmadnagar that increased Burhan Shah's stature. The confederacy against Ahmadnagar was still born.

Relations with Persia

The Persian embassy was headed by Aga Salman Tehrani and was received cordially by Burhan Shah. Subsequently it was reported that Shah Tahir had been insulted by the Persian ambassador, which made Burhan reduce the status of the Persian delegation in the court. However, Tahir managed to maintain good relations with the Persian Sultan. The on-going relationship culminated in the arrival of few Sayyids to the Ahmadabad court. The Sayyids were learned persons of noble parentage who claimed to be the descendants of the Prophet. Burhan Shah favoured some of them, giving a Nizam Shahi princess in marriage to the son of one of them, Sayyid Hasan. Burhan also reached out to Persia for military assistance, but the impracticality induced by the enormous distance between the two kingdoms precluded any such enterprise being undertaken. Further, the Safavids were pre-occupied by their interaction with the Mughals and other neighbours for any permanent contact to be maintained with a small kingdom in the Deccan. The Nizam Shahi's contact with Persia seems to have petered out thereafter.

Last Days

Burhan Nizam Shah returned from the siege of Bijapur to Ahmadnagar to recoup from the illness that had afflicted him. However, his condition continued to deteriorate on a daily basis. Burhan had six very capable sons and with his declining health being visible the struggle for succession started to come out in the open. The eldest son was Miran Shah Hussein, who was wise, generous and brave. His younger brother Abdul Qadir was also considered a model prince, but perhaps a bit more ambitious than Hussein. Both were born to the same mother, Burhan's favourite wife Ameena.

On realising that their father was actually on his death bed, the sons started to manoeuvre and continued to stay at the capital rather than at their own estates and other jagirs, presumably to be with their father during his last days, but actually to be in position to stake a claim to the throne, if the opportunity arose. Although not the eldest, Abdul Qadir had been Burhan's favourite to succeed him to the throne. However, he had fallen out with his father when the state religion was changed to the Shia sect when Qadir had refused to change his religion in accordance with his father's instructions. At this 'rebellion' Hussein was installed as the crown prince, a move that disappointed Abdul Qadir and made him anti-Hussein.

The rivalry between the two princes was reflected in the factions of the nobles, with the phirangi group supporting Miran Hussein and the Deccani faction supporting Abdul Qadir. The rivalry continued to gather momentum till it reached a stage that threatened to engulf the entire kingdom in a civil war. Alarmed at this development, Burhan ordered all his sons to leave the capital and return to their own forts and provinces. On this order being promulgated, Hussein acted decisively and took over the entire elephant and artillery corps, bringing them directly under his command. Further, he moved a few miles out of the capital and camped there. Abdul Qadir had the same thought and instead of returning to his own territory, attacked Hussein outside the capital. Hussein had anticipated such a move by his brother and was prepared for battle. He defeated Qadir's army and Qadir was forced to flee to Berar. The Imad Shah in Berar refused to give him refuge and asked him to leave his kingdom. Abdul Qadir then sought asylum in Bijapur, which was granted. He spent the rest of his life under the protection of the Adil Shah.

Hussein was shrewd enough not to pursue his defeated brother and held his army together, remaining close to the capital, in preparation to put down any other rebellious claims to the throne. Immediately on the defeat of Abdul Qadir, Hussein went to pay his respect to Burhan, who endorsed him to the throne. Burhan Nizam Shah died soon after, aged 58 years, after having ruled for 50 tumultuous years.

Burhan Shah had built many gardens and buildings in Ahmadnagar, as well as an Alms House along with many mosques with attached 'colleges' or madrasas. He was a liberal king, seeking the counsel of his nobles before embarking on any new enterprise. Burhan was methodical in his approach to governance, tactful in his decision-making and human dealings. The methodical approach translated to his taking personal interest in administrative and revenue matters. Perhaps more important to the welfare of the state was his meticulous inspection of defences and military equipment before his army went out to battle. The many successes that he achieved in consolidating the small kingdom he had inherited is testimony to his shrewd and calculated moves.

Chapter 18

TURMOIL: HUSSEIN NIZAM SHAH

On his father Burhan Nizam Shah's death, Hussein controlled his brothers and disposed off those that seemed to be rebellious, misguided and/or had the propensity to create trouble into the future. He consolidated power rapidly and commenced his rule without any anxiety, believing that any possibility of revolt had been nipped in the bud. However, this belief was proven to be without substance. Almost immediately on his assuming the throne, his position as imperial ruler was questioned. Makdum Khwaja Jahan, father-in-law of Miran Shah Haider who was one of Hussein's six brothers, was the governor of the fort at Parenda. He saw the accession of Hussein, the young prince, to the throne as an opportunity to declare independence. Khwaja Jahan had neither offered condolences on the death of his king Burhan Shah, nor had he made the traditional and formal submission to Hussein on his coronation. Therefore, he was technically guilty of rebellion on two counts.

Hussein took the counsel of his nobles and decided to crush this rebellion at the earliest. First a letter of warning was send to Makdum Khwaja in Parenda asking him to accept Hussein as the Nizam Shahi king and to pay homage to him in Ahmadnagar. Khwaja was not inclined to defy the Nizam Shahi publicly, but also did not want to travel to the Ahmadnagar court to pay homage and thereby submit to Hussein, losing his new-found independence. He put off going to Ahmadnagar on the pretext that he feared for his life in the capital since he had already been accused of rebellion. Hussein took this delaying tactics as confirming rebellion and decided to march against Khwaja. He collected an army and moved towards Parenda. Although

Makdum Khwaja initially came out to face Hussein, his nerve failed him and he fled to Bijapur, seeking refuge with Ibrahim Adil Shah. The fort at Parenda was besieged. The local commander and the forces in the garrison defended the fort stoutly with bravery, but were eventually overcome and the fort captured. Hussein did not institute any reprisals on the defenders, on account of his order there was no plunder and all lives were spared. Hussein appointed a loyal noble to rule the fort and returned to his capital.

Establishing His Rule

In Ahmadnagar an incipient rebellion by a group of dissatisfied nobles was brewing, which was crushed immediately on the return of the king to the capital. It was suspected that the Imad Shah of Berar had assisted the rebels. Hussein decided to deal with this infringement of peace by a neighbouring king through diplomacy rather than by initiating military action against the instigator of the rebellion. Accordingly he send Shah Rafi ud-Din Tahir, the eldest son of the late Shah Tahir, as the ambassador to Berar and renewed the alliance with the Imad Shah. Around the same time a contingent of Adil Shahi troops of Bijapur had invaded Ahmadnagar territory. Hussein responded by sending his own forces to oppose the Bijapur forces. The Nizam Shahi forces pushed the invaders out of their territory and also captured large booty, arms, camp tentage as well as some elephants, horses and even the royal insignia of Bijapur. This defeat further weakened an already precarious position of Ibrahim Adil Shah in Bijapur and he subsequently faced rebellion at home from a number of his nobles.

Hussein was now well-established as a strong king with no enemies of consequence and no viable threat to his kingdom. He now entertained ideas of territorial expansion—a common enough thought amongst kings who were safely ensconced in their kingdom with no immediate threat being perceived to their position. Accordingly, he captured the fortress at Galna from the kingdom of Vijayanagar without much difficulty. Vijayanagar had earlier taken the fort from Bijapur. Thereafter he sought the assistance of the Qutb Shahi king of Golconda to capture Gulbarga. The joint armies made a half-hearted attempt to capture the fort, but the result was indecisive and both the kings returned to their own countries with their forces.

The inherent nature of politics in the Deccan was one of continuous intrigue against each other by the five successor kings of the Bahmani kingdom. Since Ibrahim Adil Shah's forces had been defeated and unceremoniously pushed out of Ahmadnagar territory and Bijapur weakened, Ali Adil Shah his son who had succeeded him to the throne of Bijapur, had gradually formed an alliance with Vijayanagar to safeguard his own interests. Through this alignment, he was creating an insurance against the belligerence and growing influence of Ahmadnagar. Hussein also understood the importance of alliances. In order to counter the emerging Bijapur-Vijayanagar alliance, he initiated talks with the Imad Shah in Berar aiming to form an alliance. As a result, in order to seal the alliance Hussein married Khanzada Humayun Sultana, a princess of Berar, in 1559. Kahnzada Humayun was to play an important role in the immediate future of the Nizam Shahi kingdom.

Clashes with Bijapur-led Alliances

Once the Bijapur-Vijayanagar alliance was functioning on an even keel, the combined armies of the two countries entered Ahmadnagar territory and started to march towards the capital, devastating the countryside on the way. Hussein's advisors recognised that the enemy forces were far too large for the Ahmadnagar army to counter or hold-back. Accordingly they advised the king to leave the capital and retreat to the countryside where he could be better protected and wait for the monsoons to force the enemy to withdraw for lack of provisions. Accepting this tactful advice, Hussein left the capital under the control of a 'holding' party and left with the majority of his army, marching away from the invading forces. He crossed the River Godavari and moved to Paithan, which he established as the interim capital. The Ahmadnagar garrison continued to hold the fort against the invaders.

The king of Vijayanagar, Rama Raya (also referred to as Sadashiva Raya in some accounts; it is possible that he had a long titled name as was usual in those times) had camped outside Ahmadnagar with his army and had established a campaign of plundering the countryside while simultaneously laying siege to the capital itself. Joined by the Bijapur forces, the combined armies of the two nations instituted wanton carnage on the people of the Nizam Shahi kingdom, which affected the poor farmers the most. Then the monsoons set in with great ferocity. Almost immediately, Hussein's forces started to mount harassment raids against the Bijapur-Vijayanagar armies. Rama Raya, irritated by this affront to his command and stature, send a detachment to the River Godavari to attack Hussein's temporary camp. Hussein send a force to oppose the Hindu army. In the ensuing battle, which was extremely vicious, the Vijayanagar forces were defeated.

On their withdrawal, the Vijayanagar forces captured the fort at Kalyan fairly easily as they had overwhelming numerical and force superiority. The fort was subsequently handed over to Bijapur and remained in Adil Shahi control for long thereafter. Seeing the ease with which the fort at Kalyan was captured, Hussein felt it prudent to make peace with Rama Raya of Vijayanagar. The Hindu forces withdrew from the areas around Ahmadnagar, after which Hussein returned to his capital, now assuming a much diminished stature. This minor debacle made Hussein realise the need to strengthen his position through creating his own alliances. He made overtures to the Golconda king Ibrahim Qutb Shah and sealed the blossoming alliance by giving his daughter in marriage to the Qutb Shahi king. Almost immediately, the two kings laid siege to the fort at Kalyani that had been captured by Vijayanagar earlier and then gifted to Bijapur.

Once again the Bijapur-Vijayanagar alliance sprang into action. This time they were joined by Ali Barid ruling Bidar. Throughout the history of the successor kingdoms in the Deccan, the Barids were the most opportunistic of rulers, joining any strong alliance that was being formed in the hope of gaining some advantage for themselves. This may have been the result of Bidar being the weakest, and territorially smallest, of the five kingdoms. The Barids also lacked the legitimacy of the other four, since they were considered proxy rulers for the original Bahmani kings, whose successors still sat on the throne nominally. The reasons for their self-centred behaviour pattern are complex and extraneous to this discussion. At this stage, the typical conduct of the Shahi kings came to the fore once again. Ibrahim Qutb Shah assessed the strength of the adversaries and realised that the combination of his own and that of Ahmadnagar armies would not be able to stand up to the Bijapur-Vijayanagar combine. Promptly, he disregarded the new alliance with Hussein, as well as the matrimonial arrangements that had been made to seal it, and joined the Vijayanagar army.

At this betrayal, Hussein prudently retired to his capital in Ahmadnagar. The Vijayanagar king Rama Raya, accompanied now by the Shahi kings of Bijapur, Bidar and also Golconda, marched on Ahmadnagar. Hussein, adhering to his previous practice of withdrawing from his own capital on being attacked by superior forces, withdrew to Junafir. The invading army, again as was customary practice, laid siege to the fort and ransacked the countryside around Ahmadnagar. The contemporary reports mention atrocities committed by the 'infidel' army besieging Ahmadnagar on the common Muslims of the countryside. This claim is rather strange for two reasons. One, the Vijayanagar army and the presence of its Raya in the siege was only incidental to the main invasion that had been planned and executed by the three Shahi kings, led by Bijapur. Therefore, the majority of the besieging forces would have been Muslim. The Hindu army was present only as the contribution of an ally and partner. Second, the subjects of the Shahi kings in the Deccan were predominantly Hindu and therefore, the reporting of the atrocities of an infidel army on Muslims is a tenuous claim to make. If atrocities were indeed committed, which is a distinct possibility considering the norms of the time, then it is more likely that they were perpetrated by Muslim armies on the Hindus of the region. *[This reportage of the infidel army troubling Muslims seems to be a classic case of re-writing history for posterity.]*

Recognising the seriousness of the situation, Hussein initiated back-channel communications with Ibrahim Qutb Shah of Golconda in an attempt to break the confederacy against him. He played the religious card to bring the Qutb Shahi king to his side. He emphasised that his entire kingdom was being oppressed by an infidel army, which was not a fact but a fanciful twist of the ground reality. It was made to seem that the Vijayanagar army was singling out Muslims to commit atrocities. The two erstwhile allies met in Kalyani. Hussein's daughter, Jamil Bibi, was given in marriage to Ibrahim Qutb Shah. The Golconda king, his religious zeal fired by the exaggerated accounts of the supposed atrocities committed by the infidels on Muslims, resolved to retreat. He declared that he was no longer a party to the siege of Ahmadnagar. In order to not seem that he was abandoning his old alliance with Bijapur and Vijayanagar, he reasoned that since Hussein was totally elusive and not giving battle, there was uncertainty regarding the successful completion of the siege.

Ibrahim Qutb Shah then put forward three proposals to the anti-Ahmadnagar confederacy—all the armies retreat to their own countries and reconsider an attack next year; in case this was not acceptable to the other kings, he himself be permitted to return to Golconda to reorganise his army after which he would re-join the confederacy; and that since the war was being fought at the instigation and on behalf of Bijapur, the Adil Shahi king should compensate the others for the expenditure being incurred in conducting the campaign. Rama Raya agreed to the proposals, which was then put to Ali Adil Shah, who maintained a diplomatic silence and did not reply. This reaction was not surprising, since agreeing to the proposals would have meant he would have to compensate the other three kings from his treasury.

At this stage of indecision within the confederacy, the Imad Shahi king of Berar joined the alliance, hoping to gain some advantage from the action being taken against Ahmadnagar. At the same time, Ibrahim Qutb Shah formally left the confederacy and joined Hussein Nizam Shah. The convolutions in the Deccan kingdoms were such that even during the progress of a campaign, the kings changed sides without any thought of loyalty and integrity. This character trait was not unique to the Shahi kings and has been demonstrated repeatedly throughout the narrative of Indian history. The new Hussein-Ibrahim combine now took on the older coalition. Hussein opposed the Vijayanagar forces of Rama Raya and Ibrahim Shah fought against the Muslim forces of the Shahi kings arrayed against Ahmadnagar. Hussein did not fare well in his battle. He was defeated by the Vijayanagar army and all his artillery was captured. Hussein retreated initially towards Ahmadnagar and then fled to Junnar. Ibrahim Qutb Shah also did not have any better luck, he was conclusively defeated in battle and narrowly escaped being personally captured by the timely intervention in the battlefield of his minister Mustafa Khan Ardistani. He hurriedly retired to Golconda.

The siege of Ahmadnagar continued unabated for some more time. The allies also pursued Hussein to Junnar. However, Hussein once again adopted the Maratha tactics of never giving engaging in pitched battle, but resorting to the harassment of the main body of the adversary army with light forces. The Marathas were renowned for their hit and run tactics. Although the Nizam Shahi forces had been decisively defeated in battle, at the onset of monsoons the tables were turned. The coalition broke up, with each of the kings returning to their individual kingdoms. In the return to Vijayanagar, it is reported that Rama Raya lost 300 elephants and 12,000 cavalry who were caught in a flooded river being forded.

The Aftermath – Creating an Alliance

Hussein Nizam Shah, although peeved by the Adil Shahi's asking for Vijayanagar assistance, could not complain about it since his own father had been the first to do so amongst the Deccan Shahis. Again there is a snippet in contemporary Muslim records to state that the behaviour of the Hindu forces had 'scandalised' all the Muslims, not only the ones that were supposed to have been oppressed. While the report of widespread oppression of the general population is questionable, there are other records that describe Rama Raya's conduct during the campaign.

> ### Rama Raya's Conduct
>
> During this invasion of Ahmadnagar, the Vijayanagar Empire was at the zenith of its power. Rama Raya was an established and accomplished king, having ruled a stable and prosperous empire for a long time. He was also older than the Shahi kings who had mostly come to the throne only recently. It was not surprising that he behaved as the overlord of the entire enterprise to defeat Ahmadnagar. This attitude of the Raya has been repeatedly commented on in a number of available records.
>
> There are also reports that the Vijayanagar forces treated the Muslim forces with disdain. Further, they did not pay proper respect even to the Shahi kings, belittling them by the off-hand treatment that was meted out to them. These reports, while certain to have been exaggerated, could also have a kernel of truth in them. After all, the Vijayanagar army had not been defeated in battle for a very long time and a certain amount of haughtiness is a common trait of commanders of unbeaten armies the world over. At the same time, Rama Raya is supposed to have treated the

envoys of the Muslim kings, who were his alliance partners, as vassal agents come with supplications to him as the overlord. He even refused permission for the envoys to sit in his presence.

After the siege of Ahmadnagar was called off, when he was returning to Vijayanagar, Rama Raya forced Ali Adil Shah to cede two districts and annexed three districts from Golconda to his own territories. This action was, for the Shahi kings, like adding insult to injury. The final effect was that the Deccan kings were left with a feeling of having been wronged and, being proud kings on their own right, felt the need to avenge the actual and perceived insults.

On the withdrawal of the besieging coalition army, Hussein returned to Ahmadnagar. The one lesson he took away from this second debacle that he faced within the span of a few years was that Vijayanagar was far too powerful to be dealt with on his own and that its power was the magnet that drew the Shahi kings to seek alliances with Rama Raya, the imperial king of the empire. Hussein thought through this situation and decided that Vijayanagar power had to be whittled down and the king defeated if the Deccan Shahi kingdoms were to be really independent and have some semblance of stability and peace.

The Vijayanagar Empire

Between the 15th and 17th centuries, Vijayanagar was an empire that held extensive territories and was served by a great and powerful army, undefeated in battle by a Muslim army for centuries. The Empire had 60 sea ports and generated vast revenues, which was more than the combined revenue and income generated by all the Shahi kingdoms of the Deccan. At this juncture in history, Rama Raya was the distinguished king of Vijayanagar, ruling in pomp and ceremony for a long time; the proud and haughty scion of a venerated dynasty.

Hussein consulted with his nobles and they came to the firm conclusion that the power of Vijayanagar was such that the Nizam Shahi kingdom could not hope to defeat the Hindu kingdom on its own. This fact was magnified by the alliance between Bijapur and Vijayanagar. Hussein therefore decided to tackle the challenge through careful diplomacy tinged with the call for Muslim religious unity against an infidel but powerful king. He opened simultaneous negotiations with both Ali Adil Shah of Bijapur and Ibrahim Qutb Shah of Golconda. His proposal to both of them was to create an alliance of Muslim kings against the Hindu Empire to their south, carefully emphasising the religious aspect of the proposal. Ibrahim, perhaps because of the matrimonial alliance with Ahmadnagar and also the ignominy of the shared defeat earlier, agreed to the proposal without much debate. Ali Adil Shah was more obdurate, especially since he was still bound by the alliance to Rama Raya. He was brought around to join the Muslim coalition with the argument that even when the Deccan was ruled by a single king, the Bahmani Sultan, the region had always been open to the depredations of the Vijayanagar army and its Hindu king, who invaded and despoiled the Deccan at will. With the Deccan now divided into three major kingdoms, there was even lesser chances of standing up to stop any invasion by Vijayanagar. The argument went on to declare that in fact the Deccan was at that time at the mercy of the Vijayanagar king.

Once again the religious card was used profusely, alleging that the Muslim subjects of all the Shahi kingdoms were being persecuted and oppressed, even though the majority of the subjects of these kingdoms were Hindus. In an obtuse manner, this assertion of Muslim subjects being ill-treated could also indicate a mindset in the Shahi ruling elite that only Muslims were their legitimate subjects, even though they were a minority in all the kingdoms. The Hindus were obviously not considered worthy of being citizens of equal status to the Muslims.

A three-cornered alliance was thus created to deal with the overwhelming power of the Vijayanagar Empire. Historians are in disagreement over who was the prime mover in creating and pushing forward the alliance against Vijayanagar. They are divided over whether Hussein Nizam Shah or Ali Adil Shah was the leader of the group. There is no doubt that the initiative to create a Muslim coalition against the Hindu kingdom was taken by Hussein, after being defeated twice in a row by the Vijayanagar king. However, the alliance activities were further progressed by Ali Adil Shah who was the king to actually throw down the gauntlet to Vijayanagar, an action that subsequently led to war. Ali Shah send an envoy to Vijayanagar demanding that Rama Raya relinquish control of the Raichur Doab to Bijapur. As was expected, the envoy was unceremoniously evicted from the Vijayanagar court, which was sufficient reason for the Adil Shahi to declare war against Vijayanagar.

It is obvious that the three Shahi kings were serious about staying within the alliance and taking the fight to the Hindu kingdom by the fact they hurried to cement the coalition through creating matrimonial alliances. This was done to prevent debilitating internecine wars breaking out over trivial issues, which would then fracture the alliance. Hussein's daughter, Chand Bibi, was married to Ali Adil Shah (her exploits in Bijapur has been described earlier in the chapters that dealt with the Adil Shahi dynasty). Sholapur, the region that had been a bone of contention between the two kingdoms for long, was given as dowry to Ali Adil Shah. However, this gift of the area that was in perennial dispute did not terminate the dispute, it only laid to rest the disagreement for a brief period of time. In return for this marriage, Ali Adil Shah's daughter was married to Hussein's son Shahzada Murtaza. The three kings decided to march against Vijayanagar after one year. Burhan Imad Shah was invited to join the coalition, but declined on account his old enmity with Hussein. However, Ali Barid the opportunist, readily joined Ibrahim Qutb Shah with his forces.

A year later, the three armies met at Sholapur in late 1564 and jointly marched to the village of Talikota. (A full and detailed account of the Battle of Talikota, fought on either 23rd or 26th January 1565, will be given in the next volume of this series of books. Here it is sufficient to mention just the bare facts.) First, Vijayanagar definitely fielded the superior force. It is highly probable that they would have been overconfident of the outcome of the battle in their favour, not having tasted defeat in a long time, and never from the Deccan forces. Second, the Muslim armies were lighter in their footprint, employed more innovative tactics based on rapid manoeuvre and were able to perform much better than the heavy forces of Rama Raya. Third, from all descriptions of the battle that ensued, it is clear that Hussein Nizam Shah was considered the overall leader of the combined forces that was arrayed against the Hindu kingdom.

The Battle of Talikota was a keenly fought battle in which the Vijayanagar forces were defeated and Rama Raya captured alive in the battlefield. In the ensuing confusion a very large number of Vijayanagar soldiers were killed. The Raya was produced in captivity before Hussein Nizam Shah, who immediately ordered his execution, an order that was carried out with unusual haste. The illustrious king was summarily beheaded. The Vijayanagar Emperor's head was placed on a spear and displayed on an elephant—an undignified action that stood condemned even in the blood thirsty medieval times. The beheading of Rama Raya was done without any consultation with the other Shahi kings who were part of the alliance and was resented by them. Further, both the Adil Shahi and Qutb Shahi kings felt repentant on the treatment meted out to the Hindu king who had assisted both of them in times of their need. There was a general feeling that the beheading was an incorrect action initiated against a worthy adversary who had been defeated in honourable battle.

The three victorious Shahi kings marched to Vijayanagar and stayed there for almost four months, taking their time to destroy much of the capital, especially the architecturally magnificent temples—after all they had fought a religious war against an infidel and prevailed. They collected enormous booty and returned to their individual kingdoms. Hussein Nizam Shah claimed the victory of the alliance as his personal victory and send letters far and wide to establish the fact that this was his victory over the Hindu Empire, rather than the victory of the combined Deccan Shahi alliance. Obviously this was resented by the other Deccan Muslim kings. Hussein died on 6 June 1565 soon after returning to Ahmadnagar, because of excessive drinking and sexual debauchery according to some sources. His son Shahzada Murtaza succeeded to the throne, assuming the royal title Murtaza Nizam Shah.

Chapter 19

THE ZENITH OF POWER MURTAZA NIZAM SHAH

Murtaza Nizam Shah commenced his rule immediately on the death of his father, although the assumption of the throne was delayed on the advice of astrologers. He was officially crowned only on 26 January 1566, seven months after becoming king. At this time, Murtaza was a callow youth and a complete slave to sensual pleasures. He shunned all official business, opting to spend his entire day in the company of beautiful courtesans, indulging in every whim and fancy that appealed to him. The affairs of state was looked after by his mother, the redoubtable Khanzada (also mentioned as Khunzah in some accounts) Humayun. Her authority was such that she was obeyed by all nobles as if she was the ruling Queen and not a de facto Regent. She retained Qasim Beg Hakim as the prime minister since he had served her husband loyally and was known for his efficiency. However, she replaced him with Maulana Inayatullah at a later date. Many other changes in royal appointments were also made in quick succession by the Queen-mother.

Ahmadnagar – Bijapur Tussle

Ali Adil Shah ruling Bijapur, was an extremely ambitious king, always on the look out to improve his own status and his kingdom's territorial holding and financial position. On Hussein's death and knowing Murtaza's lack of interest—bordering on aversion—towards the affairs of state, Ali Shah disregarded the existing treaties between the kingdoms and also the matrimonial alliance that had been sealed, and invaded Ahmadnagar with a large army.

The Regent-Queen Khanzada acted decisively. At this time, Tuful Khan had usurped power in Berar, imprisoning all the Imad Shahi princes who were the traditional rulers. Khanzada Humayun initiated the forming of an alliance with Tuful Khan and marched to the Berar border with her army, where Tuful Khan joined her with the Berar army. The joint forces then moved towards Telangana where they were met by Ibrahim Qutb Shah who renewed his alliance with Ahmadnagar and joined the coalition with his army. The large combined army now marched against Ali Adil Shah who abandoned his plans of invasion and retreated to his own kingdom. The allied armies marched into Bijapur territory and ransacked the countryside, reaching the capital.

An Alternative Story

There is an alternative story to the one narrated above, which cannot be authoritatively corroborated. It is reported in one source that after the victory in the Battle of Talikota and the destruction of Vijayanagar, Ali Adil Shah took the son of Rama Raya, called Timmala, under his protection and established him as the ruler of Anagodi. (This action could have been prompted by the unwarranted and hasty execution of Rama Raya and the Adil Shahi's old and long-standing friendship with the royal family of Vijayanagar.) Anagodi being ruled by Timmala was invaded by his uncle, Venkata, ruling Nalgonda. It was obvious that Ali Adil Shah would turn to support his prodigy.

Ali Adil Shah marched to Nalgonda to punish Venkata, who in turn appealed to Ahmadnagar for assistance. Khanzada Humayun immediately prepared to besiege Bijapur, especially since Ali Adil Shah was away from his capital. He rushed back to his kingdom upon which the Ahmadnagar forces withdrew. In this recounting, there is no mention of the involvement of either Tuful Khan or Ibrahim Qutb Shah in the skirmish.

In any case, irrespective of the actual flow of events, Ali Adil Shah sued for peace and Khanzada agreed, withdrawing the Ahmadnagar army to its own kingdom.

Ali Adil Shah was nothing if not devious and self-centred. He decided to improve his relationship with Ahmadnagar and make use of it to wreak vengeance on Tuful Khan, who he felt had not been correct in joining the alliance against Bijapur. Accordingly he send a conciliatory message to Murtaza with a request to renew their mutual friendship and treaties of alliance. There is some doubt regarding who initiated the peace contact. Some reports claim that it was the Regent-Queen who started talks with Ahmadnagar in order to punish Tuful Khan for not having joined the confederacy against Vijayanagar. However this is an unlikely scenario, since Tuful Khan had joined Ahmadnagar against Bijapur just a few months back. Further, the Ahmadnagar nobles and advisors felt that peace with Bijapur was essential for their own kingdom to prosper. Therefore, the move towards peace could have been a mutual effort. The treaties of cooperation was renewed at the fort of Ausa.

At Ausa, a decision was made to make war on Tuful Khan of Berar in order to set the Imad Shahi family free and restore them to the throne. In 1567, the combined armies of Ahmadnagar and Bijapur invaded Berar. Tuful Khan was forced to flee to the fort at Gawil, which was then besieged by the alliance army. Ali Adil Shah once again resorted to his devious dealings; after some secret negotiations with Tuful Khan, he accepted a hefty bribe to lift the siege. He convinced the Ahmadnagar nobles and commanders to lift the siege and instead attack and subdue Ibrahim Qutb Shah. It was proposed that after defeating the Qutb Shahi king, Tuful Khan could be brought to book. For some unfathomable reason, the Ahmadnagar leadership agreed to this change in plans, although they commanded the more powerful part of the joint army. From a purely military point of view, this action went against the cardinal principle of war, 'selection and maintenance of aim', and was therefore bound to fail.

The combined army marched towards Golconda, with Ahmadnagar troops in the front. Some 'rebel' officers of the Bijapur army attacked the baggage train of the Ahmadnagar forces attempting to capture it for profit. In the skirmish that ensued, the forward commander of the Ahmadnagar forces was killed. Khanzada Humayun was incensed by the actions of the Bijapur forces; her wrath knew no bounds, since she may have also by now realised the double game that Ali Adil Shah had played in Berar. She determined to attack the Bijapur forces immediately. However, she was influenced by some well-meaning nobles from both the kingdoms who intervened to avert what would have been a destructive battle. Even though no battle took place, the Ahmadnagar–Bijapur alliance split and both the armies returned to their own kingdoms. Subsequently Ahmadnagar renewed its treaty with Tuful Khan and a half-hearted attempt was made to attack Bijapur, which was easily thwarted by the Bijapur forces.

Golconda Enters the Fray

To say the least, Ibrahim Qutb Shah ruling Golconda, was unhappy about the proposed invasion of his territory by the Ahmadnagar–Bijapur coalition and moved to create alliances of his own to shore up his position. Learning of the rupture between Ali Adil Shah and Murtaza (actually Khanzada Humayun, his mother, ruling on his behalf), Ibrahim offered to become an ally to Ahmadnagar. The Golconda envoy send to negotiate the treaty exposed the duplicity of Ali Adil Shah. Ibrahim Qutb Shah urged the Ahmadnagar Regent-Queen to march against Bijapur, with the assurance that he himself with the Golconda forces, Rama Raya's son now ruling a much diminished Vijayanagar, and Tuful Khan of Berar would join the expedition.

Khanzada Humayun, ordered her forces to immediately march to the banks of the River Krishna as the first step in the proposed invasion of Bijapur. She was still smarting under the earlier betrayal and duplicity of Ali Adil Shah. The Ahmadnagar forces were joined by Ibrahim Qutb Shah and the Vijayanagar forces. Tuful Khan refused to join the coalition since he still felt obliged and grateful to Ali Adil Shah for saving him during the earlier attack on Berar, even though it had been achieved with the transfer of great wealth to Bijapur. As was his customary way in dealing with disadvantageous situations, Ali Adil Shah resorted to devious diplomacy to tide over the on-coming invasion. He managed to create dissention within the coalition opposing him and succeeded in weaning Ibrahim Qutb Shah away from Ahmadnagar. Further, Ibrahim was induced to join the Bijapur forces, at least nominally, ignoring his treaty with Ahmadnagar. Having shown cursory solidarity with Bijapur, Ibrahim left the battleground and marched back to Golconda. On the way he encountered reinforcements from Ahmadnagar on their way to join the main force. He attacked and defeated them, making them disperse.

The Ahmadnagar army, realising that reinforcements had been stopped on the way, withdrew to their own kingdom. During this retreat, both Bijapur and Golconda forces harassed the Ahmadnagar forces. The Nizam Shahi forces were compelled to fight a number of pitched battles as rear-guard actions and a large number of skirmishes resulted from the hit and run tactics that was adopted by the opposing forces, especially by the Golconda army. Although no great damage was done and the Ahmadnagar forces reached home safely, the harassment caused a great deal of bloodshed and loss of life.

Murtaza Nizam Shah Takes Charge

From the very beginning of Murtaza's rule, his mother Khanzada Humayun had looked after all the affairs of state and managed the business of the day-to-day running of the court. The Queen-mother conducted the administration of the kingdom with great wisdom, dedication and extraordinary ability. Murtaza was content to continue leading a life devoted to satisfying the pleasures of the flesh.

Even though the young king was uninterested in the actual rigours of ruling the kingdom, the Queen-mother was insistent on his having access to a good education. Therefore, the Queen had appointed Maulana Husain Tabizi as the principal tutor for the young prince Murtaza. Tabizi was a remarkable person, learned and virtuous, and of 'good' birth. He was wise in his precepts, while also being well-versed in religious matters, holy law and the Quran. Within a very short time of being appointed, Tabizi was able to become an overriding influence on the young prince. Although Husain Tabizi was a 'maulana'—a learned man of God, pious and virtuous—at the end of the day, he was also a human being; and like all humans everywhere, he was also susceptible to being ambitious. With great influence over the king, he succumbed to the human craving for power, forgetting all the religious tenets that he had so far espoused. Tabizi started to poison the king's mind and altered his perceptions regarding the manner in which the Regent-Queen conducted the affairs of state.

Once he was certain that he had turned the king's opinion against his mother, Tabizi arranged for Khanzada Humayun to be seized in person and imprisoned. The Regent-Queen discovered the plot and the conspirators were forced to flee to Bijapur for shelter. However, they were gradually brought back to Ahmadnagar since they had not fallen from the king's favour. After a while, they plotted again and devised a plan to imprison Khanzada. At this time, Bijapur once again invaded Ahmadnagar. There are no details available regarding the progress or result of this minor invasion. It could be surmised that the attack was feint arranged by the conspirators while they were in Bijapur after the first attempt at deposing the Regent-Queen. The Ahmadnagar army took to the field to repel the invaders. As was her custom Khanzada Humayun accompanied the forces in their march. She had so far been part of all military expeditions of the Ahmadnagar forces.

On the march, the conspirators manage to isolate Khanzada Humayun. They captured and transported her to Daulatabad where she was kept in solitary imprisonment. She was subsequently moved to the fort at Shivner, which was isolated by itself. The complicity of the king in the capture and imprisonment of his mother has been proven beyond reasonable doubt, through independent sources. At the arrest of the Regent-Queen, her two brothers who were her staunch supporters, fled the country, one towards Gujarat and the other to Golconda. Ain-ul-Mulk, fleeing to Gujarat, was intercepted on the way and killed. The other brother Taj Mian, managed to reach Golconda safely where he took refuge. Murtaza Nizam Shah was now the undisputed king of Ahmadnagar.

On the Khanzada being deposed, the old minister Maulana Inayatullah, who had been imprisoned by her for misdemeanours, attempted to return to the capital to claim his old position as prime minister. However, Tabizi who had by now become a power-hungry and ruthless person, had the old man murdered before he could reach the capital. Murtaza removed all the nobles who had been loyal to his mother from positions of power and consolidated his hold on the administration. To entrench his position and ensure that he was unchallenged as the king, he undertook a military expedition. He attacked the Bijapur kingdom's fort at Dharur. This fort had been built by Kishvar Khan, a great general of Bijapur who was still the governor of Dharur. Kishvar was killed in the battle and the Bijapur forces suffered a devastating defeat with great loss of life. Dharur was annexed to Ahmadnagar. Since Murtaza was campaigning near Dharur and away from his capital, Ali Adil Shah started to march towards Ahmadnagar to offset the defeat that Bijapur forces had suffered. However, even in this attempt, he was not successful. The Bijapur forces were defeated and had to retreat to their own kingdom. Two consecutive victories immediately after taking over and ruling independent of his mother's advice, greatly enhanced Murtaza Nizam Shah's stature.

Other Military Adventures

Perhaps because of the military victories that Murtaza achieved, Ibrahim Qutb Shah ruling Golconda, made another overture to re-enact the bilateral friendship that had been signed earlier. Murtaza was reluctant to go into partnership with an unreliable king, but was persuaded by Tabizi to accept the proposal. Ahmadnagar and Golconda formed an alliance, primarily against Bijapur, which was reported to be in dire straits. On the advice of his nobles, Murtaza decided to recapture Sholapur from Bijapur with the assistance of Ibrahim Qutb Shah. The combined army moved out and camped at Wakdari.

Realising the difficult situation that he was in, Ali Adil Shah once again resorted to the tenet of divisive diplomacy. He send an emissary to Murtaza to appease him. The envoy was able to influence the Ahmadnagar nobles against the alliance with Golconda, who in turn managed to poison Murtaza's mind against the Qutb Shahi king. The main point against the Golconda king was his earlier abandonment of treaties and alliances with Ahmadnagar, most at critical times during military expeditions. The Ahmadnagar nobles managed to convince Murtaza to take action against the Golconda contingent, rather than proceed with the invasion of Bijapur. The Qutb Shahi army was surrounded and attacked while they were sleeping in the night. Ibrahim Qutb Shah had to flee, leaving even his royal emblems and insignia behind. The Nizam Shahi forces then captured Udgir and returned to Ahmadnagar in triumph. Murtaza established peace with Ali Adil Shah of Bijapur.

While these external engagements were taking place, the interminable palace intrigues continued unabated in Ahmadnagar.

Murtaza removed his mentor and prime minster, Husain Tabizi 'Khankhanan' and replaced him with Shah Haidar, son of Shah Tahir. Haidar was referred to as the 'peshwa', one of the earliest references to the senior minister being bestowed with this title, which was to be made famous across the sub-continent in later days with the spread of Maratha power. The king received word that the Portuguese were ill-treating the Muslims under their administration and decided to wage a 'holy war' against the foreigners. He marched to Chaul and besieged the fortress at Revanda (lower Charel). Portuguese records indicate that they faced a joint effort by Ali Adil Shah, Murtaza Nizam Shah and the Zamorin (Samoothiripad) of Calicut to expel them from the Peninsula. This claim of a joint effort by three kings to rid the foreigners form the peninsula has to be discounted since it cannot be confirmed from any other chronicle or records. Such a combined effort by the south Indian rulers would have been definitely recorded in at least one of the kingdoms involved. The siege of Revanda continued for nine months and failed because of internal treachery. All the nobles of Ahmadnagar involved in the siege, except one, were in the pay of the Portuguese. Throughout the siege they permitted supplies to be provided to the fort at night and made the siege during the day a meaningless exercise. Although the Ahmadnagar forces were far superior to the army in the Portuguese garrison, they were finally forced to abandon the siege and return home. *[The disloyalty of nobles towards their own king for pecuniary benefits is a recurring theme in the broader history of India. The majority of nobles were at all times willing to sell their integrity if the price offered was 'right'. While this abominable practice brought down many kingdoms, both large and small, the avarice, lack of upright behaviour, and inability to uphold honour, were loathsome character traits that were rampant in the nobles of the Indian sub-continent. Through the lens of a dispassionate later-day analysis, this trait is particularly galling and difficult to understand. Undermining the power of the ruling king and dynasty seems to have been the favourite pastime of the nobles in medieval India. While no unassailable proof can be offered to support this hypothesis, this analyst believes that the disloyalty could have emanated from the belief of some of the nobles that they were 'foreigners' and therefore owed a debt of gratitude to the outside invader, as opposed to being loyal to the local ruler. In the case of the Deccan Shahi rulers, religion did not play an important role in these treacherous dealings, but in North India, where the contest was almost always between invading Muslim forces and the indigenous Hindu kings, religion also played a central role in determining the loyalty or otherwise of the nobles and military commanders.]*

Invasion of Berar

The inconclusive siege of the Portuguese fort left the Ahmadnagar forces demoralised. Ali Adil Shah had by now joined forces with Tufal Khan and created a coalition against Ahmadnagar. Murtaza resorted to diplomacy, much like Ali Adil Shah, to try and break the coalition. However, he was not as adept as the Bijapur king in devious diplomacy and failed to separate Ali Adil Shah and Tufal Khan. Ali Shah had also send out feelers to Ibrahim Qutb Shah in Golconda to join the coalition against Ahmadnagar. Seeing the danger that he was in, Murtaza send out an army to march rapidly against the Bijapur forces, before the Adil Shahi king could join forces with either of his accomplices. This action was a stroke of genius. The Bijapur army was not strong enough to withstand the Nizam Shahi onslaught on its own. The Ahmadnagar forces devastated the Bijapur countryside and encamped at the village of Rui. Tufal Khan was asked to attack Ahmadnagar as a diversionary tactic in order to relieve the pressure on Bijapur, but was unable to make any headway. Individually, neither the Bijapur nor the Berar forces were a match for the might of Nizam Shahi forces.

Unable to withstand the onslaught on his kingdom, Ali Adil Shah sued for peace. Murtaza had by now set his sights on crushing Tufal Khan; after all his mother had been a princess of Berar, whose family was now imprisoned by Tufal Khan. Since he had continued to keep his mother imprisoned, the irony of the situation seems to have been lost on the young king. Murtaza wanted to keep Ali Adil Shah out of the equation and therefore agreed to the peace overture. Murtaza and Ali Shah met at village Kala Chutra to discuss future activities. In the peace treaty that was concluded, it was agreed that they would jointly capture Bidar, which would then be handed over to Murtaza; then Ali Adil Shah would march against Vijayanagar and capture territory for himself; and Murtaza would go on to annex Berar and some parts of Telangana.

The combined forces marched to Bidar and halted outside the tiny kingdom. However, true to the form of the Deccan Shahi kings, Murtaza changed his mind and decided that Berar was of a higher priority in having to be contained. He informed Ali Adil Shah of the change of plan and proceeded to Berar, asking Ali Shah to go ahead with his planned invasion of Vijayanagar. It speaks volumes of the power of Ahmadnagar that Ali Adil Shah agreed to this late change of plan without demurring. The armies split at the Golconda border with each king leaving a trusted envoy with the other. It is obvious that the envoy was meant to keep an eye on the ally's activities, a sign of the uneasy peace that was at play and the mistrust that each had for the other.

Murtaza devastated some parts of Golconda territory and settled down at Kaulas to wait out the monsoons. When the weather became conducive to military expeditions, he attacked Berar, moving in through Pathri. The conduct of the expedition left no doubts in anyone's mind regarding the Nizam Shahi's ultimate objective. It was clear that Murtaza intended to annex Berar to his growing kingdom and not devastate it—he did not permit any looting or destruction over the conquered territories. He gifted Pathri after its capture, to some of his favourite officers as personal jagirs. Tufal Khan retaliated to the invasion by trying to attack Ahmadnagar territory. However, this effort was thwarted by watchful Nizam Shahi commanders. Tufal Khan moved back to Berar and camped outside, but on being attacked by Ahmadnagar forces, fled the country towards Mahur.

The conflict continued indecisively—Murtaza chasing Tufal across the countryside, Tufal managing to avoid any pitched engagement and keeping ahead of the pursuing forces. The Nizam Shahi forces captured a majority of Berar territory, bringing most of its forts and towns under their sway. Tufal Khan was not provided refuge by any of the neighbouring kings and his counter-attack on the Ahmadnagar forces was not successful. Tufal Khan went to his own fort complex at Narnala and send his son to Gawli fort, both forts considered to be strong and extremely difficult to attack and reduce. The Ahmadnagar forces laid siege to Narnala, even though the fort was considered impregnable.

Murtaza – The Overlord

The growing power of Murtaza Nizam Shah worried Ibrahim Qutb Shah, ruling Golconda. Therefore, while Murtaza was pre-occupied with the capture of Berar, Golconda forces invaded the district of Kandhar on the Ahmadnagar border. The Nizam Shahi border forces were unable to withstand the assault and were compelled to retreat.

The arrival of reinforcements from the main body of Ahmadnagar forces made the Golconda forces withdraw. In the meantime, Narnala fort was overrun and Tufal Khan captured; the fort at Gawli was also captured and the entire family of Tufal Khan was imprisoned. Berar was annexed to Ahmadnagar.

Once again, the duplicitous nature of the Shahi kings' relationship with each other was displayed in the dealings that took place immediately after the fall of Berar. Ibrahim Qutb Shah played the role of a great friend to Murtaza and send messages to congratulate and applaud the Nizam Shahi on his victory over Berar. At the same time he was worried about Murtaza's growing power and covertly instigated the Khandesh king, Miran Muhammad Shah, to attack and capture Berar, since it was now left in the care of an Ahmadnagar noble. Accordingly, Miran Shah invaded and occupied Berar. Murtaza was consumed with dealing with other irritants—there were minor rebellions within his army and at the outer districts of his kingdom. He was unable to take immediate action. Further, he had already moved the majority of his army to the border with Bidar, which was his next target for annexation. Therefore, immediate retaliation was not possible.

Even so, annoyed with the actions of the Khandesh king, Murtaza decided to recapture Berar and accordingly manoeuvred his forces. Muhammad Shah offered spirited resistance at Burhanpur and Asir, but was then forced to withdraw to his own kingdom. Peace was established only after Murtaza Nizam Shah was acknowledged as the overlord of the region and a great deal of tribute was paid to him by the other kings.

Court Intrigues

Murtaza was reliant on his Prime Minister Changiz Khan, who was incorruptible, efficient, brave and sagacious, for the smooth functioning of the administration. Changiz Khan looked after the running of the kingdom in such a manner that Murtaza was free to indulge in his efforts to expand the borders of the kingdom and pursue his dream of becoming the most powerful of the Deccan Shahi kings. However, another noble Husain Khan was also a favourite of the Nizam Shah. Husain Khan did not have the same level of integrity as Changiz Khan, and fell prey to the machinations of Ibrahim Qutb Shah. The

Golconda king corrupted Husain Khan through heavy bribes and had him poison Murtaza against the Prime Minster, Changiz Khan. Without bothering to verify the facts, Murtaza took pre-emptive action and had his Prime Minster poisoned. After his death, Changiz Khan's innocence and loyalty was proved. Murtaza Nizam Shah was crestfallen and ashamed of his intemperate actions. As an act of repentance, he decided to withdraw from public life.

Since he was out on a military expedition at this time, Murtaza returned to Ahmadnagar and handed over the administration of the kingdom to Sayyid Qazi Beg Yazdi and himself retired to lead a secluded life. The court intrigues continued unabated, now with the nobles vying to increase their individual power and influence in the absence of the king being involved in the running of the country. He had stopped exercising direct control over the day-to-day functioning of the court. However, Murtaza continued to be engaged, not having completely 'let-go' with the withdrawal being a temporary and 'half-way' phenomenon. By this time, Berar was completely subsumed by Ahmadnagar, all rebellions being fully contained.

There is a report of the Ahmadnagar forces being placed on alert in 1576, when the Mughal Emperor Akbar started to move south from his northern citadel in Agra. His southern sojourn was however very short-lived, since he returned north in 1577. Further, there is no proof of any encounter that took place between Mughal and Ahmadnagar forces; or of any intention on the part of the Mughal Emperor to invade the Deccan. It has to be assumed that his move south was nothing more than a 'hunting' expedition, not even a scoping move to assess the strength of the major kingdoms of the Deccan.

The Mughal forces did not pose any threat to the Nizam Shahi kingdom during this minor move south. However, the Bijapur king Ali Adil Shah was ambitious, as has been stated earlier, and always looking for opportunities to enhance his own position. The victories of Murtaza and his annexing Berar rankled Ali Adil Shah. On getting to know of the ostensive withdrawal of Murtaza from public life and the running of the kingdom, and the untimely death of the efficient Changiz Khan, Ali Shah decided to invade Ahmadnagar. The Bijapur king considered the Nizam Shahi kingdom to be now in decline or at least in a relatively weakened state. However, the Ahmadnagar forces were quick to react and the Bijapur army was forced to withdraw. This Bijapur enterprise remained still-born.

While the Bijapur invasion fiasco was playing out, court intrigue continued unrelentingly in Ahmadnagar, and a different drama was unfolding in the court. Husain Khan, responsible for the murder of Changiz Khan, but still a favourite of the king, had assumed the title of Sahib Khan and was behaving as a total tyrant. His behaviour precipitated a factional fight between the Deccani and phirangi (foreigner) nobles. The animosity between the factions and Sahib Khan's oppression of the phirangis became intolerable. It reached a stage wherein the phirangi nobles fled to Bijapur. The nobles who were still loyal to Murtaza, led by Sayyid Yazdi, now requested the king to take action against Husain (Sahib) Khan before he became too powerful and it would come difficult to control or overthrow him. The king realised the seriousness of the situation and ordered his loyal nobles to bring Sahib Khan to book forthwith. The nobles used subterfuge to lure Sahib Khan to a secluded place in the pretext of their wanting to pay homage to him. He was then killed by the nobles. Murtaza once again withdrew into seclusion, although the nobles implored him to take control of the kingdom, which they feared was gradually declining into chaos.

The king however, wanted to go on a pilgrimage to Mecca and Medina after abdicating from the role of king. The nobles and other wise men of the court managed to make him change his mind and desist from undertaking such a step. Even so, he appointed Shah Haidar as the Prime Minister and once again retired to private life. He started to lead a life of ease, leisure and worldly enjoyment. Murtaza's decision to withdraw was the beginning of the turmoil that encompassed the Nizam Shahi kingdom for the next decade and more, which further led to the beginning of the decline of the dynasty. During the turbulent years that followed, successive kings and powerful nobles of the regime were almost completely unaware of the changing geo-political circumstances in North India and the rapidly increasing power of the Mughal Empire there. This would spell the doom of the Nizam Shahi dynasty.

Chapter 20

STAGNATION AND CONFUSION
MURTAZA'S LAST DAYS

Shah Haidar had been installed as the Peshwa, helped with the influence of Asad Khan who was an honoured and influential noble of the realm. However, Haidar repaid the good-will by banishing Asad to Daulatabad. Further, Haidar ignored the advice that Murtaza had given him on his appointment and started to behave in a high-handed manner. One of his first acts was to gather the jagir that had been given to his father Shah Tahir and were now in the possession of other nobles, for himself. The king had asked him to desist from such an action because it would antagonise the nobles—an advice that was also ignored. Even though compensatory grants were given to the deprived nobles, there was an undercurrent of discontentment amongst their ranks.

Murtaza Nizam Shah now removed himself to Daulatabad and once again declared his intention to abdicate the throne and proceed on the long-wished for pilgrimage to Mecca and Medina. Once again he was persuaded to give up taking such a drastic decision and acting on it. Murtaza now removed Haidar from the position of peshwa and appointed Asad Khan in his place. Haidar was appointed governor of Daulatabad. Asad Khan in turn appointed Salabat Khan as his 'deputy' in order to share the onerous duties of the peshwa. The shrewd king Murtaza, warned Asad Khan against this arrangement of sharing the duties of the Peshwa, as it could lead to the dilution of his own power and hold on the administration. Once again, the sane advice was ignored, but his warning came true in later days. Murtaza and the new Peshwa now returned to Ahmadnagar.

War against Bijapur

In Bijapur, Ali Adil Shah was murdered, leading to confusion regarding the succession to the throne since he did not have a son. His nephew Ibrahim, only nine years old, was raised to the throne with a powerful noble Kamil Khan as the Regent. There is an obscure story, not fully corroborated, that Kamil Khan murdered Ibrahim's elder brother, who had reached the age of discretion to rule on his own, so that he could become regent with absolute power. As is usual under such circumstances, the other nobles in the Adil Shahi court immediately started to plot to improve their own power and influence while trying to diminish Kamil Khan's influence.

Murtaza decided to invade Bijapur to take advantage of the prevailing confusion. As a first step, he reconfirmed the alliance between Ahmadnagar and Golconda. Ibrahim Qutb Shah send a large army contingent to assist in the proposed invasion. The combined forces were placed under the command of Malik Bihzad-ul-Mulk, a Turkish noble of the Ahmadnagar court and hence a member of the foreign or phirangi faction. There was some resentment in the Golconda army since they would be fighting under the command of a foreigner. The same sentiment was echoed in the Berar army, which was also part of the combined force since Berar had been annexed and was an integral part of the Nizam Shahi kingdom. This sentiment would play a major part in the future failure of the expedition. *[Factionalism was the bane of the Deccan Shahi kingdoms, as has been explained earlier and will also be demonstrated in the narrative of the events to come. It led to enormous divisiveness and was always one of the major reasons for the failure of the military enterprises of each of the kingdoms. The inherent division between the phirangis and Deccanis also led to civil wars, which in turn brought about unnecessary weakening of the power and stature of the kingdom itself.]*

The Nizam Shahi army and its allies marched into Bijapur, laying waste the countryside on both sides of the route. The Bijapur army, gathered under their brilliant commander Kishavar Khan, was numerically inferior but did not lack tactical capability. They intercepted the reinforcements coming from Golconda to join the Ahmadnagar army and forced that contingent to retreat in confusion. In the meantime, there was a great deal of infighting between nobles of the Ahmadnagar army, primarily regarding their individual precedence and protocol. The internal squabbles were accentuated by the fundamental and prevalent resentment at the appointment of the phirangi Bihzad as the commander-in-chief.

Bihzad-ul-Mulk was relatively young and inexperienced to have been given command of such a large and multi-national force. He was not guided and mentored by any of the more senior nobles who were relatively more competent veterans of calibre, nor was he receptive to any such initiative. There was a definitive disconnect between the commander and most of the other officers of the large army. In any case, he did not institute sufficient precautions to safeguard the forces while they were camped. Further, Bihzad kept the part of the army that he personally commanded separate from the main body, leading to a loss of cohesiveness of the entire force, a quality that should have been one of the primary strengths of such a large force.

The unfocussed Ahmadnagar army was attacked and defeated by the Bijapur forces, which was well-led and concentrated on victory, since defeat would have meant the death knell of their kingdom. The Nizam Shahi army suffered great loss in terms of horses, elephants, baggage and other warfighting resources. Even after this defeat, Ahmadnagar forces continued to be riven with factionalism and mismanaged because of internal power-rivalry, leading to the army becoming completely disarrayed. At the same time, the Bijapur forces were reinforced by the return of a contingent that had been send to suppress another minor rebellion within the kingdom.

Even though the initial engagement had gone in favour of Bijapur, the Nizam Shahi army was overwhelmingly powerful and were also assisted by the Golconda forces. Their numerical superiority continued to play an important role even when their overall strategy and battlefield tactics were inferior to their opponents. However, although the Bijapur forces presented a unified external appearance, they were also riddled with infighting amongst the nobles of the phirangi and Deccani factions. The numerical constraints and the continuous infighting of their leadership left the Bijapur forces in a demoralised state. In the ensuing battle, the first day went overwhelmingly in favour of Ahmadnagar. Bijapur attempted, in their time-honoured manner, to divide the opposing army by trying to keep the Golconda forces from joining up with the main body. However, this attempt failed. The Ahmadnagar army besieged Bijapur, which was now in dire straits. The continuing internal divisions further diminished the Bijapur army's ability to withstand the siege and the coming onslaught.

The Bijapur forces had been initially commanded by Ain-ul-Mulk, an able and loyal general. However, he had fled to Ahmadnagar for fear of his life from the African faction of nobles, called the Habshis. Seeing that the situation was becoming dire, the nobles of Bijapur induced him to return and take command of the besieged army, which greatly enhanced the morale of the Bijapur forces. Yet another ferocious battle ensued. Even though the Bijapur forces fought with great bravery, by the afternoon the Ahmadnagar forces had broken through the centre of the Bijapur army, putting them to flight. The remaining Adil Shahi forces in the fort did not have the strength or internal leadership to come out and fight, which may have turned to tide in their favour. Therefore, they shut the fort gates from within, leaving even some of their own forces outside at the mercy of the adversary. The siege continued.

Once again Bijapur resorted to dubious diplomacy and intrigue, adopting the tactic of 'divide and win'. Overtures were made to the commander of the Qutb Shahi forces of Golconda to separate him from the Ahmadnagar forces. However, in this instance the commander proved to be incorruptible and the alliance continued to hold. The failure of diplomacy to lift the siege forced Adil Shah to prepare for a prolonged war. He started to make use of the Maratha forces under his control, who were adept at guerrilla warfare. The Marathas commenced a campaign intended to disrupt the supply lines of the besieging army. The interdiction was effective and the Ahmadnagar army was forced to move away from their siege positions and ravage the countryside in order to ensure adequacy of supply. Gradually the siege started to be eased, and Bijapur heaved a sigh of relief. Realising that the siege was on the verge of collapse, the allies offered Ibrahim Adil Shah lifting of the siege and peace. This offer was promptly refused by the Adil Shahi king, who had by now sensed that the invaders were at the end of their tether.

The Ahmadnagar and Golconda forces lifted the siege and returned home, giving the impression of a Bijapur victory. They had not achieved anything for the effort that had been put in for the invasion and the siege. In addition they had lost prestige because of their perceived defeat at the hands of the inferior Bijapur forces. Throughout the retreat the combined army plundered and laid waste the Bijapur countryside at will—even at this stage the Adil Shahi forces did not have the strength to oppose the Ahmadnagar forces in direct battle. The withdrawing forced killed many citizens, wantonly destroyed many towns and villages, and collected enormous wealth through the unrestricted looting that took place. Although the armies of the two countries had remained together throughout the expedition, when they separated to go their own ways, there was some misgivings in the Golconda forces regarding the alliance and Ahmadnagar's commitment to it.

Renewed Attack on Bijapur

Ibrahim Qutb Shah died on 6 June 1580 and was succeeded on the throne by his son Muhammad Qutb Shah. Murtaza Nizam Shah was preparing yet another military expedition against Bijapur, his continuing obsession. The nobles of Golconda persuaded the new king Muhammad to take to the field and join Ahmadnagar in this enterprise—as a display of strength for the young king himself and as a show of solidarity with Ahmadnagar. In October 1581, the allies reached and camped before the fort of Naldurga. This fortress was considered impregnable and one of the strongest in the Deccan. Even so, the invading army laid siege to the fort. The siege was led by artillery—both Ahmadnagar and Golconda possessed sufficient heavy guns to continue a controlled siege successfully. However, they faced a confident defending force, who would carry out sorties out of the fort at unexpected times. These marauding raids created confusion amongst the besieging forces and resulted in heavy loss of life for the invading forces.

Reinforcements coming to the aid of Naldurga from Bijapur were able to fight their way into the fort. This was a great morale booster for the defenders who continued to hold out against a constant artillery barrage. After the walls had been breached sufficiently to permit an in-strength attack, Muhammad Qutb Shah personally led an attack on the fort. Although the walls had been broken, the approach to the fort was extremely steep and it was impossible for the soldiers to invest the fort effectively and capture it. While the attack was floundering on the steeply inclined slopes, the Bijapur Maratha irregular forces appeared on the flank of the Golconda forces. Muhammad Qutb Shah prudently withdrew from the attack, followed by the Ahmadnagar forces.

Muhammad Qutb Shah felt that he had shown sufficient solidarity with Ahmadnagar, grew weary of the campaign, and decided to return to his own country. Golconda had achieved nothing during the campaign other than the loss of some forces. It is even doubtful whether their efforts had made an impact or influenced the relationship with Ahmadnagar in a positive manner. On the withdrawal of the invading forces, Bijapur managed to recapture all the territory that they had lost. In a holistic analysis, the Ahmadnagar expedition can be counted as a total failure.

Why the State of Constant War?

At this juncture in the narrative, it is necessary to analyse the reasons that forced the three major Deccan Shahi dynasties to be in a state of war with each other on a continuous basis. What were the underlying complexities and motivation that compelled these states to fight one another, change alliances at the drop of a hat, and keep each other from prospering? Four fundamental reasons can be clearly identified for the disunity that prevailed in the Deccan during the period of medieval Islamic rule. They are not particularly applicable to one dynasty, but encompassed all three major dynasties that sprouted in the territories of the Bahmani kingdom even before the end of that dynasty.

One: the successor kingdoms to the Bahamani Empire were created by powerful nobles without much effort; the kingdoms could be considered to have been gifted to them on the proverbial platter. These nobles, the founding kings, had all been governors of the provinces that they carved into independent kingdoms with a minimum of effort at the collapse of the Bahmani dynasty. It is a universal fact that anything that is achieved with relative ease, or is gifted free, is not valued as much as a possession or prize that is hard won. The first Deccan Shahi kings and their progeny were 'accidental' kings who were elevated to the throne of minor kingdoms by a series of events that they did not initiate, but which favoured them. An innate sense of the sublime and God-given 'right to rule' was pervasive in the senior princes of all these dynasties.

Two: although the Deccan has an inhospitable appearance and is not blessed with temperate climate, it is resource-rich. Even small kingdoms of the Deccan were able to sustain themselves in a fairly opulent manner without much effort. Even under conditions of very lax economic administration, the successor kingdoms continued to flourish. The conflicts and wars did not deplete their treasuries as would have been the case in other resource-constrained kingdoms. Further, none of the kings were really welfare-oriented as such, providing the common people with minimal aid and that too only to the Muslim subjects, who were in the minority. The kings, uniformly, ruled for themselves and nothing more. They indulged in their whims and fancies and a number of them verged on the debauched—even relative to the accepted licentious ways of kings of the time—throughout their reigns.

Three: the kings had a sense of ruling an alien land because of their religion and the foreign customs and traditions that were adopted in court. This mindset was obvious and pervasive despite that fact that most of them had at least some amount of local blood in them and were 'Deccani'. By the time the Deccan Shahi kingdoms were established, sufficient intermingling of the races had happened and there was a distinct class of nobles called the Deccanis. However, the kings continued to cultivate Persian culture within the royal court and stood apart from the common people, even those of the Islamic faith. While this made the royalty standout from the plebeians, it also created a sense of insecurity within the ruling class, which translated to them being wary of the rising power of a neighbouring king. The infamous 'tall poppy syndrome' was rampantly prevalent within the Deccan throughout the three centuries of the Shahi rule. Any powerful and ambitious king had to be cut down to size—alliances were accordingly formed, based purely on ambition and jealousy of the ruler of a kingdom.

Four: since the founders of the prominent dynasties—Adil Shahis (Bijapur), Nizam Shahis (Ahmadnagar) and Qutb Shahis (Golconda)—were all derived from a group of prominent nobility of the Bahmani kingdom, they were obviously adept at administration and warfare. However, a deeper analysis brings out the fact that none of these first kings produced any successor of great merit or capability. The kings were mediocre in their ruling essence, never being able attain the level of distinction that would make them stand above and apart from the run-of-the-mill rulers of the time. They remained small-time chieftains, incapable of rising above the average. Pettiness was rampant and aspiring to prominence was not only rare but immediately punished by the others as suspicious behaviour. The Deccan Shahi kings displayed in abundance all the human frailties, which invariably bring down dynasties. Considering these factors, a state of continuous conflict that prevailed for a few centuries was unavoidable.

Internal Turmoil

In Ahmadnagar, Salabat Khan, the appointee of the Prime Minster Asad Khan, had started to increase his influence and the squabbles between the two had taken acute proportions, as had been predicted by Murtaza earlier. This contest for greater influence drew in other nobles and created factionalism, which is the beginning of chaos and confusion in any centralised administration. Dual-control is never a good system for the efficient functioning of a pyramidal organisation. In addition, division at the apex invariably invites external intervention that consistently brings further divisions and splintering of unity. Berar and Bidar started to support different factions in Ahmadnagar to add to the confusion. Around the time that the division between the two co-Prime Ministers was becoming uncontrollable, Jalal ud-Din Muhammad Akbar, the Mughal Emperor, send Khwaja Fathullah Khan as his envoy to Ahmadnagar. This appointment indicates the stature of the Nizam Shahi, at least from an external assessment, as being considered somewhat of equal status as the Mughal kingdom to the north. It is also possible that Akbar had an ulterior motive in initiating this gesture. He would have wanted his envoy to judge the power of the kingdom and assess the situation in terms of the expansionist ambition of the Mughal king. In any case, the envoy was received graciously by Murtaza Nizam Shah and housed in an appropriately grand palace in the capital.

The rivalry between Asad Khan and Salabat Khan reached its vicious height with Salabat gathering all power into his hands. However, he kept the reclusive king Murtaza in the dark regarding his activities and had him secluded in a palace in Ahmadnagar, mainly in the company of courtesans. The king was oblivious of the trouble into which the kingdom was descending. The power struggle also eventuated in the cancellation of matrimonial alliances that the Nizam Shahi kingdom had earlier entered into with other kingdoms. Miran Husain, the heir apparent in Ahmadnagar had been informally betrothed to the sister of the Golconda king, Ibrahim Qutb Shah. Salabat Khan cancelled this plan and started to negotiate a matrimonial alliance with a princess of Bijapur, to the annoyance of the Qutb Shahi king, who felt insulted.

> **The Berar Rebellion**
>
> The disunity in Ahmadnagar prompted the nobles of Berar, struggling under Nizam Shahi rule, to rebel in an attempt to regain the independence of their kingdom. A serious battle took place very close to Ahmadnagar. Salabat Khan, now the de facto ruler of Ahmadnagar, took decisive and brave action. The Berar army was overconfident and had under-estimated the warfighting qualities of Salabat Khan. They had also attempted to bribe some of the Ahmadnagar nobles to defect at a crucial moment in the battle. However, these nobles did not act according to the agreement. The combination of these factors led to a resounding defeat for the Berar army.

Although Salabat Khan was in power, the constant bickering and grab for power that characterised the royal court in Ahmadnagar continued unabated. His control was not such that he could put an end to the intrigues that were gradually debilitating the kingdom.

Meanwhile, Murtaza who was far removed from the affairs of the court was told by some astrologers that his son and crown prince, Miran Husain, would be the cause of his death. Further, it was predicted that Husain would also be the cause of the subsequent ruin of the Nizam Shahi dynasty itself. Murtaza, without considering the consequences, ordered the execution of his son Miran Husain. While these events were unfolding, the indomitable Chand Bibi—Murtaza Nizam Shah's sister and the Queen of Ali Adil Shah—re-enters the historical narrative of Ahmadnagar. She had accompanied the Bijapur princess, Khadeija Sultana who was to be married to Miran Hussein, back to her Ahmadnagar home, seeking a life of peace and quiet. However, she found that Ahmadnagar was convulsed by intrigue and strife, mainly because of the irrational behaviour of Murtaza, who vacillated between ruling and withdrawing from the royal court.

Even though Murtaza issued orders for the execution of Miran Husain, Salabat Khan was reluctant to carry out the irrational order and therefore made excuses for not carrying out the king's orders. This was the first instance of inaction by Salabat Khan that irked Murtaza and started to make him lose faith in the loyalty of the minister.

A Failed Mughal Enterprise

Seeing that there was debilitating in-fighting going on in Ahmadnagar, a rebel general Sayyid Murtaza, who was so far ensconced in Berar, went to Akbar's court and reignited the Mughal's nascent ambition to conquer the Deccan. Akbar decided to mount an campaign to the Peninsula and appointed his foster brother and governor of Malwa, Mirza Aziz Kuka, commander of the proposed expedition. Accordingly an army was gathered and marched to the town of Hindiya, situated at the junction of the borders of Malwa, Burhanpur and the Deccan plateau.

Murtaza Nizam Shah prepared to repel the on-coming assault and marched his forces to the Burhanpur border, reaching and camping on the banks of the River Tapti. The Mughal army did not give battle and is reported to have fled to safety in Gujarat. *[This may be an exaggeration, but the Mughal army did not offer battle and Murtaza was happy to let the situation rest, rather than force the issue.]* Contemporary records state that it was only providential for Ahmadnagar that the nobles of Malwa were divided on the action to be taken and therefore did not offer pitched battle. The Mughal forces were battle hardened and would have prevailed if their commanders were able to unite and agree on one course of action against the Nizam Shahi forces.

Indeed, Ahmadnagar was in no shape to face an invasion and was lucky at this stage to have avoided facing the wrath of the mighty Mughal army. The immediate reason for the Mughals not attacking may have been disunity at the local commanders' level. However, the real reason were two other strategic aspects. First, Akbar did not think that the time had come to annex the Nizam Shahi kingdom, since it was still very strongly held by Murtaza and his prime minister. An expedition to annex the kingdom would have proved too costly in lives and treasure and the Mughal was not willing to enter into battle just for the sake of a pointless victory. The strategic intent of all his military actions was expansion through annexation, not mere military victories. Second, Akbar's own assessment of the military capabilities of the Deccan kingdoms did not match the equation for an assured conquest with minimal loss and bloodshed. Ahmadnagar had survived by the barest margin, for the time being. A visionary king would have seen the writing on the wall and initiated whatever actions were required to safeguard the sovereignty of the kingdom. Sadly, the Nizam Shahis were anything but visionaries—they were immersed in the pursuit of their own happiness, steeped in self-centred pastimes. No cognisance was given to the on-coming military deluge.

Murtaza Nizam Shah – 'The Madman'

During his self-imposed secluded life, Murtaza became infatuated with a dancing girl called Tulji (also named Fathi in some accounts). In one of his magnanimous moods, Murtaza wanted to gift this dancer with two extremely costly necklaces and a large quantity of gems and rubies, from the Vijayanagar booty that was kept separately in the treasury. Worried about the high value of these gifts, Salabat Khan initially refused to agree to this gift and then substituted them for replicas of lesser value. The chagrined dancing girl complained to the king regarding this act of the prime minister.

Murtaza was enraged at the defiance of the prime minister and set fire to the entire treasury. The ensuing flames also engulfed and destroyed the royal library that had contained

> a magnificent collection of books. Only a minimal amount of pearls and gems could be salvaged from the fire-ravaged treasury. From that day onwards Murtaza was referred to as 'The Madman' by courtiers and commoners alike, obviously out of earshot of the king.

The outcome of the above episode was that the concubines, courtesans and dancing girls started to poison the king's mind against the Peshwa, Salabat Khan. They had started to exercise complete emotional control over Murtaza. The king, already suspicious of his loyalty, started to order the Peshwa to do belittling tasks, far away from the capital. Although Salabat Khan continued to be a loyal and obedient minister, the stature of the position of Peshwa was gradually diminished by these actions of an uncaring king.

The Gradually Changing Fortunes

Another issue was gnawing at the stature and power of Ahmadnagar, which was more important than the prestige of the Peshwa. At the marriage of Miran Husain to the sister of Ibrahim Adil Shah of Bijapur, a part of the dowry was to have been the transfer of the fort at Sholapur to Ahmadnagar. However, long after the wedding ceremonies were completed, Bijapur had not effected the transfer. In retaliation, Ahmadnagar kept the marriage unconsummated and threatened to annul it. The issue assumed larger proportion and became a point of contention between the two kingdoms. Ibrahim Adil Shah now deployed his forces to the Ahmadnagar border. Murtaza was unhappy with the evolving situation.

Murtaza indirectly blamed Salabat Khan for the deteriorating situation and had him imprisoned at the fort in Parenda. He appointed Bihaz-ul-Mulk and Mirza Sadiq as co-Peshwas and on perceiving a contest between them for power, imprisoned Bihaz and favoured Saqiq as the only Prime Minster. Sadiq was loyal and efficient. He managed to banish the dancing girls under whose influence Murtaza Nizam Shah had been ruling his kingdom for some time. During the time that Murtaza was appointing and removing a succession of Peshwas— Salabat Khan, Bihaz-ul-Mulk, Mirza Sadiq—the affairs of the kingdom had become completely confused. There was a rotating feast of the cycle of arrests, internments, releases and re-appointments, which repeated itself ad nauseam with nobles being appointed to positions of power and being removed within days.

The marriage of the sister of the Bijapur Adil Shahi king to Miran Husain had been an alliance initiated by Ahmadnagar. The fact that it had not been fully solemnised irritated Ibrahim Adil Shah who by now was considering the marriage a fiasco. He approached Muhammad Qutb Shah to form an alliance, which was formalised with the sister of the Qutb Shahi king being given in marriage to Ibrahim Adil Shah. Bolstered by the alliance, Ibrahim Adil Shah invaded Ahmadnagar territory and ransacked a large tract of land. The state of affairs in the Nizam Shah kingdom had reached a low that did not permit the king or his ministers to respond to the latest Bijapur invasion. The Bijapur invasion and depredations went unanswered.

Understanding the precariousness of the situation, Murtaza instituted some steps to revitalise the administration. Murtaza brought in the sons of some of the older and loyal nobles to run the administration; and appointed Maulana Habibullah, the son of Inayatullah (an earlier Peshwa), as the Peshwa, although he also did not last long in the position. The king also anointed his son Miran Husain (referred to as Mirza Khan in some accounts) as the heir apparent, ignoring the predictions that had earlier made him order the prince's execution. However, confusion continued to prevail since Murtaza could not enforce all the writs that he proclaimed—his control over the court had diminished to such an extent that the nobles could easily ignore his orders without fear of any serious repercussions. This open disobedience was led by none other than Prince Husain himself. There was no saving the administration of Murtaza who now openly blamed Miran Husain for the decline of the kingdom into chaos.

With Ahmadnagar in chaos, Miran Husain was raised to the throne by some rebel nobles at Daulatabad. On the spread of this news, the entire royal army defected to Husain and an enormous military force assembled at Daulatabad. Husain now marched to Ahmadnagar at the head of this army. On reaching the capital, Husain marched into the city in royal state and at a selected auspicious hour went to meet his father the king. It is certain that Husain met his father, who is reported to have advised and blessed him. By this time Murtaza was in a totally weakened state both physically and in spirits. The further actions attributed to Husain are speculative and unconfirmed. One narrative states that he wanted to kill Murtaza immediately, but his father told him that he, Murtaza, had but few days remaining to live and therefore he should be permitted to die of natural causes. Husain is supposed to have let this happen. The second narrative states that Murtaza was murdered a few days after the meeting on Husain's orders, by leaving him in a very hot bath for about nine hours rather than the prescribed thirty minutes or so.

Irrespective of whether Murtaza Nizam Shah was permitted to die a natural death or murdered by his son, the new king, the fact is that Murtaza died on 14 June 1588 after ruling for 24 years.

Murtaza – An Appraisal

Official records, made during various stages of his rule, state that Murtaza Nizam Shah excelled in basic kingly virtues—bravery, valour, justice and generosity. This seems to have been an exaggerated and congratulatory appraisal done during his reign and directly oriented towards currying favour from an erratic but generous monarch. The fact remains that he inherited what was an exceptionally wealthy treasury when he came to power, which he methodically bankrupted. Even though some commentators mention this fact as a tribute to his inherent generosity, the distribution of treasure and wealth was not done to help the deserving, but as gifts to people who pleased him in some inane manner or the other. State treasure was used in a self-serving manner, of course this was the accepted prerogative of the ruling king in medieval times, but that does not make the behaviour 'right'. Murtaza's use of state-treasure was wasteful with no thought given to the welfare of the common people, the subjects of the king who should have been his primary concern.

The above assessment should not be written off as applying today's standards to the medieval times when kings were self-centred tyrants. Medieval times also provide sufficient examples of thoughtful and exemplary rulers who placed the welfare of their subjects as their highest priority at all times. However, the attitude of most of the Deccan Shahi kings could not be considered anything but self-serving.

Murtaza Nizam Shah was definitely a learned person, demonstrated by the discussions that he held with philosophers and theologians. These meetings have been confirmed by multiple sources. It is also confirmed that he possessed an inquisitive and well-ordered mind as well as having great acumen and foresight. The charges of insanity and his being nick-named 'The Madman' is based on one single episode that he conducted in a fit of extreme rage while he was probably under the influence of intoxicating substances. However, a life that was led bordering on excess, was bound to have an effect on the health of the king. Towards the end of his reign, his decisions bordered on being made without any thought whatsoever and decidedly lowered his status as a capable ruler. Murtaza presided over the golden era of the Nizam Shahi dynasty and also brought it to its knees towards the end of his rule. The golden era however cannot be attributed to him, but to pure fate that decreed it to so.

Chapter 21

THE BEGINNING OF THE END

Husain Nizam Shah II was enthroned on the death or murder of his father. Whether the old king was murdered is not clear and would therefore depend on the narrative that one believes in. On becoming king, Husain bestowed favours and rewards on anyone who approached him, irrespective of the services rendered by the person appealing to the king. This was an attempt at ensuring that he was 'universally' accepted by the nobles and people as the legitimate king, especially since the reality of the death of his father was still being debated. On the third day of the new king's official reign, Ibrahim Adil Shah attempted to invade Ahmadnagar, taking advantage of the confusion of the succession. However, the Bijapur army quickly withdrew on Husain himself taking to the field to give battle.

> **A Different Story**
>
> There is also a different narrative to the Adil Shahi king's arrival in the territory of Ahmadnagar.
>
> Ibrahim Adil Shah, it is purported, was marching to Ahmadnagar to assist Husain to claim the throne and in removing the old and incapacitated Murtaza from the scene. When the Bijapur king and his forces reached Pathardi, he came to know that Husain had already assumed the throne. Ibrahim immediately send congratulatory messages and proposed that he continue to Ahmadnagar in order to visit Husain Nizam Shah II and his wife Khadeija, who was the

> Adil Shahi's sister. However, before Husain's reply to the messages were received in the Bijapur camp, Ibrahim Adil Shah got the information that Murtaza could possibly have been murdered by Husain.
>
> In a righteous rage, Ibrahim now wrote an indignant, bitter and reproachful letter to Husain, condemning him for committing patricide and clearly stating that the murder was a heinous and wrong act. Ibrahim went on to state that he personally would have removed Murtaza to Bijapur and if necessary even blinded him, but thereafter would have looked after the old Nizam Shahi king in his capital. He asserted that he could not condone murder and therefore was returning to his kingdom without visiting Ahmadnagar. The Bijapur king and his army returned to their kingdom.
>
> The authenticity of this narrative cannot be verified. Considering the avaricious nature that Ibrahim Adil Shah had so far displayed, it is more likely that he had started to move towards Ahmadnagar with some ulterior motive and to create more confusion during the succession struggle, but on Husain having assumed the throne, considered it prudent to withdraw. He could have taken the 'murder' of Murtaza as an excuse to withdraw without losing face amongst his nobles. Even this assessment is speculation, but a distinct possibility.

Husain Nizam Shah II started his reign by appointing Mirza Khan, a Phirangi noble, as the Peshwa and the commander-in-chief of the army. Husain then removed himself from the rigours of ruling and devoted his time to personal enjoyment. He did not have any appreciation of the position that he had forcibly assumed and had no time for the extreme cares that accompanied the life of a dutiful king.

Husain Nizam Shah II

With the king conspicuously absent from the day-to-day functioning of the court and the ruling of the state being left to the Peshwa, it did not take long for the traditional rivalry between the Phirangi and Deccani factions of nobles to intensify and come to the fore. It is also reported that there was some amount of in-fighting within the Deccani faction itself. The Deccanis attempted to slander Mirza Khan and poison the king's ear against him, but the youthful but astute Husain saw through the ploy and neutralised the evolving palace coup. Mirza Khan was a good administrator and unbiased, considering the norms of the times, in his dealings. In an attempt to put an end to the debilitating in-fighting in the court, Mirza Khan persuaded the king to appoint three nobles to carry out the duties of the Peshwa. The three nobles were all beholden to Mirza Khan and therefore he remained the power and controlling influence behind them—the real and effective ruler.

In a troubled and unsettled kingdom, challenges do not always have to be generated by external forces; an incompetent and self-indulgent king can also create enough troubles by himself. Husain had two intimate friends who were commoners, Ankas Khan and Ambar Khan, perhaps friends from his childhood days. In a misplaced act of magnanimity, the king promoted both these commoners, to the status of 'amirs', nobles, which was resented by the Phirangi faction of the nobles. They guarded their status zealously and obviously did not want to be equated with the lower class. In addition to this appointment, Husain regularly associated himself with courtesans and dancing girls of low-status, openly indulging in acts of debauchery. The king's behaviour was not liked by either the nobles or the commoners. Despite his initial attempts at being accepted, Husain Nizam Shah was not a popular king in Ahmadnagar.

After being promoted to the ranks of the nobles, Ankas Khan, the more ambitious of the two friends of the king, started to vie for power with Mirza Khan who was the real power behind the throne. The power struggle became acute with both plotting the downfall of the other and attempting to influence Husain to accomplish this feat. Mirza Khan was obviously more adept at such palace intrigue and also had much greater resources to fall back on. By this time the Phirangi faction of nobles, upset with the behaviour of the king who seemed to favour the Deccanis, had already started planning to get rid of Husain. As a preliminary step they had felt the necessity to find an immediate successor, so that the planned coup could succeed. In order to ensure legitimacy, the successor had to be from the royal family. Accordingly two princes were chosen as possible replacements. Through a series of calculated steps, Mirza Khan managed to lure Husain into the inner fort unaccompanied by his usual contingent of guards and imprisoned him.

On imprisoning Husain, Mirza Khan initiated the already planned steps to bring the selected princes to Ahmadnagar, so that one of them could assume the throne. There were two surviving princes imprisoned in Lohogarh—both sons of Burhan Khan who was the brother of the murdered Murtaza Nizam Shah—cousins of Husain Nizam Shah. Burhan Khan was at this time resident in Akbar's court in Agra and had been titled Sahib Qiran by the Mughal king. The two princes were secreted into Ahmadnagar fort. Although both the princes were the sons of Burhan Khan, the elder one, Ibrahim, was born to a lady of African origin and was therefore dark-skinned. The younger prince, Ismail, was fair since his mother was a fair Konkan lady and was the preferred substitute for Husain. *[The Indian pre-occupation with the colour of the skin, with fair being looked upon as handsome/beautiful can be seen to pre-date the arrival of the Europeans in numbers into the sub-continent. Perhaps this fetish went back to the days when the Central Asian hordes had started to invade the north-west of the geographic entity now known as India. Irrespective of the origin of this warped sense of beauty, fair skin-colour has always been—and continues to be—equated to beauty in the sub-continent, especially in the case of ladies.]*

With Husain imprisoned, preparations for the crowning of the 12 year-old Ismail, were hurriedly made. Since he had been captured almost on his own and thereafter kept in solitary confinement, nobody knew the whereabouts of Husain or even what had happened to him. Correctly surmising that some evil plan was being hatched by the Phirangis, the Deccan faction came together under the leadership of one Jamal Khan, who had so far been a junior and obscure military commander far removed from the centres of power. Fairly rapidly a large force assembled around the fort. Even though he had not been independent command before, Jamal Khan was quick to understand the need to ensure loyalty and promised promotions and wealth all round to the assembled force, thereby building the cohesion of the ad-hoc army.

Confident of his command over the Deccani faction, Jamal Khan send a message to Mirza Khan, now in the fort, demanding that King Husain Nizam Shah be set free. Mirza Khan was contemptuous of the upstart leader of the Deccanis and treated the message accordingly; he replied that Jamal Khan could be admitted to the fort on his own to pay his respect to the King, Ismail Nizam Shah. On receiving this answer to his demand, Jamal Khan decided to act and the bubbling civil war came into open strife. The fort was stormed.

The Aftermath

Mirza Khan now realised the seriousness of the situation and did a haphazard parade of Ismail, the young prince, under the king's canopy to prove that he had been ordained king. However, the Deccanis did not accept this show of royalty and continued to demand the release of Husain. In desperation, Mirza had Husain murdered and his severed head thrown down into the milling Deccani army inside the fort. There is a mention that Husain had already been blinded earlier, although this information is not borne out by any authentic report. The confirmation of the murder of Husain saddened the Deccani army, but they recovered sufficiently very quickly and attacked the fort with renewed energy.

The battle for control of the fort raged for more than a day, with the Deccanis gaining the advantage. Even though some of the Phirangi nobles tried to hide, but were sought out and gradually most of the Phirangi leadership were killed in the melee. The core group of Phirangi nobles formed around Mirza Khan and fought valiantly making it possible for a small inner circle group led by Mirza Khan to fight their way out of the fort and escape. Mutaza's sister Chand Bibi, the dowager queen of Bijapur for some time, had been visiting Ahmadnagar at this stage, but also managed to escape and make her way back to Bijapur. The fact that a small group of intrepid nobles were able to fight their way out of the fort, which had been breached and while they were surrounded, indicates the haphazard manner of the Deccani attack on the fort. It is obvious that there was no central plan or leadership to the storming of the fort. The rebellion was an impromptu affair, which is further emphasised by the fact that till the start of the rebellion, nothing is known of the antecedents of Jamal Khan, the nominal leader of the Deccanis.

The fleeing Mirza Khan and his small entourage reached Junnar, where they were captured and Mirza Khan executed. In Ahmadnagar, young Ismail was brought back to the throne and Jamal Khan ordered a general massacre of Phirangis. The order was followed by a great carnage of looting, burning, pillage, rape and wanton murder. The Phirangi faction of nobles were almost fully destroyed; and all their jagirs confiscated and redistributed amongst the Deccanis.

At this stage Farhad Khan, the governor of Chitapur and the de facto leader of the Habshis – the African nobles – who were aligned with the Deccanis, intervened to save the small group of Phirangis who had not yet been massacred. The Habshis were a small but powerful group within the nobles. Farhad now decreed that there would be no more slaughter, which was immediately obeyed, and he went on to play the role of the 'protector' of the now hapless Phirangis. However, this power and influence would prove transitory for Farhad Khan; Jamal Khan had other ideas. Jamal was ambitious, which was obvious, and suggested that he and Farhad become joint-Peshwas for the kingdom. However, Farhad rejected the proposal and recommended that Qasim Beg be appointed to the position.

This rejection of the offer to jointly rule the kingdom proved to be Farhad's undoing. Jamal Khan imprisoned Farhad and through hefty bribes and promise of higher positions managed to turn Farhad's army against their master—in effect buying their loyalty. Then Jamal paraded the young king through the streets of the capital, very clearly demonstrating to the people that the king was under his protection. He had Farhad Khan removed to the fort at Rajuri (Rahuri, in some accounts). Jamal Khan further entrenched his position through a matrimonial alliance with the family of a prominent noble Khudavand Khan. He also promoted many Deccani and Habshi officers to the status of nobles, or amirs, thereby ingratiating himself to both the groups.

The Phirangi Rebellion

Although Berar had ceased to be an independent kingdom, it had continued to function as an autonomous province within the Nizam Shahi kingdom. Berar was governed by a 'Phirangi' noble, Muhammad Khan, who readily gave refuge and shelter to the Phirangi nobles who had escaped the Ahmadnagar massacre. Bahri Khan was one the prominent nobles of this group under whose guidance the escapees managed to gradually build up a large force. On becoming sufficiently powerful, they decided to secede Berar from Ahmadnagar control and become independent. They set Salabat Khan, a Phirangi noble who had been incarcerated by the Nizam Shahi kings, free and unanimously declared him the ruler of Berar. The Berar forces now marched to Ahmadnagar. More Phirangis, who had either been in hiding or were scattered around the countryside in fear, started to join this rebel army of Berar.

Having established himself as the Peshwa through devious means and bribery, Jamal Khan felt that he could not fully trust the royal army. Even so, he marched with the Nizam Shahi forces to Shivgaon, taking Ismail with him to ensure that the young king remained in the Jamal camp. Thereafter, Jamal Khan resorted to bribery to break the cohesion of the rebel army. These actions should not surprise the modern reader because such actions and the following display of disloyalty by the nobles and other officers was common place in medieval Deccan. In today's modern jargon, their actions could be dismissed as being 'par for the course'.

Being a past master in the art of bribery and corruption, Jamal Khan send secret letters to the amirs, nobles, in Salabat Khan's army promising them a royal pardon as well as promotions and great wealth if they deserted the Berar army and joined the Ahmadnagar royal army. Jamal Khan also ensured that the Phirangi nobles knew that the king was in camp with him. In other words he was indicating to them that he was the de facto ruler, since the king was still a minor. Salabat Khan marched forward and reached Paithan but a number of his nobles deserted him and a few others were captured by Jamal's forces. Salabat now started to suspect the loyalty of his forces and thought it inadvisable to proceed with the proposed war on Ahmadnagar. Accordingly, in a prudent move, he withdrew towards Berar. Even during this retreat, his forces continued to bleed away through desertions to the Nizam Shahi forces that were in hot pursuit of the rebels. Salabat and a small core group of his forces managed to evade the Ahmadnagar forces and reached the border of Burhanpur, where the ruler Ali Khan provided refuge to the worn-out forces.

During the period that the regent and the boy-king were away from the capital, the ever-ambitious Ibrahim Adil Shah decided to take advantage of the situation and invaded Ahmadnagar. True to form, Jamal bought off Ibrahim by paying a huge sum of money as 'tribute', instead of confronting the invading force with his own army. The Adil Shah also insisted on his sister and the widow of Murtaza, Khadeija Sultana, being send back to Bijapur as part of the peace deal.

Even though he was reluctant to enter into battle, Jamal Khan now initiated actions that dealt a death blow to the Phirangi noble faction. He was completely disillusioned by the behaviour of the Phirangi nobles and banished the entire lot from Ahmadnagar through royal decree. He rounded up all members of the Phirangi faction of nobles, including those who were in hiding. The more important nobles of the group were forced to go on pilgrimage to Mecca and Medina; some were send to Bijapur; and some to the port at Chaul. All of them were stripped of their status and jagirs, and reduced to common people so that they could not collect forces to rise in revolt again. Jamal Khan was now entrenched as the Peshwa-Regent and the de facto ruler since Ismail Nizam Shah was still a minor. He was sublimely unaware of the on-coming war of succession.

The War of Succession – Burhan Nizam Shah II

Ismail's father and the brother of Murtaza, Burhan Khan, was at this time in the service of the Mughal king Akbar who had appointed him the governor of Bangesh. Akbar had always kept a watchful eye on the unfolding events in the Deccan and had continued to harbour ambitions of annexing the Deccan Shahi kingdoms sometime in the future. He now urged Burhan to proceed to the Deccan and lay claim to the Nizam Shahi throne. Akbar promised Burhan a Mughal army to accomplish this feat and in return extracted a promise from Burhan to cede Berar to the Mughals after he had been enthroned in Ahmadnagar. Burhan was also to formally accept Mughal overlordship, which had so far been declined by the three major Deccan Shahi rulers. In this manner Akbar hoped to gain a strong foothold in the northern Deccan as a prelude to further southward incursions.

There are two narratives regarding the origins of the army that accompanied Burhan Khan on his southward march to the Deccan. One states that he was accompanied by the Mughal forces given by Akbar, which is highly probable. The second states that Burhan was shrewd enough to realise that the nobles and the people of the Deccan would not take kindly to the arrival of Mughal forces into their kingdom, because of which he might not be able to gain popular support. Therefore, he gracefully refused the offer from the Mughal king and proceeded at the head of a small force of his own retainers towards Ahmadnagar. While this narrative sounds good and gives Burhan an undeserved reputation for astute decision-making, later events prove that Mughal forces accompanied him, at least during the early phase of the campaign. In either case, he left the court in Agra for the Deccan with the tacit approval of the Mughal king.

Having reached the border of Ahmadnagar, Burhan assumed the title Burhan Nizam Shah and send a message to Jamal Khan to present himself at the temporary court, since he was now the rightful ruler of the kingdom. For the first time, Jamal decided to give battle to protect his interests and asked a trusted Deccani general to proceed to the border at Berar. He also approached Raja Ali Khan, ruling in Burhanpur, for assistance; and also tried to get Salabat Khan to his side with the promise of a royal pardon, personal safety and great wealth. Salabat Khan readily joined Jamal Khan's forces, but was killed during a minor skirmish even before any serious battle could take place.

Burhan entered Berar through Gondwara in the Satpura ranges. He was opposed by Jahangir Khan, a Habshi noble whose jagirs lay at the border and was now under attack. Jahangir managed to withstand the attack by sheer obstinate strength of arms and continued to skirmish with great effect. During one of these skirmishes, a stray bullet killed the Mughal commander of the forces accompanying Burhan. The Mughal forces, which formed the majority of Burhan's forces, fled the battlefield. This was a setback. It took a number of months before Burhan could reorganise his forces and resume the march towards Ahmadnagar.

The rest of Burhan's campaign is a tale of alliances and betrayals, of advances and withdrawals, of avarice and generosity. Jamal attempted to dupe Burhan into coming to Ahmadnagar with minimal escorts, but Burhan refused the invitation. He started to make preparations for an onslaught on Ahmadnagar itself after establishing camp at Khandwa. Burhan also send messages to the other Shahi kings and all the minor kings and chiefs of the Deccan to come to his aid in the fight against Jamal Khan in his quest to claim his rightful hereditary position as the Nizam Shahi king. Ibrahim Adil Shah II was advised by his calculating prime minister, Dilavar Khan a Habshi noble of great influence, to join Burhan. A strong Bijapur force was send to Burhan's camp, which had now been joined by Raja Ali Khan of Burhanpur. Dilavar Khan now played an important role in deciding the fate of the Nizam Shahi throne. He had great influence amongst the Habshi nobles across the entire Deccan and on his urging, these nobles flocked to join Burhan.

Burhan entered Berar and the Habshi nobles there submitted to the 'new' king, at the behest of Dilavar Khan. This was a heavy blow to Jamal Khan since he had relied heavily on the loyalty of the Berar Habshi nobles. Jamal Khan now marched against the Bijapur army that was under the command of Dilavar Khan himself. The Habshi nobles continued to join Burhan's camp, but Jamal continued to prepare for a battle against the Adil Shahi forces. The Bijapur forces were over-confident and through sheer carelessness made a number of tactical blunders. Jamal Khan capitalised on these mistakes and defeated the Bijapur army in battle. So great was the defeat that Dilavar Khan barely managed to escape with his life. On his forces being defeated, Ibrahim Adil Shah retreated to his fort at Naldurg.

A great deal of manoeuvring and small-scale skirmishes continued while both armies prepared for the final struggle. Jamal Khan was flush with his victory against the Bijapur forces and perhaps a bit over-confident regarding his own capability as a commander as well as the fighting ability of his forces. He force-marched towards Burhan's camp and reached Rohankhed in the neighbourhood of the Ghats. On 7 May 1591, a decisive battle was fought between the two armies in which Burhan emerged victorious and claimed the throne of Ahmadnagar. Ibrahim Adil Shah send a letter of congratulations and returned to Bijapur. Following the defeat of the Bijapur forces earlier, Dilavar Khan was out of favour with the Adil Shahi king and was forced to seek refuge with Burhan Nizam Shah. He was accepted into the Nizam Shahi court since he had been instrumental in swaying the Habshi nobles towards Burhan. The commitment of the Habshi nobles in support of Burhan was a critical factor in his emerging victorious in the succession struggle.

After claiming the throne of Ahmadnagar, Burhan Nizam Shah committed an uncalculated error of judgement that influenced the further history of the Nizam Shahi kingdom. He had promised Akbar, the Mughal king, that he would cede the entire territory of Berar on becoming the Nizam Shahi ruler and also that he would formally acknowledge the suzerainty of the Mughal. On coming to the throne he did not keep his promise. This act of perceived disloyalty added to Akbar's impetus to invade the Deccan and annex the 'rebel' kingdom.

The Portuguese Interlude

Murtaza had fought the Portuguese early in his reign and been defeated because of the duplicity of some of his nobles. Burhan wanted to avenge his brother's defeat and also restore the prestige of the Nizam Shahi dynasty by righting this failure and enhance it by driving the foreigners out of the sub-continent. He decided to mount a 'holy war' against the infidels and mis-believers. While Burhan was looking for a reasonable excuse to attack the Portuguese, an opportunity fell into his lap. An Ahmadnagar trading ship returning from Mecca, sank off the coast of Bassein, which was a Portuguese port. The ship had been laden with treasure and merchandise, which the Portuguese salvaged. Even after repeated demands from Ahmadnagar, the Portuguese did not return the salvaged treasure to the Nizam Shahi king. This opened the door to initiate military action and war.

Burhan did not take the on-coming conflict with the foreigners lightly. He made detailed preparations for the campaign—he had a fort constructed at Karla hill and emplaced cannons on it; and an important port of the Portuguese at Revdanda was boxed in completely. While these preparations were being undertaken, Ahmadnagar was under pressure from the Bijapur Adil Shahis who were encroaching across their common border. Further, there were also rumours of a Mughal advance towards Berar led by Prince Murad, Akbar's son. Burhan had however characterised the attacks on foreign Christians as a holy war and therefore of greater importance than the internal squabbles of the Deccan kingdoms. He believed that the other Muslim countries would refrain from attacking Ahmadnagar while it was involved in this holy task.

After extensive preparations, the Nizam Shahi army attacked the port of Chaul. The date of this attack vary in the Deccan chronicles and those of the Portuguese. The Deccan records date this battle for Chaul as 4 May 1593, whereas the Portuguese show the date as April 1592. It is highly probable that the Portuguese took the date when the fortification at Karla Hill started as the date of the beginning of the campaign. During this campaign, the first that Burhan undertook as the king, he clearly demonstrated the inherent bias that he had in favour of the Phirangi nobles of the Deccan. This bias may have been inculcated while he was in the Agra court serving as a governor in the service of the Mughal Emperor. The initial commander of the Nizam Shahi forces undertaking the campaign was a Deccani noble who was killed in a night attack by the Portuguese forces. It is reliably reported that Burhan secretly rejoiced at the death of his commander, since he could now appoint a Phirangi noble to the position.

Burhan's Death

Burhan's belief that no political or geo-strategic strife would encompass his kingdom, externally or domestically, while he was engaged in a holy war was unfounded. Even as the campaign against the Portuguese was unfolding, there was the beginning of a rebellion in Ahmadnagar. In the Deccan, it was intrigue as usual. The expedition to capture Chaul came to a disgraceful end. The Portuguese stormed the fort at Karla with assistance from some disloyal nobles who surreptitiously left the fort gates open. There was a great slaughter of the Muslims, who were mainly Deccanis. Burhan's open apathy towards the Deccani Muslims is given as the primary reason for the open disloyalty of some of the nobles. There is a believable report that even as the kingdom was being defeated in battle at Karla, the king was rejoicing at the thought that the Ahmadnagar forces that were being slaughtered were mostly Deccani Muslims, which in a twisted manner he considered a 'victory' for himself.

The Beginning of The End

The attitude displayed by their king finally made the Deccani nobles decide to remove him and reinstate the boy-king, his son, Ismail on the throne. However, the plot was discovered and Burhan had the offending nobles flayed alive. The bias, bordering on acute hatred, that was displayed by Burhan is inexplicable—especially since his court was overwhelmingly Deccani and it was the direct support of these Deccani nobles that had brought him to power and helped in removing Jamal Khan, himself a Deccani military commander. Even after the ruthless manner in which the plotters were treated, Ahmadnagar continued to be in the grip of rebellion throughout Burhan's reign. He died of illness in 1594 after ruling for a few insignificant years. Before his death, his sister Chand Bibi was once again resident in Ahmadnagar, having returned from Bijapur to live with her brother.

Burhan Nizam Shah could be considered to have maintained the semblance of central rule in Ahmadnagar. He was succeeded by his son Ibrahim Nizam Shah, an impulsive and complex personality. On accession to the throne he insulted the ambassadors of Bijapur in the court and evicted them, exiling them back to Bijapur. This caused another war with Bijapur. The reckless and callow Ibrahim himself took to the field to lead the Ahmadnagar forces. His inexperience showed almost immediately, when he made few tactical mistakes in the battlefield, was separated from the main body of his forces with only a small troop of bodyguards, and promptly attacked and killed by the Bijapur forces.

Confusion spread throughout the Ahmadnagar army, which fled and the country descended into complete anarchy. Seeing the country in dire straits, the imperious, honourable and duty-bound Chand Bibi took charge.

Chapter 22

THE END: CHAND BIBI'S FINEST HOUR

Akbar had offered military assistance to Burhan Nizam Shah in 1590-91 to claim what Burhan perceived as his right to the throne by deposing his minor son who had been placed on the throne. In return, Burhan had made a vague promise that once he was ensconced on the throne, the Ahmadnagar kingdom would acknowledge Mughal sovereignty. This assurance had been ignored once he managed to get to the throne. Akbar had not forgotten the promise and he now send emissaries to the Deccan, demanding that the Shahi kingdoms acknowledge his overlordship and join the Mughal Empire as autonomous provinces. The three major kingdoms—Ahmadnagar, Bijapur and Golconda—unanimously refused to do so.

The demand by the powerful Mughal emperor should have acted as a warning to the Deccan Shahi kingdoms. They should have united without delay and started preparing for an invasion that was bound to come since they had defied the power of the Mughals. However, the three main dynasties of the Deccan opted to continue their internal bickering, being at odds with each other for reasons that could only be considered petty and inconsequential. Far-sightedness had never been one of the characteristic virtues of the medieval Deccan kings. They had chanced upon their kingdoms through tactical military capabilities that came to the fore when their selfish opportunistic streaks were animated. Further, the environment in the Deccan was such that it was impossible for these dynasties to produce kings of strategic calibre. The Deccan Shahi kingdoms therefore did not present a united front to what was an impending and definitive external interference. Instead, the Bijapur and Ahmadnagar forces continued to skirmish. In one of these interminable battles, Burhan's successor, Ibrahim Nizam Shah, was killed by the Bijapur forces a mere 40 kilometres from Ahmadnagar.

Succession Struggle

Even before and during the reign of Burhan, the long-standing divide between the Phirangi and Deccani factions of the nobles in the Ahmadnagar court was visually perceivable. On the death of Ibrahim Shah, the dissent between the factions became even more virulent. The Phirangi faction led by Afzal Khan wanted to place Ibrahim's infant son Bahadur Shah on the throne under the regentship of Chand Bibi, Ibrahim's aunt. The Deccanis led by Miyan Manjha feared that such a move would side-line them from power and therefore wanted to place the 12-year old son of Shah Tahir, Ahmad Shah, on the throne with one of them as the regent. Accordingly, they proclaimed Ahmad Shah as the king on 6 August 1595.

The further narrative of this succession struggle is a confusing trail of groups fighting each other and betraying allies with absolutely no thought for the future of the kingdom and an oblivious ignorance of the threat to its very existence gathering in the Mughal Empire in North India. Normally the Deccanis and the African faction of the nobles, mainly Abyssinians locally called Habshis, used to act in concert against the Phirangi faction. However, in this particular succession struggle, the Habshis led by Ikhlas Khan opposed the Deccanis. Therefore, Miyan Manjhu now courted some of the Phirangi nobles and made them join his faction in support of Ahmad Shah. Even so, the Phirangis had the upper hand in the on-going struggle.

Chand Bibi was the only person who had the sagacity to understand the threat that was being posed to her kingdom by the Mughals who were already manoeuvring to the north of Ahmadnagar. She started to settle the internal affairs of state that had been neglected for nearly a decade while in-fighting had consumed the kings, princes and nobles. The kingdom was reeling in a state of confusion and disrepair, not having been 'ruled' for a lengthy period of time. She also asked Afzal Khan to repair the fortress at Ahmadnagar in preparation for a possible assault on its ramparts. Miyan Manjha, feeling slighted, left the vicinity of the capital and took his followers to a place called Ausa where he made rebel camp.

The End: Chand Bibi's Finest Hour

The events that unfolded for the next year in Ahmadnagar are common embodiments of the long history of the sub-continent, both past and into the future—an initial succession struggle in a kingdom followed by the weaker faction seeking assistance from an external power base, normally a more powerful kingdom; the external agency attacking and defeating the legitimate rulers of the kingdom; and the kingdom itself thereafter being annexed by the external power.

While Ahmadnagar was being convulsed by the succession struggle and Chand Bibi was trying to establish some semblance of order, the Mughal Empire had already started to manoeuver in its own ponderous manner. Akbar had send his son Shah Murad to Malwa with clear instructions, to both the prince and the governor of Malwa, to invade and subdue the Deccan. Miyan Manjhu, in a sulk at Ausa, approached Shah Murad in Malwa and requested him for assistance in attacking and capturing Ahmadnagar. This invitation aligned well with the Mughal plans. By this time the central Mughal forces had already joined with the Malwa forces under the command of Abdul Rahim Khan-i-Khana, the efficient governor of Malwa. This combined force was also joined by Raja Ali Khan, ruling Mandu a vassal state of the Mughals. The combined Mughal army started its march towards Ahmadnagar.

In a side-show to this massive expedition, Miyan Manjhu had managed to defeat the Habshi faction, their rebellion against the Deccanis being short-lived. Many of the Habshi nobles deserted Ikhlas Khan and either joined Miyan Manjhu or directly defected to the Mughal army under Shah Murad. Viewing the power and might of the Mughal army, Miyan Manjhu started to have doubts about his decision to invite the Mughals to invade his own country. He regretted having joined the Mughals. It is highly likely that he was unaware of the ultimate objective of the Mughals and that the Mughal invasion of Ahmadnagar was a pre-gone conclusion, whether he had invited them or not. Irrespective of the invitation, the Mughals would have invaded Ahmadnagar soon. Miyan Manjhu, realising the threat to his country, separated from the Mughal forces, and taking Ahmad Shah the boy-claimant to the throne with him, marched post-haste to Ahmadnagar and placed himself and his forces under the command of Chand Bibi who was preparing to defend Ahmadnagar.

The Defence of Ahmadnagar

In December 1595, the Mughal forces laid siege to Ahmadnagar. Chand Bibi immediately asked for assistance from Ibrahim Adil Shah II of Bijapur and Muhammad Qutb Shah of Golconda, both of whom were her nephews by relationship. Meanwhile the Mughal forces harried and oppressed the people around Ahmadnagar, looting and pillaging the villages at will. According to the *Akbarnama*, the acclaimed biography of Akbar, Murad was outraged by the acts of plunder and wanton slaying perpetuated on the people of the Nizam Shahi kingdom by one of his subordinate commanders, Shahbaz Khan. There is also a report that states that Murad attempted to check the looting and plunder but by the time this action was initiated, the damage to the prestige and reputation of the imperial army had already been done. The people of Ahmadnagar came to believe that the Mughal army was a vicious and depraved horde and that they would not get any succour from them, even if they surrendered.

Prince Murad realised that it would be difficult to defeat Ahmadnagar if the reinforcements from Bijapur and Golconda managed to join up with the defending force. Therefore, he accelerated the siege actions by mining the fort walls in five different places. Chand Bibi was informed of this initiative by a Mughal noble who was sympathetic to the Ahmadnagar cause. She managed to excavate and remove two of the mines, but the other three were exploded by the Mughals, killing a number of Ahmadnagar troops and blowing a breech in the fort wall.

The breech in the fort wall spread panic in the Ahmadnagar forces. Seeing the confusion in her forces, Chand Bibi personally led the defence of the breech, herself fighting alongside the common soldier. The valiant Queen rallied her forces and guns were brought to bear on the invading army. Several repeated attacks by the Mughal army to force the breech were repelled and the broken walls repaired by night. During this desperate defence of Ahmadnagar, many acts of extreme bravery of the nobles of Ahmadnagar has been reported uniformly in all accounts of the siege. The Nizam Shahi forces successfully carried out many night attacks on the Mughal forces, although the *Akbarnama* refutes the efficacy of these attacks by the Deccan forces. In particular, two nobles, Miran Shah Ali and Mubariz ud-Din Abhang Khan have been mentioned in Ahmadnagar chronicles as having been extremely active and brave in their actions against the besieging forces.

The strong and determined defence of the fort by the Nizam Shahis made Prince Murad realise that capturing the fort would be an extremely difficult task. Therefore, he decided to negotiate for a settlement. At the same time the Mughal forces had started to feel the scarcity of provisions and resources necessary to continue the siege. The earlier burning and looting of the villages by the Mughal forces now started to backfire. The Mughals could not rely on any local provisions being available, which could be captured for their own use. The country was denuded of crops and habitation, making even communications with their far away home bases difficult. An uneasy peace was arrived at in February 1596, with Ahmadnagar ceding Berar to the Mughals.

Chand Bibi's courageous leadership had averted disaster for the Nizam Shahis. Her personal bravery that had so inspired the entire army to fight in a spirited manner earned Chand Bibi the sobriquet 'Sultana', and she was henceforth known as Chand Sultana. Although he was not defeated, Murad's reputation suffered a great blow since he was the one who had initiated the peace negotiations. Further, a bilaterally agreed settlement was not considered a victory for the powerful Mughal army. In a holistic assessment, the prestige of the Mughals had suffered a setback. Therefore, it was inevitable that a second attempt would be made in the near-future to humble the Nizam Shahis. The Mughals never took a slight to their status lightly. With the arrival of the Golconda and Bijapur reinforcements in Ahmadnagar, the Mughal army retreated fully from the area.

The Aftermath of 'Victory'

As soon as the Mughal threat had been warded off, Miyan Manjhu once again raised the flag of revolt, attempting once again to place his protégé Ahmad Shah on the throne. This single act demonstrates the short-sighted and selfish attitude that the nobles of the Deccan Shahi kingdoms displayed throughout the history of these kingdoms. Their inability to see beyond narrow, sectarian, and short-term interests seems astounding when examined with the advantage of hindsight from this far away in time. Even by medieval terms, their failure to see the proverbial 'wolf at the door' and the pitiable state their country was being driven to, smacks of selfish incompetence.

Chand Bibi, now Sultana, fully in control as the Regent and ably assisted by her nephew Ibrahim Adil Shah, very easily quelled Miyan Manjhu's rebellion. However, in order to avert further revolts and maintain the peace, she permitted her nephew to make Miyan Manjhu a noble of his own court and take him back to Bijapur. The unfortunate Ahmad Shah, a mere puppet in the hands of the Deccani nobles' faction, was given some estates for personal use and allowed to lead a life of leisure. Chand Sultana now formally proclaimed Bahadur Nizam Shah as the king and she herself became the Regent.

A trusted noble, Muhammad Khan, was appointed Peshwa. However, as was usual with such appointments, he attempted to usurp all power to himself by sidelining the Regent. The efforts to sideline powerful and popular regents if they were women, irrespective of their calibre, is also a common theme in medieval Indian history. Once again, Chand Sultana asked her nephew in Bijapur for help. Ibrahim Adil Shah send and army under a general, Sohail Khan, to sort out the matter—Muhammad Khan was imprisoned and the Sultana then appointed Abhang Khan as Peshwa. Thus Ahmadnagar was somewhat stabilised.

By this time, there was a common belief that the Nizam Shahis had won a 'victory' over the Mughal forces in the earlier battle, whereas the reality was something else. Buoyed by this sense of invincibility, the Deccani nobles of Ahmadnagar, with the tacit approval of both the Adil Shah of Bijapur and Qutb Shah of Golconda, repudiated the peace agreement that had been signed with the Mughals. Against Chand Sultana's advice, they recaptured Berar. The Deccanis, if they were aware of them, had not taken into account the strategic moves that the Mughals had carried out after the peace had been settled and their forces withdrawn from Ahmadnagar. On being informed that the siege of Ahmadnagar had been unsuccessful and the fort had not been captured, Akbar had personally moved south and camped at Malwa. He was personally supervising the Mughal preparations to invade the Deccan and the Peninsula. Prince Murad had died in 1599 and Akbar appointed his youngest son Danyal to command the forthcoming expedition. The Ahmadnagar nobles were oblivious of the Mughal king's focused efforts to conquer their kingdom as a first step to the broader annexation of the Deccan.

The Final Fall of the Nizam Shahis

Chand Sultana seems to have been the only person in power who was even vaguely aware of the dire threat facing her country. She prepared grimly for what she knew would be the inevitable Mughal onslaught. At this stage, some of the nobles in the Ahmadnagar court realised the close proximity of the powerful Mughal Emperor who was personally laying plans for the invasion and seeing the might of the Mughal army, abandoned Chand Sultana. Chand Sultana asked both Bijapur and Golconda to send maximum reinforcements and also asked them create a unified front to face the invaders, which she knew was an emerging common danger. The first battle between the two forces took place at Sonpat on the banks of the River Godavari—even after two days of intense fighting the battle remained indecisive.

Meanwhile, even at this juncture of mortal threat to the kingdom, internal strife continued unabated in Ahmadnagar. Abhang Khan made an effort to take the regency into his own hands and for his efforts was removed from his position by Chand Sultana. Abhang immediately became a rebel, although he did not join forces with the enemy. He faced Prince Danyal on his own with his followers and was defeated in battle. He made a feeble attempt at returning to Ahmadnagar and joining the main army, but was turned away by Chand Sultana. He and his small contingent retreated to Junnar.

The Mughal army now laid siege to Ahmadnagar. The internal divisions of the Ahmadnagar forces, especially within the ranks of the nobles, now became the fundamental cause for the final collapse of the Nizam Shahi kingdom. In very short order, the intrigue and jealousy within the court played out, leading to the fall of Ahmadnagar.

Chand Sultana was under no illusion regarding what would be the final outcome of the siege. Therefore, she had initiated peace talks through a Mughal commander, Abul Fazl who was also a reputed poet. The Sultana promised to hand over the kingdom of Ahmadnagar to the Mughals and accept Junnar as the fief of the Nizam Shahi king, her ward. However, her trusted advisor, a eunuch called Hamid Khan, advised and entreated her to continue to fight. Chand Sultana felt that she could not trust the loyalty of her nobles and the commanders of the army and took the decision to continue pursuing the peace initiative, on the terms that she had herself drawn out. In these terms she had also stipulated that no harm was to come to the people of the kingdom or to the defenders of the fort.

Hamid Khan was peeved that his advice had been ignored and betrayed Chand Sultana by leaking the peace initiatives of the Regent to the public and stoking their anger. This act by the eunuch is confirmed by Abul Fazl in his memoirs. Hamid Khan instigated the people to attack Chand Sultana's residence to stop her from suing for peace. There are two versions of the events that subsequently took place. One, that the mob rushed into the Regent's residence and put her to death and two, that Chand Sultana, seeing the turn of events, committed suicide to avoid dishonour to herself. *[Having followed the flawless behaviour pattern of the Dowager-Regent from the time of her marriage to the then Bijapur king, which itself was one of convenience and statecraft, this author is prone to believe that Chand Sultana took her own life. She would not have wanted to live on in ignominy or be killed by the rampaging public in dishonour. To the end she maintained a regal dignity befitting the best queen, aunt, sister and regent that the Deccan Shahi kingdoms ever produced.]*

After four months of siege, Ahmadnagar fell to the Mughal forces, around early 1600. Bahadur Nizam Shah, the boy-king, was captured and send as a prisoner to Akbar, then camped at Burhanpur. Akbar appointed Prince Danyal as the 'Viceroy of Deccan' and returned to Agra. The once proud and powerful Ahmadnagar kingdom of the Nizam Shahis thus came to an ignoble end, brought down primarily by the greed and ambition of petty-minded nobles who had been raised above the stations that they really deserved.

Chand Bibi 'Sultana' – An Appreciation

Chand Sultana inspired great love and respect in the hearts of the common people of Ahmadnagar. Their trust in her was such that even after her death, the commoners believed that she had only gone into hiding and that she would come out to save them and the kingdom 'when the time came' to drive the Mughals out and restore the Nizam Shahi dynasty to its rightful place on the throne in Ahmadnagar. They believed wholeheartedly that Chand Sultana would restore the kingdom to its golden years of former glory.

Chand Sultana was the only person capable of standing between the people of Ahmadnagar and Mughal imperialism. The fall of the Nizam Shahis was a powerful portent of future events that would engulf both Bijapur and Golconda. The kings there knew that their turn would come next, sooner rather than later.

The most popular image of this great queen shows her riding a horse during a hunt; a regal figure and nationalistic royal commander of soldiers, who was let down and her authority undermined by the constant bickering and in-fighting of her nobles in a male-dominated time in the history of the Peninsula.

Chapter 23

MALIK AMBAR
THE RISE AND RISE OF A SLAVE
THE HABSHI ASCENDANCY

The Ethiopian Military-Slave Tradition
The Habshis of the Deccan

Ethiopia, the early Greek name for Abyssinia, was an ancient Christian kingdom ruled by a dynasty of kings believed to have descended from the biblical king Solomon himself. The kingdom became isolated from the rest of the 'civilised' world when their connection to the Mediterranean Sea and its hinterland was cut off by the Islamic conquest of the lands in between. From about the 7th century to at least the beginning of the 15th century, Ethiopia developed and evolved without much inputs from the outside world, creating a composite culture that was a synthesis of the common Semitic culture and the Cushitic one of North-East Africa.

As early as the 12th century, there were rumours in Europe regarding a great Christian emperor called 'Prester John' ruling a kingdom in Africa, which was finally identified as the Solomonic kingdom of Ethiopia. This identification squashed the belief that the kingdom lay in the 'Indies'. Once the sea route to India had been discovered by Vasco da Gama and its oceans and lands opened up for western exploration and exploitation, the European Christian kingdoms attempted to establish contact with Ethiopia. By this time the region was also identified as the source of the slaves being sold by Arabs to the rest of the world. In 1520, the first Portuguese Christian mission reached the Ethiopian highlands and more information regarding the kingdom started to become available. Father Francisco Alvares kept a journal that provides broad information regarding the prevalent slave trade in Ethiopia.

Alvares mentions the existence of a number of semi-independent pagan states that only paid nominal homage to the ruling Christian dynasty. His journal also mentions that most of the people who were enslaved and sold were pagans—mainly belonging to the regions of Damot, Kambata and Hadya in Ethiopia. The captured people, slaves, were normally converted to Islam by the Arabs and were either sold to rich households in the Middle-East or shipped out to lands far beyond Arabia, mostly as mercenary warriors. In the Deccan there was an abnormally high demand for the services of Ethiopian slaves, mainly for employment as military-slaves and not as field labourers as was the case with the trade that flourished in later centuries between the west coast of Africa and America.

It is at times reported that the trade route between North-East Africa and the Deccan was established to facilitate the slave trade. However, this assertion is only partially correct. Definitely, the slave trade was an important factor, but other commercial activities which were less conspicuous were equally, if not more, important to the establishment of the maritime trade route. The commercial activity also supported what experts have termed the 'slave extraction system'. This was a system by which the Ethiopian high society and its minions traded for imported goods through a barter system of gold, ivory, and more importantly, slaves. Father Alvares mentions Indian cotton as being worn by the local priests and even the monarch, and also the availability of Indian silks and brocades in the region. This barter trade, called the slave extraction system by the Westerners was in existence long before the Christian missionaries arrived on the scene.

The demand for Indian textiles in North Africa provided a strong impetus for the perpetuation and entrenchment of the slave extraction system from the Ethiopian highlands aimed primarily towards the Deccan. This barter predates a somewhat similar situation that emerged in the trade between West Africa and the Americas a few centuries later. By the 15th century, before the arrival of the Christian missions, the Ethiopian highlands had already been firmly integrated into the Indian Ocean trade pattern, through long-distance caravans—mainly of Arab Muslim traders—reaching into the interior of the highlands.

These long-distance Muslim traders played a vital role in connecting the reclusive Ethiopian Christian kingdom to the outside world.

Contemporary Ethiopian law permitted enslavement of non-Christian war captives and gave the ownership of the slave children to their parents' owners. The laws were also restrictive regarding permitting Christians to deal with the slave trade, which gradually led to the trade being monopolised by the Muslim, mainly Arab, traders. However, there is irrefutable proof regarding the distinct collaboration between Christian Ethiopia and external Christian slave traders. A Jesuit account dated 1556 approximates that around 12,000 slaves were being exported from Ethiopia every year. Here, the conspicuous difference between the Ethiopian/Deccan slave trade and the later-day American slave trade can be seen. In Ethiopia, the slave extraction mainly depended on the demand for external goods emanating from the African hinterland behind the Arabian ports, whereas in the West Africa – American slave trade the demand for slaves originated from America and was almost insatiable as the commercial nature of agriculture took hold there.

The slaves brought into the Deccan were called 'Habshis'—a generic term that encompassed all ethnic tribes from the Ethiopian highlands. In the Deccan they were meant to be employed as military-slaves and formed an elite corps of warriors who maintained the political stability of the kingdom they served. They were fiercely loyal to their owners, since they were usually cut off from any of their own kin group, although in later days with the increase in their numbers they did create informal groups of their own. The masters of the slaves were normally high-ranking nobles of the court.

Why did the nobles of the court feel the need to create a group loyal to their individual masters who would at the fundamental level also ensure the stability of the state in a broad manner? The concept was based on the assumption, from the very early days of medieval Deccan kingdoms, that the overarching political system was corrupted by factionalism based on kinship and nepotism and perhaps even created by kinship affiliations. The need to have an unbiased 'outside' force to keep the peace between antagonistic groups and maintain stability was keenly felt, especially in times of turbulence normally associated with succession struggles. This force was to emanate from a group that was not politically affiliated or associated with people who populated the system as part of disparate factions. Over a period of time, the slaves' loyalty to their masters became unquestioned.

The Concept of Military Slaves

The concept of inducting warrior slaves, predominantly from the African continent is now considered to have been an Islamic tradition that was openly prevalent in the Indian sub-continent, exemplified by the so-called Slave Dynasty that ruled from Delhi for a period of time. In reality this assertion can be disputed for the following two reasons. One, the concept of military-sleaves did not occur across the entire Muslim world; and two, the tradition was in fact more the exception than the rule. The early narratives describing the tradition indicate that the phenomenon was a fallout of the frontier conditions experienced by the Islamic invaders of the Indian sub-continent. In effect, frontier conditions meant a volatile political and social condition that lend itself to instability. The military-slave system like that of the Habshis thrived in these conditions as an institution that contributed to the efforts to stabilise the conquered regions. The concept was particularly conducive to the circumstances wherein hereditary, dynastic authority was weak and therefore extremely prone to usurpation by outside agents. This instability flowed from the peculiarly Muslim tradition of leaving the succession to the throne or leadership of a clan open to anyone who felt that he was up to the task, leading almost always to a succession struggle at the passing of a tribal chief. The system also made the 'head that wore the crown' an open target for ambitious would-be leaders. Flowing from this tradition, in medieval Islamic India, there was no dearth of challengers to the throne.

Medieval Deccan can be studied as a prime example of the inherent volatility of the standard Muslim kingdoms. The reasons for instability being just below the surface in these kingdoms are many. One, there was a constant threat to the well-being of a kingdom from its neighbours. Even when external forces threatened two or three kingdoms simultaneously, the idea of joining forces to ward of the common enemy was a far-fetched concept. The second reason is peculiar to the Deccan. The nobles in the Deccan kingdoms were divided into two feuding groups of the Deccanis or local nobles and the phirangis, the adventurers who came into the region from Arab lands and Central Asia-Europe. Within this division, the Habshis maintained a tenuous neutrality, at least most of the time.

Three, the rapid breakup of the Bahmani kingdom into five separate 'Shahi' kingdoms when the central authority was in decline is a classic example of the inherent volatility of Muslim kingdoms since their leadership was always open to question and contest. Four, inevitably there was some sort of a succession struggle in all Deccan kingdoms at the death of one incumbent. The situation emanated from the peculiar Islamic tradition of permitting the elders to elect or select the next leader with no laid down customary norms to fall back on. The vagueness of the concept did away with any semblance of adhering to continuity and perhaps worked well in the context of a nomadic tribe. However, when the same custom was applied to large or even medium-size kingdoms that needed stability in administration obtained only through assured continuity, the system failed miserably. The result was chronic instability and the perpetuation of an atmosphere of tension and distrust between the king and his senior nobles, who the king considered a constant threat. In the Deccan, the situation was that no one faction could dominate the state administration for long enough to ensure at least medium term stability.

The slave trade across the Arabian Sea was, in an indirect manner, the result of the perpetual equation of demand and supply. There did exist a sort of system in Ethiopia of paying for commercial goods, at least partially, with slaves. The political demand for African slaves in the Deccan in an indirect manner perpetuated this barter trade and entrenched the process of slave extraction from the Ethiopian highlands. The demonstrated loyalty and fighting prowess of the Habshis from Ethiopia gradually raised them to almost the same level as the nobility. They started to be trusted with the most onerous of duties such as the governorship of sensitive and volatile provinces that were critical to the security of the kingdom. Their masters also trusted them with duties of an intimate and personal nature.

The change in status of a Habshi, from loyal military-slave to a second level nobility, normally took place at the death of the master. The traditional master-slave relationship came to an end and the 'freed' slave now offered his services to another noble, who was normally also a commander of troops. The relationship now changed in a subtle manner, from master-slave to patron-client, not that much different but one that emphasised the free status of the Habshi. The more talented and capable Habshis went on to create their own military contingents, usually consisting of other ex-slaves, who offered their services as individuals, on being 'freed', to the would-be commander. By creating an independent military contingent—normally free lancing forces—the chief Habshi created his own patron-client relationship with other freed Habshis. A complex system, but one that became perpetuated with time.

A contributing factor to the Habshis becoming a recognisably separate group was that on being sold into slavery, all links to their home country were forcibly severed. Further, almost all the slaves were converted to Islam, thereby alienating them from the 'old ways' and traditions of worship and social interaction. On arrival in the Deccan, the Habshis normally embraced the local culture and language and also formed matrimonial alliances with local women. In effect, they were absorbed into the local milieu and were considered part of the Deccan, even though in physical appearance they stood out as belonging to a different and separate ethnicity. Even after centuries of inter-mingling, the distinct physical characteristics of the tribes of the Ethiopian highlands are clearly visible in some of the peoples of the Deccan, although they are now not considered to belong to an independent ethnicity.

Malik Ambar – From Slave to King

In 1548, or thereabouts, a boy named Chapu was born in the Kambata region of South Ethiopia. In his early youth he fell into the hands of the slave traders in the east coast of Africa, part of a large number of Ethiopians who suffered the same fate. Captive Chapu was sold and resold a number of times. According to contemporary chronicles, sometime during this process Chapu was taken to Baghdad and sold to a rich and prominent merchant who recognised Chapu's keen intellect. The merchant converted Chapu to Islam and named him Ambar. Subsequently Ambar was taken to the Deccan and purchased by Chengiz Khan, the Peshwa of the Nizam Shahi kingdom of Ahmadnagar, then ruled by Murtaza Nizam Shah.

The commonality in origins and subsequent progression in life between Chengiz Khan and Ambar is conspicuous. Chengiz himself was a freed Habshi and one of the many nobles who recruited thousands of Habshis as personal military slaves. This was in keeping with the trend of the time when the nobles in all the successor Deccan kingdoms owned troops of Habshi military slaves, normally employing them as personal bodyguards—the system being most prevalent in Ahmadnagar and Bijapur. So Ambar joined the ranks of the military slaves of Ahmadnagar, yet another Habshi in a large group serving in the Deccan in different levels of the status-ridden forces. However, Ahmadnagar was a declining kingdom and when Chengiz Khan died in 1574-75, his widow freed Ambar from slavery.

As per the traditions of the time, Ambar now became a free-lancing military adventurer and joined the Bijapur army as a small-time commander of a minor military contingent. He was given the title 'Malik' and was also called 'Sidi Ambar'. However, within a few years he became dissatisfied with service in Bijapur and returned to Ahmadnagar with a force of 150 cavalrymen under his command. Around this time, 1595 or so, Ahmadnagar was in the grip of its death throes and the Ahmadnagar fort was under siege by the Mughals. Ambar with his small contingent joined the service of another Habshi commander called Abhang Khan within the fort. On 21 December 1595, Malik Ambar and the small cavalry troop that he commanded broke through the ranks of the besieging Mughals and escaped to the countryside.

Rise to Prominence

Politico-military instability in a country always favours men with a natural flair for leadership. Malik Ambar not only possessed inherent leadership capabilities but was also blessed with both decisiveness and bravery, while also being an astute military tactician. Once he was out of the besieged fort he started to successfully harass the Mughal forces conducting the siege. More soldiers joined him and very quickly the strength of his forces increased to 3000 horsemen, who were well-led and organised. However, after five years of continuous fighting, in August 1600, the Mughals overran Ahmadnagar fort and the Nizam Shahi dynasty came to a whimpering and inglorious end. Even though the Mughals controlled Ahmadnagar and the immediate surrounding countryside, and had started the process of officially annexing the kingdom, they still did not control the extensive territories that the Nizam Shahis had ruled over. The countryside was in chaos with no central control and the future continuance of the once flourishing Ahmadnagar kingdom as an entity hung in the balance.

Malik Ambar, now in command of around 7000 cavalry, decided to join the fight for control of the erstwhile Nizam Shahi kingdom. He ferreted out a 20-year old grandson of Burhan Nizam Shah, the second Nizam Shahi king, living in Bijapur and promoted him as the next king titled Murtaza Nizam Shah II. In order to entrench his own position, Ambar got his daughter married to Murtaza II. Murtaza Nizam Shah II was officially installed as king of Ahmadnagar in the fort at Parenda, about 75 miles south-east of Ahmadnagar, which had been made Malik Ambar's headquarters. By late 1600, Ambar had proclaimed himself as the Regent and devoted himself to stabilising the truncated kingdom and reinstating the Nizam Shahi dynasty. He concentrated on defending the kingdom from the on-going aggression of the Mughals from the north.

Malik Ambar was loyal to the Nizam Shahi dynasty and sincere in his effort to reinstate the fallen dynasty. However, he faced challenges from a number of other nobles. The lengthy siege by the Mughal forces was a chaotic period in the kingdom that had created confused loyalties amongst the nobles, with some defecting to the Mughals in the pursuit of enhanced personal positions and status. However, a number of freed slaves—the Habshis—hesitated, or even refused, to defect not wanting to follow their patrons into the Mughal fold, perhaps held back by the lingering hold of the characteristically strong sense of loyalty and integrity for which they were famous across the seas. One such was Raju Dakhani, a servant of the noble Sadat Khan who resisted defection. It is notable that in no chronicle is Raju mentioned as a slave or a freed slave, confirming the theory that he was not an enslaved person, but a servant of the noble. In any case, Raju Dakhani stuck to the age-old ethical concepts of fidelity and loyalty to the royal house, opting to forego his master when he defected, rather than his own honour.

Ambar and Raju joined hands and worked together to save the sinking, or already sunk, Ahmadnagar kingdom. Both acknowledged Murtaza II as their sovereign and conducted military campaigns to free the country, independent of each other. Mughal control continued to be restricted to the township of Ahmadnagar and surrounding countryside only, while the territories to the north and west were under the control of Raju Dakhani and to the south and east with Malik Ambar. Even though both these maverick leaders supported the Nizam Shahi king, there was simmering jealousy and antipathy between them. The differences came to a boil in 1606 and the two factions met in battle. Raju was defeated and imprisoned in the old Bahmani fort at Junnar north of Pune, which had been converted to Ambar's headquarters and de facto capital.

Ambar takes on the Mughals

Akbar died in 1605, and was succeeded by his son Jahangir. The new monarch was determined to consolidate the conquests in the Deccan and accordingly moved to effect his ambition. The Mughals considered Ahmadnagar to have already been conquered and also annexed, therefore Malik Ambar's efforts to resurrect the Nizam Shahi dynasty was considered a rebellion and not a continuation of the original war that had led of the conquest of the kingdom. A number of attempts were made to put down the 'rebel' Ambar and his puppet Nizam Shahi king. Each one of the Mughal efforts were unsuccessful—Malik Ambar had become adroit at repeatedly defeating the Mughal armies. His battlefield successes and steadfast defence of the Nizam Shahi dynasty, even if it existed in name only, had the added effect of making disgruntled and disenfranchised soldiers of the old regime flock to his banner. The ambition to fight North Indian Imperialism, embodied in the Mughal forces, ran high in the Deccan.

Fifteen years after he raised the Nizam Shahi flag outside Ahmadnagar, Malik Ambar recaptured Ahmadnagar fort and expelled the Mughals. However, instead of establishing the capital in Ahmadnagar, he moved his capital from Junnar to the old Tughluq capital of Daulatabad. This was strategically and tactically an astute move for two fundamental reasons. One was that its relative northerly location provided an early warning and also better defences for the kingdom from the incessant incursions from the north. Secondly, Daulatabad was the renamed and rebuilt old capital of the Yadava kingdom, Devagiri, and therefore was sure to stoke the pride of the local Maratha people. Maratha soldiers were an equal part of the Ambar forces by now. Malik Ambar had made impressive geo-strategic and political gains within a span of slightly more than a decade.

Domestic Discord

While the fight to retain the independence of the Ahmadnagar kingdom and save the Nizam Shahi dynasty was progressing in favour of Malik Ambar and the Deccan forces, two incidents marred the relatively peaceful domestic atmosphere. First was that Murtaza II, now 30 years old, was not content to be a puppet king anymore. He wanted to at least actively participate in, if not take over, the administration of the kingdom, which was personally controlled by Ambar. In effect, he wanted to become a king in his own right, not surprising for a prince in whose name a successful independence struggle was being waged. Ambition is not restricted to extremely capable people, it kindles the light in the heart of even pliant and humble people under the right circumstances. Murtaza II cannot be directly blamed for harbouring ambitions to become the 'actual' king of the burgeoning kingdom.

The second incident was more personal but had more lasting consequences. A family quarrel broke out in the royal harem, where a senior Persian-born wife of Murtaza II insulted Malik Ambar's daughter and went on to heap verbal insults on Malik Ambar himself. The insults, spoken in front of a number of people, involved the Persian lady casting aspersions on the race and status of the Ambar father and daughter, calling them black and slaves. Malik Ambar took immediate action and had Murtaza II and his uppity Persian wife murdered by being poisoned. However, he still did not assume the kingship, instead installing Murtaza's five-year old son from the murdered Persian wife as the nominal king with the title Burhan Nizam Shah III.

The Ethiopian Flavour in the Deccan

The activities of Malik Ambar brought into focus the manner in which the Nizam Shahi kingdom, and to a lesser extent the dynasty, had been revitalised in a uniquely Deccan manner. There is no doubt that the Mughals were just outside the borders and were a direct threat to the well-being of the kingdom. It was also obvious to even a casual observer that time was gradually running out not only for Ahmadnagar, but also for the remaining two successor Deccan kingdoms—Bijapur and Golconda.

> By now Malik Ambar was the undisputed master of Ahmadnagar and all civil and military affairs were controlled by him. In addition, his daughter was the senior dowager Queen, being the step-mother and having taken the infant king under her care. Since he was battling the Mughals in the north, Ambar wisely forged a strong relationship with Bijapur, the powerful kingdom to his south. His son Fath Khan was married to the daughter of Yaqut Khan, a Habshi and the most powerful noble in the Bijapur court. The freed Habshis had, over a period of time, built a network that was reinforced by a separate system of matrimonial alliances that thrived just a layer below similar alliances between the royal houses.

Ambar in Control

By various counts in different reports, Malik Ambar's army was now huge—it consisted of more than 10,000 Habshis, both slaves and freed men; and around 40,000 Deccani soldiers. The large number of Habshis indicate an increased influx of Ethiopians into the Deccan. A pattern of the upward mobility of the Habshis is also discernible at this time. They would come into the Deccan as military slaves belonging to high-ranking nobles, mostly Habshis; become manumitted and turning into free-lancing Habshis on the death of their master; the more capable Habshi free soldiers, went on to become commanders of small contingents of troops; and subsequently themselves becoming slave-owning nobles, fitting into the existing structure and hierarchy. Even within this 'normal' pattern of progression, Malik Ambar's rise—all the way from a slave to the Peshwa and the de facto ruler of the once powerful Nizam Shahi kingdom—has to be acknowledged as being exceptional. There can be no doubt that Ambar was endowed with extraordinary qualities, was a great warrior and military commander, and an efficient administrator.

It is reliably reported that the Mughal Emperor Jahangir detested and hated Malik Ambar, always prefixing the mention of the Habshi leader with derogatory epithets in his own writings. The enmity between the two was very bitter. Jahangir was uniformly contemptuous of the 'black-faced' Ambar, who was always mentioned in an insulting manner in all contemporary Mughal chronicles, the authors of the chronicles giving full expression to the Emperor's hatred in graphic detail. However, this hate and antagonism are also indicative of another underlying divide, which modern historians have glossed over most of the time, probably in the mistaken belief that mention of the racial divide that prevailed in medieval times would somehow bring discord in the present day. The fact remains that there was a definitive racial and ethnic divide between the light-skinned westerners, personified by Jahangir and his nobles of Central Asian origin, and the more dark-skinned and localised Deccanis, embodied by the Habshis and their descendants. Jahangir could never defeat the Habshi leader in battle, at the same time he could never accept the military genius of Malik Ambar.

End of the Habshi Enterprise

By 1624, Malik Ambar had consolidated his hold on most parts of the erstwhile Ahmadnagar kingdom and was in command of an effective and large army that was well-organised, trained and extremely disciplined. The intrepid Habshi slave, risen to the status of Regent and de facto ruler died of natural causes in 1626. His death not only marked the end of a tumultuous era in the history of Ahmadnagar, but also sounded the death knell of the Habshi enterprise in the Deccan. From here on, their fortunes were in decline till they became irrelevant to the broader sweep of history, not only in the Deccan but also in India.

On Ambar's death, his son Fath Khan became Peshwa of Ahmadnagar. Malik Ambar's death also signalled the beginning of internal squabbles within the Habshi nobles. Within about a year, a rival Habshi noble, Hamid Khan, managed to bribe the young king Burhan III into appointing him the Peshwa. In retaliation Fath Khan had Burhan III poisoned in 1632, reclaimed the position of Peshwa and placed the murdered king's seven-year old son on the throne as Husain Nizam Shah III.

Fath Khan lacked the skills and dynamism that had made his father a great leader and could not withstand the constant pressure being exerted on the kingdom by the Mughals. Unable to find a way out of the increasingly constrained circumstances, Fath Khan surrendered the kingdom to the Mughals in 1633. He was retired by the Mughals on a liberal pension in North India and the boy-king Husain III, was imprisoned for life. Thus ended the Nizam Shahi dynasty and the Ahmadnagar kingdom of the Deccan; in the end blown away by currents that it could not withstand since the leadership had decayed and atrophied beyond repair. Malik Ambar's efforts to reinvigorate the kingdom was a flash in the pan that did not yield even a semi-permanent result.

Malik Ambar – A Military Genius

Even the Mughal chroniclers, almost always commenting derogatorily about Ambar, acknowledge him as a master of guerrilla warfare. Coming from the Mughal scribes, this is indeed high praise. Throughout the conflict with the Mughals, he refused to engage their army directly in conventional pitched battles, always cleverly avoiding being pinned down. Thus he managed to avoid the overwhelming and imposing strength of the Mughal army that would have demolished the Ahmadnagar forces without any problems in direct combat. Malik Ambar was an astute strategic commander and tactical genius, able to recognise that the very strength of the Mughal army could also be made into the main contributory factor in its disadvantage—its massive strength that could push aside any adversary in battle, was also ponderous in nature and was therefore slow to respond to the tactics of fast moving attacks and withdrawals of light cavalry.

Ambar resorted to surprise attacks on the Mughal forces, carrying out rapid raids even at night. He carried out effective interdiction of supply lines, forcing the Mughal army to come out of their fortified camps into the rugged wooded areas where the light cavalry of Ahmadnagar had a distinct advantage over the heavier northern forces. Malik Ambar relied mostly on his light cavalry—manned by indigenous Marathi-speaking warriors, the Marathas—to carry out these hit and run raids. He demonstrated his military genius in the administration of the army, especially the light cavalry; all units were trained and inspected by Ambar himself or his trusted lieutenants; and the forces were paid by the central administration directly, thus avoiding the chances of an intermediary commander under-paying the forces with the accompanying loss of morale and efficiency.

These measures ensured that the cavalry remained light and swift in their application, becoming a deadly weapon against the heavy and cumbersome conventional forces. Further, the terrain of the Deccan was conducive to the tactics and the forces that Ambar employed.

By the incisive employment of the Maratha light cavalry cadre, Malik Ambar was able to push the Mughal forces all the way north to their southern headquarters at Burhanpur. Maratha cavalry was not a new addition to the Deccan Shahi armies, they had been used since the time of the Bahmani kings. However, it was under Malik Ambar that they were used extensively, growing into a recognisable and evidently extremely effective and ruthless force. At the height of Ambar's power, around 1624, the Maratha cavalry numbered around 50,000 in the Ahmadnagar army. During his de facto reign, Ambar had founded the township of Khirki, later to be called Aurangabad, near the capital Daulatabad. It is a testimony to the important role that the Maratha cavalry played in the struggle against the Mughals and of Malik Ambar's complete reliance on them that the different suburbs of this new township, Khirki was named after prominent Maratha military chieftains.

The central role that the Maratha forces played in keeping the Mughal forces at bay and ensuring the 'independence' of the Nizam Shahi kingdom had the unforeseen effect of gradually diminishing the importance of the Muslim nobles, both Deccani and Phirangi, in the administration of the kingdom. This downward slide in status was obviously accompanied by the increasing stature of the Maratha chieftains. Malik Ambar's Ahmadnagar kingdom was truly a Habshi-Maratha enterprise. The military forces and the warfighting enterprise, critical to the survival of the kingdom, was dominated by the Maratha chieftains; and the political base was gradually filled by Habshi nobles who were personally loyal to Malik Ambar. Unfortunately for the kingdom, this combine lasted only for a few years after Malik Ambar's death in 1626.

A Travesty

For some unknown reasons, Indian historians do not give Malik Ambar the importance that he deserves—perhaps because of his foreign origin, that too as a black Ethiopian slave. Even when he is mentioned, Ambar is brushed aside, almost swept out of the way disdainfully, as a governor of the Mughal Emperor. This assertion, as has been explained in detail above, is not only factually incorrect but a blatant travesty in reconstructing medieval Deccan history. The racial, religious and ethnic bias and snobbery, resting just below the surface even in modern India, can be seen to percolate into the narration of history of the sub-continent.

The reality is very different. From the time of his manumission, Malik Amber tenaciously clung to his personal independence. Throughout his life as a military commander and the de facto ruler of Ahmadnagar for most of that time, he reigned over his own territories, never subservient to anyone else, other than acknowledging the nominal suzerainty of the Nizam Shahi king. He was in continuous and constant conflict with the Mughals, gradually recapturing almost the entire Ahmadnagar kingdom, and never a Mughal governor. Ambar was held in great respect in the Deccan during his own lifetime and there are instances, carefully recorded, of both Bijapur and Golconda voluntarily paying him tribute. Without doubt, Malik Ambar was the last capable defender of the Deccan. His passing, of natural causes and not in battle, ushered in the end of the independence of the successor kingdoms of the Deccan. Malik Ambar may have suffered battlefield reverses and even few defeats, but he was never conquered.

> 'In warfare, in command, in sound judgement, and in administration, he had no rival or equal. He well understood that predatory (*kazzaki*) warfare, which in the language of the Dakhin is called *bargi-giri*. He kept down the turbulent spirits of that country, and maintained his exalted position to the ended of his life, and closed his career in honour. History records no other instance of an Abyssinian slave arriving at such eminence.'
>
> Mutamad Khan, in 'Iqbal-nama-yi-Jahangiri',
> As translated in *History of India as Told by its Own Historians*, Vol VI,
> Henry M. Elliot & John Dowson (ed & trans)

The Marathas

The Maratha forces and their chiefs were the right-hand personnel of Malik Ambar throughout his extended defiance of the Mughal might. Initially, the Maratha chief Maloji and then his son Shahji Bhosle led the Marathas in support of Ambar and were the most successful of the Maratha chieftains during this period. *[Shahji's son Shivaji would go on to found the mighty Maratha empire. The narrative of the detailed history of the Marathas will be provided in a forthcoming volume of this series.]*

After Ambar's death, when the Mughals recaptured Daulatabad and imprisoned the boy-king, Shahji took up the cause of the Nizam Shahis and became the leader of the loyal forces still ready to battle the Mughals. He placed an 11-year old 'prince' on the Nizam Shahi throne and proclaimed him Murtaza III. However, the circumstances were such that the throne was in perpetual movement, being established and removed from the many hill forts of the Sahyadri ranges that the Marathas controlled, according to tactical requirements, since the fight with the Mughals was an on-going enterprise. Shahji continued this rear-guard action for nearly three years, all the while appealing to both Maratha and Habshi leadership for support and entreating them to unite the various fractured military units in order to present a consolidated front to the Mughals.

Once again the base character trait, which has always been the bane of the Indian psyche, the inherent inclination to betray one's own countrymen and side with external elements who are bent on destroying the strength of the local opposition, raised its head. When Shahji and his indomitable Marathas were fighting off the Mughals in many fronts simultaneously, The Adil Shahi king in Bijapur, positioned to the south of the Maratha enterprise made a pact with the Mughals who were amassed to the north of the Nizam Shahis. The Bijapur king coveted Ahmadnagar territory, which he could not invade or capture as long as Shahji remained powerful and in control. Between the Adil Shahi king and the Mughal prince leading the army, they managed to wean away the Habshi and other Ahmadnagar nobles from Shahji, bribing them with the promise of wealth and position. This was a death blow to the Ahmadnagar kingdom.

Shahji was finally isolated in his fort at Mahuli, watching helplessly as the Ahmadnagar kingdom that he had served so assiduously and ably was dismembered and parcelled between Bijapur and the Mughals. In 1636, a decade after the death of Malik Ambar, the territories of the Nizam Shahi kingdom were divided and annexed—Ahmadnagar as an independent kingdom was formally dissolved.

Shahji was coerced to join Bijapur forces, where he once again did splendid service; and the boy-king became the latest to join the two earlier Nizam Shahi 'kings' who had already been imprisoned, in 1600 and 1633, in the Gwalior fort—an ignominious end to a once splendid kingdom.

Conclusion

Malik Ambar's de facto rule was the golden era of Habshi influence that peaked during this period and could be actually termed the time of 'Habshi greatness'. Immediately after Fath Khan surrendered the kingdom to the Mughals and accepted their pension, the institution of military slavery went into sharp decline and disappeared completely from the Deccan by late-17th century. Three main reasons can be identified for the rapid decline in the fortunes of the Habshis, starting with the death of their principal patron and the foremost amongst them—Malik Ambar.

The first reason was mainly political, tinged with racial bias—the collapse of the Ahmadnagar kingdom, even though the Maratha leadership under Shahji made a valiant effort to reinstate the Nizam Shahi rule. The collapse put an end to the primary source of patronage for the tradition of the induction of Ethiopian military slaves into royal service. As a policy, the Mughals did not recruit military slaves. More importantly, they favoured people of the Iranian-Turkish race for service. Their treatment of the dark-skinned people was deplorable and bordered on racial bigotry. Second was socio-cultural in nature. The Habshis were brought to the Deccan without any Ethiopian female slaves accompanying them. It was but natural for them enter into alliances with the local women. Such inter-racial marriages were at time encouraged by the masters of the military slaves to ensure that they remained loyal to the master's household. The off-springs of these liaisons also married locally putting in motion a process of gradual absorption into the local society over generations of co-habitation.

Third, is purely societal in nature and is connected to the custom of local marriages. The Habshis, even though slaves, became normal house-holders in the Deccan, gradually losing their separate identity and integrating into the racial and social hierarchy of the region. Over a period, the length of time required to become a 'localised' Habshi reduced, even for newly arrived slaves. Further, slavery could not be sustained in the prevailing process of slaves being manumitted on the patron's death and becoming free-lancers. This process paved the way for the rise of a slave to nobleman. In the broader analysis, military slavery as practised in the Deccan was a self-terminating process. Through its support for the Habshi system, the Ahmadnagar kingdom made a fundamental contribution to the socio-political evolution of the Deccan.

The Nizam Shahis founded the kingdom in 1496 and ruled it for nearly two centuries till the final collapse in 1636. Although officially ruled throughout by the Nizam Shahi dynasty, history shows that below the surface of their tenuous control, many groups were constantly fighting each other for the actual control of the kingdom. Initially the struggle for power was restricted between the Deccani (local) and Phirangi (Iranian-Turkish) groups of nobles. The Habshis pushed these groups into the background and brought into prominence the Maratha chieftains as the king-makers.

Historically the most momentous function that the Ahmadnagar Kingdom carried out, especially during the Habshi ascendancy phase, was to serve as an incubator for the rising Maratha power. From a political viewpoint, it was during the struggle for Ahmadnagar that the foundations for the great Maratha empire-to-come was laid and nurtured. Of course, the Maratha Empire was built on much more than the political institutions left behind by the failed Ahmadnagar kingdom. The Nizam Shahi rule and their institutions were only a small contributory part of the large number of inputs that went into the making of the great Maratha Empire.

Section V

THE SUCCESSOR KINGDOMS OF THE DECCAN

THE QUTB SHAHIS OF GOLCONDA – HYDERABAD

With the failure of the last desperate defensive fight led by Razak Lari, Abul Hasan knew that the end had come. It is reported, by chroniclers from both sides of the equation, that Abul Hasan's act of surrender that ended the reign of the Qutb Shahi dynasty was done with a 'collectedness and composure' that is very seldom seen and has no parallel in Indian history. It is said that even the haughty Mughal commanders were uncharacteristically compelled to defer to the nobleness of the king and his royal demeanour. Abul Hasan, the Meek, had acquitted himself as a king better than any of his more powerful ancestors.

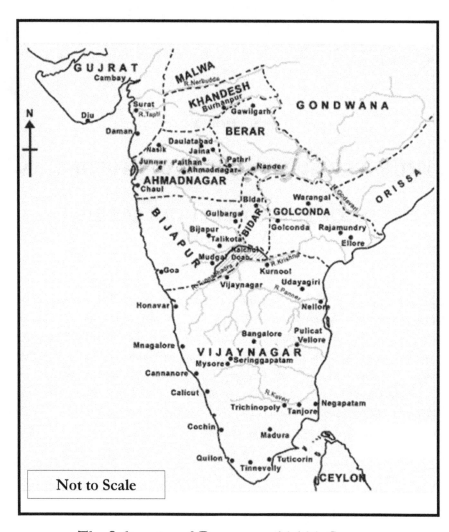

The Sultanates of Deccan – mid-16th Century

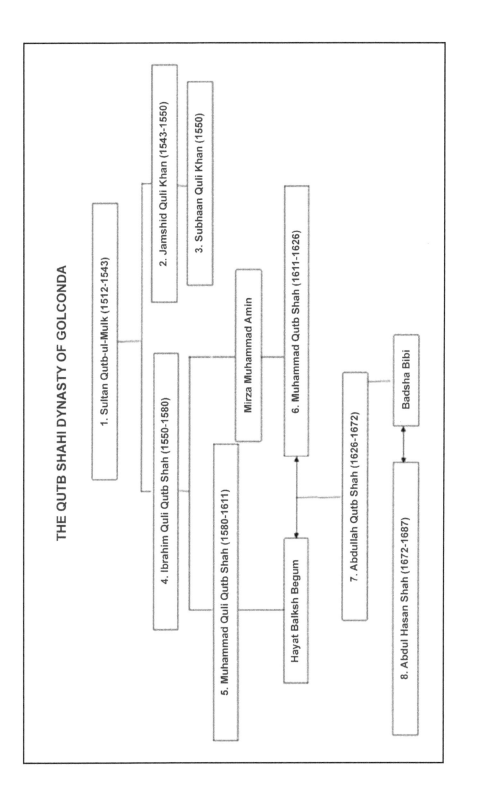

Chapter 24

A KINGDOM IS ESTABLISHED

In medieval times, the tribe of Qara Quyunla held sway over some territory that was spread between Armenia and Azerbaijan. Timur defeated the tribe during his devastating conquest of Central Asia and the Quyunla were forced to flee to Egypt. On Timur's death and the subsequent disintegration of his empire, the tribe returned and re-founded the kingdom, establishing its capital at Tabriz. However, the tribe was riven with internal dissensions as opposing groups vied with each other for the position of chief. More importantly, the tribe was not overtly warlike, instead being content to lead a life of comparative peace. Very soon after their return from exile in Egypt, the Quyunla was defeated by a rival tribe and the leadership put to the sword. Of the chieftain's family, only one branch headed by Pir Quli was spared, mainly because the Pir and his immediate family were peace-loving and did not claim any patrimony for the leadership of the tribe. Pir Quli had a grandson called Sultan Quli. Here the term Sultan was used purely as a proper name and did not indicate any positional title or royal dignity that flowed from it.

Since Sultan Quli was a descendent of the ruling elite of a Turkman tribe, from an early age he was instructed in the many arts that was considered required learning for a future ruler. He was also taught theology to a very high standard. Even though Pir Quli had willingly surrendered his patrimony on the tribe being defeated, when a new chief succeeded to the throne, the conquering tribe resorted to renewed persecution of the Quyunla. Fearing for his son's life, Sultan Quli's father send him to India under the protection of his brother and Sultan's uncle, Allah Quli, to seek his fortune. The uncle-nephew Quli team came to India as traders in horses, but also brought with them rich and valuable presents as well as money to ease their way and gain favour when necessary.

Sultan Quli Qutb-ul-Mulk

Early Days in the Deccan

Although the Quli duo came to India through the land route in the north-west, they did not tarry long in North India, where the Lodis were ruling from Delhi. They proceeded south and reached the Deccan. These were the fading days of the Bahmani kingdom and they were reasonably well-received in the capital Bidar, ensured no doubt with the help of the 'presents' that would have passed hands. The balkanisation of the Bahmani kingdom was already underway and it was not difficult for a foreign aristocrat to find gainful employment in the court. Sultan Quli rose gradually in the service of the Bahmanis—the rise in status being a gradual process rather than a spectacular one. Sometime during this period, the Bahmani king conferred the title Khawas Khan on Sultan Quli and also granted him the jagir of Kurangal, in small holding in today's Mahbubnagar district.

A Romantic Twist

In some of the narratives regarding the rise of Sultan Quli, a romantic twist has been given. In these accounts, Sultan Quli is mentioned as a slave of the Bahmani king, an inherently wrong assumption. The story continues that since he was well-versed in mathematics, Sultan Quli was a favourite with the ladies of the harem who entrusted him with keeping accounts and looking after their personal financial matters. At this time, The Bahmani dynasty was faltering and the kingdom was in turmoil. It was definitely on a downward spiral with law and order deteriorating on a daily basis. Dacoity and highway robbery had become commonplace occurrences and a direct rebellion was brewing in Telangana. The king therefore decided to send a military contingent to put down the nascent rebellion.

A Kingdom is Established

> Sultan Quli was at this time romantically involved with one of the ladies of the royal household. Through her influence in the court, Sultan managed to get appointed as the commander of the military forces being dispatched to Telangana. The campaign was successfully completed and brought Sultan Quli accolades from the Bahmani king, accompanied by royal favour and the title of Khawas Khan.
>
> This account cannot be corroborated with any reputed source and therefore must be dismissed as embellishments in a later day account, after Sultan Quli had become more powerful and an independent ruler. Even so, the narrative is not completely improbable and there could be some grain of truth in it.

In December 1487, the Bahmani king was ambushed by some rebel Deccani nobles and Sultan Quli is mentioned by name in all accounts as being personally responsible for saving the king's life. Two facts become apparent from this mention of Sultan Quli. First, it becomes obvious that he was not any longer a non-entity or a hanger-on in the Bahmani court, but a noble with sufficient individual stature and recognition to have been mentioned individually. Second, he had risen in the hierarchy of nobles to a position to have been moving around within the small entourage that accompanied the king on his personal outings. In effect, he had become part of the inner circle of courtiers. It is obvious that a grateful king bestowed further favours on the brave noble who had saved his life.

Governor of Telangana

The Bahmani kingdom was fast descending into chaos. The governor of Goa and the provinces of the Konkan coast, Bahadur Gilani, grabbed this opportunity and revolted, declaring independence. Sultan Quli led a contingent of soldiers and was effective in putting down the rebellion. The king bestowed the title Qutb-ul-Mulk on him. Sultan Quli, continued the campaign in Goa even after the revolt was controlled and went on to defeat Bahadur Gilani who was killed in battle in November 1494. Even though the nominal Bahmani king was a virtual prisoner in Bidar and the kingdom was controlled by Qasim Barid, the king made Sultan Quli Qutb-ul-Mulk, the governor of Telangana and also granted the Golconda fort to him as his personal jagir.

At this time the entire Deccan Plateau was in the grip of a continuous wave of intrigue that led to regular skirmishes between the emerging successor kingdoms to the Bahmani Empire. Further, these newly forming entities were harried by the strong and powerful Vijayanagar Empire to the further south. The Vijayanagar king, Immadi Narasimha, was a minor and therefore the kingdom was ruled by an able minister Naraya Nayak. The weakness of the Bahmani kingdom and the on-going disunity of the emerging rulers provided the impetus for Vijayanagar to take over the Raichur Doab, a territory that had always been a point of contention between the two kingdoms. However, Yusuf Adil Shah, ruling Bijapur, recaptured the Doab. The Raichur Doab, between the Rivers Krishna and Tungabhadra, continued to change hands regularly. While the control of the Raichur Doab was being keenly contested, Qutb-ul-Mulk managed to free the Bahmani king from Qasim Barid's control.

It is an interesting fact that even though the Bahmani kingdom, and more importantly the king, did not wield any power over the various provinces of the Deccan, Qutb-ul-Mulk continued to be loyal to the Bahmani throne. The Bahmani king ruled only in name and other governors had declared independence and forged new dynasties, but Sultan Quli did not declare independence. The Qutb-ul-Mulk was a completely autonomous ruler of Telangana but even after the death of the last Bahmani king, he did not declare independence or assume the title of 'Shah' indicating the establishment of a new kingdom and dynasty.

Qutb-ul-Mulk's professed loyalty to the Bahmani king stands out as an aberration in the annals of the Deccan. It must be surmised, that Sultan Quli, now Qutb-ul-Mulk, was under-confident regarding his ability to chart an independent course and become a 'king' in his own right. This assessment is corroborated by the fact that even when the powerful Vijayanagar king, Krishnadeva Raya, conquered and annexed Telangana territories, Qutb-ul-Mulk did not take any action to either resist invasion or recapture the lost provinces. Krishnadeva Raya went on to capture Warangal and his conquering march reached as far north as Cuttack. Prataparudra, ruling in Warangal, was forced to sign a treaty that ceded Andhra country to the south of River Krishna to Vijayanagar. Qutb-ul-Mulk, 'governing' from Golconda did not take any action against the invaders.

The Telangana Campaigns

On the death of Krishnadeva Raya, a number of Vijayanagar's vassal states rebelled and even declared independence. However, Qutb-ul-Mulk did not act in haste and bided his time. He waited till 1532, when the Vijayanagar kingdom was further weakened by internal strife before advancing to the eastern regions to recapture lost territory. Abundant caution and a certain amount of timidity were the watchwords for Qutb-ul-Mulk. However, the hesitation to take offensive action is belied by his tactical excellence and personal bravery in battle. If anything, Qutb-ul-Mulk was a complex person.

Before embarking on a recapturing march, Qutb-ul-Mulk strengthened the Golconda fort, once again an act of immense caution. He then captured the fort at Devarkonda. This annexation was contested by Achyuta Raya, now ruling Vijayanagar, who took umbrage to Qutb-ul-Mulk's actions. The Vijayanagar and Golconda armies met for battle at Panagal. Achyuta Raya was defeated although he commanded a numerically larger force. Qutb-ul-Mulk proved to be a superior tactician and a master at the employment of reserves during the battle, accurately judging the timing to throw them into battle in order to swiftly change the tide of the fighting. He kept a large and manoeuvrable force of cavalry in reserve and brought them into battle at decisive points and critical times during the battle. The intervention of the reserves at critical junctures almost always turned the tide of the battle in his favour. However, the employment of this tactic needed astute observation of the battle and the inherent ability to make the decision to commit the reserves at the right time and place. Qutb-ul-Mulk repeatedly displayed these astute battlefield capabilities.

The Golconda forces went on to annex a number of other forts. Qutb-ul-Mulk differed from other chiefs, governors and rulers in the Deccan in his treatment of defeated opponents. He almost always showed clemency, permitting the defeated opponents to depart with their personal property and at times even letting them continue to rule as vassals. This behaviour is in sharp contrast to the norms of the day when the defeated chief or king was invariably beheaded or at least imprisoned after being blinded. The origin of this sensibility in Qutb-ul-Mulk's behaviour pattern is difficult to unearth and must be considered a personality quirk. The annexations made Golconda to have common borders with Bijapur and Vijayanagar.

Next, Qutb-ul-Mulk defeated the Berar army and occupied Haft Tappa and then came up against Shitab Khan then in control of Warangal and surrounding areas as an autonomous chieftain. Shitab Khan was defeated and fled to join forces with Ramachandra ruling an Orissa kingdom from Kondapalli, his territory flowing to the north and east. (This Ramachandra is not to be confused with the Ramachandra ruling Vijayanagar.) Qutb-ul-Mulk once again found himself in familiar circumstances, facing a large army with a small but well-led and better organised force. The Golconda forces prevailed against the combined Ramachandra-Shitab army and a peace treaty was enacted with Ramachandra, accepting the River Godavari as the border between the two kingdoms.

While Qutb-ul-Mulk was busy in the north-east of his territories, Vijayanagar forces under their king Achyuta Raya, invaded Golconda territory and occupied the areas near Kondavidu. Qutb-ul-Mulk retaliated almost immediately and was victorious against the Vijayanagar army. He then occupied the doab of the Rivers Godavari and Krishna as far as Ellore and Rajamundri. The Vijayanagar forces attempted to recapture lost territory, but were once again defeated on the banks of the River Godavari. Throughout the Telangana campaign, Sultan Quli Qutb-ul-Mulk made tactically astute moves that made his forces victorious in all battles, prevailing over numerically superior forces. He also personally led the forces from the front on the battlefield, although by this time he was a septuagenarian.

Taking advantage of the incessant fighting that continued between the Bahmani Successor States in the Deccan, Achyuta Raya joined forces with Ismail Adil Shah of Bijapur and incited him to lay siege to the fort at Kovilkonda, a Golconda possession. The relentless and persistent quarrels, leading to bitter enmities between the three major Shahi kingdoms in the Deccan kept them divided and without sufficient strength to deter external invasions. This inherent disunity was the fundamental reason for their subsequent downfall, when they were unable to withstand the inexorable attacks from the north that started to blow into the Deccan. The Vijayanagar-Bijapur combine was not able to capture Kovilkonda and had to withdraw, Qutb-ul-Mulk being victorious by not having been defeated. During this skirmish, Ali Barid controlling Bidar, had assisted the Bijapur Adil Shahis and therefore Qutb-ul-Mulk now laid siege to the Barid stronghold in Bidar. However, the Golconda forces were unable to bring the siege to a successful conclusion and Qutb-ul-Mulk agreed to a treaty of peace that favoured him. Around this time Raja Harichand, a proclaimed vassal of Golconda exploited Qutb-ul-Mulk's preoccupation and declared independence in Nalgonda. The rebellion was expeditiously put down.

Qutb-ul-Mulk's Death

After the campaign against Bidar, Qutb-ul-Mulk managed a relatively peaceful rule for about nine years, during which period he attempted to bring about some administrative reforms to the 'kingdom'. However, any changes that were made were minor in nature and one is left with the feeling that Qutb-ul-Mulk was a tired man wanting to rest and enjoy the fruits of his long labour of over fifty years. He wanted nothing but a tranquil dusk to his tumultuous life. However, this was not to be.

Mystery surrounds his death and there are many narratives regarding his last days. However, there are some irrefutable facts that can be listed—he ruled the de facto kingdom for 24 years; he was fairly old, probably in his early 80s at the time of his passing; and he did not die of natural causes, but was murdered. The accounts of his murder also vary between sources. One states that he was murdered by a slave on the orders of his son Jamshid and the other that Jamshid himself beheaded his father. The place where the dastardly act is supposed to have taken place also varies in different accounts—from a mosque during afternoon prayers to the palace garden where Qutb-ul-Mulk was relaxing.

Prince Jamshid had been imprisoned earlier by Qutb-ul-Mulk for some misdeeds and was considered an impetuous, violent and harsh person. Qutb-ul-Mulk's eldest son and preferred heir apparent, Haidar Khan, had been killed in battle earlier. Jamshid was suspected of conspiring against his other elder brother Qutb ud-Din who had been elevated to crown prince by Qutb-ul-Mulk, which has been quoted as the reason for his earlier imprisonment. Considering the circumstances it is difficult to assign a reason for Jamshid's desire to murder his father, especially since Qutb-ul-Mulk was already old and would not have lived for more than a few years more. Even in those times when degeneration of the succession struggle into murder, blinding and imprisonment of adversaries was accepted as normal, patricide still carried a stigma that was difficult to shake off. Therefore, only his impetuous nature points a finger at him; Jamshid's complicity in his father's murder cannot be confirmed with assurance.

Qutb-ul-Mulk died (was murdered) in September 1543, leaving behind a large territory for his successor to rule.

Sultan Quli Qutb-ul-Mulk – An Assessment

Qutb-ul-Mulk was the contemporary of perhaps the most powerful of the Deccan rulers from each dynasty in the region. During the time that he was carving out a kingdom and establishing a kingdom, Orissa was ruled by king Purushottam; the great Krishnadeva Raya ruled in Vijayanagar; and Burhan Nizam Shah reigned in Ahmadnagar. For a first time appointed and relatively minor governor to hold his own against these established rulers was a singularly great achievement. Further, Qutb-ul-Mulk proved to be an astute opportunist and managed to expand his borders eastwards till he reached the Bay of Bengal.

Qutb-ul-Mulk was a military genius at the operational level and a person who understood diplomacy and statesmanship as well as, if not better than, most of his contemporaries. It is noteworthy, that before he undertook any military campaign and before going into battle itself, Qutb-ul-Mulk provided a considered and definitive offer to the adversary to avoid actual combat. In doing so, he did not consider the religion of the opposing ruler, the peace offer being extended to both Muslim and Hindu alike. Throughout his career Qutb-ul-Mulk preferred to settle disputes through negotiations and other peaceful means, resorting to military action only as a last resort when it became inevitable. In medieval times and anywhere in the world, this was a novel approach to securing the kingdom. Across the world, recourse to the sword to put right any wrong, actual or perceived, and to ensure the prosperity of one's own kingdom, was a natural and normal action of ruling chiefs, princes and kings. Sultan Quli Qutb-ul-Mulk once again proved the complexity of his personal character by his considered actions prior to going to war.

The other noteworthy feature of Qutb-ul-Mulk's character is that he treated the defeated adversary with compassion and forgiveness, at times even re-instating the defeated ruler as a vassal. He took a measured approach to the command of the army, personally leading them into battle even when he was in his late 70s. He was an avid student of military tactics, repeatedly besting his opponents in battle after battle, most of the time fighting numerically superior forces. This statistic provides an insight into the fact that Qutb-ul-Mulk must have been blessed with a great power of perception regarding understanding the adversary commander's intent at the beginning of the battle and being able to revise it as the battle progressed.

Religion was not an important cornerstone for Qutb-ul-Mulk, unlike a number of his contemporaries. Born in Central Asia, he was a Shia, but was loyal to the Sunni Bahmanis till his death. The official religion of Golconda was declared as being Shia only because by early to mid-1500s, Iran had come under the rule of a Shia monarch, Shah Ismail Safawi.

Qutb-ul-Mulk established a kingdom in the Deccan that would endure for slightly more than two centuries. He was first and foremost a tactical military leader and a shrewd strategist, more than anything else. He could not be counted as an accomplished ruler, even though he brought a large part of Andhra country under one rule, consolidating disparate regions and territories. There is some amount of uncertainty whether or not Qutb-ul-Mulk declared independence. All available information point to his not having declared independence, unlike the other three Shahi kings of the Deccan. At least formally, and nominally, he continued to profess his allegiance to the Bahmani king, who was himself a prisoner in his own capital. In fact, historians are still divided regarding the timing of the actual declaration of independence by the Adil and Nizam Shahis, the other two greater dynasties of the Deccan.

The debate regarding the independence of the successor kingdoms continues to be contentious.

Sultan Quli Qutb-ul-Mulk outlived the last Bahmani king by at least five years, but did not declare independence even then, nor did he assume royal stature and regalia. The reason for this reluctance to declare his independence and to assume royal stature is unfathomable. Even lesser persons with smaller holdings and hardly any achievements to their credit attempted to become 'king' in the confusion that emanated from the decline and fall of the Bahmani dynasty. Only his inherent timidity outside the battlefield, perhaps inherited from his grandfather Pir Quli, can account for the decision not to crown himself king. Qutb-ul-Mulk died and is buried not as a king, but as the senior-most nobleman of the territory, denoted by the title 'Bare Malik'; as Qutb-ul-Mulk, and not Qutb Shah as was the case with every other ruler from the dynasty that he founded.

Chapter 25

CONTAINING INSTABILITY

Sultan Quli Qutb-ul-Mulk was succeeded on the throne by his son Jamshid, who was not the appointed heir apparent. Jamshid had come to the throne by force after capturing and blinding his elder brother Qutb ud-Din. In combination with the rumours of his involvement in the murder of his father Qutb-ul-Mulk, it gave him a reputation of being harsh, violent and unscrupulous. On ascending the throne he ordered his younger brother, Ibrahim, to present himself at Golconda. Fearing for his life, especially after having seen the way in which Jamshid dealt with his elder brother, Ibrahim fled to Bidar instead of going to the Golconda court as ordered.

Jamshid followed his father's reluctance to assume royal regalia and declare himself 'king', not claiming the title of 'Shah'. Throughout his reign, he preferred to be referred to as Jamshid Khan. The reason for this display of humility is difficult to fathom and the contemporary records do not elaborate on the issue. Based on available, and scanty, records it is difficult to determine whether Jamshid was inherently a humble person or he did not want to draw too much attention to himself and therefore did not assume the royal title. The story of his accession to the throne point towards the non-assumption of royal prerogatives being more of a calculated move to remain uncontroversial rather than real humility. Jamshid also faced a hostile neighbourhood. From the beginning of his rule, the other Deccan Shahi kingdoms continually conspired to break up the cohesiveness of the Qutb Shahi rule in Golconda.

Ibrahim's Fight and Flight

After having been given refuge in Bidar, Ibrahim instigated Ali Barid, then ruling the kingdom, to invade Golconda and lay siege to the citadel. Knowing that the invasion was undertaken under the influence of Ibrahim, Jamshid tried to appease Ibrahim with many offers of friendship, and extensive jagirs. However, Ibrahim remained unrelenting and continued the pursuit of military action. Jamshid then asked Burhan Nizam Shah of Ahmadnagar for assistance in warding off the invasion. Accordingly, a Nizam Shahi army started to march towards Golconda. Ali Barid, fearing that he would be trapped between the Golconda and Ahmadnagar armies, hastily withdrew to Bidar. This left Ibrahim in a vulnerable position without the support of a strong military force. He immediately fled to Vijayanagar, taking refuge with the Raya there, returning to Golconda only after Jamshid's death. The Vijayanagar Raya received Ibrahim cordially and granted him a jagir, making him stay in the country as his personal guest.

Ibrahim's flight to Vijayanagar is indicative of the political environment of the Deccan and the Southern Peninsula at that time. It is obvious that there was enmity and adversarial activities between the various kingdoms, but equally obvious is that there was also co-operation and co-existence, demonstrated by the formation of alliances and coalitions. It is noteworthy that religion did not play any part in the formation of alliances, till a much later time. Both Hindu and Muslim nobles played equal parts in the administration and the military, as well as in determining the forward course of action of a particular kingdom. Therefore, Ibrahim fleeing to Vijayanagar and living under the protection of the Hindu king there till he felt it was safe to return to his country was not an extraordinary event, as it would have been in a later period. From the conditions in the Deccan during this time it becomes clear that religious persecution and bias came to the Peninsula at a later stage in the historical narrative of the region.

Jamshid Khan's Reign

As Jamshid was consolidating his position, the alliance groupings in the Deccan were also solidifying. However, the alliances in the Deccan were notoriously fickle in their character and prone to rapid restructuring and for the pettiest of reasons. At the time of Jamshid coming to the throne, Burhan Nizam Shah of Ahmadnagar, Darya Imad Shah of Berar and the Qutb Shahis in Golconda formed one bloc, while the Adil Shahis of Bijapur, Ali Barid in Bidar and Ibrahim in self-exile in Vijayanagar, formed the opposing group. Considering the history in the Deccan of restructuring alliances, the term 'solidification' is perhaps overstating the case. Suffice it to understand that the blocs mentioned remained so for a few years.

Once the threat to Golconda had vanished as quickly as it had emanated, Burhan Nizam Shah wanted to reclaim Sholapur that had earlier been lost to Bijapur and asked Jamshid for assistance. Jamshid had no option but to send Golconda forces to assist the Nizam Shahi army, since earlier Burhan had promptly come to his aid. On the combined Ahmadnagar-Golconda forces moving towards Sholapur, Ibrahim Adil Shah led his forces towards Parenda. A fierce but indecisive battle ensued. Although no victory was claimed, the Bijapur forces withdrew at the culmination of the fighting. A number of skirmishes continued between the two forces but none of them led either to larger battles or to any further decisive actions. The Golconda forces under Jamshid clashed directly with Ali Barid, and was more successful although even in this case, the Bidar army was not conclusively defeated. Jamshid managed to capture some Bidar territories around Kaulas and then retired to his kingdom.

Unique Aspects of Wars in the Deccan

There are some peculiar, and unique aspects of wars that were fought in the Deccan during medieval times, especially during the period when the Shahi kings were ruling most of the region.

In all of the battles that were fought where decisive outcomes were achieved, the victorious forces never pursued the defeated, and normally fleeing, adversary. Neither did they put to death the captured leadership of the defeated adversary. A sense of 'forgiveness' seemed to be all pervasive. At the culmination of a battle, the defeated adversaries were permitted to 'go away', at times even being allowed to take their personal effects with them. Normally, it is seen that the victorious army did not inflict any serious or lasting punishment on the adversary. In the case of defeated kings, they were normally permitted to return to their capitals after having ceded some territory to the victor.

This lenient attitude towards the opponent could have been inculcated because of the fact that the all Shahi kingdoms fought each other in combinations of different alliances, with today's friend being arrayed against an ally the next day. At some time or the other, each of the kingdoms fought against the others in alliance with some other kingdom. There were no permanent friends or enemies. Unusually harsh treatment of defeated opponents would have invited spirited revenge and reprisals. Even so, the attitude of forgiveness was fundamentally wrong in terms of warfighting and socio-political stability.

Permitting the adversary to go away after a defeat invariably led to rebellion and attacks a few months or years later, since the defeated leader would always want to prove his capability and not continue to live in ignominy for long. Defeated forces also tended to join up with other disgruntled elements to foment trouble against the victor. In all cases, lenient dealings with the defeated forces inevitably led to further trouble for the victorious forces and their king. Considering that the disadvantages of 'forgiving' the opponent far outweighed the advantages such dealings provided, it is difficult to fathom the behaviour. It could only have been the prospect of being defeated themselves at a future date that made the winning side so tolerant and merciful.

The two alliances continued to feud and Jamshid was still keen to defeat Ali Barid. He therefore once again approached Burhan Nizam Shah for assistance. Ahmadnagar and Berar forces were already marching to Bidar and Jamshid joined them with glee. In the ensuing battle, Bidar forces were defeated—Ausa was captured by Burhan and Udgir by Ala ud-Din Imad Shah who had succeeded Darya. Jamshid Khan occupied Medak.

The changing characteristics of alliances and the inherent intrigue that plagued the Deccan was now demonstrated. Ibrahim Adil Shah resorted to political manoeuvring to drive a wedge between the three members of the confederacy attacking Bidar. He ceded some of his own territory to Burhan Nizam Shah and appeased Ramaraja, the Vijayanagar prime minister by giving him a great amount of treasure. After having ensured that the Nizam Shahi and Vijayanagar forces would not interfere in the battle, Ibrahim Adil Shah send his army to attack Jamshid Khan, who was forced to retreat to Golconda. Ibrahim then imprisoned Ali Barid and annexed Bidar to Bijapur.

Golconda Diplomacy

With the annexation of Bidar by Ibrahim Adil Shah, Burhan Nizam Shah became uncomfortable with the growing power of the Bijapur ruler. Even though some sort of a non-aggression pact had been arrived at between the two kings earlier, Burhan send his forces to advance on Sholapur, the area of perpetual contention between Ahmadnagar and Bijapur. At Sholapur, Adil Shahi forces halted Burhan's further advance. It is at this stage in the political developments in the Deccan that one gets a clear indication of the emerging influence of Golconda on the affairs of the region. Both the Nizam Shahi and the Adil Shahi kings, now confronting each other, asked for Jamshid Khan's assistance—he had become the deciding factor in the region, perhaps in a de facto manner. His further actions from this point forward cemented the position.

Jamshid Khan went to Sholapur and through diplomatic negotiations diffused the situation. He persuaded Ibrahim Adil Shah to release Ali Barid and pay a large 'donation' to Burhan Nizam Shah while withdrawing voluntarily to Bijapur. Jamshid then proceeded to Bidar and reinstated Barid, giving him control of Bidar once again. The stature and power of the Telangana throne in Golconda was clearly visible—both the other major Deccan Shahi powers acceded to his 'requests', making Golconda an acknowledged and more than equal power. Considering that Jamshid had not crowned himself king, his position could be best described as the 'uncrowned' king of Telangana in the literal meaning of the term.

Immediately after this signal triumph of diplomacy, Jamshid Khan was struck by cancer and died about two years later in January 1550.

Jamshid Khan's Achievements

Although he had ruled only for a brief period of time, Jamshid had managed to get himself 're-instated' in the good graces of the other kings of the Deccan, managing to wipe away the taint of patricide apportioned to him, correctly or otherwise. Through his personal bravery, astute statesmanship and his application of military strategy he had made it necessary for the other kingdoms and dynasties to recognise not only his own personal competence, but the position of the dynasty itself. That the establishment of the position of Telangana was achieved without having to declare himself 'king' is a great achievement and testimony to Jamshid's calibre as a ruler.

When Jamshid inherited the throne and came to power, he could not count a single friend amongst the Deccan kings and chiefs. The strength of his character shone through at this difficult time; instead of becoming despondent at the unsavoury situation that he was in, he faced it calmly, took the bull by the horns and by sheer fortitude turned his fortunes around. His achievement in firmly establishing the dynasty was demonstrated during the almost two years of his debilitating illness before his death. Even though he was almost fully bedridden, not one of the squabbling and warring kings of the region attacked his kingdom, a silent testimony to the stature that he had attained in a short period of time. It can indeed be speculated that had Jamshid reigned for a longer period of time, the history of Telangana and the Golconda dynasty would have been very different to what transpired after his death.

Two far-reaching trends started during Jamshid Khan's brief reign in Golconda. First, from the very beginning of his reign, Jamshid was a patron of Persian literature. While such patronage itself was not out of the ordinary, the Golconda patronage encouraged and later led to a distinct literary development. The royal support was unflinching and the literary efforts later blossomed into the development of the local Telugu language. More importantly, the trend led to the development of the Dakhni language and literature in the Golconda court that spread further to all of the Deccan.

The second was the beginning of administrative reforms in the Telangana region. Jamshid was the first to establish districts in Telangana and make them the basic units for administrative purposes. The emphasis on administration initiated the later creation of a core administrative cadre in the Golconda kingdom. Hindus played an increasingly important role in the general administration of the kingdom, which remained a hallmark of the Golconda kings throughout their dynastic rule. The lesser Hindu aristocrats, called 'naikwaris', became a predominant section of the administrative machinery. They were personally loyal to the king and many of them rose to prominence amongst the nobles of the kingdom.

Unstable Aftermath

On the death of Jamshid Khan, his minor son Subhan was elevated to the throne. Subhan was between two and seven years old at this time, according to different sources. Inevitably, as has been seen repeatedly through the history of the sub-continent, the placement of a minor on the throne almost immediately declined into palace intrigues and power struggles. Although two nobles were instrumental in ensuring that the minor prince was crowned as the nominal ruler, the Queen-mother appointed her favourite noble, Saif Khan, as the Peshwa. Obviously the power struggle intensified with this partisan appointment and one of the squabbling factions requested Ibrahim to return from his self-imposed exile in Vijayanagar and take over the kingdom.

Jamshid Khan had appointed Jagadeva Rao, a Hindu naikwari, as the governor of Kaulas, who now came into prominence. There was another brother of Jamshid and Ibrahim, Daulat Khan, who was considered mentally 'ill' and had been imprisoned in Bhongir by Jamshid. Jagadeva Rao had Daulat released on the condition that he would hold the Golconda throne only till the time when Ibrahim returned to claim it. Daulat agreed to the condition and accordingly was proclaimed king. Jagadeva also asked Tufal Khan, the de facto ruler of Berar who had usurped power from the Imad Shahi king, for assistance, which was provided in the form of 3000 cavalry forces. However, Saif Khan now titled Ain-ul-Mulk, marched to Bhongir and defeated the Jagadev Rao-Daulat Khan army in a keenly fought battle near the village of Sunigram. Bhongir was starved into submission and both Daulat Khan and Jagadeva Rao were imprisoned.

With the defeat of Jagadeva Rao, Saif Khan was in virtual control of Golconda. However, he had not made any friends in the court, especially since he dealt with the nobles in a high-handed manner. Saif Khan could not appreciate the ground swell of animosity towards him. A large number of these nobles who were still loyal to the emerging Qutb Shahi dynasty would not support Saif Khan. The same group who had placed Subhan on the throne invited Ibrahim to come out of exile and Ibrahim finally obliged, marching out of Vijayanagar towards Golconda. The Naikwaris led by the imprisoned Jagadaeva Rao also supported the move. Ibrahim was accompanied to the border of Vijayanagar Empire by Ramaraja himself, the powerful minister ruling Vijayanagar. This action is indicative of the esteem in which Ibrahim was held in Vijayanagar, although he had been a refugee in that court for seven years.

Ibrahim reached the fort at Kovilkonda in the early summer of 1550 and arrived at Golconda in July of the same year. At Kovilkonda, Ibrahim appointed Mustafa Khan the Mir Jumla of the kingdom, the first time this appointment and title appear in Deccan history. The appointment subsequently became the most important one in the kingdom, combining administrative, financial and military responsibilities in one position—a super prime minister. It can be assumed that the establishment of this position diluted the power and prestige of the 'Peshwa' who had so far been considered the senior-most noble in court. Prior to Ibrahim arriving in Golconda, Saif Khan Ain-ul-Mulk absconded from the fort with a body of troops, paying homage to the new king through a messenger. He took refuge in Ahmadnagar with the Nizam Shahis. It is reported that Ibrahim conducted ritual mourning for his father and also prayed at his tomb before being crowned as king—Ibrahim Quli Qutb Shah.

Chapter 26

IBRAHIM QULI QUTB SHAH
INCREASING POWER AND STATURE

Ibrahim Quli Qutb Shah was the first of the dynasty to assume royal regalia and the title 'Shah', the accepted title for a king. He was also the first to be accepted by other contemporary kings as the ruler of the newly established kingdom with Golconda as the capital—the Qutb Shahi kingdom. It is not surprising that he was also the first of the dynasty to mint his own coins as well as to have the royal name embossed on his tomb.

Political Manoeuvring

By the time Ibrahim came to the throne, Burhan Nizam Shah had died and been succeeded by his son Husain Nizam Shah. In 1557, with the reluctant assistance of the Golconda army, Husain marched to capture Gulbarga from the Adil Shahis of Bijapur. Ibrahim Qutb Shah was advised by his friend and benefactor, the Vijayanagar minister Ramaraja, to desist from providing assistance to Husain in this endeavour. He also cautioned Ibrahim against straining his relations with the Bijapur king. Meanwhile, Gulbarga fort proved to be vested with very strong defences and extremely difficult to breech. Ibrahim Adil Shah wrote a letter to Ibrahim Qutb Shah asking him not to be part of the siege of Gulbarga, upon which the Qutb Shahi monarch withdrew with his troops to Golconda.

The tide of events now started turn in unexpected ways. Almost immediately after the withdrawal of the Golconda forces, Ibrahim Adil Shah died and was succeeded by his son Ali Adil Shah. Ali was immature and impetuous, and invaded Qutb Shahi territory in a sort of revenge attack, with the assistance of Vijayanagar. Once again, the fickleness of alliances in the Deccan and the Peninsula is demonstrated in this quick change of loyalty by the Vijayanagar forces. While this realignment was unfolding, Ramaraja's brothers rebelled in his kingdom and captured the fort at Adoni. In an about turn, he now asked for Ibrahim Qutb Shah's assistance, which was readily given. The combined Vijayanagar-Golconda army recaptured the fort at Adoni and forced the rebels to surrender.

This turn of events is full of paradoxes and clearly indicates the confused and complex state of political affairs and military alliances in the Deccan. Vijayanagar even while continuing to attack Golconda territory, asks the Golconda Qutb Shahi king for assistance to put down a domestic rebellion. In a sort of stranger than fiction situation, the requested assistance is readily given and the Vijayanagar rebellion is contained. It is obvious that within the Deccan, alliances were made, broken and then reinvigorated, at times within the span of a single year. In an obtuse manner, these manoeuvrings could be seen as the outward display of the lack of sincerity towards the forging of alliances. It also placed on display the utter lack of earnestness with which these kings looked at the serious business of ruling a country—a mockery of the exalted concept of kingship.

Jagadeva Rao, who had been the prime mover in bringing Ibrahim back into Golconda at the death of Jamshid, was used to exercising control over the court and the administration at his will and fancy. Jagadeva had got used to issuing independent orders, without the kings permission, even to high officials. After Ibrahim took control of the kingdom, Jagadeva felt constrained and started to feel a loss of power. In keeping with his volatile nature, Jagadeva moved away from the court in a semi-rebellion and established his headquarters at Elgandal; moving later to the Imad Shahi capital of Ellichpur. He became overbearing in his attitude at the Berar court and was subsequently expelled from Imad Shahi territories. Jagadeva then collected an army to oppose Ibrahim Qutb Shah, which was defeated in battle by

Golconda forces. Jagdeva fled and sought refuge in Vijayanagar. This episode was the consequence of blatant personal ambition taking over the good sense of an otherwise shrewd and capable noble.

Wars against the Nizam Shahis

Vijayanagar was virtually controlled by the powerful minister Ramaraja who kept the actual king Sadasiva Raya in close confinement and ruled on his behalf as a dictator. Ali Adil Shah of Bijapur joined forces with Ramaraja and started a campaign to recover Sholapur and Kalyani from Ahmadnagar. Ramaraja in turn requested Ibrahim Qutb Shah for assistance, although he had given Jagadeva Rao refuge when the latter was fleeing after rebelling against Ibrahim. Once again the Qutb Shahi forces joined the alliance against Ahmadnagar. Considering all the facts on the ground, this was an act that defied any logic in such matters. Ahmadnagar was under siege with all the other major kingdoms arrayed against it. However, Ibrahim Qutb Shah maintained contact with the Nizam Shahi king besieged in the fort. This act indicates that Ibrahim was not interested in fighting Ahmadnagar. He had been left with no choice but to join the coalition since the Vijayanagar strongman had asked him to do so. The power of Vijayanagar was such that none of the other kings could deny the wishes of its virtual ruler.

This campaign sowed the seeds for the later formation of a confederacy against Vijayanagar, which ultimately brought down the great empire. There are many reports of the depredations that the invading army visited on the countryside around Ahmadnagar where the siege was being conducted. Some of the chronicles of the time mention separately that the Vijayanagar forces oppressed the 'Muslim' population and hurt their religious sensibilities by their wanton acts of cruelty. This is one of the first instances when religious sentiments have been mentioned in relation to military campaigns in the Deccan. Till this time, reports only mentioned oppression of the people of a territory. The introduction of the religious angle into what was almost a routine campaign led to further actions and events in the Peninsula that would have long-lasting consequences. It is to be noted that this was one of the earliest instances of religion, and the divisions it would bring, entering the Deccan and South India.

Ibrahim Qutb Shah was unhappy about the manner in which the Ahmadnagar people were being treated by the invading forces and privately devised a plan to have the siege, of which he was part, lifted. He voluntarily surrendered the fort at Kondapalli to Vijayanagar and advised Ramaraja, presumably in private, of the possibility of an intervention from Gujarat to assist Husain Nizam Shah. Under these circumstances, Vijayanagar felt it prudent to raise the siege without having achieved anything. Ibrahim lost a fort in the bargain. Even so, contemporary chronicles laud the raising of the Ahmadnagar siege as a diplomatic victory for the Golconda king. This claim of victory could be because the all-powerful Vijayanagar army was 'forced' to retreat into their own territory through negotiations. The reports are also indicative of the animosity that had developed against Vijayanagar in the other kingdoms, primarily born of jealousy in its power and stature, and the arrogant and wilful nature of its rulers.

The reason for Ibrahim joining the anti-Ahmadnagar coalition being the fear of Vijayanagar is confirmed by the fact that he married Husain Nizam Shah's sister in 1563 and went on to forge a close alliance with Ahmadnagar. The Golconda-Ahmadnagar combined forces captured Kalyani, which had been under Bijapur control for a long time. In retaliation, Bijapur forces, aligned with the Vijayanagar army besieged Kalyani. They were joined this time by Ali Barid from Bidar and Tufal Khan who was the de facto ruler of Berar. Kalyani was recaptured and went back to the Bijapur fold.

The Bijapur-Vijayanagar alliance then marched to Ahmadnagar and laid siege to the Nizam Shahi capital. During this march the countryside was ransacked and after the siege was laid, the surrounding areas were once again pillaged and destroyed. The siege this time was much fiercer than the previous attempt and Husain was forced to remove his family from Ahmadnagar to Ausa and he himself fled to Junnar, which was the original seat of power of the Nizam Shahis. Alongside the continuing siege of Ahmadnagar, the Bijapur-Vijayanagar combine also moved into Golconda territory, coming close to the capital itself. The extensive power of Vijayanagar was once again in full display. There were only three major kingdoms in the Deccan—Bijapur, Ahmadnagar and Golconda—and Vijayanagar could lay siege to the capital of one and maraud the territory of another almost to its capital. During the Vijayanagar incursion into Golconda territory, Jagadeva Rao who was now fully integrated with the Vijayanagar king, fomented trouble across the entire Telangana region.

Ibrahim Qutb Shah was in a quandary. According to some reports he wanted to fight the invasion. However, his council of ministers prevailed in dissuading him and Golconda once again returned to the negotiating table with Vijayanagar and Ramaraja. The senior ministers knew that Golconda could not withstand the might of the Vijayanagar forces. A treaty was arrived at; Golconda surrendered two forts to Vijayanagar, while Ramaraja returned all the forts that his forces had captured during their sojourn into Golconda territory. Ramaraja was now supreme in the Deccan and South India. Although peace had been enacted, it was at best strained and Ramaraja continued his efforts to whittle down the strength of Golconda and neutralise the power of Ibrahim Qutb Shah. It speaks volumes about the sagacity of Ibrahim that despite concerted efforts by Ramaraja of Vijayanagar, he was able to ride out the intense turmoil that was being generated in his kingdom, by conclusively putting down rebellions wherever they broke out.

A Union of the Successor States

For more than a decade Vijayanagar had been treating the Bahmani successor dynasties, the Deccan Shahis—Adil Shahis in Bijapur, Nizam Shahis in Ahmadnagar, Imad Shahis in Berar and Qutb Shahis in Golconda—with ill-concealed disdain, at times even as vassal kings. By the mid-1560s each one of these kingdoms had some score or the other to settle with the high-handed and arrogant Vijayanagar dynasty and leadership. Ali Adil Shah of Bijapur had aligned himself with Vijayanagar against Ahmadnagar on the stipulated condition that the invading army would not harm the common people of the kingdom, the non-combatants, nor desecrate religious monuments and places of worship. The Vijayanagar army had reneged on this promise and done both during the invading march as well as during the subsequent siege. Husain Nizam Shah of Ahmadnagar had the misfortune to have his people put to the sword indiscriminately and he himself had to flee the capital with his family in front of the Vijayanagar onslaught. Ibrahim Qutb Shah of Golconda was enraged that Vijayanagar had given shelter to Jagadeva Rao who had rebelled against him and later permitted him to enter Golconda territory to spread discontent. He had also had to cede few forts to Vijayanagar to ensure peace and stability in the region.

The antagonism ran deep against Ramaraja, the dictator who had usurped power in Vijayanagar, converting the actual Raya or king into a mere puppet. In an once-in-a-lifetime effort, the Deccan kingdoms decided to unite against the might of Vijayanagar. Ali Barid, the de facto ruler of Bidar, had no personal animosity against Vijayanagar as such, but was willing to go with the initiative of the rest of the Muslim kingdoms. He was an opportunist who was on a perpetual lookout to better his own position. Only Tufal Khan, the minister who had usurped power in Berar, refused to join the coalition or confederacy. However, his dissent was not because of any liking for Vijayanagar but because of the humiliation that had been heaped on him by Ibrahim Qutb Shah after he had been humbled in battle earlier. Effectively Tufal Khan was sulking in his small kingdom.

1564-65 were epoch-making years in the history of South India—the Deccan and the Southern Peninsula. This was the only time period during which the perennially warring Bahmani successor kingdoms united to face a common adversary. Only the unity of purpose—the defeat and elimination of Vijayanagar as the predominant regional power—kept the alliance united. The three major kingdoms were earnest and serious about the unity of purpose, thus managing to keep the cohesiveness of the confederacy till the objective was realised. In order to put an end to minor irritants between them, the three major kingdoms enacted a number of initiatives. Ali Adil Shah married Husain Nizam Shah's daughter, Chand Bibi, and Ali's sister Hadia Sultana was married off to Husain's son Murtaza. (These events have been described in detail in the earlier section on the Nizam Shahis of Ahmadnagar.) Husain also gave away control of Sholapur to Ali Adil Shah, thus bringing to an end a perennially contentious issue between the two kingdoms.

The confederacy, some historians have labelled it the 'League of Four Sultans', gathered and moved south, arriving on the northern banks of the River Krishna. The famous Battle of Talikota ensued.

> ## A Wrongly Named Battle
>
> The critical battle that once and for all extinguished the greatness of Vijayanagar was fought on 23 January 1565. However, it has wrongly been called by historians as the 'Battle of Talikota'. For a little while after the battle it was referred to as the Battle of Raksasi-Tangadi, which is also a wrong name.
>
> Factually, the battle was fought at a place called Bannihatti, a small hamlet about 34 miles south of Talikota. Some historians have also called this important battle, the Battle of the River Krishna, since it was fought on its banks. The three places mentioned in relation to this battle—Talikota, Rakasgi and Tangadgi (the last two places are incorrectly spelt as Raksasi and Tangadi in the early reports)—are all on the north bank of the River Krishna. The actual fighting and the defeat of Vijayanagar, it has been confirmed, took place in the south-bank of the river, where the village of Bannihatti is located.
>
> There is no valid reason not to call this historically pivotal battle, the Battle of Bannihatti.

In the Battle of Bannihatti (Talikota), Vijayanagar was conclusively defeated. The powerful minister Ramaraja was either killed in battle or captured and almost immediately beheaded. (The details of the battle itself will be explained in the next volume, which will also elaborate on the fall and sacking of the glorious Vijayanagar Empire and its prominent towns.)

It is reported that at the end of the battle, a Vijayanagar noble called Tirumala managed to remove great wealth, mentioned as being in excess of one hundred million sterling worth, the royal insignia and crown from the capital and installed them at the fort in Penukonda, which was then made the new capital of the defeated kingdom. Tirumala is reported to have imprisoned the king Sadasiva Raya. It is no exaggeration to state that the Battle of Bannihatti (Talikota) was disastrous for the great Vijayanagar Empire and its ruling dynasty. Before moving on to the further actions of the Deccan Shahi kings, an attempt to 'white-wash' history by some biased historians must be put right here.

Some modern-day historians have vociferously mentioned that after the defeat of Vijayanagar and the ensuing sacking of its capital, no temples were desecrated or destroyed. They point to the few temples that exist today in the territory that was the erstwhile Vijayanagar kingdom as proof of this assertion. This claim has to be considered a blatant attempt at re-writing history for the sake of bringing out the victorious Muslim rulers as paragons of virtue and religiously tolerant rulers. These narratives are untrue. The assertions of the Hindu temples being spared are incorrect. Considering that religion and religious differences with the powerful neighbour were the underlying principles that united the confederacy and that religious hatred percolated the armies of the Deccan, it is certain that the temples were looted, desecrated and then destroyed. The few temples that today spread across the countryside that was once Vijayanagar was definitely rebuilt at some later date. Religiously biased persecution indeed took place in the aftermath of the Battle of Bannihatti (Talikota).

The Aftermath

Not long after the momentous victory, the confederacy fell apart, because of the normal bickering between the kings on trivial matters. This development is not surprising, considering the inherent and common character of the Shahi dynasties of selfish pettiness. The immediate cause for the breakup was the procedure adopted to divide the captured territories, which did not meet the approval of all the participants. The real reason was the fundamental and underlying disunity brought about by individual aspirations, ambition and the exaggerated sense of self-worth that each of the Shahi kings cultivated within highly overstated egos. They were petty beings, and continued to be mean and frivolous in all their dealings. There are descriptions of the magnanimity of the Deccan rulers in a large number of books and articles and these may indeed be true to some extent. However, there is no evidence to prove that any of these kings were able to rise above their self-centred behaviour at any stage during the nearly three centuries during which the Deccan was under their control.

One must therefore surmise that their magnanimity was displayed for some ulterior motive that concerned them at that moment when these actions were supposed to have been taken.

Ibrahim Qutb Shah played a pivotal role in maintaining the balance of power between the three major Deccan kingdoms. Further, he was also instrumental in keeping in check the ambitions of both the Barids of Bidar and the Imad Shahis in Berar. Although both these kingdoms were relatively weaker than the other three, they were continually initiating actions to disrupt the stability of the region with an eye to gaining some advantage for themselves from the ensuing chaos. With the Vijayanagar power almost completely neutralised, Ibrahim undertook the conquest of the region around Rajamundry that had earlier been parcelled out to minor chieftains. The territorial extent of the Qutb Shahi kingdom was enhanced by this move.

Other Military Exploits

Vijayanagar had also been partitioned between few chiefs, the most prominent of them being a noble called Vidhyadhar. On Rajamundry being invaded, he ensconced himself within the fort at Qasimkota, although he was ousted by the Qutb Shahi forces who surrounded and captured the fort. After settling the Rajamundry region, the Qutb Shahi army moved to southern Orissa where they seized some territory and a few forts. The forces were commanded by Malik Naib and his objective seems to have been to secure the north-east borders of the country. Malik Naib continued his victorious march till the Deccan army reached the Bengal border, where the king Vasnadeo was ruling. Vasnadeo sued for peace, accepted Ibrahim's nominal suzerainty, and paid a large tribute to the Qutb Shahi commander. This was the northern-most limit of the Golconda army's march.

Berar had been going through some turmoil for almost a decade. Tufal Khan, who had not joined the confederacy against Vijayanagar had become the de facto ruler and was keeping Burhan Imad Shah under palace arrest. Tufal had so far enjoyed the tacit protection of Ahmadnagar. However, in 1572, Murtaza Nizam Shah demanded that Burhan be released, without citing any reason for the ultimatum. Starting with the founder of the dynasty, Qutb-ul-Mulk, the Qutb Shahi rulers of Golconda had always attempted to maintain the balance of power between Bijapur, Ahmadnagar and Golconda. Ibrahim, also involved in the same endeavour, felt that Murtaza had become too powerful and was acting in an overbearing manner. Accordingly, he send a message to Ali Adil Shah in Bijapur stating that Murtaza's pretensions to being the lead power in the Deccan should be checked before it became a threat to them. Ali Barid in Bidar supported the Bijapur-Golconda initiative.

Murtaza Nizam Shah proved to be agile in diplomatic manoeuvring. Before any action against him could be initiated, he embarked on a personal visit to Bijapur. He proposed to Ali Adil Shah that by joining forces they could enhance their individual territorial holdings—Murtaza would annex Berar and Ali could annex some territories of the defeated Vijayanagar, although the three Shahi kings had jointly decided, after the Battle of Bannihatti (Talikota), that Vijayanagar territory was not to be invaded or annexed. Subsequently, the combined Ahmadnagar-Bijapur armies could also invade and capture Qutb Shahi territories.

The Ahmadnagar forces easily overran Berar and the kingdom was annexed, even though the initial pretext for the invasion was the necessity to free its rightful ruler Burhan Imad Shah. This annexation marked the end of the independent existence of the Imad Shahis, a minor dynasty amongst the Bahmani successor states of the Deccan. Bijapur armies went into the Karnataka region and annexed a swath of territory that had been part of the Vijayanagar Empire. Ibrahim Qutb Shah was now placed in a situation wherein Golconda was forced to share a border directly with Ahmadnagar, with the annexation of Berar; and also with Bijapur, with the territorial expansion that the Adil Shahi kingdom had undertaken. The buffer states between Golconda and the other major Deccan kingdoms had been swallowed by Ahmadnagar and Bijapur.

Last Days

Forever the keeper of the balance of power, Ibrahim had to check the burgeoning strength of Bijapur, since Ali Adil Shah had made deep inroads into erstwhile Vijayanagar territory and bolstered his own power. Since Ali Adil Shah was campaigning deep in Vijayanagar territory, Ibrahim agreed to help Sriranga, the ruling chief of the truncated Vijayanagar kingdom. He send an army to invade Bijapur territory as a diversion. This ruse worked and Ali Adil Shah returned to Bijapur to safeguard his kingdom. Further incursions into Vijayanagar by the Bijapur army was curtailed.

Ibrahim saw the withdrawal of the Bijapur army from South India as an opportunity to enlarge his own kingdom and the Qutb Shahi forces ventured into Vijayanagar territory. He changed his policy towards Sriranga and captured the province situated around Udayagiri. The Qutb Shahi forces went on to capture few sundry forts in the region and in April 1579 occupied the Kondavidu fort. At this stage, Ali Adil Shah died in Bijapur and was succeeded on the throne by his minor son Ibrahim. Ahmadnagar and Golconda took this opportunity to attack Bijapur with a combined force, once again demonstrating the in-built opportunistic trait of the Deccan Shahi kings. In this invasion, the Qutb Shahi forces won many skirmishes. (The siege of Bijapur has been covered in detail in an earlier section.)

While the Qutb Shahi forces were still engaged in Bijapur territory, Ibrahim Qutb Shah died in Golconda—5 May 1580.

Ibrahim Quli – An Assessment

Ibrahim Qutb Shah—the first to assume the title and rank—ruled for 31 years, essentially as a man of peace, which was a rarity in those times. There are only two recorded instances of his initiating major offensives against any of the other kingdoms of the region. It can be assumed that the provocation was extreme for the Golconda forces to have been deployed offensively. Ibrahim was also the first king from the dynasty to mint his own coins, although only a few of them have survived to this day. It is noteworthy that none of the Bahmani successor states struck gold or silver coins of their own; they used the Vijayanagar coins for gold and the Mughal rupaya for silver coins.

From available records it is seen that Ibrahim's administration followed the same pattern as those of the other Deccan Shahi kingdoms. The Qutb Shahi country was not sub-divided into provinces or districts till much later in the dynastic rule and was centrally administrated as one entity. As was common in the Deccan kingdoms, there were ministers appointed to look after the important functions of the state such as the army, treasury etc., and also a prime minister; an advisory council of the more senior nobles was also a common element in the Deccan.

A factor to note, which was unique to the Qutb Shahi kingdom, was the complete harmony that existed between the Hindus and the Muslims within the Golconda territories. Even though there were almost continuous clashes with the Hindu kingdom of Vijayanagar to the south, the discord was not religious and has to be considered enmity and competition that is bound to exist between immediate neighbours. Ibrahim, as a ruler, did not display any bias between his Deccani, Hindu or phirangi nobles, a really notable achievement in a time when religion and race-based factionalism had started to become the norm.

Ibrahim himself was a lifelong student and built schools in all the villages across the countryside, making attendance compulsory for the children of the kingdom. This was a revolutionary concept at a time when education was restricted to the upper strata of the society. By imparting free education to his subjects, irrespective of social and economic class, Ibrahim Qutb Shah laid the foundation for the building of a great cultural edifice that Golconda became in the later years of the Qutb Shahi rule.

Chapter 27

MUHAMMAD QULI QUTB SHAH
FOCUS ON CULTURAL DEVELOPMENT

Ibrahim left behind six surviving sons and was succeeded by his third son, Muhammad Quli. Obviously some palace intrigue took place, as the eldest did not automatically ascend the throne. It is highly likely that Muhammad was elevated to the throne by ambitious nobles since he was pliable and could be manipulated to their will. He was therefore 'elected' by the nobles and placed on the throne in 1580 as Muhammad Quli Qutb Shah. There is a report that Muhammad had been chosen by Ibrahim to be his successor, although there is no evidence to support this conjecture. It is highly probable that this report was generated as an embellishment at a later date to improve the legitimacy of Muhammad's accession.

First Foray

Muhammad inherited the on-going conflict with Bijapur—the Qutb Shahi forces were besieging the fort at Naldurg even as he was being crowned. The commander of the forces in Naldurg, a foreign (phirangi) noble called Mir Shah Mir invited the new king to the frontlines in Naldurg, to bolster the morale of the forces and also to establish his credentials with the army. Muhammad proceeded to Naldurg and while he was there, it became clear that the siege would not be successful. Muhammad was disgusted with this failure and returned to Golconda after removing Mir Shah Mir from command and also exiling him back to Persia.

Mughal Interlude

From the very beginning of their rule, the Qutb Shahi rulers had been in contact with the Mughal rulers in Agra. Qutb-ul-Mulk, the founder of the dynasty, had send envoys to the Mughal court and although a flattering response had been received in return, the Qutb Shahis had kept their own counsel and not accepted any orders or followed any suggestions from Agra. In fact, the Deccan kingdoms had maintained sporadic contact with the Mughals from the time of Babur establishing his rule in North India. By 1579-80 the Mughal incursions into northern Deccan had become regular and frequent. Khandesh had become a vassal state of the Mughals and they had also overrun and annexed Gujarat. It was impossible not to feel the virtual Mughal presence in Golconda.

The die was cast for serious Mughal intervention in the Deccan in 1595, when one party in the Ahmadnagar civil war invited the Mughal Emperor Akbar's son, Prince Murad, to intervene on their side. It took only a few months for the Mughal forces to invest Ahmadnagar. Both Bijapur and Golconda responded to the Nizam Shahi appeal for assistance by sending strong forces, which joined together at the fort of Naldurg, while the indomitable Chand Sultana was entrenched in the fort at Ahmadnagar. However, the city per se had already fallen to the Mughals. Since the combined Bijapur-Golconda forces were formidable and they occupied some strategic forts which were considered impregnable and were stoutly defended, the Mughal prince thought it prudent to accept a treaty of peace and withdrew to the northern extremity of the Deccan.

This episode should have been a signal lesson for the Deccan Shahi kingdoms on the necessity to remain united, especially since it had been demonstrated that their combined armies could stand up to the might of the Mughal power. However, not surprisingly, considering the inherent character traits of the rulers and their dynasties, the lesson was not heeded. Factional disagreements, mutual distrust and self-centred ambition clouded their individual and collective judgement. The result—Ahmadnagar and the Nizam Shahi dynasty were eliminated after a heroic struggle that was also tainted by internal betrayal.

Ahmadnagar's final struggle and death throes do not form a direct part of the narrative of the Qutb Shahi dynasty. Muhammad Qutb Shah studiously kept away from the Ahmadnagar war for survival in the face of the final Mughal onslaught. The further story of Malik Ambar's exploits and attempts to keep the Nizam Shahi dynasty alive is covered in another chapter and is not a direct part of the Qutb Shahi history. However, it is important to note that the Mughals—nemesis of the Deccan Shahis—had physically moved much closer to Golconda.

Military Actions – Political Challenges

The Adil Shahis invaded Golconda territory and were beaten off with the assistance of Murtaza Nizam Shah. The Golconda-Ahmadnagar army conducted guerrilla warfare against the invaders, compelling the Bijapur forces to withdraw to their own territory. However, this three-cornered fight resulted in making the existing matrimonial alliance between Bijapur and Ahmadnagar a more considered relationship—Ali Adil Shah was married to the famous Chand Bibi, who was Murtaza's aunt.

Muhammad faced a serious rebellion towards the end of his reign. Earlier, he had appointed a noble Ali Khan Lur as the commander of the important fort at Kondavidu in the south. Ali Khan however defected to Vijayanagar and joined the ruling Raya, Venkata II. Subsequently, he broke away from Venkata because of some disagreements and became a free-lancing independent commander with a sizeable force under his command. He captured a number of forts from both Golconda and Vijayanagar territory, but was killed in a battle against Bijapur forces. Even after his death, Ali Khan's earlier activities continued to create instability in the region.

Muhammad Qutb Shah believed that Venkata II had been instrumental in turning Ali Khan Lur against him and that the Vijayanagar ruler had egged the rebel on against Golconda. He also wanted to recapture the forts that Ali Khan had captured earlier and were now within the territorial control of Vijayanagar. Muhammad himself led the military campaign to the south, which was a great success. Golconda forces recaptured the fort at Musalimadugu, south of the River Krishna, which in turn resulted in a number of chieftains surrendering other forts to the Qutb Shahis. Buoyed by the easy success of this campaign, Muhammad decided to directly attack the truncated Vijayanagar kingdom. The Golconda army marched to the new Vijayanagar capital Penukonda and laid siege to the fort there.

Venkata pretended to be giving in and requested a three-day truce as a prelude to accepting a longer term peace treaty and also in order to prepare for receiving the Golconda king. Muhammad was naively taken-in by what he believed was considerate behaviour and not only agreed to the temporary truce, but also lifted the siege in anticipation of Venkata's surrender. Venkata used the reprieve to rapidly stock the fort with food and other provision, arms and ammunition, and a large contingent of soldiers—enough to withstand a long siege. Realising that he had been tricked, Muhammad renewed the siege. However, the fort and its defences proved to be formidable and the Golconda forces were unable to break-in. As the monsoons were about to start and the Qutb Shahi forces were south of the River Krishna, Muhammad had to hurriedly lift the siege and withdraw to the north bank, which was Golconda territory before the river flooded and became unfordable. It is reported that the withdrawing Golconda army was repeatedly harassed and defeated in skirmishes by the Vijayanagar forces. The retreat must have been a harrowing experience for the Golconda forces and their king.

On the departure of the Golconda forces, Venkata consolidated his position and recaptured all the lost territory south of the River Krishna with the exception of Kondavidu. Muhammad Qutb Shah lost all his territories south of the river. This debacle was a great blow to Muhammad's prestige in the Deccan. The Golconda army had proved its mettle in the battlefield, but their king had failed as a diplomat and statesman. Through his leniency, the king had forfeited all the gains that the military campaign had accrued—he had permitted the enemy to become entrenched in their own stronghold.

The disastrous end to a somewhat easy and successful military campaign demonstrates the immaturity, impetuousness and the indecisive soft nature of Muhammad Qutb Shah. These were the same character traits for which the nobles had elected Muhammad to the throne—he was simplistic by nature and pliable since he was straight forward and trusting in his dealings. From this display of characteristics it becomes obvious that the nobles of the kingdom had harboured ulterior motives in selecting Muhammad to ascend the throne. It is apparent that their loyalty to the Qutb Shahi kingdom and concern for its well-being were questionable, at best.

Rebellions in the East

In the early 1590s, three chiefs controlling the south-eastern provinces of the Golconda territories bordering Vijayanagar, jointly rebelled against Qutb Shahi control. No doubt the debacle in the campaign against Venkata II must have been a contributory factor, along with their ambition, for them to have initiated this action. The rebels also requested Venkata for assistance, which was given in the form of a 10,000-strong cavalry force. Muhammad send a force under a seasoned military commander, who put down the rebellion and returned to Golconda. Almost simultaneous to this rebellion, the north-eastern province, southern Orissa, also revolted. This province had been a Qutb Shahi protectorate from the time that Ibrahim Qutb Shah had overrun the region.

Muhammad wanted to lead the counter-campaign into the rebelling provinces, but was dissuaded by the council of nobles from doing so. Perhaps, they feared a repeat of the Vijayanagar campaign if the king himself went out to battle. The Golconda force met the rebels led by Mukundaraj at Rajamundry. The rebel forces were defeated and Mukundaraj fled to Qasimkota pursued by the Qutb Shahi commander, Amin-ul-Mulk. Mukundaraj appealed for help from the chiefs of the region, but no one ventured to assist the rebel. He was then driven out of the region and took refuge in Bijapur.

Around the same time, an imposter declared himself as one of Muhammad's elder brothers in Bidar and claimed the Golconda throne as legitimately being his. Although no conclusive proof of his involvement is available, since the claimant was resident in Bidar, it is certain that this person was supported by Ali Barid, who was a known destabilising influence in the region. The imposter crowned himself the king of Telangana on the banks of the River Krishna and managed to collect a large army in preparation for a march to Golconda. Qutb Shahi forces under the command of Itibar Khan defeated this large but fledgling army and nothing more is heard about the imposter, who was presumably killed in the battle or beheaded after defeat and capture.

This episode was only a prelude to a continuous stream of rebellions, especially in the north-east of the kingdom. Rebellions and revolts erupted routinely and were put down, also in much the same routine manner, by the Qutb Shahi forces. It is obvious that the Golconda forces were better trained and led, as compared to the rag-tag armies that the rebels were able to put together. It is equally obvious that the Qutb Shahi control over their territories was not as strong as it would have been under a strong king. Muhammad was an ineffective ruler.

Last Days

When the rebellions in the east were somewhat contained, Muhammad appointed Muhammad Amin as Mir Jumla on the advice of the council of ministers and other nobles. Amin proved to be an efficient prime minister with a great sense of loyalty and high level of integrity. In a short period of time he managed to stabilise the turbulent kingdom. Around 1590, the capital of the kingdom had been shifted to the newly built city of Hyderabad. (The building of Hyderabad and the shift of the capital is covered in detail later in the chapter.) In 1603-04, Hyderabad was visited by Prince Aghuzlu Sultan as the envoy of Shah Abbas the Great, the Safawi king of Persia. The envoy brought a matrimonial proposal for the Qutb Shahi dynasty, suggesting that Muhammad Qutb Shah's daughter be married to 'one of the great Sultan's sons'. Obviously Muhammad did not take kindly to this vague proposal and had this particular princess married off to a noble while the Persian envoy was still residing in Hyderabad.

Refusing a proposal of matrimonial alliance with the Shah of Persia was not a trivial action. However, it is probable that Muhammad's decision was obviously influenced by the great distance between the two kingdoms that would in turn have acted as dampener for any action that the Persian king would have wanted to undertake in retaliation for the insulting refusal of his 'magnanimous' offer—that too by a minor king ruing a marginal kingdom at the extremity of the greater Islamic world.

The palpable rift between the Deccani and Phirangi nobles was a perennial challenge to the stability of each of the Shahi kingdoms, almost throughout their existence. In fact, the in-fighting between the two groups could be counted as one of the core reasons instrumental for the collapse of the Nizam Shahis in Ahmadnagar. The same challenge raised its head in Golconda during the last days of Muhammad Qutb Shah. Here the confrontation was aggravated by the presence of the Mughals who were in the process of infiltrating the Golconda court in order to weaken the administration. An internal attempt to bring these trouble-makers, from both sides of the equation, to book resulted in few desultory riots in Hyderabad that were quickly put down. The Deccani faction brought out yet another brother of Muhammad and attempted to place him on the throne. Even this rebellion was quickly contained and the brother imprisoned in Golconda.

Even though the minor rebellions were being regularly put down, they did not stop. Further, the Mughals were concentrating on advancing into the Deccan and were being held back only by the valiant efforts of Malik Ambar who was fighting to save the Ahmadnagar kingdom. (Malik Ambar's efforts have been covered in detail earlier.) The Mughals continued to instigate rebellions in Qutb Shahi territories, all of which were quelled and contained by a strong military commander Changiz Khan. A notable rebellion was that of a Hindu naikwari chieftain in Bastar, which was also efficiently put down. While the rebellions were indeed being contained, their occurrence so regularly indicate a deeper malaise in the kingdom—one of a faltering and inefficient administration, gradually moving towards a final collapse.

In early January 1612, Muhammad Qutb Shah fell ill at the age of 47 and died after a few days, on 11 January. He had ruled for a long 33 years from the age of 14 and died without leaving a son to succeed him. He was followed by his nephew and son-in-law to the Qutb Shahi throne.

Muhammad Qutb Shah's Personality

There is definitive evidence that Muhammad led a life of ease and luxury. His love and commitment to the 'good life', leading a life of sensuality and near-debauchery, has been attributed as the reason for his early demise. This assertion cannot be confirmed as true since there are no medical records available to confirm the actual illness that led to Muhammad's death after a few days of being sick. However, it is true that he concentrated on his private life and forayed into real-politic and military campaigns only a couple of times during his long rule. He left the administration and security of the kingdom in the hands of capable ministers, without any interference, himself taking no active part. This attitude, which the nobles must have detected in the young 14-year old prince, could have been the fundamental reason for Muhammad being chosen, from a group of six princes, to become the king.

Muhammad was essentially an artist, with all the extreme sensibilities that go with being one. He must be credited with recognising the severe congestion and unhealthy living conditions faced by the common people in Golconda and making the decision to build a more open and larger capital. In creating an outlet for the new capital across the River Musi and laying out the new township Muhammad was intimately involved. He took personal interest in building the capital and was involved in supervising the construction as it progressed. He was also a great patron of literature—both prose and poetry—as well as dance and music. In encouraging literature, he made no differentiation between endeavours in Persian, Telugu or Dakhini, supporting each of them equally. In a time when Persian was considered the more sophisticated language and the local tongue was shunned as being coarse, the king's patronage to Telugu gave it an impetus to develop into a refined language capable of expressing higher emotions in a sophisticated manner. With the king's support, uninhibited poetry emanated from the court in all three languages. This body of work has in later, more puritanical, days been attributed to the 'loose morals' that is supposed to have prevailed in Muhammad's court—a not so subtle attribution to the king's commitment to sensual living.

Muhammad was inherently a gentle and forgiving person, character traits that sit at odds with the normal mean and bloodthirsty characteristics attributed to a medieval monarch. There is no doubt that the king's mild manner and lack of understanding of the intricacies of court politics and external diplomacy created a great deal of trouble for the kingdom. The domestic rebellions that plagued his entire reign and undermined the strength of the kingdom can be attributed to his lenient nature. Further, almost all the reverses that the Golconda army suffered is believed to have been the result of Muhammad's immature but humane character and inability to enforce his will. He lacked decisive leadership focused on battlefield victory and to ensuring the stability of the kingdom—at best being vacillating and weak in his decision-making and follow-on actions. Muhammad was lucky that he had a group of nobles loyal to him and the kingdom to clean up after him and run the state as a well-administered entity. Even though he was removed from the daily running of the court and the kingdom, he was astute enough to realise the threat that was posed by the proximity of the Mughals and there interference in the affairs of the Deccan. He therefore insisted on burying the hatchet with Bijapur and initiated a period of peace between the two countries. He also assisted Malik Ambar, to the extent possible without directly confronting the Mughals, when the latter was fighting the Mughal forces.

With all his faults, fads and foibles, Muhammad Quli Qutb Shah must be given credit for achieving something that none of the other Shahi kings managed to do with as much success as he did. Although the Qutb Shahi kingdom was at war with the Hindu kingdoms of Vijayanagar and Orissa for the better part of Muhammad's rule, within the Golconda kingdom there was no animosity between the two religious groups. On the contrary, there was a great deal of cooperation between the two communities in supporting the sovereignty of the kingdom. This completely non-communal approach to alliances was not restricted to the loyal subjects of the king, but also percolated into the formation of rebel groups that tormented the Qutb Shahis on a perpetual basis. The kingdom was almost completely free of religious and communal divisions, other than the perennial rivalry between the local and foreign nobles. The kingdom lived in a visible spirit of harmony. The gentle and tolerant attitude of Muhammad had a great deal to do with the religious harmony that prevailed. This should be considered a singular achievement of this 'gentle', if ineffective, monarch.

The Building of Hyderabad

Golconda was always a crowded city, situated at the cross roads on an important trading route that connected the Deccan hinterland with the port of Masulipatam. By the 1570s it had become unmanageably congested and Muhammad decided to expand the capital. His father Ibrahin Qutb Shah had already built a wide bridge over the River Musi that flowed south of Golconda and encouraged the people of the capital to settle on the south bank. In 1578, Muhammad followed up this initiative by deciding to build a new capital across the river. The building of this new capital—named Hyderabad—is covered later in this chapter.

Ibrahim Qutb Shah had experimented with extending the capital, Golconda, towards the west that had been unsuccessful because of the region being arid. However, the flat grounds on the southern banks of the River Musi on which Golconda stood promised to be a favourable region to move to and ease the congestion of the capital. In 1589-90, Muhammad made the decision to construct a new capital in this area. The nucleus was planned on the gridiron system in the form of a giant cross. Already a major road existed that passed west from Golconda, all the way to the port at Masulipatam. This road was intersected by a planned north-south road and the Charminar was built at the point of intersection to become the centre of the new planned city.

The region that was considered for the new capital was however not virgin territory. Archaeologists have unearthed an Iron Age site, dating to about 500 B.C. in the region, and also indications that the place was part of the great Mauryan Empire in the 3rd century B.C. When the Mauryan dynasty fell into decline, the Satavahanas, feudatories of the Mauryas declared independence and also took over their Deccan territories including the Golconda-Hyderabad region. The Satavahanas were based out of Kotilingala in Telangana and controlled the region up to Junnar (near modern day Pune) and Prathisthan (modern Paithan) in Maharashtra. Later the Hyderabad region came under the control of the Ikshvakus who were followers of Mahayana Buddhism. However, throughout the ancient times, no settlement of significance were built in the Golconda-Hyderabad region.

During medieval times, the region changed hands initially to the Chalukyas of Kalyani and then to the Kakatiyas. It was the Kakatiyas who built the fort at Golconda as a part of their western defences, in line with the Kondapalli fort. Successive rulers, particularly Rudramadevi and Prataparudra, strengthened the Golconda fort. Even though Warangal fell to the Tughluq army after a protracted fight, Golconda fort by itself was not taken over and retained a dubious status in terms of control for some time. During this time the fort was controlled by

Musunuri Nayaks who had defeated the Tughluq force and controlled the region around Warangal-Golconda. In the 1350s, Golconda was overrun by the Bahmani forces, while it was under the control of Kapaya Nayak. From then on, Golconda increased in importance and became a district headquarters where governors started to reside. It is through this process of being governors that the Qutb Shahis established themselves as the rulers of the region, making Golconda their capital at the break-up of the Bahmani kingdom.

The Charminar as completed in 1592 and consists of four minarets and four arches that face the four cardinal directions, with four roads flowing outwards from the structure. It remains even today one of the grandest structures in India. Hyderabad became the official capital of the Qutb Shahis sometime after the construction of the Charminar. Construction of the royal palace commenced along with that of Charminar and the better part of it was completed around 1610, just before the death of Muhammad Quli Qutb Shah.

> ### The Bhagmati Story
>
> The process by which the new capital was named has created no end of controversy, with no universally accepted solution being provided even now. There are a number of stories regarding the naming of the capital.
>
> The most common is the one regarding a courtesan named Bhagmati. It appears that Muhammad Quli was besotted by a courtesan named Bhagmati who became his favourite. He is supposed to have named the new capital Bhagnagar after her. She is supposed to have subsequently converted to Islam and assumed the name Haidar Mahal, upon which the king changed the name of the capital to Haidar-abad. The story of the courtesan is most likely a flight of fantacy for the following reasons. First, not one contemporary chronicle provides even a passing reference to Bhagmati or mentions the king's infatuation with a famous courtesan. Second, Muhammad has been acknowledged as a well-known and good poet. He has written odes to all his

> mistresses, numbering 17, and there is not one ode that is dedicated to Bhagmati. This would not have been the case, if he was as taken in by this courtesan as the stories mention. By a process of elimination, the story of the courtesan can be discounted. However, the legend of Bhagmati continues to percolate even today, with no real evidence to support it.

Irrespective of the story of the courtesan and the king, European travellers of the time who visited the city mention the name Bhagnagar. Thevenot (1633-1667), a French traveller in the East who wrote extensively about his travels, visited the capital in 1666 and mentions that, '...the capital city is called Bagnagar, while the Persians call it Aidar-Abad'. The explanation seems to be that the name Bhagnagar is an allusion to the fact that the entire city was just 'one big garden' and therefore Baghnagar—a city of gardens, which got perverted colloquially to Bhagnagar and subsequently became linked to Bhagmati the courtesan. What is certain is that in the initial formative years after the creation of the city, it was known by two names, of which only Hyderabad remained for posterity.

Chapter 28

PLATEAUING AND DECLINE

Muhammad Quli was succeeded to the throne by Muhammad Qutb Shah, the son of his brother Muhammad Amin who had pre-deceased him. The nephew Muhammad was also Muhammad Quli's son-in-law, having married his daughter Hayat Bakshi Begum in 1607. There was some fear amongst the nobles that other contenders to the throne may contest the succession, since Muhammad Quli had died without a direct male heir. The fear was founded on the fact that another of Muhammad Quli's brothers, Muhammad Khudah Banda, had rebelled earlier and had been imprisoned in Golconda. Although he too had pre-deceased Muhammad Quli, his name was still revered by a section of influential nobles as well as by some of the general population. The Sunni population of the kingdom was particularly inclined towards supporting Khudah Banda and his progeny. In these circumstances, a succession struggle would not have been considered out of the ordinary.

In order to ensure that not even an incipient rebellion marred the succession, the efficient Peshwa, Mir Munim, had the crowning ceremony of the new king conducted on the same day that Muhammad Quli died. Such alacrity in crowning the new incumbent was not normal or standard practice. Even with all the precautions that were taken, the new king Muhammad Qutb Shah, inherited a crisis. Venkata II who had diplomatically bested Muhammad Quli when Golconda had earlier invaded the truncated Vijayanagar kingdom, now invaded Qutb Shahi territories. It is unclear whether the new ruler of Golconda had the wherewithal to respond effectively—both in terms of personal capability and also the strength and readiness of the Golconda army.

Before the ruler and the army could be put to the test, providence interfered; Venkata II faced some domestic unrest in his capital Penukonda and he was forced to hold back the invasion before it could take hold; a fortunate turn of events for Golconda.

Muhammad Qutb Shah

On Muhammad's ascension to the throne, the Persian Emperor send an embassy to Golconda to congratulate him, which paved the way for enhanced cooperation between the two kingdoms. Both Bijapur and Daulatabad, now the capital of the Nizam Shahis under Malik Ambar, also send envoys with gifts to Muhammad thus accepting his right to rule. The only military venture that was initiated during Muhammad Qutb Shah's tenure was against Bastar, where a Golconda army under the command of Asva Rao had been trapped. A large relief force was send to relieve the trapped forces; the rebel ruler of Bastar, Partap Shah was defeated and surrendered; and the Golconda forces were successfully brought out. Partap Shah was subsequently reinstated by the Qutb Shahi king and permitted to continue ruling Bastar as a vassal.

The Mughal Threat

Muhammad Qutb Shah very consciously followed a policy of peace. There are few reasons for this somewhat inexplicable attitude, especially during an era in the sub-continent that was known for a universal expansionist attitude of the major dynasties, their ruthless acts and extreme bloodshed that accompanied all battles. The first reason was that temperamentally the king was inclined towards keeping the peace, being attuned to peaceful times from his youth. More important was the second reason—even though Muhammad has historically been considered a light weight as a king, he was acutely aware of the continuous rush of Mughal invasion from the north, that at times thrust deep into the Deccan, which was considered an existentialist threat. In view of this extreme challenge, Muhammad was keen to consolidate the existing kingdom and create, as well as strengthen existing, defences rather than attempt to expand his dominion. This was a pragmatic approach to the beginning of his rule.

At the same time, the Mughal invasion and their concerted fight against Malik Amber continued unabated. Ambar had successfully held

Plateauing and Decline

off the Mughal force, confining them to Ahmadnagar and surrounds, before evicting them even from there. The mainstay of his forces was the Maratha army which was well-versed in the art of guerrilla warfare that was ideally suited to counter the heavy forces of the Mughals. Since the Ahmadnagar forces were not yet defeated, the Mughal Emperor Jahangir himself moved south to Mandu and also brought his son and heir apparent, Prince Khurram, with him to command the next invasion of Ahmadnagar. The threat to the Deccan had suddenly become very high.

Malik Ambar also realised the increasing danger that was approaching and asked both Bijapur and Golconda for assistance. However, both the kingdoms and their rulers were overawed by the might of the Mughal Empire that was on open display. Instead of helping their fellow-Deccan king, both the rulers opted to approach Prince Khurram entreating him to sign peace accords and paying him tribute. Realising that he was abandoned and left alone, Malik Ambar evacuated Ahmadnagar, once again withdrawing to Daulatabad. The Mughals again occupied Ahmadnagar and Jahangir titled his son Shah Jahan to honour this fairly easy triumph. However, Malik Ambar was highly regarded as a military commander by the Mughal forces and Shah Jahan did not press home the advantage that had been gained. In fact, Shah Jahan considered Ambar the only one capable of defending the Deccan and accepted a peace treaty with him.

Immediately after the signing of the peace agreement, Shah Jahan fell from favour with the Emperor as a result of some court intrigue. He wanted to retreat to Bengal, where he felt he had some allies who would rally to his cause. Muhammad Qutb Shah permitted Shah Jahan's entourage to pass through Golconda territory and Orissa, facilitating this flight of the Mughal prince. However, forces supporting Jahangir defeated Shah Jahan on his way to Bengal and he was forced to return. He had to spend the period of being out of favour in the Deccan. Seeing the divisions in the Mughal royalty and hoping to take advantage of the situation, Malik Amber welcomed Shah Jahan into his territories. However, before this intrigue could play out, Shah Jahan was reconciled with his father and the situation returned to normal in the Mughal court.

Trading with Foreigners

The Dutch East India Company was incorporated in 1602 and signed a treaty with Qutb Shahi officials in 1606 to establish 'factories' and trade with and in the Golconda kingdom. By 1610, the Dutch had established their factories, in reality warehouse, in Masulipatam and later in Pulicat. The English East India Company, that was later to 'own' India, had been established on 30 December 1600, but was slow to make inroads into the Deccan, establishing their factory in Golconda territory in Masulipatam only in 1611.

The diamond mines of the Golconda kingdom was initially a monopoly of the Dutch, who operated them on lease. In 1623, Muhammad Qutb Shah decided to cancel the lease and started to work the mines on his own, through royal officials posted to the mines permanently. He also established a strong maritime force to patrol the coastline and enforce law and order. This was the beginning of establishing regulations under which the foreigners were permitted to trade within the Deccan.

1626

At this juncture, the entire narrative of Deccan history was overshadowed by three deaths—Muhammad Qutb Shah died on 30 January 1626; Malik Ambar died four months later on 11 May 1626; and Jahangir died 18 months later on 28 October 1627. 1626 was the end of an epoch in the Deccan. The precarious balance of power that had been maintained between the various kingdoms—mostly through military action by the others against any one of them becoming too powerful—had finally come to an end with these three deaths.

Shah Jahan became the Mughal Emperor; within a few years Ahmadnagar was finally and fully annexed after being dismembered; no obstacle now stood in the way of the Mughals in pursuing their expansionist strategy; and the two surviving Deccan kingdoms were not capable of putting up an insurmountable struggle against the Mughals—individually or even if they combined—who were now at the zenith of their power.

Abdullah Qutb Shah – The Onset of Decline

Muhammad dad three sons, of whom Abdullah the eldest succeeded him. Abdullah was born in 1614 and was being groomed to be the heir apparent, educated and brought up to assume the kingship at a future date, when his father died. He was only 12 years old when he came to the throne. However, the boy-king was accepted by both the Bijapur Adil Shahis and the Ahmadnagar Nizam Shahis. Surprisingly, he was also congratulated by Prince Khurram—now titled Shah Jahan by Jahangir—who was still having difficulties in his relationship with his father. The intimate, and sometimes nurturing, relationship with Iran also continued.

Following the death of Jahangir, a Mughal war of succession ensued, which brought a certain amount of relief for the entire Deccan since it loosened the stranglehold of the northern army and diluted their presence in the region. However, this relief was short-lived, as it was bound to have been. As soon as Shah Jahan won the succession and assumed power, the imperial attitude towards the Deccan changed— the Mughals would not rest until the entire region was annexed under the their banner.

Mughal Intervention

Shah Jahan was a demonstrated expansionist. He was not only determined to exterminate the Nizam Shahis of Ahmednagar who were already in their death throes, but had plans to annex both Golconda and Bijapur. While direct assaults were being mounted on Ahmadnagar, he also initiated moves to gain a foothold in Orissa from where he could harass the Qutb Shahis in the north-east. Accordingly, parts of Orissa were annexed and a Mughal governor appointed. The ultimate aim was to squeeze the Deccan kingdoms from two directions, into submission. Shah Jahan, now the all-powerful Mughal monarch, in full control of the vast empire after having settled the vicissitudes of the succession struggle, marched to Burhanpur in 1630 to personally guide the Deccan campaign. By 1633, the last Nizam Shahi king was imprisoned in the Mughal fort at Gwalior and his attention turned to the remaining two Deccan Shahi kingdoms.

The main thrust against the Qutb Shahis came for the north-east, where their fort at Mansurgarh, which was considered impregnable because of its formidable defences, was overrun and captured by the Mughal governor with relative ease. Buoyed by this victory, and perhaps because of the ease with which the campaign was concluded, Shah Jahan now send two 'firmans'—one to Bijapur and one to Abdullah Qutb Shahi. Firmans were orders that contained a list of demands to be fulfilled by the receiving kings, which were in effect ultimatums—a sort of, 'do this and this and I will not send my army to attack you', kind of documents. Implicit in a firman was the un-stated threat of the use of force and the intimidation that if the firman was not adhered to, the kingdom would be laid waste. Shah Jahan's firmans were also unilateral in nature in terms of the demands and did not leave any latitude for negotiations.

The firman to Abdullah was followed up by an 'Inquiyad Nama', which could be translated to mean a 'Deed of Submission' that he was supposed to sign latest by May 1636. This Deed had provisions incorporated in it to make the Qutb Shahi fully subservient to the Mughal Emperor. Immediately after the Deed was presented, Abdullah was served with an 'Ahd Nama'—this was not a firman, but more a treaty, which was nonetheless unilateral—that had already been signed by Shah Jahan on 29 August 1636. The Ahd Nama was not the final treaty document, but a preliminary to it. However, this treaty made, by unilateral Mughal decree, the Qutb Shah agree to accept a position of subservience. In this preliminary document, Qutb Shah was shorn off all his exalted royal titles and named only as Qutb-ul-Mulk and referred to as the 'hereditary disciple' of the Mughal Emperors.

Abdullah Qutb Shah of Golconda-Hyderabad was now reduced to an abject vassal, an object to be ordered about at will by the imperial Mughal monarch. He was also not master of his own mint, with all his coins being issued in the name of the Emperor. This was a debilitating blow to the prestige of the kingdom, for coins were one of the greatest privileges of medieval kings and indicated the independence, sovereignty and strength of the kingdom and its ruler. Along with the instructions to mint coins only on the Emperor's name also came orders that the Qutb Shahi was not to indulge in foreign policy initiatives of his own, but that the Qutb Shahi's relations with other kingdoms would be 'looked after' by the Mughal enterprise. There was now no difference between the Golconda king and a Mughal governor of a conquered province. It is remarkable that all this had been achieved by the capture of a single obscure, albeit strong, fort in the north-eastern extremity of the Qutb Shahi territories. Pure fear of the Mughal power had paralysed the Qutb Shahi leadership and reduced an already effete kingdom to the status of a protectorate of the Delhi monarch, without having offered any resistance or raised a single sword to protect its honour.

This abject surrender without even a token resistance brings to the fore the question of the appropriateness and acceptability of the Qutb Shahis ever having become 'kings' in their own right. It can be surmised that the so-called 'dynasty' was established because of the driving ambition of a single individual, who was endowed with above average capabilities and had the capacity to grasp an opportunity when it was presented, to carve out some territories and establish personal control. The fact that the territories were rich in natural resources and also included diamond mines were added advantages to maintaining control as a kingdom. The fact that the Golconda dynasty did not produce a single king of exemplary calibre, unlike the other two major Deccan Shahi kingdoms, speaks volumes about the mediocrity of the Qutb Shahi lineage.

The Next Twenty Years

Shah Jahan returned to Delhi after Abdullah had signed on the dotted line, accepting his vassal status to the Mughals without demurring. He left the Deccan in the hands of his 17-year old son, Aurangzeb, who was appointed the Viceroy of the Deccan. However, he had ruled for about eight years, the Mughal Emperor removed or retired Aurangzeb from his position as the Viceroy in 1644. In the next eight years, Shah Jahan appointed and removed five viceroys before re-instating his son once again into the powerful position in the Deccan. This slightly tumultuous period in the Deccan also paved the way to a sort of proxy control of the region, consciously permitted by the central authority in Delhi. During this period of nearly a decade, the Mughals were content to let the South Indian affairs be handled and controlled by vassal kingdoms and some strong men with proven loyalty to Delhi. The return of Aurangzeb to favour and his reappointment as the

Viceroy in 1652 once again changed the flavour of the Mughal attitude to the Deccan. Importantly, it marked a concerted push to establish Mughal suzerainty over the entire Peninsula. Aurangzeb left no doubts in anyone's mind that he would personally control and rule the Deccan and thereafter the entire South Indian peninsula.

Golconda, now a vassal state of the Mughals, was under the virtual control of its Mir Jumla, Muhammad Said. Through calculated actions, he had amassed great wealth and become the real power in the kingdom. He had also made Gandikotta as the headquarters for his vast estates, which naturally became an alternative and virtual capital of the kingdom. Under direct instructions of Shah Jahan, Muhammad Said invaded and captured most of the remaining free territory of the old Vijayanagar Empire, the truncated parts now named Karnataka.

Abdullah Qutb Shah in the meantime had become completely servile and fawned on the Mughal Emperor—he wrote long and effusively abject letters to Shah Jahan wooing favours from him; and paid inordinate respect to the Mughal envoys in the Golconda court, hoping to remain in the good books of the Mughals. He also wrote entreating letters to Prince Dara Shikoh, the heir apparent to Shah Jahan and also the principle advisor to the emperor. These letters, some of which have survived to this day, confirm the conquest of Karnataka by Muhammad Said. Gradually, but certainly, Golconda had become subservient to the Mughals, accepting and readily adjusting to this new and bitter reality. Even though he assumed a servile position when dealing with the Mughals, Abdullah continued to try and assert his independent power within his kingdom. Muhammad Said's assumption of great power and status, with the tacit support of the Mughal representatives, was resented by Abdullah who continually tried to curtail the power and position of eminence of his Mir Jumla.

A petty and avoidable incident brought this brewing rivalry between king and prime minister into open confrontation. Muhammad Said's son, Muhammad Amin, was arrogant and accustomed to being a wastrel based on his father's position and power. One day, when he was dead drunk, he went to the palace and sat on the throne. If that act itself was not a grave provocation, he was also violently sick while sitting on the throne. Abdullah had no option but to act—Muhammad Amin was arrested and confined in the fort at Kovilkonda, all his property was confiscated and annexed to the royal estates, and Abdullah send out summons for Muhammad Said to present himself in the royal court.

The Mir Jumla refused to obey his king or to apologise for the behaviour of his son. Instead, he established contact with Aurangzeb and started negotiations for the Mughals to invade the Qutb Shahi kingdom. Muhammad Said was also shrewd enough to think about alternative courses of action in case the Mughals did not come to his aid and send messages to both the Adil Shahi king in Bijapur and the Shah of Persia, seeking asylum in their respective domains. It is a separate matter that both the kings refused to provide him asylum. Muhammad Said requested Aurangzeb to invade and annex the kingdom of Golconda, of which he was Mir Jumla, the prime minister. He also promised to defray the costs that the Mughal army would incur in the campaign, calculated at 50,000 rupees per day. In today's terms the situation would look very awkward, in that the Prime Minister of a sovereign state was asking its sworn enemy to attack and annex the state so that he could continue to be a powerful person. Such a person's loyalty, integrity, love of country and the sense of independence would all be under a cloud. However, the medieval Deccan was a strange region, such actions seemed common place—one's roots and country did not seem to have been held in high esteem and their betrayal to further self-interests was common place.

By now Shah Jahan also ordered Aurangzeb to march on Hyderabad, although the army was already on the move. The Mughal army was commanded by Aurangzeb's son Prince Muhammad Sultan and reached Husain Sagar, the lake outside Hyderabad, on 22 January 1656. Throughout the development of this invasion, Abdullah had been servile and conciliatory towards the Mughal viceroy, only requesting that the invasion be stopped and indicating that he was willing to pay tribute/ransom to ensure that his kingdom was left alone. However, when Hyderabad was encircled, he showed some initiative and fled to Golconda, the older capital of the kingdom. The Mughals occupied, pillaged and burned Hyderabad in short order. Aurangzeb now carried out a great feat of military manoeuvre. He undertook a number of forced marches and personally reached the scene of battle, having covered 630 kilometres in just 18 days. Thereafter, the Mughals marched to Golconda and laid siege to the city.

Abdullah, realising that Aurangzeb was personally conducting the campaign now, send tribute and begged for the cessation of hostilities. He also requested an audience for his mother with the Mughal viceroy of the Deccan. Haughty Aurangzeb declined both and instead tightened the siege even further. However, Shah Jahan had been following the sequence of events from Delhi and appreciated the helplessness of Abdullah deep in the Deccan. On the sane advice of Dara Shikoh, he granted Abdullah a free pardon. Now Aurangzeb's duplicity and cunningness, which was to later become hallmarks of all his dealings, was put on public display and also chronicled meticulously by both Mughal and Deccan scribes.

Aurangzeb suppressed the document, firman, which gave a free pardon to Abdullah, even though it had come direct from the great emperor himself. He coerced Abdullah, who was unaware that he had already been pardoned, into promising to have his daughter married to Prince Muhammad Sultan with a large accompanying dowry. Aurangzeb then condescendingly granted an audience to the Queen-mother, Hayat Bakshi Begum. The meeting took place on 8 March 1656. Even after coercing the hapless Abdullah and keeping him in the dark about the royal pardon, Aurangzeb was not finished. He demanded, and got, one crore rupees as payment for not looting Golconda and more importantly, got a promise from the Qutb Shahi matriarch that his son Sultan, betrothed to Abdullah's daughter, would succeed to the throne of Golconda on Abdullah's death. On the acceptance of these terms, Abdullah was given the free pardon firman and within less than a month the marriage was solemnised, on 4 April.

The initiator of this entire sequence of events, Muhammad Said now arrived at Bolarum in the outskirts of Hyderabad and was received by the Mughal nobility and given a robe of honour. He went on to join Aurangzeb's camp and was granted the title Muazzam Khan. The defection of the Mir Jumla and his instigation of actions against his own kingdom and king is an important point in the history of Golconda and one that would reverberate across the entire Deccan. Betrayals were not unknown, but betrayal on this grand a scale was the opening of a new door in the diminishing moral stature of the nobility of the Deccan.

The Mughal War of Succession

Almost immediately after this demeaning peace was agreed upon by Aurangzeb, in 1658-59, the Mughal Empire was shaken by the vehemence of a succession struggle that erupted. Aurangzeb was the victor—he inflicted military defeat on his brothers and subsequently murdered all of them; imprisoned his father in a small part of Agra fort; and crowned himself Emperor on 5 June 1659. While the turmoil in the Mughal Empire was gradually stabilising, another momentous event was taking place in South India. A rebellion was successfully waged in the western hinterland of the Peninsula, which saw the phenomenal rise and rapid establishment of Shivaji as the Maratha chieftain of an emerging kingdom. The first Maratha-Mughal encounter took place around the same time. A bit later Shivaji was crowned as the 'Chhatrapati', king of the Marathas. (The history of the Marathas will be covered in a forthcoming volume in this series.)

Aurangzeb, now the emperor, was pre-occupied with controlling other parts of the vast empire that he had forcibly taken over, and therefore the minor Qutb Shahi territories in the Deccan were not a priority anymore. The neglect was also because Muhammad Sultan, the heir apparent foisted on the Qutb Shahis, had unfortunately joined the wrong side of the Mughal succession struggle and had been captured and imprisoned for life by his father, Aurangzeb.

Muhammad Said's defection created another schism between the Mughals and the Qutb Shahis. Since Aurangzeb was busy in the north, Abdullah decided to claim the conquered Karnataka territory for the Qutb Shahis, since the areas had been captured by his Mir Jumla. The Mughals, however, also laid claim to the territory since Muhammad Said was now a high-ranking Mughal noble. In affirmation of this claim, the Mughals once again overran the entire Karnataka region, barring the forts at Siddhoust and Gandikota, which continued to remain within the Qutb Shahi kingdom.

The war of succession and subsequent diversions had initially held Aurangzeb's inclination and ambition to annex the Golconda kingdom in check, and the rise of Shivaji had further delayed the project. In effect, the Qutb Shahis had survived as a dynasty for some time now purely because of a sequence of events over which they had no control or influence. Such are the vagaries of history, clearly visible when viewed through the prism of hindsight.

Bijapur Interlude

The Mughals, under the guidance of the new emperor Aurangzeb, renewed their efforts to annex the remaining two Deccan Shahi kingdoms, starting with Bijapur. The Mughal army under Raja Man Singh moved south and engaged Bijapur forces in December 1665. Man Singh adopted a strategy of diplomatic initiatives to neutralise would-be allies, first by concluding a treaty with the Marathas and then by attempting to do the same with Golconda. Shivaji studiously kept away from interfering with the Mughal army and its invasion of Bijapur. However, Abdullah did not sign the treaty of neutrality and when Bijapur asked for assistance, he decided to go to his brother-in-law Ali Adil Shah's assistance. A Qutb Shahi army of 12,000 cavalry and over 40,000 infantry under the command of Neknam Khan joined forces with the Bijapur army.

In the face of this large force, the Mughal army was forced to retreat without indulging in any major battle, or being defeated in the battlefield. They withdrew initially to Dharur and then to Aurangabad. On the withdrawal of the Mughal army, the Qutb Shahi forces were ordered home.

The Deccan Shahi kingdoms, especially Bijapur and Golconda, shared a somewhat strange relationship with each other. The royal houses were closely connected through matrimonial alliances, which were more often than not, marriages of convenience organised by the kings for sealing treaties and ensuring assistance. By the late-1500s, it had become natural for the Adil Shahis and Qutb Shahis to seek alliances with each other since no other successor state to the Bahmanis existed. These two houses were the last remaining bulwarks of the fast vanishing Deccan Shahi royalty. The underlying reason for marriages between the royal houses can therefore be easily understood. Layered on top of this was the pragmatic and expansionist ambition of the ruling kings that almost always led to border disputes and frontier clashes, which in turn turned into avoidable military incursions. Therefore, even though marriages were routinely conducted between them, the Deccan Shahi kingdoms mostly remained at loggerheads with each other from a security perspective. The coming together of the three kingdoms, as in the formation of the confederacy against the Vijayanagar Empire, was the exception and not the rule.

There was also a redeeming factor, at least in the earlier history of the successor states. If a foreign army entered the Deccan, the internal quarrels were forgotten and the Shahi armies came together to ward off the intruder. However, immediately on the threat being diffused, the kingdoms went back to their bickering and quarrelling ways, sowing the seeds for disunity in the long term. The Mughals, from the time of Akbar, had studied and understood the dynamics of Deccan Shahi politics. They would later use this knowledge and serve ultimatums simultaneously to the multiple Deccan rulers in order to stop them assisting each other. By being placed under threat simultaneously, the Mughals denied the Shahi kings mutual help and the ability to present a unified front to a common enemy.

Ever since the great Vijayanagar Empire had been reduced to a mere stump of a kingdom, both Bijapur and Golconda had aspired to annex the remaining territories. Bijapur was the first to act, invading and capturing Ikkeri and surroundings; while at the same time the Golconda army under Muhammad Said overran the Karnataka region (mentioned earlier). In 1662, Abdullah named Riza Quli Beg, titled Neknam Khan, the governor of Karnataka. The simultaneous invasion brought Bijapur and Golconda into direct confrontation with each other. Abdullah, always a peace-loving person adopted a more conciliatory approach rather than continue the confrontation, thereby avoiding the necessity for military action. This action of his has been described as 'weak-kneed' by contemporary chroniclers and even later-day historians have portrayed Abdullah as being placid and non-aggressive by nature, based on this episode. *[One wonders whether the fact that the Qutb Shahi ancestor in Persia would not fight even to claim his own patrimony, preferring peace to conflict, has anything to do with the unusually soft attitude that seemed to have been a common character trait among the Golconda kings.]*

Abdullah's Last days

The peace overtures and the Qutb Shahi assistance to Bijapur at the Mughal invasion combined not only to cover the rift between the two kingdoms, but also assisted in cementing the relationship. At this stage, the Mughal attempts to annex the Deccan and Karnataka and make them appendages of the great empire faltered. Aurangzeb was preoccupied with running his vast monarchy with little time to concentrate on the Deccan. Muhammad Said, who in the first place had assisted Aurangzeb to gain traction in the region was now concentrating on Bihar and Bengal and there was no one in the Mughal hierarchy interested in guiding the actions in South India. From this perspective, a semblance of stability percolated over the Deccan Shahi kingdoms.

It was around this time that the Dutch and English trading companies had started to assert themselves in the Madras region. Neknam Khan, the Qutb Shahi governor of Karnataka under whose jurisdiction the region fell, was an astute negotiator and a resourceful military commander. Actually the Dutch and English factories were located at the edge of the outskirts of Qutb Shahi territories. Both did not want to be controlled by Neknam Khan and challenged his authority to control and regulate them. However, Neknam managed to contain the Dutch traders, somewhat amicably. Then he blockaded Madras twice, the second time in 1670, and then established a Qutb Shahi warehouse within Fort Saint George after a brief siege of the fort that lasted little more than a month. He forced the recalcitrant English governor to accept Qutb Shahi terms for the continuation of trade in the region.

Neknam Khan died in March 1672, immediately after the arrangements with the English were ratified by the king. Three weeks later Abdullah Qutb Shah also died, leaving only three daughters and no male heir to follow him to the throne.

Chapter 29

THE OBLITERATION OF A DYNASTY

Abdullah Qutb Shah left no male heirs to succeed him. He had three daughters—the eldest was married to the Mughal prince Muhammad Sultan, who was imprisoned for life by his father during the succession struggle for the Mughal throne. The second was married to Mirza Nizam ud-Din Ahmed of Mecca who had been assisting Abdullah in matters of the state for a few years. The third had been betrothed to Syed Sultan of Najaf, however the engagement had been broken off. She had therefore been married off to Abul Hasan, a recluse living outside the Qutb Shahi capital, but with some vague and unexplained connection to the royal family.

> **A Twist in the Succession**
>
> Even before Abdullah took ill, his second son-in-law, Nizam ud-Din had become the right hand man of the king. He advised the king on all matters of state and was considered the obvious choice as the next king. When Abdullah was on his deathbed, Nizam ud-Din was certain that he would be anointed the next king and started to display his inherent autocratic character. He started to curtail the power vested in the nobles, particularly targeting the senior nobles holding positions of influence and authority. He also started to be rude to the nobles and became haughty in all his dealings.

> Abul Hasan, the other son-in-law available as a contender to the throne, was almost an ascetic with no pretensions to royalty or ambition to be powerful. In fact he was meek by nature and courteous to all. The senior nobles, led by Syed Muzaffar, decided to take action against Nizam ud-Din. They produced Abul Hasan in front of Abdullah and had the king proclaim Hasan as his chosen successor before he died. Nizam ud-Din did not have any support and therefore was removed from the equation.

On Abdullah's death, the nobles wanted to avoid a debilitating succession struggle within an already weak kingdom and found it expedient to crown Hasan immediately. On 21 April 1672, Abul Hasan Qutb Shah became king by default. Syed Muzaffar assumed the role of Mir Jumla.

Syed Muzaffar was an efficient and strict administrator and controlled the treasury and disbursement of funds with a tight fist. Muzaffar also appointed a trusted Hindu and an acknowledged learned man Surya Prakash Rao aka Madana Pandit as his personal secretary. Muzaffar's zeal to stabilise the administration brought him into conflict with the new king. Abul Hasan, who had lived his entire life in a simple, almost abstemious manner wanted as king to spend money lavishly. Muzaffar on the other hand, was miserly with the allocation of funds for the king's pleasure. The resistance from the Mir Jumla to the king's more egregious demands for funds gradually becoming a bone of contention between him and the king. This division continued to fester as Hasan's rule progressed.

Syed Muzaffar believed that had it not been for him, Abul Hasan would have continued to be the relatively poor recluse outside the capital and therefore could not get himself to treat Abul as the king with sufficient respect. He approbated all power to himself, was full of pride regarding his position in the kingdom, and became unbearably overpowering in his dealings with the king. Historical narrative is over-crowded by instance such as this, where a noble starts to consider himself the de facto ruler, and completely oversteps his remit. The fundamental difference between being a noble, even the highest ranking one in the kingdom, and belonging to the royal house gets diluted in these cases and invariably it is seen that the noble finally gets cut down by the higher authority vested in the royal dynasty. The same turn of events took place in Golconda.

With the Mir Jumla Muzaffar taking over almost the entire administration of the kingdom, Abul Hasan perceived and felt his power waning on a daily basis. He wanted to rectify the situation and took into confidence Madana Pandit, who advised the king to start filling all key positions in the court by people who were personally loyal to him. Hasan started to gradually send nobles belonging to the Muzaffar faction to the outlying districts and replacing them in court with nobles loyal to him. When Abul Hasan had altered the constitution of the court sufficiently and was confident that he could act and enforce his orders, he asked Syed Muzaffar to vacate the position of Mir Jumla and retire to his jagir. Hasan promised that Muzaffar's jagirs would not be confiscated and the powerful Mir Jumla was reduced to the status of a retired noble. Hasan then appointed Madana Pandit as the Mir Jumla.

Madana Pandit – Prime Minister

Madana Pandit's first action as the Mir Jumla was to pay tribute to the Mughal Emperor and then send a petition to Aurangzeb with a request to recognise Abul Hasan as the legitimate ruler of Golconda. The petition was acknowledged by the Mughal, but not in the manner that Madana had anticipated. In his reply, the Mughal Emperor firmly placed Hasan in the ranks of the vassal rulers, calling him Qutb-ul-Mulk, the title by which the founder of the dynasty, Sultan Quli, had been known throughout his life. The royal 'Shah', indicating independent rule and sovereignty, was completely omitted from the acknowledgement. More important in the long term than the dropping of the title of Shah, was the fact that the Mughal reply clearly mentioned that although Hasan was governing ancestral property, he had promised that on his death the territories would revert to the control of the Mughals, becoming part of the imperial Mughal Empire. The fact that the Qutb Shahi dominions had never been Mughal territory did not merit a mention in the Mughal missive. Obviously such 'minor facts' were below the level of consideration of the emperor. Abul Hasan was also instructed to send 40 lakh rupees (Rupees 40,00,000) per annum to Delhi as tribute. Hasan was left with no choice but to accept the terms in the most abject manner.

Even if Hasan did not realise the implicit threat in the Mughal reply, the shrewd Madana Pandit did, and he immediately set about strengthening the fortifications of the capital. Further, he started to strengthen the forts on the western borders of the kingdom from which direction the Mughal invasion, when it eventually came, was anticipated. As is obvious from his background, Hasan was not inclined to pursue military and security matters. However, in the gradual build up to what the nobles of Golconda knew would be the eventual show down with the Mughals, Hasan was persuaded to visit Vijayawada and inspect the Kondapalli fort—an effort to raise the morale of the people and the military.

It is clear that Madana realised the threat to the kingdom and started to prepare for an impending invasion and the siege that would invariably follow. However, at the same time, he also displayed a streak of nepotism and inherent corruption that was to dilute the defence preparations. First, he appointed his kith and kin to positions of power and influence in the court. Perhaps more debilitating to the organisational structure of the kingdom was his asking for and receiving monetary benefits personally for himself in return for the appointment of nobles to coveted positions. In one blow, he had killed the concept of meritocracy in the kingdom. The result was the unchecked spread of endemic corruption and bribery throughout all level of the bureaucracy—from the highest to the lowest. Madana's acts of personal corruption that led to inefficiency and chaos has been recorded by the English agents in court as well as by some local Brahmins who were themselves aligned with Madana Pandit.

Interaction with the English

In his single-minded pursuit of nepotism, Madana Pandit also made changes to the various governorships—notably in Karnataka and Poonamalai. Neknam Khan, the efficient and honest governor of Karnataka had died and was replaced, initially by Madana's brother and then his nephew Podili Linganna. Almost immediately on assuming governorship Linganna, an avaricious person by all accounts, raised the rent of the English in Fort Saint George for their use of Qutb

Shahi territories. He told the English that the petty rent being paid by them was not sufficient and that he, the Governor, would be the authority who would determine the correct rent. While this change in the administrative process was being played out, Linganna also enforced a surreptitious embargo on rice and other food stuff entering the fort without paying the newly established and exorbitant custom duty.

The English initially tried to reach King Hasan directly to appraise him of the situation and clarify matters by attempting to make contact with him during one of his infrequent travels outside of Golconda. However, this attempt did not work out. The English were forced to move out the recalcitrant governor and bring in someone with a more diplomatic and tactful approach to the situation. The new governor managed to bribe his way out of the tricky situation, which must not have been difficult considering the greed that was displayed by Madana's family. Linganna was removed from the governor's position subsequently, during the turmoil that rocked Hyderabad at a later date.

The Rise of the Marathas

The rise of the Maratha people as a regional, and then an Indian, power was of direct import to the successor Deccan Shahi kingdoms. (The trajectory of the upsurge of the Marathas and the establishment of one of the grandest empires in the sub-continental history is not being covered here, as the narrative is only peripherally connected to the events taking place in medieval Deccan. The history of the Marathas will be the central topic in a forthcoming volume.) A brief summary of the Maratha influence in the Deccan, particularly as it pertains to the narrative of the Qutb Shahi history, is given below.

In 1672, when Abul Hasan ascended the throne, Shivaji, the Maratha chief and king, was the most prominent figure in the whole of the South Indian Peninsula. Further, he was crowned as Chhatrapati—a title that can be roughly translated to 'all-encompassing monarch'—at Raigarh on 6 June 1674. The Deccan was now divided between the Marathas, the Bijapur Adil Shahi and Golconda-Hyderabad Qutb Shahi kings. On Abul Hasan coming to the throne, Shivaji had demanded and received 20 lakh (20,000,000) pagodas from the Qutb Shahis as a peace offering, to ensure his non-interference. This single episode demonstrates the enhanced and predominant status of the Maratha king without any doubt.

By 1676, Shivaji had already planned a campaign that would ultimately give him control over all the territories in the Peninsula to the south of the River Tungabhadra all the way to Bangalore and Tanjore (Tanjavore). The indirect objective of this campaign was also to restrict the increasing influence of Bijapur in the extreme southern region. In order to achieve this objective, he wanted to neutralise the Golconda kingdom first and accordingly send an emissary, Raghunath Narayan Hanumante, to Hyderabad. A year later Shivaji himself descended on Hyderabad on an official visit and forced Abul Hasan to sign a treaty of peace. As per this unequal treaty, the Qutb Shahi was required to pay a tribute of Rupees 3000 per day to the Maratha king, for the entire duration of the Maratha campaign in South India.

Shivaji's sojourn to the southern part of the Peninsula was a great success from the Maratha point of view. He managed to contain both Bijapur and Golconda and put down a nascent rebellion by one of his step-brothers. Perhaps more importantly, he was able to fortify the southern part of the peninsula against Mughal incursions by bringing the warring factions together under his overall suzerainty. From a holistic perspective of Indian history, it was unfortunate that Shivaji died a few years later at the relatively early age of 53. His son who succeeded him had rebelled against his father at one stage and was in any case not as astute as his father.

The Mughals Extinguish the Qutb Shahi Dynasty

When the Deed of Submission had been signed and accepted without demur by the Qutb Shahi ruler in 1636, the dynasty had forfeited their claim to suzerainty and independence as well as surrendered the sovereignty of Golconda as a kingdom. Nearly forty years later when Abul Hasan signed the Agreement with Aurangzeb to hand over the Qutb Shahi kingdom to the Mughals on his death, he was in effect driving the last nail into the coffin of the dynasty. Even so, Abul Hasan the reluctant king, felt the necessity to strengthen his kingdom's defences in view of the unabated progress of the Mughal army into the Deccan. He was also acutely aware of his own precarious situation, both in person and that of the kingdom. The alignment with Shivaji, the Maratha king, was an attempt at breathing a fresh lease of life into

The Obliteration of a Dynasty

the moribund kingdom that he was ruling. It was also an endeavour to retake some of the territories from the Karnataka region that had been lost earlier to the Mughals.

Hasan also started to think about creating a united front against the advancing Mughals by joining hands with Bijapur, now ruled by a child-king. He offered military and economic assistance to Bijapur. Contemporary chroniclers and later-day historians often wonder at the audacity displayed by the meek Abul Hasan in attempting to create a common front against the Mughals. In less than two years after signing off his inheritance and accepting the reduced status of a vassal and 'disciple' of Aurangzeb the Mughal Emperor, Abul Hasan was now signing a pact with Shivaji and a bit later providing active help to the beleaguered Bijapur. The newfound assertiveness of the Qutb Shahi has to be marvelled at, if not for anything else, but for the assertion of an 'independent' foreign policy that he was displaying. (The assistance provided to Bijapur by Abul Hasan and the tumultuous events taking place in that kingdom have already been enumerated earlier.)

Abul Hasan's actions however had unintended effect on the evolving overall situation. The assertion of independence by both Bijapur and Golconda; their coming together to present a joint and united front against the Mughal army; and the continuing intransigence by Shivaji and the Marathas made Aurangzeb personally march out of Delhi towards the Deccan. He was never to return to his imperial capital. The Mughal entourage reached Aurangabad on 22 March 1682 and Ahmadnagar a little over a year later, in November 1683. Aurangzeb send a message, actually an order, to Abul Hasan to desist from providing assistance to Bijapur. However, the once meek king had grown brave, perhaps knowing fully well that his independence was already forfeit and that he and his kingdom would not last long as autonomous entities. He disobeyed the Mughal edict and continued to assist Bijapur—the last hurrah of the Qutb Shahis. So while Bijapur was being ground down by the Mughal forces, Golconda continued to attempt to send military assistance. The communications between Bijapur and Golconda were intercepted by the local Mughal commander.

Aurangzeb decided to conquer both Bijapur and Golconda-Hyderabad simultaneously, without waiting for Bijapur to capitulate. Just this one presumptive action is indicative of the strength of the

Mughal army—the emperor did not consider it a difficult task to annex two major kingdoms in faraway Deccan, simultaneously, through military action.

The Battles of Malkher

Aurangzeb ordered Prince Muazzam (mentioned as Muhammad Azzam in some records), the commander of the Mughal forces in the Deccan to attack Qutb Shahi territories with a force that included more than 35,000 cavalry. Madana Pandit, monitoring the movements of the Mughal forces, ordered his commanders to move the Qutb Shahi forces to the border with the Mughals near Ahmadnagar. The two armies met at Malkher. In the ensuing battle, the Qutb Shahis won the initial skirmishes. However, the engagement lasted a number of days but was indecisive in the end, although the Mughals had gradually started to become ascendant as the battle progressed. The First Battle of Malkher was an impasse.

Aurangzeb was angry at this stalemate, especially since the Mughal forces had not taken advantage of their better position and superior strength to defeat the adversary. He send word to the commander of his displeasure at the emerging situation; the message immediately led to the Second Battle of Malkher. This battle involved very heavy fighting and loss of life. The Qutb Shahis knew that they were fighting for the survival of their kingdom and were especially valiant in their actions. However, they were pushed back, one step at a time, retreating to the capital Hyderabad in early October 1686.

At this critical juncture in the struggle, the age-old Indian malady of betrayal rose its head in the Qutb Shahi kingdom. Khalilullah Khan, one of the two senior Qutb Shahi military commanders chose this time to defect to the Mughals and joined Prince Muazzam. It is certain that he was enticed with bribes and promises of a position of power and prestige. While he was one of the top echelon in the Qutb Shahi kingdom, it is possible that he knew in his heart that the struggle would only have one outcome—the defeat and annexation of the Golconda-Hyderabad kingdom. Therefore, he obviously hedged his bets and went over to the winning side at an opportune time, when his defection would have been considered by the Mughals to have created the maximum effect. As anticipated, for his defection the

Mughals immediately gave him a mansab of 10,000-horse and the title of Mahabat Khan.

Khalilullah's defection was just the beginning, it was followed almost immediately by a series of betrayals and defections—minor to ones of serious consequence. These increasing number of incidents finally culminated in Abul Hasan fleeing Hyderabad for the ancient citadel of Golconda with just his immediate entourage. In turn, the king's departure from the capital opened the floodgates and started a veritable deluge with almost the entire population hurriedly leaving the city by any and all means at their disposal. The city of Hyderabad was now open to the Mughals. Prince Muazzam gave instructions that the city was not to be despoiled, an order that was obeyed in the breach. Hyderabad was looted, pillaged, burned and destroyed in short order by the victorious Mughal army. Only an empty shell was left of the once magnificent city.

The Final Fall of Golconda

After the sacking of Hyderabad, Prince Muazzam gathered his forces and started the short march towards Golconda. He send his ultimatum to Abul Hasan in advance. The demands placed on the Qutb Shahi king was straight forward, if strict—the Qutb Shahi was to pay an annual tribute of 120,000 rupees to the Mughals; he was to vacate all the palaces in the Mughal conquered areas of the Golconda kingdom; and the Mir Jumla Madana Pandit and his brother Akkanna, who the Mughals considered the strength behind the Qutb Shahi resistance, were to be immediately dismissed. While negotiations were still on-going, both Madana and Akkanna were murdered on the streets of Golconda. Madana's severed head was immediately despatched to Emperor Aurangzeb camped at Sholapur. Hasan also send gifts direct to Aurangzeb in an effort to gain favour with him and pleaded for clemency.

Aurangzeb was, however, in no mood for reconciliation and firm of purpose, which was to annex Golconda to the growing Mughal Empire, continued his march. The Mughal was in Sholapur in October 1686; by November he was already in Bidar; in January 1687 he had reached the outskirts of Golconda; and was taking charge of the siege. The siege of Golconda lasted eight months and must be included in the list of great sagas of the medieval ages. The siege is to be remembered for the stubborn resistance of the Golconda army and people; equally for the tenacious manner in which Abul Hasan, the meek and reluctant king, led his people; and for an exemplary display of organisational ability by the king. Abul Hasan had all through his reign suffered the demands of the Mughals in silence and acquiesced to being treated as a vassal and a 'chieftain' of no consequence. However, in the last days of his turbulent rule he demonstrated exemplary king-like qualities that stands even today as a beacon of greatness to lesser mortals.

The defences of the Golconda fort were entrusted to Sheikh Minhaj and two other commanders, who tenaciously held fast. An year earlier, Bijapur had been overrun and had freed the entire Mughal army to concentrate on Golconda and the on-going siege.

Of Heroes and Brave Hearts

The defence of Golconda is suffused with admirable tales of bravery, heroism and absolute loyalty to the crown. In an era when betrayal and cowardice were the more common traits, these tales provide a glimpse of the better traits of human beings. The stories are heart-warming as exemplars of human dignity and selfless valour—of Khwaja Abid Qilich Khan, an old general whose arm had been severed from the shoulder blade, sitting and sipping coffee with the other hand while the surgeons were suturing the wound without anaesthetics; of tired and near starving Qutb Shahi guards waking up at night to defend and push back a night attack by the Mughals because of the barking of a pariah dog; and the stories go on.

By now the interdictory missions that were continually mounted behind enemy lines by the Golconda forces led by Mustafa Khan had started to create semi-famine conditions in the Mughal camp. Along with these rids, Sambhaji's Maratha forces were laying waste the countryside, thereby making sure that the Mughals were not able to gather provisions, which could have helped the army. Gradually the

Mughal army was being pushed into a stressful situation. At the same time Abul Hasan continued his diplomatic initiatives, approaching the Mughal Emperor through emissaries, entreating Aurangzeb to 'pardon' him; promising that he would rule Golconda according to the Mughals whim and fancy if only the siege was lifted and his people spared. However, Aurangzeb was unrelenting—he demanded that Abul Hasan present himself in the Mughal camp with his hands tied behind him and a rope around his neck, in order for any negotiations to even start. The siege was tightened. The Mughal army now came under further stress with the unseasonal and heavy monsoons assisting the Qutb Shahis in following their interdiction and scorched earth policy.

At this critical juncture in the battle for survival, when their very existence hung on the balance, the Qutb Shahi kingdom was once again plagued by internal betrayal. The prolonged siege had started to unnerve some of the leadership, meaning the nobles, within the fort. Sensing the unease, the Mughals had been quick to bribe the wavering nobles with promise of high titles and wealth. Gradually some of the Qutb Shahi nobles started to defect to the Mughals. While the initial defections were not debilitating to the defence, they were the beginning of more serious moves. In September 1687, Abul Hasan's adopted son defected and paid homage to Aurangzeb—a great blow to the morale of the besieged fort that was already in dire straits.

Militarily, Golconda remained impregnable and unconquered with the garrison continuing to make effective sorties into the Mughal forces with great effect, especially after the monsoon had set in. Even as the defenders of Golconda were resisting the siege effectively, the leading nobles of the regime had come to the conclusion that in the end the siege would succeed, considering the might of the Mughal army. They continued to defect in small numbers till such times that only two senior nobles were left loyal to Abul Hasan and supporting the defences of the fort.

One of the nobles, called Abdullah Khan Panni, had earlier been in the service of the Adil Shah of Bijapur and then an employee of the Mughals. His loyalty to the Qutb Shahis now severed completely—he betrayed the beleaguered citadel by leaving a gate open on a pre-arranged night through which the Mughal forces were able to storm the fort and invest it after a bitter struggle. The other noble who had remained loyal, Abd-ur-Razak Lari, was on the other end of the spectrum on the loyalty scale—he fought the invading army with a handful of faithful followers, attacking the triumphant Mughal forces inside the fort, till he was overwhelmed by the sheer numerical superiority of the invading forces and beaten down. Lari's act of significant courage and loyalty was indicative of the manner in which the fort finally fell to the northern army.

With the failure of the last desperate defensive fight led by Razak Lari, Abul Hasan knew that the end had come. It is reported, by chroniclers from both sides of the equation, that Abul Hasan's act of surrender that ended the reign of the Qutb Shahi dynasty was done with a 'collectedness and composure' that is very seldom seen and has no parallel in Indian history. It is said that even the haughty Mughal commanders were uncharacteristically compelled to defer to the nobleness of the king and his royal demeanour. Abul Hasan, the Meek, had acquitted himself as a king better than any of his more powerful ancestors. Perhaps because of the manner in which Abul Hasan conducted himself as the king, Aurangzeb himself treated the Qutb Shahi with the dignity that he deserved, taking him to Bijapur, where the Mughal monarch was heading.

Later, on Abul Hasan's request to be allowed to live in the Deccan rather than be transported to Delhi, Aurangzeb set him up in the Nizam Shahi palace at Daulatabad. Abul Hasan spend his last days in splendid isolation as a virtual prisoner and died around 1699-1700 after a brief illness. There is no doubt that, despite his individual character flaws, he met the final defeat and annexation of his kingdom with the grace and dignity that could not be bettered by any other king.

Abul Hasan left four daughters and a son named Khudah Banda who was born while he was a captive in Daulatabad. Aurangzeb, always shrewd and ruthless, perceived a threat from the young prince who could become the spearhead for a rebellion in the now subdued Deccan, and had him removed to an unknown place. Nothing more is heard about the prince named Khudah Banda. Thus ended the Qutb Shahis. The only epitaph that can be written for the Qutb Shahi dynasty is that they faced the end with great dignity and that they were ultimately brought down by the collective avarice and disloyalty that led to betrayal of the kingdom by its nobles.

Section VI

DECCAN SHAHIS – OTHER ASPECTS

The Deccan Shahi military forces were spawned by the Bahmani military organisation because the founders of each of the successor dynasties had been successful military commanders of the Bahmani kings. Their success as military leaders had been the fundamental reason for their rising to positions of influence and power.

Chapter 30

ADMINISTRATION, MILITARY AND FOREIGN AFFAIRS

The Deccan was ruled for more than three centuries by Muslim kings, starting with the Bahmanis in early to mid-1300s during their highly centralised independent rule and continuing even after the splintering of the Bahmani kingdom into the five successor states—of these, Bijapur, Ahmadnagar and Golconda were the more prominent. Even though Islamic tradition and practice permitted, and at times even encouraged, succession to the leadership position by the most capable contender with the right credentials and if he had sufficient support, like elsewhere in the medieval world the throne had gradually become a hereditary position. In the Deccan this development took only the span of about two generations to become entrenched as being customary.

Administration

The details of the administration—the methodology used for actually controlling the kingdom—has not been elaborated in any of the available Bahmani or Deccan Shahi chronicles. However, there are snippets that can be gathered from the historical narrative of the major kingdoms, which can be strung together in a collective fashion to obtain a picture of the administrative ethos of the kingdoms in a generic manner. This effort is made easier by the fact that all the administrative initiatives originated centrally at the king's court and all the kingdoms followed similar principles in administering their territories. Further, the Nizam Shahis of Ahmadnagar left behind a large number of petitions from the provincial councils to the king at the royal court that provides an insight into the working of the administrative machine. The picture that emerges is not extraordinary in any manner and broadly adheres to the common practices of the time.

The Deccan Village

As had been the practice even in earlier times, in medieval Deccan also the village formed the basic unit for administration as well as the nucleus of the local economy. The administration was conducted by the village head, in the Deccan normally a Reddy, assisted by an account keeper. The professions that were fundamental to the well-being of the village in terms of the quality of life—such as the washerman, cobbler, blacksmith, potter, barber, carpenter and waterman—were given free land to practice their trade. An interesting fact that emerges, more by omission than direct mention, is that the village priest did not have a distinct role in the administration. A collection of villages was called a Pargana.

A council of learned Brahmins, called the Brahmasabha, arbitrated all religious cases within the village and the Pargana; while the age-old tradition of the Panchayat continued to function to enforce all other local laws and customs. Both the Brahmasabha and the Panchayat were feudal in character and there are no indications of any sort of elections being held for membership to the councils. It is notable that the Muslim kings of the Deccan did not interfere in the personal law of the Hindus, leaving it to the Brahmasabha to pronounce judgement in all cases of dispute. However, the Muslim rulers instituted the system of the Mirasidar tenure for controlling the land, which was very similar to the earlier practice of the Sthalakari tenure. Mirasi was a term derived from the Persian that meant 'hereditary rights', and a Mirasidar was a traditional land lord who held the land hereditarily, passing it on to his successor within the same family. In the case of the Deccan, the system was predominated by the Reddys. The Mirasidars formed a deliberative and consultative body to take care of the affairs of the village called Gotsabha, the term presumably derived from the word gotra, meaning family.

Central Administration

The Muslim rulers instituted a new council called the Pargana Majlis alongside the Gotsabha in the villages. These were the only two councils permitted to approach the king's royal court with petitions. Mahmud Gawan, the great administrator and an extremely religious person, is credited with establishing the Majlis to provide judgement and arbitration to the people in accordance with Islamic Law. The decision of the Majlis, called Mahzar, was normally a sort of recommendation to higher authorities to enact or perform some local action, which was beyond the capacity of the Pargana administration to achieve. The Majlise was an Islamic introduction and was headed by an appointed Qazi or judge. The Majlis and Gotsabha often met in joint sessions to govern the Pargana, indicating the mixed religious composition of the Deccan Parganas.

The chain of administrative unit(s) that connected a Deccan Pargana, at the lower end of the totem pole, to the central administration of the king is not clear, a sort of vacuum exists in the information spread. The Bahmanis had very vaguely defined provinces, called tarafs, for example the Taraf of Telangana. Later the Taraf seems to have been renamed and is seen to be referred to as Wilayat, most likely a term acquired through the increased interaction with the Persian Empire. However, both the terms are absent in the available literature on the Qutb Shahis of Golconda. This situation creates a sort of ambiguity. That the kingdoms of the Deccan were sub-divided into administrative units—provinces and smaller holdings—consisting of several Parganas cannot be doubted, especially considering the available information on the Bahmani administration. The Deccan Shahi kingdoms also must have been sub-divided into 'provinces' but there is no information available regarding the exact nature of these divisions, their probable boundaries, and the manner in which they were administered.

In all cases, the king was the pivotal personage in the administrative set-up. He was assisted by an advisory council, normally called Majlis-i-Kingash, consisting of the senior nobles of the kingdom who held positions of power and authority, essentially the 'wazirs and amirs'. The Majlis assembled when called by the king to settle matters of importance to the kingdom, including foreign affairs. The power of the Majlis waxed and waned dependent on the king's personality and his inherent hold over the administration—in certain cases the Majlis was strong enough even to decide who would succeed to the throne on the death of an incumbent. In the beginning, the membership of the Majlis was decided by the king who nominated nobles to the council. Gradually the system was altered and the ad-hoc character of the council disappeared with nobles holding designated appointments being automatically inducted. Along with the appointments themselves becoming hereditary, as the administrative system became moribund, the Majlis also became a council whose membership was itself hereditary. In Golconda under the Qutb Shahi dynasty, the council evolved into the Majlis-i-Diwandari, the equivalent of a Privy Council.

There was an accepted hierarchy within the appointments in the court with the Mir Jumla being considered the senior-most appointment, a position that could be equated to the traditional role of the prime minister. In some accounts the Mir Jumla is reported as being the oldest recognised appointment within the Deccan kingdoms, although this assertion could be disputed. The Bahmanis had a position titled the Peshwa which was at times considered to be next to the king himself. In later days, the Peshwa was relegated to being the second in the hierarchy. Even so, there is some confusion regarding the precedence of the Mir Jumla and the Peshwa and it is evident that the relative seniority was determined by the king. It can be accepted that in the hierarchy of the court generally the Mir Jumla was considered the senior-most followed by the Peshwa.

In the medieval Deccan kingdoms and the Peninsula, the religious divide between the Hindus and the Muslims had not yet become clearly apparent, although North India had already been visibly divided on religious lines by the policies of the Mughal emperors who followed Akbar—the last, and perhaps only, secular Mughal monarch. In the Deccan, a partnership between the Hindu and Muslim population existed—a secular approach that transcended social status and percolated upwards from the village all the way to the nobles in court. In most cases, no religious bias to appointments, high or low, can be discerned. In fact the division in the Deccan was between the Phirangi nobles of foreign origin, and the nobles of local extraction, the Deccanis, and not normally on religious grounds between Hindus and Muslims. Even in the Majlis, Hindus were equally represented. However, it is not to be thought that there was no religious persecution or that religious bias was not displayed, especially when wars were fought. The joint campaign that the Deccan Shahis mounted against Vijayanagar, which was instrumental in the eventual destruction of that great kingdom, is a prime example of a religious war. The co-existence of Hindus and Muslims in the Deccan was a product of pragmatism—the Hindu population was far too large to be 'controlled' by a minority Muslim population. It was evident to the Muslim 'conquerors' that a kingdom could not function without the assistance of the majority population who performed most of the minion roles critical to administering large swaths of territory.

Judicial Administration

The delivery of justice to the common people in the Deccan kingdoms emanated from a highly centralised system, flowing from the king who personally judged cases that were considered important. In theory, no one was considered above the law, a tenet that was practiced by all powerful kings. Also, in theory, all illegality within the kingdom was punished. The king was assisted by the Chief Sadr and the Chief Qazi in judging cases, by actually delivering judgments or by advising the king regarding the law in designated cases. All cases relating to Muslims were decided according to the Sharia, the Muslim religious law, and non-Muslims were judged according to the prevalent secular law, unless a Muslim was involved in the case in which case the Sharia was applied. In the villages, justice was dispensed by the Panchayat. A secular law applied to trade, sale, contract and other matters of a generic nature normally associated with commerce and was made equally applicable to Muslims and non-Muslims alike.

Punishment for misdemeanour was usually very severe in the medieval Deccan kingdoms. Even very ordinary crimes could be punished with the death sentence that was carried out almost immediately after the pronouncement of the judgement and without any appeal. Heavy fines that would bankrupt the offender was another way of punishment. This attitude of extreme punishment was perhaps meant as a deterrent to would-be offenders. The fundamental principle of delivering justice that was followed was oriented towards curtailment of crime through coercive deterrence. No attempt at reformation of the offender is visible in the nearly four centuries of Deccan Shahi rule in the Peninsula.

The source of law was primarily Qur'anic injunctions, interpreted and applied by the Sadr and the Qazi, the severity of the sentence being almost completely dependent on the common sense of the individual delivering the judgement. Muslim law for a long period of time was almost fully the 'will of the king' tinged with actual or imagined royal traditions. The Deccan did not have any lawyers until the arrival of the Westerners, particularly the British, in positions of power and influence. Therefore, the roles of the judge, defence and the traditional jury were all carried out by the officials of the court. Litigations were short, judgements delivered concisely, and justice dispensed swiftly.

Organisation of the Military Forces

The Deccan kingdoms were born out of the balkanisation of the Bahmani kingdom that took place because of the revolts of powerful military commanders. It is therefore obvious that the most important and powerful arm of the State was the military forces. Without a strong and viable military force at his command, no king could have considered ruling his kingdom with poise and composure. The common heritage from the Bahmanis and the fact that each of the Deccan kingdoms were carved out by sheer military power also became the root cause for the lack of trust between the successor kingdoms. The mutual distrust resulted in almost uninterrupted border skirmishes and constant wars between the Deccan Shahis, from their inception as independent entities to their final eclipse as the Mughals swallowed them piecemeal. The endless conflict was also the result of mutual jealousy and the imperative that each kingdom felt to keeping the balance of power between them, not permitting any one kingdom to become overwhelmingly powerful. The military forces were obviously the binding glue that maintained the kingdoms as independent holdings.

The Deccan Shahi military forces were spawned by the Bahmani military organisation because the founders of each of the successor dynasties had been successful military commanders of the Bahmani kings. Their success as military leaders had been the fundamental reason for their rising to positions of influence and power.

The Deccan armies were essentially feudal in nature. Initially the Bahmani kingdom had been divided into four provinces, tarafs, under a tarafdar who could be equated to a military governor. He had complete control of the administration and military forces of the province and was given separate jagirs to defray the cost of maintaining the necessary force levels. In return, he was fully responsible to the king for the recruitment, training and maintenance of the military forces in his province. This was a system that had been traditionally followed in the sub-continent for ages and continued to be open to being abused, as was seen in earlier times. The tarafdar could deplete the military forces and use the jagirs to financially benefit himself personally, thereby endangering the broad security of the kingdom or alternatively, he could build up a strong force and become powerful enough to threaten the king himself. The division of the kingdom into provinces under tarafdars left very little direct income for the king to create a centralised force making him vulnerable to the schemes of ambitious nobles. Further, the king's lack of control of most of the military forces left him exposed to internal rebellions and revolts.

Mahmud Gawan, always loyal to the throne, attempted to reform the civil-military structure in favour of the king, and was murdered for his troubles. The Bahmanis attempted to de-feudalise the army, at a later date and on a smaller scale, but the effort was a case of 'too little too late' and could not save the failing and floundering dynasty. The kingdom had already descended into chaos and the more prominent tarafdars had already started to act independent of the central administration and few had even declared independence. History has repeatedly shown that feudal armies function well only when the central authority, the king, is strong and decisive. A weak or faltering king within a feudal military system invariably led to diminishing central control and the gradual but ultimate break-up of the kingdom.

All the Deccan Shahi kingdoms were founded by tarafdars who clearly understood the pitfalls of the feudal military system, after all they had all benefited from the inherent lacuna in the system. Therefore, they were careful to maintain direct control over the army and did not parcel out the military to secondary nobles to maintain and operate. Within a generation, the feudal character of the Deccan armies had been replaced by military forces that were centrally controlled by the king. At this stage, artillery made its appearance and forever changed the deployment tactics of the army. Artillery assumed a central role in military campaigns of the time since most conflicts invariably led to the siege of a fort at their culmination. Artillery was capable of breaking down fort walls that could otherwise withstand a siege of several months and they were useful in breaching battlements. In medieval Deccan, the artillery component was almost always commanded by Turk officers. This could have been because of the technical nature of the equipment and the complexity involved in calculating the azimuth and elevation required for the positioning of the guns to ensure accuracy. Being a new and imported form of warfare, the local soldiers may not have been proficient in this technical element. It can also be speculated that the kings were not comfortable leaving control of this new and powerful arm in the hands of local officers whose loyalty could be open to doubt.

Tactics in Battle

The Marathas introduced the concept of guerrilla warfare and its predatory nature into the Deccan. The basic concept is prevalent even today, in a much refined manner, although the core of the Deccan Shahi armies did not adopt this mode of warfighting. Medieval Deccan battles continued to be fought in the traditional manner with the army divided into three main sections—the main central section and the two flanks. The centre was normally commanded by the king himself and formed the nucleus of the army. When the king personally did not take to the battlefield, he appointed a Sipah-Salar, sort of commander-in-chief to command the forces. However, in the Deccan this appointment has been recorded in the chronicles infrequently, more exception than the rule. The Deccan kings however appointed Sarlashkars, commanders who were selected on an ad-hoc basis to lead a particular campaign, normally expeditionary in nature, so that the king would not have to be away from the capital for long periods.

The most important military appointment was the Quilahdar, the commander of the fort. In an indirect manner this commander decided the rise and fall of a kingdom's power and prestige, especially when the kingdom was under attack. A beleaguered fort held its own or fell to the enemy depending on the fortitude and expertise of the Quilahdar and the fate of the kingdom often hung on the fate of a single critical fort. In addition there were the Nayakwaris, Hindu chieftains who exercised a great deal of local power, especially since they influenced the majority Hindu population.

The customary Islamic military reliance on horses and cavalry permeated to the Deccan kingdoms also. In pitched battles, the Bahmani and its successor states relied heavily on out-flanking movements and rapid manoeuvres of the cavalry to succeed. It was from this initial use of the cavalry that the Marathas developed the concept of the irregular cavalry, adapting the use of horses to their own peculiar and favoured style of warfare that relied on hit and run tactics. In turn, the guerrilla warfare tactics that became the hallmark of the Maratha forces was developed—an astute combination of rapid cavalry manoeuvre and a stealthy approach to surprise the adversary. The Marathas became masters of the use of light, irregular cavalry in classic guerrilla fashion, throughout the middle-ages.

In analysing the development of battle tactics in medieval Deccan and South India it comes as a surprise to note that the Vijayanagar Empire continued to depend heavily on the traditional elephant corps, which had been the mainstay of the Hindu armies before the advent of the horse and cavalry, even as its neighbours moved on to focusing on the cavalry as the main element of the army. This static approach to battle tactics that should have been evolving is doubly surprising in Vijayanagar since the kingdom was renowned for its progressive approach to all aspects of nation-building, including the organisation of the military and national security strategy. (This aspect of the Vijayanagar Empire will be studied in greater detail in the next volume in this series that analyses the great kingdom.)

From the time of Alexander the Macedon's victory over the legendary Indian king Porus, elephants have repeatedly proven themselves to be unreliable animals to be taken into battle. Mass in combination with unpredictable behaviour can very rapidly become a liability from being an asset and therefore the risk associated with employing elephants in critical battles must be considered a questionable strategy. The risk increases exponentially when the adversary is an unfamiliar quantity and their tactics unknown, as was the case when the invading forces were reliant on the cavalry and rapid movements to isolate and destroy crucial elements of the defending Indian armies. In the long history of invasions of the Indian sub-continent, the vaunted elephant corps of the Hindu kings played an important and often decisive role in deciding the outcome of critical battles.

Foreign Relations

The Deccan Shahi kings followed the traditions that were established by Mahmud Gawan in dealing with neighbouring kingdoms. However, there was one fundamental difference between the foreign policy initiatives pursued by the Bahmanis and the successor kingdoms. The Bahmanis controlled the entire Deccan and therefore had to deal only with Vijayanagar, Orissa and Malwa since the Mughals had not yet started to covet the Deccan. However, the Deccan Shahis had to initially content with each other and in later days with the Mughal Empire. It was Mahmud Gawan who first realised that the Shahi kingdoms must cooperate with each other in order to keep the northern invaders at bay. He was murdered before his concepts could be put into practice.

In medieval Deccan there was no tradition of permanent envoys being placed in courts of neighbouring kingdoms. Special envoys were send to represent their kings for special occasions such as coronations etc., and their stay in the host country was restricted to the time of the celebration. They did not conduct any diplomatic mission during their visit. Discussions regarding alliances, treaties or peace initiatives were conducted by special representatives and minutes of the discussions were made and mutually accepted. Permanent ambassadors were still not on the horizon.

During times of trouble in a kingdom, nobles of influence and holding high positions in the administration were appointed as special envoys and send out to seek assistance from friendly neighbours. This was a universal practice in medieval Deccan. It was also a universal practice for these envoys to also have personal dealings with the king and/or nobles of the host kingdom that may not have been authorised, and worse, may not have been in the best interest of the envoy's own kingdom. The duplicitous nature of such diplomatic missions is displayed repeatedly in the dealings between the Deccan Shahi kingdoms.

After the successful combined Deccan Shahi attack on Vijayanagar, the major Shahi kingdoms adopted the practice of keeping an accredited permanent envoy in each other's courts. They were more like military attachés and doubled as diplomats during times of relative peace. Even so, they were not guaranteed diplomatic immunity by the host kingdom with some even being beheaded for their involvement in local trouble-mongering. The successor kingdoms evolved a process of issuing an ultimatum to the would-be adversary before actually taking to the field and conducting a war. Over a period of time this developed into a tradition that was honoured most of the time. Essentially, the sending of a demand or ultimatum provided an opportunity for the adversarial kingdoms, and also other parties, to negotiate a settlement on mutually agreeable terms without unnecessary bloodshed. It also provided the prospect for a more powerful kingdom to interfere and enforce a peace without the two antagonists going to war, with the accompanying instability and chaos. The Deccan Shahi kingdoms conducted inter-state relations within a broad set of principles that did not have laid down stipulatory rules.

Chapter 31

THE CULTURAL FRONT

The Deccan Shahi kings were generally great patrons of art and literature and some of the kings were poets and litterateurs of some repute. This patronage was particularly demonstrated in Golconda under the Qutb Shahis who assiduously cultivated the arts.

Languages

Medieval Deccan saw the development of a hybrid language, much like Urdu in North India, which was named Dakhani. The development of the Dakhani language started with the Bahmanis. It became an independently spoken and literary language during the period of rule by the successor dynasties—the Deccan Shahis. Dakhani sourced its repertoire of words from Arabic-Persian, Marathi, Kannada and Telugu, in later years being referred to as Dakhani Urdu in order to distinguish it from the more widespread and prevalent North Indian Urdu. The enormous patronage of Dakhini provided by the Qutb Shahi kings encouraged learned persons from overseas to come to Golconda with some of them settling their permanently if they found sufficient support from the royal house. In a climate of royal patronage for literature, with a number of languages burgeoning simultaneously and competing for patronage, it was not surprising that a hybrid language would develop and then flourish. Through the Qutb Shahi rule, Dakhani rapidly matured into a literary language of merit.

The kingdom of Golconda also actively supported the development of Telugu language and literature. Ibrahim Qutb Shah, who had lived in the Vijayanagar court for seven years of self-imposed exile, spoke the language and is reported to have been passionate about it. He also married an Andhra woman named Bhagirati. On becoming the Golconda king, Ibrahim invited a number of Telugu poets to his court and also appointed a Telugu poet laureate, Gangadhara Kavi, for the kingdom. Ibrahim, in turn, was also given a Telugu title by the poets—Malkibharam. The Qutb Shahi reign made an enormous contribution to the development of Telugu, gradually bringing it up to the same level as Persian and Dakhini or proto-Urdu as it is sometimes referred.

Dance – The Kuchipudi Story

The Deccan Shahis, particularly the Qutb Shahis, extended their patronage to almost all aspects of cultural endeavours and development. Of particular note in this respect is Abul Hasan Qutb Shah's grant, in perpetuity, of a village to the Brahmin troupe performing a dance form that came to be called Kuchipudi—named so since it originated in and centred on a small town called Kuchipudi, situated between Vijayawada and Masulipatam. This grant was of enormous import since the support it provided to the impoverished troupe was the only reason for the continued presence of the Kuchipudi dance form in the Indian classical dance repertoire. The origin, development and refinement of the Kuchipudi dance-drama tradition is an interesting story. The earliest mention of the Kuchipudi dance-drama is seen in the records of a village called Machupalli on the Coromandal coast.

The Origins of Kuchipudi Dance-Drama

If the prevalent story regarding its origins are to be believed, then without doubt, Kuchipudi as a dance form goes back at least seven centuries. The story goes:

An orphan, Siddappa, who lived sometime between 1350 and 1450, had been married as a child of six months to another child, a tradition that was normal during that period. He lived on one bank of the great river that flowed through the kingdom (probably River Krishna) and his prospective wife's family on the other bank. When Siddappa came of age, his father-in-law asked him to come and get proper nuptial ceremonies completed. Accordingly, Siddappa set course to his bride's place. While he was swimming across the river, he was caught up in a storm and he was sure that he would drown. He prayed for survival and vowed that if he was saved he would devote his entire life to the service of Lord Sri Krishna and remain a 'sanyasi'—a celibate—for the rest of his life. He was miraculously saved from the storm.

On reaching his father-in-law's house on the other bank, Siddappa was honour bound to remain a sanyasi. However he also had to honour the marriage vows that had been taken on his behalf when he was an infant. As a via media, he and his bride saw themselves as the embodiment of Satyabhama and Sri Krishna and enacted the celestial love between them. Siddappa is credited with having founded the Bhama cult. He went on to compose a large number of songs in praise of Lord Sri Krishna and himself danced to the songs. The ensemble that he founded began to be called Bhama-Kalapam or Parijatam and was the beginning of a distinctive dance form based in and around the village of Kuchipudi in the Telugu country.

Kuchipudi is one of the eleven major Indian classical dance forms and traces its roots to the ancient Indian text Natya Shastra.

The Natya Shastra

The Natya Shastra is an ancient Sanskrit text on performing arts, which is considered to have been written by the sage Bharat Muni. It has been dated to between 200 B.C and 200 A.D, although estimates vary between 500 B.C and 500 A.D. The book influenced all dance, music and literary traditions in India. Its most important contribution is the introduction of the 'Rasa Theory' into the Indian performing arts. The Rasa Theory postulates that even though entertainment is a

> desired outcome of the performing arts, it cannot be and is not the primary goal. The primary goal of performing arts is to transport the audience, individually, to a make-belief reality that in turn makes the individual experience the essence of his/her consciousness, forcing the individual to ask or reflect on spiritual and moral questions.
>
> It is an exhaustive encyclopaedia, a dissertation on the performing arts, which acknowledges the divine origins of the arts and the central role of performing arts in achieving divine goals.

Like most Indian art forms, Kuchipudi also developed in connection with cultural activities that focused on the temple and religious beliefs. The Kuchipudi tradition credits the modernisation of the dance in terms of it being systemised, around the 17th century, to a Vedantic 'sanyasi', poet and musician named Tirtha Narayana Yati and his devoted disciple Siddendra Yogi (the Siddappa of the folklore given above). Siddendra Yogi composed the Bhama-Kalapam, also called Parijatam, which is the main or pivotal drama in the entire repertoire of the dance. The composition tells the story of Satyabhama, who considered herself the favourite consort of Lord Sri Krishna and induced him to transplant the heavenly tree Parijatam, of the never-fading flowers, into her private garden. The composition and its enactment in the dance form is exalted in the Bhama cult of Siddendra Yogi—the loving devotion of Lord Sri Krishna realised though the conjugal love of Satyabhama for her lord.

> ### Support of the Raya of Vijayanagar
>
> Records show that a small troupe of Kuchipudi dancers went to Vijayanagar to perform before the king. On their way they were harassed by the ruler of Siddhout, named Sambata Guruvarayu. Having reached Vijayanagar, the troupe introduced this episode into their performance before the king. The Raya—probably Vira Narasinha

> Raya—was enraged by his vassal's behaviour in harassing his performers. The Raya is recorded as having summoned the erring vassal king and beheading him for his temerity. This episode would have happened around 1507.

When Vijayanagar fell and the patronage was abruptly cut off, the travelling troupes moved to Tanjavore in search of alternative royal support. Since the Bhama-Kalapam dance was very sensuous in nature, it was not considered proper for women to come on stage and enact the poems, especially the theme of Krishna-Bhama love. Gradually, women were completely excluded from the performance of the Kuchipudi dance form and men and boys enacted the female roles.

The name of the village, Kuchipudi, is probably derived from the word 'Kusilava', meaning travelling troupe of artistes, from there to Kusilavapur or Kuchilapuri, the village of the Kusilavas, which subsequently became Kuchipudi in the local language over a period of time. Much like Kathakali, all-night performances were normal in Kuchipudi recitals. Each of the performers were singers, dancers and actors with great emphasis being laid on pantomime or abhinaya. Kuchipudi enjoyed a privileged status and great patronage during the reign of Abdullah Qutb Shah. During this time some changes to the footwork of the dance was introduced which is prevalent even today. Towards the end of the Qutb Shahi rule, the then king Abul Hasan stayed overnight in Kuchipudi accompanied by his prime minister Madana Pandit, where the core troupe put on a show for him. Pleased with the performance, he granted an entire village for the sustenance of the people dedicated to this art form. Thus, it was the last scion of the Qutb Shahi dynasty who ensured the continuation of an age-old dance form that had originated in the Deccan. Without this royal support, it is conceivable that the art form may well have died out and gradually vanished.

Architecture – The Legacy

The architectural legacy left behind by the Deccan Shahi kings is a growing field of study. Although there is a common thread of

Indo-Islamic architectural development that can be noticed in the medieval Deccan architecture, the individual elaborations in the style that is unique to the three major Deccan Shahi kingdoms—Bijapur, Ahmadnagar and Golconda—confirm their support for architectural innovation. Running side-by-side with the Mughal initiatives in North India, the Deccan elicits less attention because of the magnificent splendour and spread of the Mughal architecture.

The importance of the Deccan architecture lies not only in appreciating the developments in their own right, but in the strong relationship that the Deccan Shahi kingdoms share with each other, yet manage to remain refreshingly distinct in their final creations. Perhaps more important is the connections, both political and economic, that the Deccan Shahis had with other parts of the world, especially the Middle-East and East Africa, which in turn greatly influenced the architectural developments. These connections, made through the Indian Ocean trade route and thriving ports like Chaul, was denied to the land-locked North Indian kingdoms.

The connections of Indo-Muslim architecture meanders across the developments in architecture through the entire period of the more than three centuries of the Deccan Shahi rule in the Peninsula. The study of the developments in architecture, within the confines of a particular period, also provides a clear indication of the thrust of social development and creates an understanding of the convulsions in society. They also elaborate on the economic process of the period and therefore cannot be ignored when examining the history of the period in question.

While all three of the major Deccan Shahis were attuned to support of architectural endeavour, the Qutb Shahis perhaps displayed a much more acute sense of societal requirements vis-à-vis buildings and architecture. Golconda was already a built-up town and fort when the founder of the dynasty, Qutb-ul-Mulk, took over its governorship. His realisation of the overcrowded nature of the city and attempt to expand it westwards, speaks volumes about his civic awareness. The later construction of Hyderabad as the Qutb Shahi capital flows from this fundamental awareness. Moreover, the Charminar, constructed by the Qutb Shahis, is still considered a masterpiece of architecture across the entire sub-continent. The Deccan Shahis left the region dotted with palaces, both large and small; tombs of kings and noblemen, elaborate and carefully planned; and a large number of mosques that are still seen spread across the landscape of the plateau.

Conclusion

The Deccan Shahis may have individually 'arrived' at their role of being kings through historic accidents and without any great personal merit per se. However, they managed to hold on to a majority part of the Deccan Plateau for close to three centuries—through incessant infighting, intrigue, betrayal and the ever-present danger of obliteration by the more powerful northern power, the Mughals. Measured by any yardstick, this is not a petty achievement. On the other hand, almost all the Deccan Shahi rulers were uniformly self-centred and a majority were pleasure-loving enough to forsake the kingdom for worldly pleasures. The overall picture that emerges is that of a group of self-indulgent people who had suddenly been given the opportunity to rule over a rich land with a multitude and diverse population. This remains the enduring image of the Deccan Shahis.

Any amount of retelling of history, done by later-day historians for a variety of reasons, cannot and will not erase this hard truth. Even by medieval Indian standards, the Deccan Shahis behaved abominably in pursuing their completely self-absorbed ways. The 'religious tolerance' that is at times pointed out as a virtue, especially by historians attempting to provide a 'cleaner' picture of the Deccan rulers, was a default attitude because the king could not be bothered to persecute someone, when he could use that time to fulfil some of his baser instincts. Persecutions were left for the nobility and lesser officials to perform and therefore not considered worthy of reportage by contemporary historians. The Deccan Shahi rule has no parallel in Indian history as a period when so much could have been achieved. However, a long list of rulers managed to squander every opportunity which pointed towards bettering the status of the dynasty and the kingdom that came their way. The land was rich and the people generally of a subdued nature—but nothing of importance or significance came of the Deccan Shahi rule, primarily because of the mediocrity of the rulers.

Section VII

MEDIEVAL DECCAN – A CONCLUDING ANALYSIS

The arrival of the Turko-Afghans into the sub-continent in medieval times, which was the last of the major people movement into India, changed this congenial attitude between races and religions that were coming together, at times under duress. All the previous entrants into the sub-continent had, over time, merged with the existing Indian society in a mutually beneficial manner. The outsiders had adopted the Indian religion, social customs, languages and even values, becoming an indivisible part of India, merging with the local people and creating a ready mix. Both the outsiders and the local people were enriched in this process. The Turko-Afghans were, culturally and religiously, antithetical to the all-encompassing Hindu ethos and therefore had no tendency to mix and merge.

Chapter 32

CHAOTIC ADMINISTRATION

Medieval Indian kings and sultans were almost completely focused on waging war, which was considered their primary responsibility, to the exclusion of all other duties. They waged war to suppress rebellions, to expand the territorial holdings of the kingdom and to seize the wealth from other kingdoms in order to enrich their own. It was believed that only through war could the king better the lives of his subjects, who in most cases lived in abject poverty and continued to do so irrespective of the number of wars fought and won. Therefore, it is obvious that the king did not wage wars to alter this abysmal situation, but to better his own and the nobility's circumstances. In most cases the common people and their situation in life did not matter and was never considered a factor in the broader calculations and decision-making process. Stability of the kingdom, brought about through efficient administration held a very low priority, if it was considered a necessity at all. The welfare of the common man was a concept that was to come into consideration at a much later time in humanities progress. Medieval India was waking from a centuries-old slumber during the dark ages, which had enveloped the sub-continent after the enlightened rule of great monarchs, emperors and kings when kingdoms and empires had flourished as near-utopian entities. The situation in medieval Deccan was the same as everywhere else—people's welfare was hardly a concern of the rulers.

In the Bahmani kingdom and its successor states, almost all kings were mere warlords. When warlords rule neighbouring kingdoms, peace and stability take a backseat and therefore it is not surprising that in the more than three centuries of their combined rule, there is no recognisable period of peace and stability in the Deccan. Throughout the three centuries violence was the norm and when no wars were being fought, it lurked just below the surface of a thin veneer of diplomacy and attempts at peaceful co-existence.

The borders of the medieval Deccan kingdoms were ill-defined at best, with no fixed frontiers; the borders were what the army of the kingdom established and controlled. Further, central control of territorial holdings was a direct function of the power and stature of the king, which waxed and waned dependent on the individual capacity and capability of the ruling monarch of the time. Provinces were controlled, the term control being used in a very lose manner, by royal favourites who were permitted to collect taxes on their whims and fancies. The only requirement of the provincial administrators, if they could be called that, was for them to pay a pre-determined amount into the royal treasury. Provinces were sub-divided into districts and taluks and were afforded considerable autonomy in their administration. The village continued to be the basic unit and there was absolutely no central or royal interference in the working of the village as long as the dues were paid on time.

Corruption

Like all medieval courts, the Deccan royal courts were also steeped in corruption. Corruption was endemic, rampant and open and percolated from the highest to the lowest levels. It is reliably mentioned that the king himself was not above seeking recompense, in terms of presents, for granting favours, which was not considered bribery. The case of the last Mir Jumla of the Qutb Shahis, Madana Pandit, 'selling' appointments in the provinces is an illustrative example of this system. The giving of presents to the person granting a favour by the person being conferred a favour was a euphemism for bribing the higher official. The system was based on a two-way transaction—presents given to superiors in gratitude for favours granted to subordinates, which was a method to ensure their continued loyalty. The system prevailed across the spectrum of society, emanating from the king and flowing downwards.

The end result of the system becoming entrenched was that probity in public life became an unaffordable luxury that even the king could not indulge in; the other side of the coin being the fact that loyalty was openly put on sale in medieval India.

Slaves and Foreigners

By the time Islam arrived in the Deccan, the egalitarian ethos so apparent in the early times of the religion had already washed-off. Further, a number of the early nobles of the region were manumitted slaves and/or their descendants. In the early medieval period, being a slave was not a disgrace or a handicap in rising in the social hierarchy. It was obvious and an accepted fact that no one became a slave willingly and that most of them were sold into slavery as children or captured and enslaved as adults. While there was no embargo on a slave rising in stature, it was equally obvious that a large number of slaves lived degrading lives, suffering abject poverty and ill-treatment. However, being a slave was by itself not considered a disgrace or a disability.

The medieval Muslim kings in India, both in the north and in the Deccan, tended to favour foreigners—Turks, Arabs, Persians and Afghans—for service at the higher levels of the administration and the military, as opposed to local Indian converts to Islam, even second or third generation Muslims and at the higher levels of society. This attitude and preference reflected their disdain for native Indians and in the Deccan sowed the seeds of discord within the bureaucratic nobility. *[This discrimination is visible even today in the Islamic world, where the Muslims from the Indian sub-continent, as well as from South-East Asia, are treated as inferior in the Muslim majority nations of the Middle-East and elsewhere. This discrimination is not only based on race, but also the perceived inferiority in the actual practice of the religion as such.]* In medieval India, the native Muslims, almost all of them Hindu converts, were considered suspect in the sanctity of their religious practices by the orthodox Muslim clergy. This lurking suspicion regarding the local converts of the sub-continent has never been fully cleansed in the larger Islamic world.

Religion in the Administration

It is wrong to think that the administration and military forces of the medieval Muslim rulers in the sub-continent were serviced by either Muslims who came with the invading forces or by local converts to the religion. The Hindus played a major and important role in both the administration and the military forces. This tradition goes back to the time of the repeated invasions of Mahmud of Ghazni. It has been recorded that several Hindu chieftains acted as captains in the invading army, mostly leading their own contingents that were predominantly Hindu in their constitution.

In medieval Muslim kingdoms, or rather kingdoms ruled by Muslim rulers, the preponderant majority of the administrative staff was Hindus. In fact, other than for the top two layers of the bureaucracy, the entire administrative machinery was staffed by Hindus in the Deccan kingdoms. The fact was that the Muslim rulers did not have the necessary number of Muslims to man the entire administration by their own people. The Indian Muslim kingdoms, even the relatively smaller ones, were vast and diverse and the invading rulers and their descendants did not have the necessary depth of local knowledge necessary to be effective in running the lower level administration. In a real sense, the Hindus ran the government of the Muslim rulers. Foreign visitors to the medieval Muslim kingdoms of the Deccan have chronicled and commented on this aspect; some even going to the extent of stating that both the Hindu and Muslim kingdoms of the sub-continent were under 'Brahminical rule', since Brahmins held most of the crucial positions in the administration. In North India, most of the Hindus were placed in subordinate positions in the hierarchy, which was not the case in the Peninsula.

In medieval Deccan, the Hindus held positions dependent on their demonstrated capabilities, reaching the top echelons of the government with some even rising to the position of wazir, the equivalent of the administrative head of the central government. The lot of the common people hardly altered with the change in the ruling hierarchy from Hindu king to a Muslim sultan. This was so because the newly installed Muslim ruler did not have the administrative depth, knowledge, capacity or the inclination to be fully intrusive at the rural village level of administration. However, even though the lower level administration was left untouched in the hands of the Hindu officials, there were subtle changes that manifested over a period of time that resulted in the power, influence and prestige of the Hindu elite being gradually eroded and diminished at the local level.

Military Vicissitudes

There has been, and continues to be, a great deal of debate regarding the defeat of Hindu armies by the numerically inferior invading Islamic armies. This was true of even the great Vijayanagar Empire at the height of its power, when the combined armies of the Deccan Shahi kingdoms were able to defeat a numerically superior Hindu army. (In this case, the 'Hindu' army also consisted of Muslim troops who were serving Vijayanagar as mercenary forces and also as citizen soldiers.) Over the years of debate, a number of theories have been put forward to describe this inexplicable turn of events. Some of them could be considered as contributory factors but some have to be dismissed as fanciful thoughts, purely aimed at myth-building.

The first contributory factor is the superiority of the Muslim cavalry, which has been alluded to earlier in this narrative. Without doubt, the invading Muslim armies depended on their cavalry to make rapid manoeuvres the centre-piece of their battle tactics. However, the superiority of their cavalry being the prime reason for their success is not entirely true since there was no difference in the quality of the horses and men that came with the invaders and those that served in the local cavalry. In fact Vijayanagar had inducted Muslim cavalry into their military forces and yet fared no better against the Muslim cavalry of the Shahi kingdoms. Therefore, there must have been some other factors that made the invading armies more efficient. The second factor is perhaps more important in its contribution to Islamic victories and at times could have been decisive in determining the outcome of crucial battles and at critical stages in combat. This was the fighting spirit of the army as a whole which is the product of a number of elements interacting with each other. The invading armies maintained their fighting spirit at a very high level through the direct involvement of their commanders and the princes of the royal house in the day-to-day functioning of the army. Further, the personal stature of the princes depended on their valour and bravery in battle, which automatically made them a bit more aggressive and brave in the face of actual danger. These circumstances made a positive difference to the performance of the invading Muslim armies.

The third factor was that the Muslim armies were much more disciplined and the rules that made the military a fighting entity were better enforced within the force, making them a more cohesive entity. The enforcement of discipline was easier because of the homogeneity of the force and the underlying religious fervour that spread across the rank and file of Muslim armies. This factor is intangible and made the Muslim soldiers more ferocious in battle and less inclined to be kind and forgiving. In addition, the invading armies knew that they had nowhere to flee to in case of a defeat and therefore, the options were stark—victory or death. In comparison, the Hindu armies, especially the infantry, were large in numbers but not trained well. The fourth factor was that the Hindu armies were more akin to mobs with hardly any specialised military training and therefore prone to disintegrating at the slightest pressure being applied on them in battle. Essentially, the debate regarding the one-sided success of Muslim armies when pitted against the local Indian forces have always been about four indefinable factors—the competence of the cavalry, the fighting spirit of the opposing forces, the numerical comparison and the discipline of the force as a whole.

Repeated defeats are bound to have created a cumulative demoralising effect on the Hindu armies and they often went into battle expecting to be defeated. In this thought process, the battle and warfighting became mere formalities paving the way towards eventual defeat. The inevitability of defeat seemed to have pervaded the senses of the Hindu armies from the invasions of Mahmud of Ghazni. Both the Hindu and Islamic armies were far from cohesive units. However, the Muslim forces made up for the lack of cohesion through tight discipline that was enforced rigidly. The Islamic armies were on one end of the spectrum, where religious fervour overcame any other divisive forces within the army, integrating them through a sense of religious brotherhood. The Indian forces lacked not only discipline but also did not possess any integrating spirit, so essential for success in hard-fought battles. No emotional bond integrated them to the king and his commanders and therefore unity was the first casualty when a standing Hindu army went into battle. The caste differences further divided the Hindu army. All these disparate factors joined together to create a situation where the Indian forces did not possess even a slight amount of group discipline. Winning battles with such forces was an impossible task.

The Hindu Disconnect

The Hindu armies could not connect the result of battle directly to its impact on the kingdom. Victory or loss in battle had consequences only for the king and what happened to the king hardly ever made a difference to the common people. What happened to the State, the kingdom, did not play an important role in the thinking process of the common Hindu people. In reality, nothing roused the Hindu to fight, to put his life on the line, since race, tribe, caste, sect and even religion divided them rather than uniting them. The Hindus lived in the villages scattered across the rural landscape and the invading Turko-Afghans confined themselves to the urban areas after their battlefield victories. The king/sultan had no direct input into the rural regions and their rule was limited to the important towns and population centres. The same system had prevailed during the Hindu rule and therefore the common people remained unconcerned about the religious affinity of their rulers. This apathy of the commoner to who ruled them was carefully exploited by the invading Muslim rulers. They ensured that there was no popular revolt against them, which would have been catastrophic if it happened.

The above explanation however should not be taken to mean that the Hindus lacked in bravery and valour. The individual valour of the Hindu soldier and commander alike was not a shade lesser than that displayed by the Turko-Afghan invaders. Hindu valour was second to none in the medieval world. However, the peculiar philosophy of the Hindus that exhorted them to do their duty without consideration of the return permeated into the warfighting ethos. Over millennia the warfighting ethos of the Hindu soldier was attuned to ensuring individual valour and extreme bravery, laced with an incorruptible sense of honour, without the necessity to achieve overall victory for the kingdom ever influencing battlefield decisions.

Living within this disconnected kingdoms, the Hindus were completely unaware of the peculiar and unique features of the Turko-Afghan invasion, which was totally unlike any of the previous invasions of the sub-continent. This invasion was intent on displacing the existing political system and replacing it with one that was completely alien to the prevailing ethos of the sub-continent. It involved the superimposition of a different, unfamiliar and foreign culture and religion over the local and centuries-old religion and the civilisation that it had spawned. Since there was no awareness of the direction the new invading victors were about to take, there was no unified opposition put up by the Hindu kingdoms.

Even as kingdom after kingdom was being subjugated and destroyed, Hindu kings continued their petty squabbles and betrayals. It was common to find that minor Indian chieftains were in the lead in commanding Turkish forces to betray their own neighbours or even their own king. In a very broad manner, it could be surmised that by the medieval times, the sub-continent had reached a stage of decay that any external intrusion would have succeeded. It just happened that this time the invasion that came to the gates of the sub-continent was by a more rigid and unrelenting force, strengthened by an inner fibre provided by a religion that did not believe in tolerance. It was inevitable that the societal environment would be changed, by force and not through assimilation, as in earlier cases.

Chapter 33

THE SOCIAL ENVIRONMENT

Medieval chroniclers, even those who had not visited the sub-continent, described India in poetic fantasy, extolling its wealth, opulence, abundance and beauty. India was placed at par with all other exemplary places and then raised a bar above, even being described by some as the heaven on earth. All medieval mention of India exaggerated not only its wealth but also its importance in the known world and its unparalleled beauty. This trend continued well into the pre-modern world. The descriptions were such that even Indians, who should have known better, became prone to believing the descriptions and myths that abounded. The arrival of the Europeans in sufficient numbers, and not the few travellers who came in a dribble before the sea-route was established between Europe and India, started the trend of providing believable and realistic reports. Even so, there were some fanciful reports and descriptions of India that were widely circulated in Europe and other places.

These exaggerated reports fired the imagination and avarice of the medieval Central Asian nobility who believed that India was a country fit to be raided since it was so rich—proverbially 'ripe for the plucking'. The other side of the coin was the belief that the sub-continent, while rich and susceptible to being raided, was not a country to be conquered and settled. This belief emanated from the conviction that the purity of their race would be diluted by interaction with the kafirs, the non-believers, who inhabited the sub-continent; and that in turn this dilution of the core qualities leading to the ultimate degeneration of the race and that their strength and valour would diminish over the generations. The tinge of self-proclaimed racial superiority is clearly visible in these recorded perceptions. The Islamic Turko-Afghan disdain for the Hindus of India is very evident in this demonstrated attitude.

There is a plethora of accounts, reports and travel writings by medieval Muslim chroniclers that provide detailed and minute information of the political aspects and activities within the sub-continent. They also provide accurate analysis of the impact and influence of external invasions and interference in the political developments in medieval India. However, detailed as these reports are, they provide almost no information about the society of the sub-continent, especially the rural areas and mofussil towns in which the majority of the common people lived. A modern-day historian is left with very limited information regarding the way of life and day-to-day struggles of the people of the land. Even the more fastidious European travellers give but few random sketches of places and people that only partially alleviates the dearth of information regarding such matters.

Settlements

By early 13th century, Delhi had becom the centre of all political activity in North India with the establishment of the Delhi Sultanate. (For details of the political activity of this period, see Volume V *The Delhi Sultanate*, in this series.) In South India, Vijayanagar was the most prominent of the cities, while in the Deccan Plateau, Devagiri in the north, built by the Yadava dynasty in the 12th century and renamed Daulatabad by the Muslim invaders, was considered the urban centre. Daulatabad has been described in contemporary reports as rivalling Delhi itself in splendour. Further, Daulatabad Fort was considered impregnable and therefore an asset to possess on the borders of one's kingdom. Some of the reports describe few other towns, such as Gwalior, but the rest of the sub-continent remains shrouded in a lack of information, as far as a later-day historic chronicler is concerned.

Between the late Classical Period and the establishment of the Delhi Sultanate, the Indian economy was in steep decline and accordingly the great urban centres of the ancient times had gradually been hollowed out. Even during the Delhi Sultanate period, the revival of the economy and the towns were minimal. The improvements did not amount to a strong revitalisation of the economy and neither did it bring about a renaissance of decayed urban centres.

Medieval Indian villages were normally secluded settlements of a few huts in the forest and were almost unreachable. These collection of huts were for the most part temporary, since a constant population shift in the perennial search for agricultural land was a common reality. Babur, the first Mughal king, notes in his 16th century autobiography that the villages, and even towns of Hindustan could be depopulated and also set up 'in moments'. The temporary nature of settlements is evident from this comment. The fundamental fact is that medieval India did not have permanency of population centres. The society and the way it was set up and governed varied from region to region, making India's vastness and diversity clearly visible even in medieval times. Further, it is clear that Indian villagers led isolated, secluded and self-contained lives.

Travel

Travel within the sub-continent also varied with the regions. The best roads were found in the Gangetic Plain with both the east-west and north-south arteries passing through Delhi. The arterial roads into the Deccan and the South were also equally travelable and were used as the basic trade routes. The ancient and traditional practice of planting shady fruit trees along the roads for the assistance of the traveller was continued well into medieval times. The Ganga-Yamuna river system was used as a primary artery for the transportation of goods and long distance travel in medieval times had become commonplace. Similarly, the rivers of the Peninsula were also used for travel and transportation, although they were not inter-connected and did not form a grid covering the entire region. Travel along the arterial roads was well-organised and devoid of any unusual hazards.

As regulated and relatively easy as was the travel across the main arteries, travel into the interior, outside the main roads, was equally hazardous. Roads were ill-maintained, there was a constant threat from highwaymen and shelter was almost non-existent. Thieves operated even close to urban centres and their audacity or civility varied with the strength or weakness of the government then in power. Even in the case of interior travel, the safety of the wayfarer varied from one region to another. Essentially, the picture that emerges is that other than for the major roads, the vast country remained trackless in a majority of the regions. For reasons of safety and security, travel was almost always undertaken in large groups. Nevertheless long distance travel, especially on pilgrimages was a common practice in medieval India. The mode of transportation also varied regionally—from using horses or ox-carts to walking. Obviously, the pace of travel was slow in medieval India.

The Evolving Society – Co-existing while Drawing Apart

Over millennia, diverse races and ethnicities flowed into India through the passes in the Hindu Kush Mountains and made the sub-continent their homeland. They assimilated with the local population, both the hosts and the foreigners drew from each other's customs, traditions and even religious practices to create a holistic and mostly harmonious society. Acrimony between the 'outsiders' and the local community was minimal and most often settled amicably. One of the primary reasons for this fairly agreeable and good-humoured attitude towards each other was the fact that the religious practices of both the parties were flexible and open to adaption. Importantly, there was no critical analysis of each other's practices nor did they indulge in downgrading the other as inferior.

The arrival of the Turko-Afghans into the sub-continent in medieval times, which was the last of the major people movement into India, changed this congenial attitude between races and religions that were coming together, at times under duress. While Hinduism continued to maintain its flexible attitude towards external aggression and intervention, the new invasion was spearheaded by the followers of one of the most rigid religions to emerge from the Middle-East. This latest people migration, brought about through military invasion, changed the socio-cultural profile of the sub-continent unlike other earlier invasions. Although the later rule by the British also made a similar impact, the coming of the English people cannot be equated to a migration. They never had any intention of making India their homeland and the socio-cultural impact was mush lesser than the earlier Islamic invasion.

The Social Environment

All the previous entrants into the sub-continent had, over time, merged with the existing Indian society in a mutually beneficial manner. The outsiders had adopted the Indian religion, social customs, languages and even values, becoming an indivisible part of India, merging with the local people and creating a ready mix. Both the outsiders and the local people were enriched in this process. The Turko-Afghans were, culturally and religiously, antithetical to the all-encompassing Hindu ethos and therefore had no tendency to mix and merge.

The Hindu religion was polytheistic and was capable of adapting and absorbing anything that it encountered by way of concepts, philosophy and even physical practices. It was capable of reaching far back into the recesses of its collective memory to find a parallel to a recent event and then modifying the historical antecedent to suit the current purpose. This fantastic and inherent flexibility was, paradoxically, the creation of the vast diversity of the Hindus and the numerous divisions that collectively bound the religion together. Islam on the other hand was monotheistic, worshiping only one God and therefore extremely cohesive. It had only one set of beliefs and practices and propounded a uniformly egalitarian society, whereas the Hindu society was multi-layered through the insistence on birth conferred status and positions.

Similarly, the attitude of the Hindus and Muslims towards each other was also poles apart. The Hindus viewed the Muslims with an extremely tolerant attitude, similar to how the different castes in the Hindu society viewed and interacted with each other. The Hindus had no objection to the Muslims observing their religious beliefs and practices, as long as no inter-mixing took place between the two religious communities. Although the Hindus had absolutely no objection to serving under Muslim officers, they did not interact socially with their Muslim colleagues. The high-caste Hindus, who were involved in dealing directly with the conquering Muslims equated the people of the Islamic faith with the untouchables of their own religion. Muslims, on the other hand, had no prejudices based on birth, at least theoretically. In their religion, even the lowest 'caste', on conversion to Islam would be treated at par and as an equal to everyone else. Personal status and position was a function of individual ability and achievement and nothing else influenced the rise of an individual to higher levels of society—in effect, at least in theory, Islam was a practising meritocracy. A person from the lowest rung of the Hindu society, after conversion to Islam could aspire to rise to the highest rung in Muslim society. Whether such promotions actually took place or not is an irrelevant detail in this discussion of the underlying philosophies of the two religions.

Since these differences were fundamental in nature and irreconcilable, the two communities had only very limited socio-cultural interaction with each other. This stand-off continues despite centuries of co-existence in the Indian sub-continent. In medieval India, Hindus and Muslims lived separately—the Muslims were concentrated in the towns where they served the government and the Hindus were content to populate the villages, continuing to be farmers and landlords and pursuing other occupations focused on villages. When the Hindus gradually moved to the towns in order to work in the bureaucracy, they lived in independent wards or suburbs that were separate; creating in effect, an extension of the original Hindu town that had always been segregated according to the castes. The minority of Muslims who moved to the rural areas, normally created their own villages independent of the existing Hindu ones. It is true that there was some amount of interaction and mutual influence, as it is bound to happen when human beings are forced to share the same land. However, such interactions remained at the superficial level such as adoption of Islamic dresses by the Hindus and at the mystic level of religious practices. The communities co-existed but did not interact in a manner that would have made assimilation necessary and possible. The reason lay with both the religions—which were truly inimical to each other at the fundamental philosophical level.

Muslim Rulers

Irrespective of whether a Muslim ruler was a celebrated king/sultan controlling a vast empire, or whether he was a small-time chieftain in-charge of a minor taraf or district, the attitude of the ruler towards the Hindus was generally one of tolerance. This attitude was assumed for purely pragmatic reasons. In order to continue to garner the support of the Muslim soldiers and the influential religious teachers who accompanied the invading armies, the leadership—sultan, noble, military commander—had to demonstrate that they were devout followers of the Islamic faith. The sultans clearly understood that in their role as devout Muslims, they were expected to vigorously suppress Hinduism and any other system of religious apostasy that did not adhere to the rigid tenets of Islam. On the other hand, as practical rulers they also understood the need to patronise the Hindus in order to effectively govern the kingdom that had been won through military power and exploits. The conquering Islamic army did not possess sufficiency in numbers or the required local knowledge to organise and govern the captured lands as their fiefdoms or kingdoms.

The practical side of the sultans therefore created a situation wherein the Hindu zamindars, landlords, were made into a group of 'protected non-Muslims', provided they supported the newly entrenched ruling elite. In some cases the zamindars were reluctantly permitted to enter the inner circle of power with the sultan at the centre. These Hindus were permitted to continue to adhere to their own social customs and religious practices, including the questionable practices of sati—the self-immolation of the wife on her husband's funeral pyre—and human sacrifice that were abhorrent to the Islamic creed. This process of excluding designated groups from forced religious conversions was known as the 'zimmi system' and had initially been extended to Jews and Christians in the Middle-East and Central Asia. They were considered 'people of the book' and their Prophets were also accepted as prophets of God in the broader Islamic narrative, and therefore they were 'acceptable'. In the Indian sub-continent, similar privileges was extended to select Hindus who were critical to the administration. The Muslim rulers had no other choice in the matter. The sheer vastness of the country that they were invading and the diverse and numerically vast number of local people made it impossible to even contemplate either conversion or extermination, which were the only two lines of action recommended in the Islamic code of conduct. The Muslim conquerors needed the Hindus to establish their rule in the sub-continent.

Perpetuation of Fallacies

Second-Class Citizens. While it can be verified that selected Hindus were extended privileges and exemptions by the Muslim rulers, the fact remains that all Hindus remained second-class citizens within the medieval Muslim kingdoms. This was so irrespective of the fact that Hindus formed the majority in all the kingdoms, provinces and districts that the Muslims ruled. A number of modern historians have revelled in this situation of the Hindus being relegated to second-class citizen status by stating that it was great for the Hindus to be treated as such, since they were not deprived of citizenship completely—that they were being treated at least as 'citizens', albeit second-class ones in their own country. Further, they go on to add that the discrimination could not have troubled the Hindus 'that much', stating that the Hindus were used to discrimination since their own society was hierarchical in nature.

These are insulting explanations meant by modern historians to create a feeling that the medieval Indian sub-continent lived harmoniously and that the broader society was at peace with itself. All proof point to such assertions being wrong; as soon as Muslim invaders decided to settle down in the sub-continent rather than invade, loot and go back, the broader societal environment became one steeped in reciprocated suspicion. The Hindus and the Muslims were made into two mutually exclusive groups directed by religion and ruler. However, it is true that the discriminatory practices were felt mainly in the towns because the Hindu villages were made to pay a collective tax and thereafter left to their own devices.

Persecution. Some modern historians tend to play down the persecution that was heaped on Hindus. These historians try to portray Islam as a religion of 'peace' and tend to explain the severe persecution of non-Muslims by the victorious invaders as the work of few 'over-zealous and hyper-orthodox Muslim clerics'. This assertion is difficult to believe for two reasons. First, the Muslim clerics functioned under the control of the rulers and did not take such steps unless given royal permission or ordered to do so. Second, the general attitude of Muslim rulers and nobles towards the Hindus was one of scorn and disdain. In such an atmosphere and when religion percolated into every nook and corner of Islamic society, the claim that persecution of the Hindus was the work of a few clerics is far-fetched and difficult to believe. Further, the claim of tolerance flounders in the face of the fact that Islam gives an injunction to all Muslims to attempt the conversion of all non-believers, failing which their lives would be forfeit. It is obvious that the Muslim military leaders and rulers would have wanted to subscribe

The Social Environment

to this exhortation in order to ensure continued loyalty of their troops and the support of the clergy to legitimise their rule.

Conversions. Some modern historians even go to the extent of stating categorically, without giving any statistics or proof, that forced conversions were few and far in between in the sub-continent. The conversions by the sword in India, a process which was fundamental for the establishment of the religion in the Middle-East, is conveniently swept under the carpet. The fact is that in medieval India conversions were common place. When the lower caste Hindus converted, contemporary chroniclers, and especially some later-day historians, report them as 'voluntary', without mentioning the coercion and enticements that preceded and facilitated these conversions. Of course, it is also true that the harsh treatment meted out to the lowers caste Hindus by the Brahmins did not help the Hindu cause. There are also reports that a small number of upper caste Hindus also converted, mainly to gain socio-political and material advantage. These reports also indirectly point to the discrimination heaped on the Hindus, which enticed upper caste Hindus to forgo their religious beliefs. Further, the conversion of some of the trading class to take advantage of the preferential treatment given to Muslims in trade practices also confirm the discrimination that was practised.

Destruction. Even the modern historians who try at all times to prove the tolerant nature of Muslim rulers and nobility agree and accept that several instances of mass slaughter of Hindu men, women and children did take place in medieval India. They also confirm the wanton destruction of Hindu temples, reported and recorded with unbridled glee by contemporary Muslim chroniclers. Modern apologist-historians have attempted to dilute the vehemence of even these factual reports by Muslim writers of the time. They have attempted to play down the reports by stating that they were written by overzealous chroniclers trying to gain royal favour by exaggerating and eulogising the destruction and slaughter. These historians believe that the reports were mechanisms to emphasise the king's prowess and commitment to Islamic ideals.

Treating proven reality with 'kid gloves' and attempting to smoothen the aberrations and inherent violence that inevitably accompanied medieval military conquests does not serve any purpose in a historic analysis, if the analysis is meant to be unbiased. If anything, such attempts only tend to distort history and warp modern understanding of the reasons, motives, logic and judgements of individuals, and the collective society, which went into the creation of what is seen today.

Irrespective of the many attempts at white-washing the gruesome details of the Islamic invasion of the sub-continent, the fact remains that almost all Muslim rulers in medieval India were overtly religious and virulently anti-Hindu. They may not have been fanatics, but needed to display their anti-kafir antecedents to ensure the continued support of the powerful religious contingent that accompanied all Islamic armies. Islam traditionally was, and continues to be, an aggressive and proselytising religion. It is by nature and practice completely intolerant of any contrary doctrine and non-believers. No amount of attempts at playing down this aspect of the religion will make it into one that is tolerant and compassionate towards people of other faiths—every attempt to do so, whether by re-analysing history or providing explanations to contemporary events today, will ring hollow. The medieval Muslim rulers who were trying to establish their kingdoms in India were practical military commanders, pragmatic enough to realise the futility of trying to exterminate all the non-believers and particularly aware of the need to tolerate the Hindus in order to put a functioning practical administrative system in place. The Hindus survived largely because of their numbers and perceived usefulness.

Intelligentsia – The Contrast

Both the invading Muslims and the local Hindus boasted of a group of people who were considered the intelligentsia—a class of educated people engaged in the complex mental process that critique, guide and lead the development of the religious discourse, culture and politics of their society.

In the case of the Muslims and the Hindus, the two groups were the complete antithesis of each other—the Muslim intelligentsia were totally and actively hostile to the Hindus; and in contrast, the Hindu intelligentsia were passive and ambivalent towards the Muslims, the new religion, and efforts to establish a religion-based central rule.

The Hindu intelligentsia's reflexive and pliable attitude was so pervasive that there is not even a mention of the Turko-Afghan conquest of most of the sub-continent in any of the Sanskrit texts of the medieval times. This attitude of being distanced from reality could be attributed, to some extent, the 'spiritual' outlook amongst the Hindus, especially the intelligentsia, that viewed life in a fatalistic and cyclic manner—a belief that 'what is to happen, will happen', which can be noticed even today in India. This detached attitude further entrenched an already apathetic attitude to their circumstances, which was considered an individual or society's God-given status in life.

This fatalistic attitude was a major contributory factor that led to a relatively small group of Turko-Afghans ruling over a majority Hindu population for several centuries.

The Muslim Society in the Sub-continent

By Islamic traditions, the Muslim society was ideally an extended brotherhood, with a person's status determined by individual ability and competence, with the society having only functional divisions. This is the Islamic ideal—an Utopia. The reality of the Muslim society in India was something completely different. The Muslims were divided based on race, clan and sect that in turn decided an individual's social status. The entire society itself was a layered hierarchy. The Sayyids, considered to be the direct descendants of the Prophet Muhammad's lineage, held birth-determined high caste within the Islamic society anywhere in the world. This system was enforced irrespective of the individual merit of a Sayyid, much like the Brahmins of Hinduism. In India, next to the Sayyids came the foreigners—Persians, Arabs, Turks, Afghans—in that pecking order, who also formed the upper crust of Muslim society. They were followed by the upper class Hindus who converted to Islam, and the lowest in the totem pole were the lower caste Hindu converts.

The divisions of status and class did not end in the broad segregations mentioned above, it percolated into each of the sub-groups. Amongst the foreign migrant Muslims, the older or early migrants and their offspring were looked down upon, with the third or fourth generation almost completely losing their privileged 'foreign' position in society. The later a migrant had entered the sub-continent, the higher in society they were. The class divisions, which in the case of Hindu converts were a manifestation of their previous Hindu castes, were rigidly enforced and determined the social status of an individual in the Indian Muslim society. Families from the same class intermingled and marriages were arranged within the same class. The egalitarian ideal of a classless society was purely a theoretical exercise, at least in the sub-continental Muslim society.

Islam did not have any ordained priests, but had religious leaders—Imams—who led the congressional prayers and were extremely influential in society. The Muslim aristocracy in medieval India were almost all in royal service, their status being determined by the position an individual held in court. All of them led extravagant and profligate life styles, most often in complete debt, since they lived off state-provided estates that were not hereditary, at least in the beginning of Islamic rule in the sub-continent. This situation prompted the nobles to live beyond their immediate means since their wealth was ephemeral and they were, as families, expendable. Information is available in plenty about the somewhat debauched lifestyle of the nobility, but unfortunately there is no elaboration in any of the reports regarding the lives of the common people, both Muslim and Hindu.

While there were few clearly noticeable differences between followers of the two religions in social norms and practices, in the area of marriage there were similarities. While Muslim men were permitted four wives at the same time, all of whom could be divorced at will by the husband, polygamy was accepted among the Hindus. Although Hindu divorce proceedings were cumbersome, effectively there was very little difference between the two religions in the sphere of marriage and legitimacy of procreation. The theological argument that the Muslim system was a better arrangement does not stand up to scrutiny and really cannot be logically justified. However, the Hindu practice of committing ritual suicide—on permanent disability, old age and on widowhood (the practice of sati)—was considered a cardinal sin in Muslim eyes and could not be reconciled. The only interaction between the two religiously divided communities remained the adaptation of each other's dresses to cater for the weather and also the sensibilities of the other community.

Medieval Demography

The Indian sub-continent was relatively densely populated even during medieval times.

> '...the population profile of India was highly complex, because of the racial, linguistic, social, cultural, religious and sectarian diversity of Indians, resulting from the socio-cultural-religious developments within the country, as well as from the migration of very many different races into India over millennia.'
>
> Abraham Eraly,
> *The Age of Wrath*, p.331.

During medieval times, the inward migration continued unabated as the Turko-Afghan rulers actively encouraged Muslims from the Central Asian regions to migrate to the sub-continent in order to boost Muslim numbers and also to strengthen the army, which was the mainstay of their often tenuous hold on power. The Muslim rulers suffered from a lack of belief in the loyalty of local recruits into the army, often with sufficient reason. This invitation and the preferential treatment meted out to them by the Muslim rulers in India suited the restive Central Asians well, especially since they were under the constant threat of Mongol invasions from their north and east.

The Hindu society at this time was already polymorphic in nature and therefore had become highly tolerant of the different practices of other religions, sects and cults as long as they did not interfere with the fundamental rites of the Hindu religion. The use of the term 'tolerance' in this context can be debated. Was the Hindu religion being tolerant or was it displaying a kind of indifference to other religions and their practices? It could be surmised that it was indifference, bordering on a self-induced superiority complex, since Hindu tolerance of other religions was one of non-interference and non-interaction and not one of deliberate and calculated actions to ensure an acceptable social exclusion. This assumption is strengthened by the fact that even within Hinduism, the deliberate caste separations did not normally yield to any kind of oppression, but only to a fatalistic acceptance of the prevailing circumstances.

The fact remains that before the advent of the Turko-Afghan Muslim invasion, the traditional Hindu society was exceptionally peaceful and harmonious. Each individual was accepting of his birth-given status and station in life without demur, leading to a social cohesion that was not seen anywhere else in the world. The foreigners who dissected the Hindu society in the firm belief that there would be a simmering underbelly of discontent in what they believed to be an inequitable caste-ridden society, was aghast at the philosophy of Hinduism and the stoic acceptance of its adherents to a deep philosophical approach to life. The challenges within Hinduism started with these foreigners stocking the apparent divisions that existed from their viewpoint and opposition to what they perceived as injustice, without having even superficial knowledge of the deep philosophical foundations of the religion.

Chapter 34

ECONOMY, TRADE AND COMMERCE

By the end of the first millennium C. E., India had slid into somnolence, brought about by a sort of arrogant superiority complex that led to ignoring developments outside its immediate sphere of interest. India and its once thriving civilisation was sliding from the dusk of arrested development into what can only be called the medieval dark ages. The cultural effervescence, economic prosperity and visionary sovereignty that had been the hallmark of a flourishing Indian sub-continent that had assisted it in informally assuming the leadership of civilisational achievements had risen to opulent glory that had then gradually receded to the background, giving way to decadence, decay and progressively reducing the sub-continent to irrelevance. Although the sub-continent continued to be resource-rich and therefore a prime target for external aggression, India's commercial enterprise had collapsed and it had retreated into a state of deep slumber, almost comatose, indulging in desultory activities of little import. India's civilisational collapse was evident from all relative aspects of development.

The Domestic Economic Situation

Like all medieval societies, there was a great deal of economic disparities visible in India also—the nobles were rich beyond comparison and lived lives of extreme opulence and luxury whereas the common people existed at the edge of abject poverty. Since there was a constant risk of the common people slipping into real poverty at any given time, they lived frugally, consciously saving for the proverbial rainy day and almost always tending to hoard their limited wealth. The rulers of medieval India, both Hindu kings and Muslim sultans, were all warlords and therefore natural predators. They had no interest in either guaranteeing or creating a system that catered for the welfare of the people. The corollary to this situation was that by the same token, the common people did not identify with a king or sultan and did not care when a king was defeated in battle, deposed or killed. Essentially there was a total emotional disconnect between the ruler and the ruled.

The economic disparity between the ruling elite and the common people, combined with this emotional disconnect meant that there were no people's rebellions in India. The people did not care whether they were ruled by a local king or by a foreigner since their lot did not fluctuate, diverge or improve in either case. The poverty of the common man was such that although he lived at the subsistence level, he did not starve, had adequate shelter and a modicum of security.

Medieval India lived in the villages, where life remained the same—unchanged over the centuries. India had by then been looted beyond belief, but still abounded in natural resources. The enormous horde of natural resources led to greatly exaggerated reports of the wealth in the sub-continent that in turn invited spirited adventurers to attempt repeated invasions, even when the initial attempts were less than successful. This romantic view of India started to change only with the arrival of the early European travellers who reported the stark reality of poverty in the Indian villages and rural population on the whole. They tended to compare the 'static' medieval India with the 'progressive' Europe. In an almost about-face, the reports now highlighted the abject poverty of rural India and the common people, even exaggerating it most of the time.

The fact remained that medieval India continued to be fabulously rich. The issue was that most of the wealth was held by a small percentage of the ruling class and the left-over was only just sufficient to keep the common people out of complete poverty but not to provide them with any luxuries or ease of living. The visible disparity between the unfathomable, and at times vulgar, wealth and luxury enjoyed by the ruling elite and the mundane, almost dreary life of the common people was shocking for an external Western observer to witness. Therefore, they tended to exaggerate this aspect of medieval India, glossing over the fact that this disparity in wealth distribution was a common feature in all medieval societies across the world—the life of the underclass was definitely dismal on a global scale. The early Europeans on the scene in India was very aware of the concentration of wealth in few hands and the widespread poverty, but also realised that the actual wealth of the sub-continent lay in its vast and as yet unexploited natural resources. Further, they were shrewd enough to also realise that the endemic and widespread poverty of the common people made invasion and conquest easy to achieve. The domestic economic situation in India was ripe for the picking.

Agriculture

Agriculture was rain-fed and therefore totally dependent on the monsoon rains across the entire sub-continent, although the methods of cultivation varied across the region. The Peninsula was both arid and verdant with fertile patches interspersed with non-cultivable areas. The irrigation system was primeval and its efficiency improved only with the Turkish influence that came with the invading Muslim armies. The building of water tanks was a tradition across the sub-continent but it was in the Deccan that these structures took on a more widespread usage. These tanks were normally constructed by damming a minor tributary stream and then further flooding the dammed part with a system of pipes and canals that brought water from either a nearby lake or by making it a catchment for rain water. In the Deccan, great reservoirs were built by powerful kings both to assist the people and also to demonstrate the power and status of the king. There are reports that such a reservoir existed in the great kingdom of Vijayanagar.

Even though some kings attempted to create rudimentary irrigation systems, direct support for agriculture in the Deccan was sporadic at best. Farming was dominated by the Hindus who continued to live in the villages and cultivated small holdings. Landlords owned larger holdings that they sublet for farming or farmed the land through the employment of hired labour. It was also customary for temples to own large tracts of land which were rented out with the funds so obtained being normally used to support farmers through the provision of loans and other assistance in times of need.

Reliance on agriculture also directly influenced the movement of people and at times led to mass migrations. Examples are the movement of farmers from the dry areas of Karnataka to the more fertile Cauvery valley and the movement of Telugu farmers from the arid Deccan to the Tamil country.

Urban Trade and Commerce

Between the Classical Age and the medieval era, there was a general collapse of commercial activity across the sub-continent. The urban prosperity so obvious in ancient India had completely vanished. Textile production, which was one of the major industries of the sub-continent, had also suffered a downturn. However, the Turko-Afghan invasion brought about a gradual revival of the industry and the introduction of the spinning wheel started to speed up production. Thereafter, cloth-weaving and textile production dominated the industrial activities in India. There was also a revival of metal works, especially for the manufacture of military equipment. Majority of these equipment were produced in state-run industrial works, a peculiar development in the Deccan that subsequently percolated to North India. Over a period of time Indian exports brought the craftsmen to prominence and their skills were appreciated and held in high esteem in Central Asia.

After the collapse and disintegration of Empires and the end of the Classical Age, internal trade had almost completely collapsed and the economy had been fully ruralised. The establishment of the Delhi Sultanate started a slow process of revival, which was accelerated slightly by the creation of the Bahmani and Deccan Shahi kingdoms in the Peninsula. One of the direct influences in uplifting the domestic economy was the demand for luxury goods and items, created by the newly established nobility, who had disposable incomes that could not be invested in any other enterprise. The large estates which generated the extraordinary incomes of the nobility were a direct gift from the king and normally not hereditary family holdings. This situation made most of the noblemen spendthrifts in a class by themselves. The advantage to the economy was only a by-product of a slightly skewed system.

The Turko-Afghan empire building efforts were based on political integration and the creation of large centrally controlled kingdoms, which in turn necessitated integration of the economy. Centrally integrated economies tend to coalesce around towns and also to the creation of new urban centres, which would further enhance domestic trade and commercial activities. However, the trade pattern in both North India and the Peninsula remained within the traditional concepts and therefore did not bring about any marked societal changes.

One of the positive impacts of the Islamic conquest in medieval times is the fact that it facilitated the economic recovery of a moribund economy across the sub-continent. First, the consolidation of political and territorial integrity of the kingdoms, relative to the previous several centuries, which brought about relative stability made economic recovery an easier process. Second, the king invariably supported the traders since they brought about economic prosperity to the general public that in turn permitted the entrenchment of the king's preeminent position. This created a cycle of self-perpetuating mutual support between the traders and the king. Since royal support for trade was visible and steadfast, the affluent class of Muslim ruling gentry also provided patronage for trade and commerce, further enhancing trade possibilities. Trade also doubled as a tax revenue source for the kingdom that could not be ignored by any king. There were sufficient number of reasons for the kings to support the activities of the traders and be partial to them.

The increasing wealth of the traders also made them an important group, leading to their gradually growing involvement in the political activities in the Peninsula. An economically strong trader even played the role of a king-maker for some time in the Pandya kingdom. The premium placed on the status of traders in the broader community can be understood from this example.

Commercial taxation policies varied between the different kingdoms and at times even between successive rulers of the same dynasty within the same kingdom. Even so, a number of kings attempted with varying levels of success, to establish fair trade, especially in the sale of essential commodities. The success or failure of these attempts were a direct demonstration of the strength or weakness of the king's hold on power. In medieval Deccan, as elsewhere in the sub-continent, all commercial or profit-creating activity was taxed by the king. The logic for this was the ingenious explanation that since all activities were undertaken at the pleasure of the king, and depended on his protection for its success, he was entitled to his share of the profits and transactions. Even under these circumstances, in medieval India commercial taxation was much lesser than agricultural tax, which was the major source of revenue for most kingdoms. The kings normally protected the traders since they were a direct source of immediate wealth for the king and indirectly for the kingdom as a whole itself.

Maritime Trade in the Peninsula

Traditionally, the peninsular kingdoms had been part of the ancient Indian Ocean maritime trade, particularly with South-East Asia and China. This trade was carried out by Indians, Arabs, Chinese and South-Eastern Asians. However, the Arabs tended to dominate the Arabian Sea and the Indians had been forced to withdraw from that region and concentrate on trade with China and the South-East Asian kingdoms. In this compromise realignment, the Indians started to dominate the Malacca region—the influence of Peninsular India can be seen in the region even today.

The Arabs were extremely active and competitive as traders but the commercial activity did not involve any military activity. This was the case before the arrival of the Western powers into the Arabian Sea, throughout the ancient trade with Greece and Rome, then with the nomadic Arabs and subsequently with the Arab Muslims after Islam had become embedded in the Middle-East. The Peninsular kings—uniformly both Muslim and Hindu rulers—patronised the traders, particularly the Arabs, for two reasons. One, they contributed to the prosperity of the kingdom; and two, they were the primary source for the supply of Arabian horses to the Peninsula. Since all the rulers were practising warlords, horses were in perennial demand in the Peninsula and very highly valued.

This status quo, of understanding the importance of trade and also in conducting these activities within customary rules and in a spirit of peaceful competition, was an age-old tradition in the Arabian Sea and Indian Ocean. The recourse to military power and the use of force to enhance trade was introduced to the region only after Vasco da Gama entered the Arabian Sea with a crew of brigands and pirates in the late 15th century. The Portuguese attempted to declare the Arabian Sea and the Indian Ocean their sovereign territory and enforce their claim through acts of piracy and military action against the ruling house

Economy, Trade and Commerce

of Calicut, the Zamorins (Samuthiripad). They managed to establish a hegemony, which lasted nearly a century until it was questioned and demolished by other Western powers. The incessant wars for control, initiated and instigated by Western powers, also gradually brought down the once supreme Zamorin of Calicut to the level of a local chieftain.

By the 16th century, the peninsular ports had become the most prominent trading centres in the sub-continent, gradually making maritime trade replace the land-route-centred trade through the north-western passes that had so far been the primary entry ports into India. The western coast of the peninisula—from Kerala to Gujarat—boasted a number of natural ports that supported an explosion of trade and commercial activities. In almost all foreign travelogues of the period, Kollam (Quilon) and Kozhikode (Calicut) in Kerala and Khambat in Gujarat are mentioned as being great port cities, almost beyond comparison in their trading grandeur. Similarly, the entire Coromandal coast was a hive of trading activity with commerce reaching hitherto unknown levels of prosperity. The sub-continent exported spices like pepper, cloves, and ginger; other natural products such as sandalwood, sugar, rice and saffron; precious stones and particularly beautiful seed pearls; and fine cotton and fabrics. The fabrics were manufactured all over the sub-continent but the special ones that were made in Bengal were particularly sought after.

The exports far outweighed the imports with horses being the most expensive import item. There were other minor items of dubious value brought in from both the Arab lands as well as China. The demand for these so-called luxury items increased as the lifestyle of the kings and nobles changed and vulgar displays of wealth became a sign of status and power. A variety of ships visited the ports to trade, with the Chinese junks being the largest, followed by Indian ships. The Chinese junks were large enough to carry a crew of a 1000 men—600 sailors and 400 soldiers. The European ships were the smallest, but were more robustly built and could withstand much more punishment in a battle than the relatively fragile Chinese junks. The Asian ships, including the Indian ones, could not go into the open seas in rough weather, something that was almost second nature to European ships that were manufactured to venture into faraway shores in uncertain sea conditions.

The European ships were not only hardier than the other ships, but always carried artillery that proved to be more effective than any of their possible adversaries. The superiority of their shipborne artillery was one of the main reasons for the eventual domination of the Arabian Sea and Indian Ocean by the European nations. This domination was one of the fundamental cause for the maritime trade off the coast of the Indian sub-continent gradually becoming a European monopoly. The impact of European maritime power on the further political developments in the Indian sub-continent could already be surmised even in a casual analysis of the events that followed immediately after the initial arrival of the Portuguese at the Kerala coast.

Chapter 35

THE CAULDRON BUBBLES...

There is general agreement within the community of historical analysts—including most Western historians who dabble in Indian history—that the Hindu and Islamic civilisations developed with strongly independent traditions. However, they mixed and mingled freely in an unprecedented manner when Islam made its appearance in the Indian sub-continent. The impact that one had on the other has no parallel in world history and is worthy of a lifetime study. By early medieval times, India had withdrawn into itself, content to be inward looking and to plod along an undistinguished path that led to and also demonstrated a plateauing of its once glorious cultural development. This insularity was facilitated by a relatively long period of time when the regular and serious migrations and invasions from the north-west had greatly reduced in number. Perhaps this period of lethargic languish was a harbinger of the cultural and religious collision that was to occur across the sub-continent within a few decades. However, the early medieval period was one in which India was moribund with no visual indication of cultural, aesthetic or literary effervescence. India was in a somnambulant state with absolutely no forward knowledge of the jolting shock that it was about to receive.

India – Devoid of Reality

During the centuries when Islam was gradually encroaching into the sub-continent, both as purely plundering raids and then as territory capturing invasions, India remained unconcerned about these developments. It is highly likely that the ruling elite and the nobles of the land considered the onslaught as 'yet another' invasion by foreigners that would in turn be assimilated into the core Hindu societal ethos, as had traditionally been happening for centuries. The fundamental Hindu resilience had withstood numerous invasions, attacks and raids, finally subsuming the external elements within its own system through a somewhat peaceful process of adaption and assimilation. The completely different attitude of Islam to other societies, cultures and religious beliefs had not become apparent to the complacent Hindu religion and people of India. Therefore, India remained completely unaware of the tremendous power of Islam—both physical and spiritual—that impacted and influenced all aspects of life, equally for the believers as for the non-believers. More important was the fact that the challenge of Islam came at a time when the once-jubilant Hindu culture was at its jaded worst.

India was immersed in the belief that its ancient knowledge and wisdom made the Indian-Hindu culture superior to all others and considered any contact with a foreign civilisation or culture to be degrading and unnecessary. This conceited attitude was bound to get a tremendous shock when it came into contact with the rigid and strong beliefs of the Islamic civilisation. The Hindu culture that faced the Islamic offensive in the sub-continent was one that was almost at the end of its decline, most of it brought about by its own arrogance. There are any number of accounts explaining the Indian cultural arrogance that made even the common people vain and full of disdain for all external influences, however pertinent they may have been to the place and time.

It is true that during the medieval times, there was a downturn in innovation and forward looking conceptual thinking across the world. There was also a decline in learned debate within the intellectual elite of the world. However, by late 12th century, the world was witnessing a renewed push towards greater creativity in all fields of human endeavour—scientific, cultural, philosophical and aesthetic. India was absent from this 'renaissance' of thought and creativity. It continued to live, in splendid, overconfident and conceited isolation, completely confident in its past glory as a civilisation where wisdom and great cultural, academic, scientific and philosophical achievements were common place. *[This malaise of believing that the Hindu culture is the acme of achievement, based on ancient glory is prevalent even in modern, independent India.*

This thought process is narcissist and has never assisted any nation transition from ancient glory to modern stability, power and a place in the sun. Unfortunately India has suffered from this syndrome of self-importance and self-delusion for centuries.]

Medieval India lived devoid of reality with a sense of superiority pervading all aspects of its normal existence. The complex was such that the Indian-Hindu culture considered even exemplary ideas and achievements from the outside to be either of no use or to be an improbable lie. India's creative vitality had oozed out of its core. Scholarship, once the cornerstone of the Hindu society, also became rare with a gradual, but discernible, decline in creativity. The decline took place despite a thriving tradition of patronage from the kings, which says a great deal about the decline in intellectual standards. The medieval Hindu 'intellectual' was reduced to learning old texts by rort without any thought to understanding them in order to advance knowledge. Progressive thinking was lost sight of and over a period of time not considered worth the effort. This attitude had disastrous effects. The old texts, admittedly full of knowledge, were orally transmitted in most cases. With the decline in academic excellence, the transmission of these texts also became corrupted. Knowledge being passed down the generations became flawed with no one available to set it right—there was a continuous and unstoppable decay in the veracity of information. Indian-Hindu knowledge, once the best that was available anywhere in the world, became questionable and untrustworthy.

The pathetic situation of Sanskrit scholarship was not arrived at as the result of some catastrophic incident. It was a gradual, but unchecked, decline brought about and even exacerbated by the mediocrity of the scholars. Sanskrit writing and scholarship had, over a period of time, been made into literary acrobatics, form taking precedence over substance. Some of the writings had become incomprehensible even to some of the so-called scholars themselves. By the time of the Persian arrival on the scene, Sanskrit had proven itself to be the dead language of a dying civilisation.

From a military perspective, medieval Indian kingdoms had become traditionally defensive in nature. Gone were the days of the conquering marches of a Chandragupta Maurya, an Asoka or a Harsha Vardhana, triumphant in battle. Medieval Hindu kings thought that offensive action was abhorrent, even if the battle or war had been forced on them. They were content to protect their geographic borders and did not give any thought even to an immediate future security situation. No Indian king of medieval times stepped out of the confines of his kingdom to attack and annex, turning an essentially defensive mindset into a virtue. *[This non-aggressive stance was the core reason for the easy conquest of the sub-continent by the soldiers of Islam. Hindu kings who defeated the invading armies never followed through the victory to annihilate the adversary, permitting them to regroup and attack again. The once mighty strategic armies of India had been reduced to mere border guards. The exhortations of the Bhagavad Gita to '…wage war with all your might and annihilate the enemy' were completely forgotten. The same attitude pervades modern India, wherein non-aggression is proclaimed with great fanfare as a virtue, rather than a strategic liability. The repercussions on the security of modern India is open for all to see.]* In the medieval Indian context, the vehemence of the Turko-Afghan invasion completely destroyed the limited self-confidence that was prevalent in some of the Hindu states. In the proverbial manner, the Islamic armies wiped the slate with the Indian armies.

Turko-Afghan Influence

The Turko-Afghans who predominated the invading group, were of a nomadic and mixed racial origin. Their Islamisation process had also made these Turko-Afghans culturally more Persian. By the time these people had started to invade India in earnest, they had already evolved into a fairly sophisticated group, especially the ruling elite. Even so, their fundamentally base nature persisted as a group in matters of religion, giving rise to the cruel imposition of their new and uncompromising beliefs in conquered lands. This attitude provided an added impetus and edge to the teaching of Islamic values and its proselytising that accompanied their military conquests.

The establishment of the Delhi Sultanate created a tradition of patronage to Muslim learning, with the sultans and nobles spending huge sums of money in the support of scholarship. In fact many sultans and nobles themselves were extremely learned men. Sporadically some Muslim kings also attempted to spread learning across their domains by establishing educational institutions and providing continual support to them. This sort of benefaction was aimed and oriented mainly towards furthering Islamic education, although Hindu scholars also benefitted from the largesse on the periphery. These efforts gradually started to lift India out of the cultural, scholastic and literary stupor that it had sunk to during the previous few centuries. A large number of Indian scientific texts, considered by the Islamic scholars to be devoid of any religious intonations, were translated into Persian by the sultan's orders. This provided an opportunity for a so-far insular Indian/Hindu knowledge to be spread outside the sub-continent. This patronage, which was essentially a continuation of an age-old Indian tradition, managed to cushion, in a somewhat obtuse manner, the decline of Hindu cultural development.

The greatest impact of the Islamic invasion was brought about through the spread of Persian language and literature, which automatically brought with it certain cultural aspects. Since Persian was the preferred language of the ruling elite of the invading forces, the language and the associated cultural intonations started to be cultivated by the upper class Hindus who had the maximum interaction with them. Gradually Persian influence could also be noticed in the dress of the Indian nobility.

Persian scholars wrote extensively about medieval India—the customs and traditions, dress, inheritance laws, marriage traditions, all of which are explained in detail in these works. Al-Biruni and Amir Khusrau are two stellar examples of the genius of Persian scholar-writers, whose works have left a lasting impression on the understanding of medieval India. Khusrau, whose works are of great beauty, also used a number of Hindi words in his writings, initiating a process of cautious assimilation of the languages that was to last for centuries. From the literary interaction and mingling of the languages, a particular factor of note emerges. The Persian scholars who came into the sub-continent bend themselves to the task of learning Sanskrit and subsequently to translating noteworthy texts from that language to Persian. However, this initiative to learn the other great language was one-sided. In contrast to the Persian scholars' enthusiasm, almost no attempt was made by the Hindu scholars to learn Persian. This attitude alone stands as silent testimony to the arrogant and insular attitude of the Hindi intelligentsia. The lack of inquisitiveness towards external developments heralded the beginning of the end of the greatness of Hindu learning and culture. Knowledge assimilation and cultural development in the Hindu system has not been able to keep up with external developments from this time forward, languishing in the sidelines ever after.

The Turko-Afghan invasions announced the arrival of a dominant culture into the sub-continent. It clearly broadcast its intentions of subsuming the existing culture by the forced and rapid pace of its spread through the sub-continent. The Hindu society did not even seem to be disturbed by the spread of this alien culture, continuing its insolent and secluded way with not a breath of change. Not one Sanskrit text of the time even casually mention the arrival, establishment or spread of Islamic culture in the sub-continent. There is no explanation for this neglect other than extreme cultural arrogance based on an insular conceit and haughtiness in the greatness of Hindu knowledge, culture and societal arrangement. There is no greater demonstration of this self-assumed superiority than the recorded fact that when the last great Hindu empire of North India and its king, Jayachandra, was being conclusively destroyed by Islamic forces, his court poets were engaged in churning out great romantic poems in Sanskrit. The situation was similar across the sub-continent. The Hindu kingdoms imploded like over-inflated balloons at the slightest prick by a needle, brought about by their own foibles and incompetence.

There was a silver lining in this dreadful circumstance where Sanskrit was moribund and almost in its death throes as a living language. The inaccessibility of Sanskrit even to some of the higher caste Hindus opened the door of literary space to local regional languages, which started to grow and flourish in the widening gap being left by a receding Sanskrit tradition. This revival of local languages was initiated by Buddhist and Jain priests in their attempt to connect with the common people in order to ensure the spread of their own gospel. The spread was gradual but firm. In medieval India, the earliest writers in some of the regional languages were Buddhist monks, like in the case of the dominant regional languages of Bengali and Telugu. The second positive fallout from the dormancy of Sanskrit was the spread of the Bhakti movement within the folds of Hinduism that in turn added an urgency to the revival and spread of regional languages.

South Indian Languages

Other than for Sanskrit, Tamil resident in the south of the Peninsula, was the only ancient language with a recognisable literary tradition of its own. While turbulence was encompassing the politico-social atmosphere, Tamil had remained vibrant, not having fallen to slumber like Sanskrit, and charting a course of its own. During the classical age, Tamil literature had created many sensitive and secular works that bore the striking influence of Buddhist and Jain thought process. From the classical age to medieval times Tamil literature did not stay static, it evolved with the times and remained pulsating and energetic. In medieval times, Tamil moved to concentrate on religious writings that were both devotional and exploratory in nature, a direct influence of the Hindu revival and the Bhakti movement. The writings were infused with religious fervour, only meandering into philosophical discussions sporadically, unlike in the classical age when philosophical discussions were the main theme of almost the entire plethora of writing.

By the end of the classical age, Tamil had created three main offshoot regional languages, Kannada, Telugu and Malayalam. All three went on to produce impressive literature collections during medieval times and were, to a certain extent, influenced by Sanskrit traditions; whereas Tamil continued to remain completely unaffected and independent in its developmental trajectory. The Chola period could be considered the golden age of the revival of Tamil literature in the medieval era. During this period, local nuances were introduced to the core literature, including the retelling of ancient classics like the *Ramayana*.

The path to independence of the three main offshoot languages was irreversibly assisted by the Bhakti movement in their different regions of influence as well as by the patronage of local rulers and nobility. Kannada, receiving a great deal of royal patronage was the first to attempt charting an independent course and develop outside the Tamil circle of influence. Its early works were produced to influence the common folk, mainly by the Jain monks who were active in the Kannada region. Telugu, for politically historic reasons, had been aligned with Kannada and initially shared a common script with it. By the 6th century however, Telugu had started to develop its own distinctive characteristics, moving along to being a separate language and finally entrenching its own script by the 10th century. From this point onwards Telugu came under the influence of Sanskrit and as a result became estranged from the common people. However, the patronage of the Vijayanagar kings during the 16th century, while being a high point in the history of Telugu, also curtailed its headlong dash to obscurity along with Sanskrit. Malayalam was the last to break away from Tamil but its script has continued to be a variant of the Tamil. Malayalam also became the most Sanskritised of the three regional languages and evolved as a separate entity only in the 11th century.

The Struggle for Dominance – Disharmony in Architecture

The architectural basics of the Hindu and Islamic building traditions were completely different to each other. Hindu temples were complex structures with secretive passages and sanctums and inners sanctums built around columns and architraves. Mosques, on the other hand, were generally meant to be open, with simple lines based on the concept of arch and vault. Attempts to combine the two did not create any graceful structures and did not lend itself to a harmonious blend of the two traditions. However, it has been noted by analysts that the adoption of the Islamic cultural aspects and architectural forms into the Hindu tradition was easier than the other way around. Some have attributed this to the inherent flexibility and diversity of the Hindu religious traditions themselves, as opposed to the rigidity and orthodoxy of Islam. This reason may indeed be true, but the fact that the Islamic invasion of the sub-continent was gradually succeeding and the forceful nature of the religion and its rulers cannot be discounted as contributory factors for the Hindu traditions being 'adapted' to accept Islamic architectural and cultural practices.

The establishment of the Delhi Sultanate permanently altered the architectural scene in North India. The Indo-Gangetic plain became, and continues to be, dotted with Muslim forts, mosques, tombs and palaces. The building material for these monuments usually came from demolished and destroyed temples, especially for the building of the mosques. There are reliable reports that confirm that the most sacred of the temple stones were normally laid as the stepping stones to the mosque, as a calculated affront to the Hindus. Later-day and modern historians have attempted to dilute the brutishness and savagery of these activities and to underplay the inherent viciousness of these actions that were instituted by the conquering Islamic warlords. These apologist historians have repeatedly tried to explain the use of the temple stones and other material for the building of mosques by stating that their use was necessitated by non-availability of other building material and that it was necessary to build a mosque for Friday prayers. This explanation is an attempt at 'whitewashing' the behaviour of the invading armies—so much balderdash. The use of temple stones, idols and other material to construct mosques was nothing but an overt and symbolic demonstration of the superiority and power of Islam, nothing less. These actions were consciously carried out by the adherents of the rigid and orthodox Islamic traditions.

Even though the wanton destruction of Hindu temples was pre-calculated and conceived, the employment of Indian artisans for the construction of Muslim palaces, mosques and tombs became common practice out of sheer necessity. The Indian artisans gradually gave the buildings a distinctive Indian appearance by incorporating Hindu designs and motifs into the broader building blueprints. However, this reverse influence was short-lived and did not take firm root, since Muslim masons and other artisans started to migrate to India from Central Asia.

Peninsular India, where Islam made inroads at a slightly later stage in relation to the onslaught in North India, followed the pattern that had been set in the north. The Muslim rulers of the Deccan built ever larger mosques to accommodate the increasing numbers of Muslims in their prayer congregations. They also built urban centres of commerce and trade dominated by Islamic architecture. Gradually, the Islamic style influenced the Hindu architectural practice, which particularly adopted the arches and domes. However, as seen in other aspects of cultural influence, South India managed to keep their temple architecture somewhat outside Islamic influence and also managed a sort of revivalist renaissance in temple building and architecture. While Hindu kings had disdained to create grandiose palaces and there was no Hindu tradition of building tombs, the Muslim rulers of the Deccan had gone into a frenzied spasm of building palaces and tombs, each grander than the previous. Almost like an anti-dote to this hyperactive building flurry, the remaining Hindu kingdoms of Peninsular India, went into the last post-modern spurt of temple building, creating some temples that continue till date to be considered the acme of Hindu temple-building architecture.

Conflicting Art Forms

The art forms of the Hindus and the Muslims could not have been more different from each other. In Islamic art, there can be no representation of living beings, whereas Hindu art is almost completely figurative, both in paintings and in sculpture. In the Muslim mosques one finds only calligraphy and geometric and arabesque designs, while the Hindu temples are replete and rich with painting and sculpture of life forms and also of men and women in erotic play, something that is abhorrent to Islam. Muslims consider paintings inappropriate to be displayed in a place of worship. However, some of the Muslim rulers of the Deccan patronised painting and sculpture of the Hindu school, even placing them in their palaces. By the early medieval period, miniature paintings and their more stylised approach had made its appearance; and further, the arrival of paper as a medium in the 15th century altered the entire practice of painting and the production of books. The Hindu and Islamic style of painting and sculpture continued their own separate paths in the Indian sub-continent, hardly influencing each other.

The Clash of Religions

While Hindu and Islamic literature, sculpture, painting and architecture differed in tradition, they could co-exist, even if with some difficulty. However, when it came to religious beliefs, customs, traditions and practices, the differences between the Hinduism and Islam were almost irreconcilable. Hinduism had over the centuries transformed itself from one adhering to Vedic formulations into one that could be termed Puranic Hinduism, which was polymorphic and unlike any other in the world. It was not a religion in the common meaning and understanding of the term. Hinduism was a loose confederation of distinctly different and disparate creeds of diverse socio-cultural make up.

There are two distinctly different opinions within the scholars regarding the origins of Hinduism. One school of thought insists that Hinduism was imported to the sub-continent by the invading 'Aryans' from Central Asia. Diametrically opposed to this view is that of another faction of scholars who insist that the Aryans were indigenous to

India. The common ground between the two groups is that Hinduism was the 'religion' that was observed by the Aryans, irrespective of their origins. From the very beginning Hinduism was open to being flexible in accommodating other socio-cultural and religious systems with which it came into contact with. It took and gave to the traditions of Judaism, Christianity, Zoroastrianism and even early Islam that was brought to the peninsular shores by the Arab traders. However, this amicable acceptance of socio-cultural and religious differences came to an abrupt end with the establishment of the Delhi Sultanate. This arrival of harsh Islamic traditions was an event that Hinduism had not thought through, let alone prepared for, in advance. The Hindu religion had continued on its merry way, assessing, assimilating and attempting to influence the new socio-religious groups that were butting against its ancient beliefs, completely unaware of the orthodox rigidity that it was soon to confront.

The Turko-Afghans who founded the Delhi Sultanate came to the sub-continent already imbibed with an aggressive and uncompromising stance against all religions other than their own orthodox version of Islam. They did not attempt, even at the beginning, to co-exist with the local religion or culture. Their attitude to Hinduism, Buddhism and Jainism was one of extremely arrogant antagonism that translated to an intense urge to destroy anything connected with these local religions, customs and culture. The Indian religious tradition and the Islamic tradition were opposing philosophies and it was obvious even at that time to any observer that they could never reach a real harmonious blending.

The differences were far too many: Islam was monotheistic, Hinduism was polytheistic; Islam was mono-layered and immutable, Hinduism was multi-layered and in a state of constant flux; Islam believed in aggressive proselytising and was totally intolerant of all other belief systems, Hinduism was passive and was prone to looking for ways to co-exist with all other religions; and Islam as a religion was exclusive in an inclusive society, whereas Hinduism was the exact opposite, it was inclusive in an exclusive society. Any amount of research will not reveal two religions so completely unlike each other in all aspects—lifestyle, religious practices, social customs, cultural traditions, et al.

It was, therefore, not surprising that there was no synthesis of Hinduism and Islam in the Indian sub-continent or elsewhere. Further, the two religions did not influence each other in any manner other than in limited and superficial ways, the differences were far too entrenched to permit any such utopian movement. In the Indian context, although conversion of the lower caste Hindus to Islam became a common practice, the numbers were never sufficient to create a Muslim majority, other than in small geographic pockets of the sub-continent. Medieval India lumbered on, much like an elephant does, taking no cognisance of the dramatic changes taking place in the socio-religious and politico-economic spheres and the intermingling of the two that was creating large waves in the placid atmosphere of the sub-continent. Nothing had changed in the imperturbable attitude of the Hindu to life, even though the waves of repression and brutal suppression by militant Islam were bringing about unusually high turmoil in the sub-continent.

> 'Three different lines of evidence—Muslim chronicles, the account of Ibn Batutah and contemporary Indian literature—all agree in testifying to the fact that the basic and fundamental differences between the two communities continued, as before, during the period under review. [medieval times]. No doubt, mutual understanding was developed and there was a greater amount of cordiality in the normal social relation between the two. Each was influenced by the other, in varying degrees, not only in different spheres of life, but also in ideas, beliefs, and even superstitions. But all these merely affected the external and superficial in man and society, and left untouched the core of the heart and mind. It was only necessary to scratch the skin to bring out the Hindu and Muslim in every Indian, individually or collectively.'
>
> R. C. Majumdar, 'Hindu Muslim Relations',
>
> In *The History and Culture of the Indian People*, Volume VI, 'The Delhi Sultanate', p. 636.

BIBLIOGRAPHY

Books

Allchin, Bridget and Raymond, *The Rise of Civilization in India and Pakistan*, Cambridge University Press, New Delhi, 1996.

Avari, Burjor, *India: The Ancient Past*, Routledge, London, 2007.

Chandra, Satish, *Medieval India: From Sultanate to the Mughals (1206-1526) Part I*, Har-Anand Publications, New Delhi, 2006.

_____ *A History of Medieval India*, Orient Blackswan, Hyderabad, 2007.

Chirol, Sir Valentine, *'India Old and New'*, Macmillan and Co., Limited, London, 1921.

Chopra P.N., Ravindran T.K., and Subrahmanian N. *History of South India (Ancient, Medieval and Modern) Part I*, Chand Publications, Delhi, 2003.

Danielou, Alain, *A Brief History of India*, (Translated from the French by Kenneth Hury), Inner Traditions International, Vermont, USA, 2003.

Davis, Paul K., *100 Decisive Battles: From Ancient Times to the Present*, Oxford University Press, Oxford, 1999.

Day, U. N., *Some Aspects of Medieval Indian History*, Low Price Publications, Delhi, 1971.

Devi, Ragini, *Dance Dialects of India*, Motilal Banarsidas Publishers, Delhi, 1990.

Devi, Yashoda, *The History of Andhra Country 1000 A.D. – 1500 A.D.*,

Gyan Publishing House, New Delhi, 1993.

Eaton, Richard Maxwell, *The Sufis of Bijapur 1300-1700*, Volume I, University of Wisconsin-Madison, USA, 1972.

Edwardes, Michael, *A History of India*, The New English Library, Thames & Hudson, Great Britain, 1961.

Elliot, H. M. & Dowson John, *The History of India: As told by its own Historians*, The Muhammadan Period, and Several other Volumes, Trubner & Co, London, 1867. Digitised by MSN and Cornell University Press, Vol VI available online at https://archive.org/details/in.ernet.dli.2015.458719 (also reprinted by Kitab Mahal, Allhabad and digitised in 2015), OR at http://www.rarebooksocietyofindia.org/book_archive/196174216674_10153808785141675.pdf

Gautier, Francois, *'Rewriting Indian History'*, India Research Press, New Delhi, 2003.

Gribble, J.D.B., *History of the Deccan*, Rupa Publications India Pvt Ltd., New Delhi, 2002. (First published Vol I-1896, Vol II – 1924.)

Grousset, Rene, *The Civilisations of the East: India*, Volume 2, Munshiram Manoharlal, Delhi, 1969.

Gupta, Harsh K., Parasher-Sen, Aloka., & Balasubramanian, D., (eds), *Deccan Heritage*, Universities Press (India) Ltd., Hyderabad, 2000.

Haidar, Navina Najat & Sardar, Marika (eds), *Sultans of Deccan India: Opulence and Fantasy*, The Metropolitan Museum of Art, New York, 2015.

Haig, Lieut-Colonel Sir Wolseley, *The History of the Nizam Shahi Kings of Ahmadnagar*, The British India Press, Mazgaon, Bombay, 1923. Reprinted from 'The Indian Antiquary', https://archive.org/stream/in.ernet.dli.2015.72241/2015.72241.The-History-Of-The-Nizam-Shahi-Kings-Of-Ahmadnagar#page/n1/mode/1up accessed between 28 July and 5 September 2018.

Jaques, Tony, *Dictionary of Battles and Sieges*, Greenwood Publishing

Group, Santa Barbara, California, 2007.

Jayapalan, N, *History of India*, Volume II, (Four Volumes), Atlantic Publishers and Distributors, New Delhi, 2001, accessed on line on 18 April 2018.

Jenkins, Keith, *Re-Thinking History,* Routledge, London, 1991.

Kamath, Suryanath U., *A Concise History of Karnataka: Frome Prehistoric Times to the Present*, Jupiter Books, Bangalore, 1980.

Keay, John, *India: A History*, Harper Collins Publishers, London, 2000.

_____ *India Discovered: The Recovery of a Lost Civilisation*, Harper Collins Publishers, London, 2001.

Khalidi, Omar, *A Guide to Architecture in Hyderabad, Deccan, India,* Aga Khan Program for Islamic Architecture, Massachusetts Institute of Technology, MIT Libraries, Cambridge, Massachusetts, 2009.

Kothari, Sunil & Pasricha, Avinash, *Kuchipudi*, Abhinav Publications, Mumbai, 2001.

Law, Narendranath, *Studies in Indian History and Culture,* B. R. Publishing Corporation, New Delhi, 1985.

Majumdar, R. C., (General Editor), *The History and Culture of the Indian People Volume V: The Struggle for Empire*, Fifth Edition, Bharatiya Vidya Bhavan, Mumbai, 2001.

_____ *The History and Culture of the Indian People Volume VI: The Delhi Sultanate,* Fifth Edition, Bharatiya Vidya Bhavan, Mumbai, 2001.

Majumdar, R. C., Rauchaudhuri, S. C., & Datta, Kalikinkar, *An Advanced History of India,* Third Editon, Macmillan India, 1946, Digital Library India Texts, Free download, https://archive.org/details/in.ernet.dli.2015.279506 accessed on 20 September 2017.

Michell, George., & Zebrowski, Mark., *The New Cambridge History of India I:7 Architecture and Art of the Deccan Sultanates,* Cambridge University Press, Cambridge, UK., 1999.

Mukerjee, Radhakamal, *The Culture and Art of India*, Fredrick A. Praeger Publishers, New York, 1959.

Nehru, Jawaharlal, *The Discovery of India*, Penguin Books, New Delhi, 2004.

Nizami, Khaliq Ahmed, *Some Aspects of Religion and Politics in India During the Thirteenth Century*, Asia Publishing, New Delhi, 1961.

Owen, Sydney, *From Mahmud Ghazni to the Disintegration of the Mughal Empire*, Kanishka Publishing House, Delhi, 1987.

Panikkar, K. M., *A Survey of Indian History*, Asia Publishing House, Bombay, 1960 (first published 1947).

Prasad, Durga, *History of the Andhras up to 1565 A.D.*, P.G. Publishers, Guntur India, 1988.

Prasad, Iswari, *History of Medieval India: From 647 A.D. to the Mughal Conquest*, The Indian Press Ltd, Allahabad, 1925.

Robb, Peter, *A History of India*, Palgrave Essential Histories Series, Palgrave Macmillan, Great Britain, 2011.

Sastry, Nilakanta, K.A., *A History of South India*, Oxford University Press, Indian Branch, New Delhi, 1975.

Schwartz, Susan L., *Rasa: Performing the Divine in India*, Columbia University Press, NY, 2004.

Sen, S.N., *A Textbook of Medieval Indian History*, Primus Books, New Delhi, 2013.

Sherwani, H.K., *History of the Qutb Shahi Dynasty*, Munshiram Manoharlal Publishers Pvt Ltd., New Delhi, 1974.

_____ and Joshi, P.M., (eds), *History of Medieval Deccan 1295-1724*, Government of Andhra Pradesh, Hyderabad, 1973,

Shyam, Radhey Dr., *The Kingdom of Ahmadnagar*, Motilal Banarsidass, Delhi, 1966.

Spear, Percival, *India: A Modern History*, University of Michigan Press, Ann Arbor, USA, 1961.

Spear, Percival (ed), *The Oxford History of India* (4th edition) by late Vincent A. Smith, C.I.E., Oxford University Press, New Delhi, 1958. (First Published 1919 by Clarendon Press Oxford).

Talbot, Cynthia, *Precolonial India in Practice: Society, Region, and Identity in Medieval Andhra*, Oxford University Press, New York, 2001.

Thapar, Romila, *A History of India*, Volume I, Penguin Books, London, 1966.

Theodore de Barry, Wm, (ed), *Sources of Indian Tradition*, Columbia University Press, New York, 1958.

Tucker, Spencer C., (ed), *A Global Chronology of Conflict: From the Ancient World to the Modern Middle East*, ABC-CLIO, Greenwood, USA, 2010.

Watson, Francis, *India: A Concise History*, Thames and Hudson Ltd, London, Revised edition, 2002.

Wolpert, Stanley, *A New History of India*, Oxford University Press, New York, Sixth Edition, 2000.

Wood, Michael, *The Story of India*, BBC Books, UK, 2007.

Zinkin, Taya, *India*, Thames and Hudson Ltd, London, 1965.

Others (Reproductions, Articles, Lectures etc.)

Websites

This book incorporates information gleaned from the *Encyclopaedia Britannica*, Eleventh Edition, now available in the public domain on-line.

Encyclopedia.com, Dictionary of Women Worldwide, https://www.encyclopedia.com/women/dictionaries-thesauruses-pictures-and-press-releases/chand-bibi-1550-1599, accessed on 5 September 2018.

Articles

Balakrishna, Sandeep, *The Indian Conception of History*, http://prekshaa.in/the-indian-conception-of-history/ 16 June 2016, accessed on 11 November 2018.

Kulkarny, A. R., *Maratha Policy towards the Adil Shahi Kingdom*, https://www.jstor.org/stable/42930290?seq=6#page_scan_tab_contents accessed on 4 June 2018.

Kulkarni, G. T., *Deccan (Maharashtra) Under the Muslim Rulers from Khaljis to Shivaji: A Study in Interaction*, Bulletin of the Deccan College Research Institute, Vol 51/52, 1991-92, pp. 501-510.

Raman, Anuradha & Pathak, Vikas, *History is not written by committees but by individual historians, says Romila Thapar,* The Hindu, 28 March 2018, http://www.thehindu.com/news/national.history-is-not-written-by-committees-but-by-individual-historians/article23366668.ece accessed on 08 January 2019.

Stewart, Courtney, A., *Feminine Power of the Deccan: Chand Bibi and Mah Laqa Bai Chanda*, The Metropolitan Museum of Art, New York, 2015, https://www.metmuseum.org/blogs/ruminations/2015/feminine-power accessed on 5 September 2018.

The Madras Courier, *Chand Bibi: The Deccan's Warrior Queen*, https://madrascourier.com/insight/chand-bibi-the-deccans-warrior-queen/ accessed on 2 September 2018.

The Madras Courier, *Ikhlas Khan: The Abyssinian Who Ruled The Deccan*, https://madrascourier.com/biography/ikhlas-khan-the-abyssinian-who-ruled-the-deccan/ accessed on 27 September 2018.

Index

A

Abdullah Qutb Shah   355, 356, 358, 364, 365, 395

Abyssinians   91, 135, 150, 155, 156, 278

Adil Shahi dynasty   121, 131, 132, 134, 135, 138, 151, 155, 171, 175, 177, 181, 182, 184, 185, 186, 187, 188, 230

Adil Shahis of Bijapur   vii, xxx, xxxii, xxxvi, 130, 163, 200, 321, 327

Afzal Khan   169, 170, 183, 278

Ahmad Shah Bahmani   77, 193

Ahmad Shah Vali   85, 93

Ahmad Shah Vali's Tomb   85

Ain ud-Din Junnaidi   187

Ain-ul-Mulk   74, 139, 238, 250, 326

Ajanta and Ellora   xxi

Ala ud-Din Ahmad   82

Ala ud-Din Bahman Shah   55, 60

Ala ud-Din II   84

Ala ud-Din Imad Shah   202, 205, 211, 212, 213, 323

Ala ud-Din Khilji   xxi, 18, 135

Ala ud-Din Mujahid Shah   67

Ali Adil Shah   143, 144, 145, 146, 148, 152, 153, 168, 170, 173, 183, 184, 185, 223, 226, 228, 229, 230, 233, 234, 235, 236, 239, 240, 241, 242, 244, 248, 255, 328, 329, 331, 332, 336, 337, 341, 362

Amiran-i-Sada   53

Athanasius Nikitin   109

B

Babaji Naik Punde   183

Babur   xxiv, xxxii, xxxiii, xxxiv, 103, 109, 210, 212, 340, 411

Bahadur Shah   211, 212, 213, 214, 215, 216, 278

Baha ud-Din Garshap   40

Bahmani dynasty   xix, xxiii, xxiv, xxv, xxvi, xxvii, xxxvi, 5, 9, 49, 53, 54, 64, 70, 71, 83, 93, 98, 102, 103, 105, 108, 109, 119, 132, 182, 194, 206, 252, 310, 318

Bahman-nama   83

Bahman Shah   9, 55, 56, 57, 58, 59,

60, 61, 64

Ballala Hoysala III   44

Barid ul-Mulk   103

Battle of Bannihatti (Talikota)   333, 334, 336

Battle of Mahendramangalam   29

Battle of Talikota   107, 231

Battles of Malkher   372

Bedar Nizam-ul-Mulk   74

Berar Rebellion   255

Bihzad-ul-Mulk   248, 249

Boobaji Khanun   129, 130

Building of Hyderabad   347

Burhan Nizam Shah II   xxxiv, 270

C

Capture of Tanjore   174

Chalukya   xix, xxx, 6, 9, 13, 27, 43

Chand Bibi   viii, 146, 153, 154, 155, 156, 157, 158, 160, 162, 230, 255, 267, 275, 277, 278, 279, 280, 281, 282, 285, 332, 341, 448

Charminar   xxx, 348, 349, 396

Choda Tikka   30, 31, 32. See also Gangagopala

Chola dynasty   6, 33

D

Dakshinapatha   xix

Daud Khan   67, 68, 202

Daulatabad   xxi, 4, 40, 41, 44, 54, 57, 64, 71, 76, 82, 110, 121, 165, 172, 198, 199, 210, 211, 212, 213, 238, 247, 259, 295, 300, 302, 352, 353, 376, 410

Deccani Muslims   xxx

Deccan Plateau   xiv, xix, xx, xxi, xxxi, xxxvi, 3, 14, 97, 181, 202, 312, 397, 410

Delhi Sultanate   vi, xx, xxi, xxiv, xxv, xxviii, xxx, 4, 5, 7, 9, 18, 20, 21, 22, 23, 24, 34, 39, 40, 41, 42, 43, 44, 45, 54, 82, 110, 202, 410, 426, 434, 438, 441, 442, 445

E

Eyn-ul-Mulk   160, 161

F

Faruqi dynasty   xxxii

Fathullah Imad-ul-Mulk   99, 103

Fatimid Caliphs of Egypt   208

First Vijayanagar Campaign   71

Firuz Shah   xxiv, 62, 71, 73, 76, 97, 102, 144

Firuz Shah Bahmani   xxiv, 144

G

Gandagopala. See also Choda Tikka

Ghiyas ud-Din Muhammad Shah Damaghani   45

Ghiyas ud-Din Tughluq   39, 55

Index

Golconda Diplomacy 323

Gol Gumbaz 167

Gulbarga Revolt 124

H

Habshi military slaves xxxiii, 293

Habshis of the Deccan 287

Haidar Mahal 349

Harihara I 58

Hindu civilisation xi

Hosadurgh 41

Hosiar Ain-ul-Mulk 74

Hoysalas 7, 8, 13, 27, 28, 31, 32, 33, 36, 37, 40, 45, 46

Humayun Shah 93, 94, 95, 96, 97

I

Ibrahim Adil Shah 135, 136, 140, 143, 153, 157, 158, 159, 161, 162, 163, 182, 184, 217, 218, 222, 223, 250, 258, 259, 263, 264, 270, 272, 280, 282, 321, 323, 327, 328

Ibrahim Quli Qutb Shah viii, 326, 327

Ibrahim Qutb Shah of Golconda 225, 229, 331

Imad Shahi dynasty 92

Imad Shahi ruler of Berar 132, 138

Imad-ul-Mulk 99, 103, 125, 205, 206, 207, 211

Iqta System 23

Ismail Adil Shah 126, 130, 133, 206, 209, 210, 211, 212, 213, 314

J

Jahangir Khan 196

Jalal ud-Din Ahsan Shah 44

Jatavarman Kulasekhara 27

Jatavarman Parakrama Pandya 37

Jatavarman Sundara Pandya 31

K

Kadava Kopperunjinga 29

Kakatiya xxx, xxxii, 11, 12, 13, 14, 15, 16, 17, 18, 19, 20, 21, 25, 28, 31, 32, 36, 39, 40, 44

Kamil Khan Deccani 153

Kampili 40, 41, 42, 43

Kampilideva 40, 41, 42, 43

Kannanur Fort 32

Kapala Nayaka 9

Kapaya Nayaka 43, 44, 45, 54, 58

Khalaf Hasan 75

Khandesh xxxii, 5, 74, 80, 82, 201, 202, 204, 206, 211, 212, 243, 340

Khawaja Imad ud-Din 120

Khilji dynasty 34, 39

Khilji Sultanate 18

Khusrau Khan, General 20

Khwaja Gisu Darag 74

Kishawar Khan 154, 155

Kulasekhara Pandya 33, 34

Kulottunga III 27, 28

Kuttulugh Khan 54

M

Madurai Sultanate 45, 46, 53, 58

Mahmud Adil Shah 166, 167, 168, 174, 175

Mahmud Gawan 88, 94, 95, 96, 97, 99, 100, 101, 102, 108, 114, 121, 186, 193, 194, 198, 381, 385, 388

Makhdumah Jahan 95, 96, 97

Makhdum Khwaja Jahan 209

Malik Ambar- From Slave to King 292

Malik Hasan 99, 100, 101, 102, 103

Malik Kafur 7, 8, 19, 34, 35, 37

Malik Saif ud-Din Ghuri 70

Malik-ul-Tijar 82, 86

Malik Zada 41

Maratha Revolt 151

Maravarman Kulasekhara Pandya I 33

Military Slaves 290

Mir Rukn ud-Din 208

Mongol invasions xx

Mughal Empire xxxv, 169, 181, 183, 186, 187, 212, 216, 218, 245, 277, 278, 279, 353, 361, 367, 373, 388, 446

Muhammad-bin-Tughluq xxiii

Muhammad Qasim Firishta 3

Muhammad Qutb Shah 251, 252, 259, 280, 341, 342, 344, 345, 351, 352, 353, 354

Muhammad Shah I 60, 61, 211

Muhammad Shah II 68, 69, 70, 71

Muhammad Shah III 97, 102

Mustafa Khan 146, 151, 154, 155, 226, 326, 374

N

Najm ud-Din Mahmud bin Muhammad Gawan Gilani 94. *also known as* Mahmud Gawan

Narasimha II 30

Nasir ud-Din Ismail Shah 54

Nizam Shah viii, xxxiv, 92, 96, 97, 138, 143, 144, 146, 147, 148, 158, 159, 160, 161, 162, 195, 197, 201, 202, 203, 205, 208, 210, 212, 214, 215, 216, 217, 219, 220, 221, 226, 227, 229, 231, 233, 237, 238, 239, 240, 242, 243, 244, 247, 251, 254, 255, 256, 257, 258, 259, 260, 261, 263, 264, 265, 266, 267, 270, 271, 273, 275, 277, 278, 282, 284, 292, 294, 296, 298, 316, 320, 321, 322, 323, 327, 330, 331, 332, 335, 336, 341

Nizam Shahis of Ahmadnagar viii,

Index

xxxii, xxxvi, 183, 200, 332, 379

Nizam-ul-Mulk   74, 100, 120, 193, 195, 196, 214

P

Pallava dynasty   6

Panchayat system   xxiii

Pandya-Chola conflict   28

Pandya dynasty   7, 34, 36, 37, 38

Parakramabahu II   32

Parakramabahu III   34

Phirangi Rebellion   269

Prolaya Nayaka   9, 43

Q

Qara Quyunla   309

Qasim Barid   xxviii, 122, 123, 124, 129, 312

Qutb Shahi Dynasty   370, 446

Qutb Shahis of Golconda   xxx, 127, 133, 143, 335

Qutb ud-Din   45, 316, 319

Qutb-ul-Mulk   103, 166, 199, 310, 311, 312, 313, 314, 315, 316, 317, 318, 319, 335, 340, 356, 367, 396

R

Rajaraja III   30

Rajendra Chola III   33

Rama Raya   xxix, 110, 223, 224, 225, 226, 227, 228, 229, 230, 231, 234, 236

Rameswaram   xxi, 9

Rashtrakutas   xix

River Krishna   9, 40, 64, 71, 121, 131, 147, 236, 313, 332, 333, 341, 342, 343, 392

River Tungabhadra   6, 8, 9, 40, 64, 79, 370

S

Sambuvaraya dynasty   44, 45

Sayyid Murtaza   256

Second Vijayanagar Campaign   72

Shahi Kingdoms   xv, xxvii

   Adil Shahis in Bijapur   xxviii

   Barid Shahis in Bidar   xxviii

   Imad Shahis in Berar   xxviii

   Nizam Shahis in Ahmadnagar   xxviii

   Qutb Shahis in Golconda   xxviii

Shah-nama   83

Shah Nimat Allah Wali   111

Shah Tahir   208, 209, 210, 214, 217, 218, 219, 222, 240, 247, 278

Shaikh Nizam ud-Din Aulia   56

Shaistha Khan   183

Shivaji   141, 168, 169, 170, 171, 172, 173, 174, 175, 176, 177, 182,

183, 184, 185, 186, 302, 361, 362, 369, 370, 371, 448

Sultan Damaghani 46

Sultan Hasan Bahmani 104

Sundara Pandya 27, 28, 29, 31, 32, 33, 34, 37

Svayambhusive Temple 21

T

Taj ud-Din Firuz Shah 71

Tanjore Maratha dynasty 175

Tarafdari xxvi, 91

Third Vijayanagar Campaign 73

Timurid dynasties xxxi

Tufal Khan 148, 241, 242, 243, 325, 330, 332, 335

Tughluq dynasty xxiii, 20

U

Ulugh Khan 20, 21, 37

V

Vasco da Gama 109, 126, 287, 428

Vijayanagar Empire xxii, 1, 5, 9, 21, 46, 47, 53, 58, 122, 145, 147, 181, 210, 227, 228, 229, 312, 326, 333, 334, 336, 358, 363, 387, 405

Vindhya Mountain Ranges 3

Vira Ballala II 8

Vira Ravivarman Kulasekhara 8

W

Warangal xxi, xxx, 44, 45, 61, 62, 78, 80, 96, 313, 314, 348, 349

Y

Yusuf Adil Khan 99, 102, 103, 119, 121. *See also* Yusuf Adil Shah

Yusuf Adil Shah vii, 119, 122, 123, 124, 125, 126, 127, 181, 198, 200, 201, 312. *See also* Yusuf Adil Khan

CPSIA information can be obtained
at www.ICGtesting.com
Printed in the USA
BVHW031308250719
554278BV00002B/2/P